James Henry

Aeneidea

Or, Critical, exegetical, and aesthetical Remarks on the Aeneis - Vol. II

James Henry

Aeneidea

Or, Critical, exegetical, and aesthetical Remarks on the Aeneis - Vol. II

ISBN/EAN: 9783337180348

Printed in Europe, USA, Canada, Australia, Japan

Cover: Foto ©ninafisch / pixelio.de

More available books at **www.hansebooks.com**

AENEIDEA,

OR

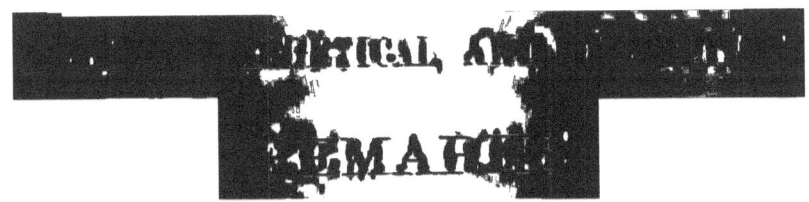

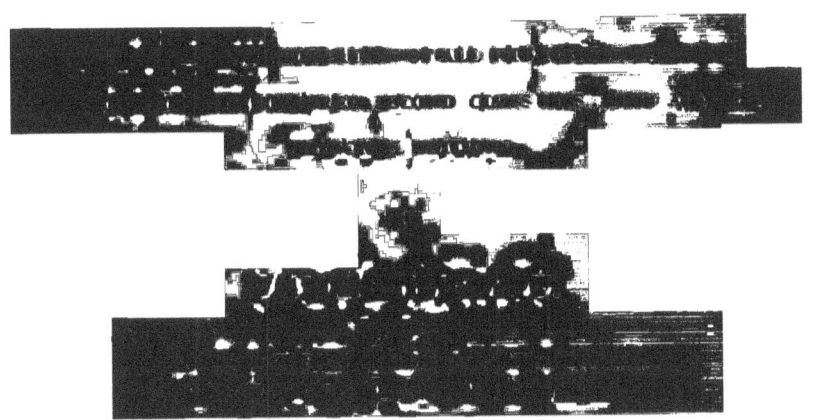

AENEIDEA.

II.*

1.

CONTICUERE OMNES INTENTIQUE ORA TENEBANT

Commentators and translators alike understand this verse to express by its first clause the silence, by its second the attention —manifested by the fixed countenances of the audience—with which Aeneas was heard: "Et tacuerunt et desiderio ducebantur audiendi," Donatus. "Aut ora intuebantur loquentis, aut immobiles vultus habebant, ut *Georg. 4. 483:* '*Tenuit*que inhians tria Cerberus *ora*,' i. e. immobilia habuit; aut intenti tenebant, habebant, ut sit figura, et intelligamus ora intenta habebant," Serv. "INTENTI ORA TENEBANT, ornate: erant intenti, habebant vultus et oculos intentos et conversos in Aeneam," Heyne. Επει δε και σχημα προσωπου μαλιστα προσοχης εμφασιν εχει, ουδ' εκεινο παρελιπε, του μη και οφθαλμοις αυτοις, οσα και

---

* As to the source of the second book, see Macrob. *Saturn. 5. 2*, who introduces Eustathius saying: "Diuturnumne me putatis ea quae vulgo nota sunt? quod Theocritum sibi fecerit pastoralis operis auctorem, ruralis Hesiodum? et quod in ipsis Georgicis, tempestatis serenitatisque signa de Arati Phaenomenis traxerit? vel quod eversionem Troiae, cum Sinone suo, et equo ligneo, ceterisque omnibus, quae *librum secundum* faciunt, a Pisandro paene ad verbum transcripserit?"

ωσι, χρησαμενους, μονονουχι των χειλεων εξαρτησαι του λεγοντος τους ακουοντας, προσθεις οτι και ενητενιζον· τουτεστιν·ατενως προς αυτον ταις οψεσιν ειχον, Eugen. de Bulgaris. "IN-TENTI ORA TENEBANT ut, 8. 520, 'defixi ora tenebant,' explica: 'sie richteten aufmerksam den blick,'" Gossrau. "INTENTI ORA TENEBANT: ergo ut solent intenti, in ipso ore apparebat intentio," Wagner (1861). "Ora tenere is not, as in *Georg*. 4. 483, equivalent to linguam continere, but means to hold the countenance in attention, as in 7. 250 (where observe the epithet 'defixa,' and compare 6. 156), 8. 520," Conington. "INTENTI ORA TENEBANT: habebant vultus et oculos intentos, et conversos in Aeneam," Forbiger (1873).

> "they ceissit all attanis incontinent,
> with mouthis clois and vissage taking tent." Douglas.

> "they whisted all, with fixcd face attent." Surrey.

> "they whusted all, and fixt with eies ententive did behold."
> Phaer.

> "stavan taciti, attenti, e disiosi
> d'udir già tutti." Caro.

> "taciti tutti, e con volti bramosi
> d'udire, immoti stavansi." Alfieri.

> "still war's und jedes ohr hing an Aeneens munde." Schiller.

> "rings war alles verstummt und gespannt hielt jeder das antlitz."
> J. H. Voss.

> "each eye was fixed, each lip compressed,
> when thus began the heroic guest." Conington.

The interpretation is false, and there is not one of all this brilliant field of philologist truth-hunters whose horse has not shied and thrown him on the kerb of the deep dark well in which his vixen game so loves to lurk, and down into which, audax—not in iuventa but in senecta—and cheerily barking-in with Hermes' and Athena's* " whoop, whoop, halloo!" I propose now at all risks to pursue her. Let him who has a taste for such adventure draw on his spatterdashes and accom-

---

* This Rem. was written for, and first published in, the *Hermathena* of Trinity College, Dublin.

pany me. I promise him sport, if nothing more. "Allons! Vive la chasse de la vérité!"

ORA is here neither *the face,* nor *the mouth* literally, but *the mouth* figuratively, *i. e., the speech, voice,* or *utterance* (exactly as (verse 423) "ora sono discordia," *sound of voice or speech, disagreeing with assumed appearance.* Compare also Ovid, *Met. 6. 583* (of Procne):

  . . . " dolor *ora* repressit,
  verbaque quaerenti satis indignantia linguae
  defuerunt"

[*grief repressed her utterance*]); and ORA TENEBANT is neither *were holding their mouths closed,* literally, nor *were holding their faces fixed,* but *were holding their mouths closed,* figuratively, *i. e., were holding-in (withholding) their voice, speech, or utterance;* in other words, *were remaining silent;* exactly as (*a*), " dolor ora repressit" (just quoted), *grief repressed her mouth,* i. e., *her utterance;* and as, still more exactly (*b*), Ovid, *Met. 9. 513:*

  . . . "poterisne loqui? poterisne fateri?
  roget amor, potero; vel si pudor *ora tenebit,*
  littera celatos arcana fatebitur ignes"

[*shame will hold my mouth (voice);* i. e., *will keep me silent*]; and more exactly still, and even word for word (*c*), Lucan, 4. 172:

  . . . " *tenuere* parumper
  ora metu; tantum nutu motoque salutant
  ense suos. mox ut stimulis maioribus ardens
  rupit amor leges, audet transcendere vallum
  miles, in amplexus effusas tendere palmas.
  hospitis ille ciet nomen, vocat ille propinquum"

[*they held their mouths,* i. e., *their voice, speech, utterance*]; also (*d*), Senec. *Troad. 521:*

  " *cohibe* parumper *ora,* questusque opprime;"

and, however differently expressed (being prose), still precisely the same thought (*e*), Seneca, *de Vita Beata, 27:* "Ut quotiens aliquid ex illo proferetur oraculo, *intenti* et *compressa voce* audiatis," where we have the very INTENTI of our text, and where "compressa voce" is our text's ORA TENEBANT.

How truly this is the meaning of the ORA TENEBANT of our text is further shown, and scarcely less strikingly, **on the**

one hand by Servius's own quotation, *Georg. 4. 483:* "tenuitque inhians tria Cerberus ora" [*neither*, surely, with Servius, "kept his three faces fixed," "immobilia habuit" (a picture bordering on the ridiculous), *nor* "kept his three mouths closed" (literally), for he has them partially open ("inhians"), as it is right he should have them, the mouth being always partially open whether in the passions of wonder and admiration or in the expectation inseparable from attentive listening, as Val. Flacc. 5. 469:

>   . . . " postquam primis *inhiantia* dictis
> agmina, suppressumque videt iam murmur Iason,
> talia miranti propius tulit orsa tyranno ;"

Shakespeare, *King John, 4. 4:*

> " I saw a smith stand with his hammer, thus,
> the whilst his iron did on the anvil cool,
> with *open mouth swallowing a tailor's news*,
> who, with his shears and measure in his hand,
> standing on slippers, which his nimble haste
> had falsely thrust upon contrary feet,
> told of a many thousand warlike French
> that were embatteled and rank'd in Kent ;"

Milton, *Par. Lost, 5. 353:*

>   . . . " in himself was all his state,
> more solemn than the tedious pomp that waits
> on princes, when their rich retinue long
> of horses led and grooms besmeared with gold
> *dazzles* the crowd and sets them all *agape ;*"

Sir W. Scott, *Lady of the Lake, 1. 17:*

> " the maiden paused, as if again
> she thought to catch the distant strain ;
> with head upraised and look intent,
> and *eye and ear attentive bent,*
> and locks flung back and *lips apart,*
> like monument of Grecian art,
> in listening mood she seemed to stand
> the guardian naiad of the strand ;"

and Mr. Conington's " lip compressed" being a mistake not merely with respect to Virgil's meaning, but with respect to the natural phenomenon, and descriptive of the *habitus*, not of a pleased and attentive listener, but of a pugilist, or the Coryphaeus of a party—some Cromwell or some Gladstone—who throws down his bill on the table and defies you to reject it], **and on the other hand** by the general use of *solvere ora, resolvere ora, movere ora, aperire ora*—all plainly opposites of *tenere ora*—to express the breaking of silence, the beginning to speak. Nor is direct testimony to the same effect altogether wanting, the passage having been thus paraphrased by Sulpicius, *Anthol. Lat.* Burm. (ed. Meyer), 223. 7 :

"conticuere omnes, intentique ore loquentis
ora tenent,"

where—"intenti ore loquentis" expressing fully and unmistakably the intentness with which the hearers look the speaker in the face—the remaining words, viz., "ora tenent," can hardly by possibility be anything else than *keep their mouths quiet*, i. e., *say nothing*.

Ora tenere is thus the Latin representative of the Greek στομα εχειν, equally figurative, and equally signifying to keep silence, as the two following examples sufficiently testify, Eurip. *Suppl. 513* :

. . . σιγ', Αδρατ', εχε στομα,
και μη 'πιπροσθε των εμων τους σους λογους
θης.

Soph. *Trachin.* 976 (Senex to Hyllus) :

σιγα, τεκνον, μη κινησης
αγριαν οδυνην πατρος ωμοφρονος.
ζη γαρ προπετης. αλλ' ισχε δακων
στομα σον.

And the ORA TENEBANT of our text is our author's usual modified repetition in the latter part of his verse—whether for the sake of the greater impressiveness, or the greater ease and fluency of versification, or the less difficult introduction of an additional thought (on this occasion, INTENTI), or whether for all three purposes at once—of the thought just expressed in the former part (on this occasion, CONTICUERE). Compare (*a*), Soph. *Trachin.* 976 (just quoted), where the thought σιγα is repeated in the same figurative form in which the thought CON-

TICUERE is repeated in our text (σιγα, ισχε στομα : CONTICUERE, ORA TENEBANT), the thought δακων being added to the repetition in the Greek, in the same manner as the thought INTENTI is added to the repetition in the Latin. (*b*), Eurip. *Suppl. 513* (just quoted), where the thought σιγα is not only repeated in the same figurative form in which the thought CONTICUERE is repeated in our text (σιγ', εχε στομα : CONTICUERE, ORA TENEBANT), but re-repeated and enlarged upon throughout the whole of the next verse. (*c*), Eurip. *Androm. 250:*

ιδου, σιωπω, καπιλαζυμαι στομα,

where the thought σιωπω is repeated in the same figurative form in which the thought CONTICUERE is repeated in our text: σιωπω, επιλαζυμαι στομα : CONTICUERE, ORA TENEBANT. **And** (*d*), Plochiri *Poematium dramaticum:*

σιγα, σιωπα, σφιγγε τοδε λαυρον στομα,

where the thought σιγα, already repeated in σιωπα, is re-repeated in the same figurative form in which the thought CONTICUERE is repeated in our text (σιγα, σιωπα, σφιγγε τοδε λαυρον στομα : CONTICUERE, ORA TENEBANT), the thought λαυρον being added to the re-repetition in the Greek, as the thought INTENTI is added to the repetition in the Latin. That the repetition, so manifest and unmistakable in these examples, has so long escaped detection in our text is owing to two causes: first, to the ambiguity of ORA, a word equally significant of *face* and of *mouth;* and, secondly, to the modification of the repetition by the change of time: CONTICUERE, TENEBANT—they *have* become silent and *were* holding—a change of time necessary to the full expression of the thought : *they ceased to speak and were continuing silent.*

Nor is a right interpretation of our text the sole fruit of a right understanding of the expression *tenere ora*. The interpretation of other passages, not only of Virgil, but of other authors also, is rectified at the same moment, *ex. gr.* (**1**), *Aen. 11. 120:*

. . . . " illi *obstupuere* silentes
conversique oculos inter se, atque *ora tenebant;*"

not *they stood in silent astonishment looking at each other, and held their faces* (fixed), but *they stood in silent astonishment looking at each other, and held their mouths* (quiet), i. e. *withheld their utterance, or speech = said nothing*—" ora tenebant" being a modified repetition (variation) of the theme " obstupuere silentes," as ORA TENEBANT in our text is a modified repetition (variation) of the theme CONTICUERE; and " conversi oculos inter se," a third thought thrown in between theme and variation, and attached to the former (" silentes et conversi oculos inter se obstupuere"), as INTENTI in our text is a third thought thrown in between theme and variation, and attached to the latter (ORA TENEBANT INTENTI). (**2**), *Aen. 8. 520*:

  . . . " defixique *ora tenebant*
  Aeneas Anchisiades et fidus Achates,
  multaque dura suo tristi cum corde putabant,"

where the meaning is: *standing fixed in one position, kept their mouths* (quiet), i. e., *said nothing, and revolved many hardships with their minds*; and where the silence referred-back-to in the words " multaque dura suo tristi cum corde putabant" has not been mentioned at all, if the words " defixi ora tenebant" be rightly interpreted *kept their faces fixed*. (**3**), Ennius, ap. Cicer. *de Divinatione, 1. 48* (ed. Orelli) :

  " sic expectabat populus atque *ora tenebat*
  rebus, utri magni victoria sit data regni;"

not, *the people expected and held their faces fixed*, but *the people expected in silence*. **And** (**4**), Val. Flacc. 4. 322 :

  . . . " qua mole iacentis [Amyci]
  ipse etiam expleri victor nequit, *oraque* longo
  comminus obtutu mirans *tenet* ;"

where, far more than either in our text or in any of the just cited examples, *ora tenere* might (on account of the superadded " obtutu") be suspected of meaning *to hold the face fixed* (*admiring, holds his face fixed in a long gaze*) ; but where, nevertheless, the " obtutu ora premit" of Statius [*Theb. 1. 490* :

  . . . " stupet omine tanto
  defixus senior, divina oracula Phoebi
  agnoscens, monitusque datos vocalibus antris,
  obtutu gelida ora premit, laetusque per artus
  horror it "

(plainly incapable of being understood of the face at all, and equally plainly nothing more than an emphatic " obtutu ora tenet")] forbids us to find other meaning than *keeps silence in a long gaze of admiration—gazes long in silent admiration*. And so, precisely, " obtutu tenet ora," *Aen. 7. 249:*

> " talibus Ilionei dictis defixa Latinus
> obtutu *tenet ora*, soloque immobilis haeret,
> intentos volvens oculos"

—the very passage which has been put forward as demonstrative that the expression *ora tenere* signifies *to hold the face fixed*—is not *holds his face fixed in a gaze, rolling his eyes intently*, but (as sufficiently shown by the examples just now commented upon, viz.: Val. Flacc. 4. 322, and Stat. *Theb. 1. 490*) *holds his mouth fixed in a gaze, rolling his eyes intently*, i. e., *gazes with fixed and silent mouth, and rolling eyes intent*. Or, if to any one those examples be unsatisfactory, let him compare Stat. *Theb. 11. 49:*

> " stabat in Argolicae ferrato margine turris
> egregius lituo dextri Mavortis Enipeus
> hortator; sed nunc miseris dabat utile signum,
> suadebatque fugam, et tutos in castra receptus ;
> cum subitum obliquo descendit ab aere vulnus,
> urgentisque sonum laeva manus aure retenta est
> sicut erat; fugit in vacuas iam spiritus auras,
> iam gelida *ora* tacent, carmen tuba sola peregit,"

where there is no ambiguity, and no matter in which of its three senses—*mouth, face, head*—" ora" be understood, not *fixedness of feature* but only *silence* can by any possibility be meant ; just as not *fixedness of feature*, but only *silence, profound silence* can by any possibility be meant in the exact Ovidian parallel, I might almost say repetition, of our text, *ex Ponto, 2. 5. 47:*

> " cum tu desisti, mortaliaque *ora* quierunt,
> clausaque non longa conticuere mora,"

where " conticuere" is the modified repetition (variation) of the theme " ora quierunt," as the ORA TENEBANT of our text is the modified repetition (variation) of the theme CONTICUERE ; and where to the variation are added the thoughts " clausa" and " non longa mora" in the same way as to the variation in our text is added the thought INTENTI.

With the active *tenere ora*, *premere ora*, compare the passive *ora quiescere*, *ora requiescere*; Ovid, *ex Ponto*, 2. 5. 47 (just quoted):

"cum tu desisti, mortaliaque *ora quierunt*;"

Aen. 6. 102:

"ut primum cessit furor, et rabida *ora quierunt*;"

ibid. 6. 300:

"ut primum placati animi et trepida *ora quierunt*;"

Propert. 3. 10. 9:

"Alcyonum positis *requiescant ora* querelis,
increpet absumptum nec sua mater Ityn"

—in which passages "quierunt" and "requiescant" express *quiet*, *rest from action*, exactly as "quievit," last word of the third book, expresses *quiet*, *rest from action*; with this only difference, that, the subject of "quierunt" and "requiescant" being "ora," quiet of the mouth only is meant; whereas in the third book, the subject of "quievit" being Aeneas, quiet both of mouth and limbs is meant: *Aeneas not only ceased to speak, but ceased to gesticulate;* and the thought which so appropriately and impressively closes the third book is neither, with Burmann and Wunderlich, "somno se tradidit," nor with Wagner in his edition of Heyne (1832), "narrare desiit," but with Wagner (1861)— studiedly, however imperfectly, translating, as is his wont, from my "Twelve Years' Voyage" (part 2, p. 53), and my paper in the Goettingen *Philologus* (vol. 11, p. 480)—"Non cubitum ivit, sed finita narratione rediit ad habitum compositum et quietum." How much more in ancient times than at present the notion of motion was contained in the notion of speech appears less, perhaps, from the so frequent expressions: *tenere ora*, *premere ora*, εχειν στομα, and their opposites: *solvere ora*, *resolvere ora*, *movere ora*, *aperire ora*, διαιρειν το στομα, λυειν το στομα, ανοιγειν το στομα (for similar expressions are not uncommon either in our own or other modern languages), than from the strong pictures of immobility of mouth, face, and even of the whole person, so often presented to us by ancient writers along with the picture of silence. Some of these pictures, viz., *Aen. 11. 120; 8. 520; 7. 249*, will be found cited above; another is *Aen. 6. 469:*

> "illa solo fixos oculos aversa tenebat,
> nec magis incepto vultum sermone movetur
> quam si dura silex aut stet Marpesia cautes."

Compare also Ovid, *Met. 13. 538:*

> . . . "obmutuit illa dolore,
> et pariter vocem lacrymasque introrsus obortas
> devorat ipse dolor, duroque simillima saxo
> torpet."

Ibid. 6. 301:

> . . . "orba resedit
> exanimes inter natos natasque virumque,
> diriguitque malis. nullos movet aura capillos.
> in vultu color est sine sanguine. lumina moestis
> stant immota genis. nihil est in imagine vivi.
> ipsa quoque interius cum duro lingua palato
> congelat, et venae desistunt posse moveri.
> nec flecti cervix, nec brachia reddere gestus,
> nec pes ire potest : intra quoque viscera saxum est."

Philemon, Fragm. 16 (*Anthol. Pal.*):

> Εγω λιθον μεν την Νιοβην, μα τους θεους,
> ουδεποτ' επεισθην, ουδε νυν πεισθησομαι
> ως τουτ' εγενετ' ανθρωπος· υπο δε των κακων
> των συμπεσοντων του τε συμβαντος παθους
> ουδεν λαλησαι δυναμενη προς ουδενα
> προσηγορευθη δια το μη φωνειν λιθος.

Paul. Silentiar., *Anthol. Pal. 7. 588:*

> Δαμοχαρις μοιρης πυματην υπεδυσατο σιγην·
> φευ το καλον μουσης βαρβιτον ηρεμεει.

In this last, however, the quiet, rest, or stirring no more, which accompanies and completes the silence of the musician, is not the musician's own, but his instrument's.

CONTICUERE. "Conticuerunt, non tacuerunt, quia omnes," La Cerda. That CONTICUERE expresses not that they were all silent *together*, but that the silence of one and all (of the OMNES) was *deep* and *perfect*, appears **firstly**, from "conticuit" being the very word used (*a*), in the last verse of the third book to express the silence of Aeneas—of Aeneas singly and alone :

"*conticuit* tandem factoque hic fine quievit ;"

and (**b**), in verse 54 of the sixth book, to express the silence of the Sibyl singly and alone ("talia fata *conticuit*"); as well as the very word used (**c**), by Apuleius to express the similar silence, or ceasing to speak, of Psyche, *Met. 4. 87:* "Sic profata virgo *conticuit*," not to insist on its being the very word (**d**), by which Statius, *Theb. 8. 267*, expresses the silence on board a ship at sea in the dead of night :

> "sic ubi per fluctus uno ratis obruta somno
> *conticuit*, tantique maris secura inventus
> mandavere animas, solus stat puppe magister
> pervigil, inscriptaque deus qui navigat alno :"

and the very word (**e**), by which Severus (see below) sets before us the deep silence observed by Latin Eloquence mourning the death of Cicero; **secondly**, from the well-known general use of the particle *con* to intensify the action of an individual; **thirdly**, from the little occasion there was that the idea expressed by the very next word should be anticipated; **and**, more than all, from "conticuere" being the precise word used by Ovid (*ex Ponto, 2. 5. 47*) to express the complete silence of his friend Salanus's one only mouth :

> "cum tu desisti, mortaliaque ora quierunt,
> clausaque non longa *conticuere* mora."

But CONTICUERE is not merely *they were entirely silent*, it is something more; it expresses the passage from the state of speaking to the state of silence : *they have become entirely silent*, or, which is the same thing, *they have entirely ceased to speak*, exactly as 3. 718, "conticuit tandem," *at length he has become entirely silent*, or, which is the same thing, *has entirely ceased to speak*. Compare *Eleg. in obit. Maecen. 52:*

> "postquam victrices *conticuere* tubae"

[*after the trumpets have entirely ceased to sound*]. Severus, *de morte Ciceronis Fragm., Anthol. Lat.*, Burm. (ed. Meyer), 124. 10 :

> "abstulit una dies aevi decus, ictaque luctu
> *conticuit* Latiae tristis Facundia linguae"

[*Latin Eloquence, sad and mourning, has entirely ceased to speak*].

Strong in itself, and no matter where placed, CONTICUERE is doubly strong owing to its position before, not after, its nominative; still stronger owing to its position, first word in the verse; and stronger still, owing to the verse in which it is first word being first verse of the book.

INTENTI. Not, with Conington and the commentators generally, "to be taken adverbially and as part of the predicate," but to be taken adjectively and as equivalent to a predicate : *intent*, i. e., *being intent : the whole company ceased talking, and being intent was silent*, exactly equivalent to *was intent and silent;* INTENTI being as thoroughly in form and more thoroughly in sense an adjective than was ever any one of Horace's four unquestioned and unquestionable adjectives, "invidus," "iracundus," "iners" and "vinosus." Settled the grammar, what is the meaning of the term? Of course, *intent*, Germ. *gespannt :* both of them, terms expressive of a state intermediate between the state expressed by lentus and that expressed by gnavus or sedulus; that intermediate state between slack and full-drawn, which a harper, speaking of his harp, might designate by the term *strung;* that intermediate state between remiss and excited, in which, according to Roman historians, Roman soldiers, prepared and on the *qui vive*, used to await the enemy ; Liv. 30. 10 : "Parati atque intenti hostium adventum opperiebantur." Except for this word, it might have been supposed that Aeneas took advantage of a hush or lull in the conversation—a moment of accidental silence—to begin his story. This word, informing us that when Aeneas began, the minds of the company were already in a fitting state to hear, prevents the mistake. All present had heard the queen's command, and perceiving it was about to be obeyed, had become silent and—not *attenti*, for, no word having yet been spoken, there was as yet nothing to attend to, nothing to justify an *ad*, but—INTENTI, intent, *strung*, if I may so say, not to *make*, but to *hear*, the music.

2.

INDE

This word and the change from perfect to imperfect in the preceding verse point out the precise time when Aeneas began to speak, viz., *after* the company had ceased talking, and *while* they were silent and on the *qui vive*. Had *cum* been used, as it might have been used by an inferior writer endeavouring to express the thought which Virgil has expressed by INDE, the meaning might have been supposed to be that it was only *when* Aeneas began his narrative the company ceased to talk and became silent and intent. INDE makes [say rather *should make*, for have we not

"all were attentive to the godlike man,
when from his lofty couch he thus began,"

and

"each eye was fixed, each lip compressed,
when thus began the heroic guest"?]

such misapprehension impossible : *all have entirely ceased to talk, and were continuing silent and intent;* INDE (*then—thereafter—next*) TORO PATER AENEAS SIC ORSUS AB ALTO.

3-6.

INFANDUM—QUIS

VAR. LECT.

[*punct.*] DOLOREM. TROIANAS . . . FUI—QUIS ▮▮▮ Haeckerm. (Muetzel, 1852); Ladewig.

[*punct.*] DOLOREM, [or ;] TROIANAS . . . FUI. QUIS ▮▮▮ All editors previous to the appearance of Haeckermann's observations in Muetzel's *Zeitschr.;* Wagner (1841), *Lect. Virg.* and *Praest.*, the former containing the author's very weak defence of the ancient punctuation.

[*punct.*] DOLOREM. TROIANAS . . . FUI, QUIS ▮▮▮ Haupt; Ribbeck.

3–5.

INFANDUM REGINA IUBES RENOVARE DOLOREM
TROIANAS UT OPES ET LAMENTABILE REGNUM
ERUERINT DANAI

Haeckermann (Muetzel's *Zeitschrift*) separates TROIANAS, &c., from the preceding by a period placed at DOLOREM, and Ribbeck has followed the example—a bad example, as I think. No doubt it may be urged in favour of his view that Aeneas's proem, thus confined to a single verse, becomes more emphatic, more modest, more graceful, and more touching; and the woes and fall of Troy—beginning a new sentence and a new line, and in the objective case, preceding the tears of the Myrmidons and Ulysses' soldiery—occupy a more dignified position than tacked to the tail of Aeneas's grief. Compare Silius's imitation, 2. 650 (of the fall of Saguntum):

"quis diros urbis casus, laudandaque monstra,
et fidei poenas, et tristia fata piorum
temperet evolvens lacrymis? vix Punica fletu
cessassent castra, ac miserescere nescius hostis,"

where the tears and their object occupy the same relative position as, according to Haeckermann's punctuation, they occupy in our text. But I strongly incline to the other punctuation given in the *Var. Lect.* above, (**1**), on account of the monotony of three successive verses terminated each by a period. (**2**), because three successive verses terminated each by a period are, when first verses of a book, worse than monotonous; disappoint the reader impatient to get on; make him feel as if he had stumbled three times on the threshold, or as if the door had been shut three times in his face. (**3**), because at 9. 66, where see Rem., "dolor" followed by "qua temptat ratione aditus" affords a very exact parallel for DOLOREM followed by UT ERUERINT DANAI TROIANAS OPES, not to speak of the so similar structure, 2. 120 :

" obstupuere animi, gelidusque per ima cucurrit
ossa tremor, cui fata parent, quem poscat Apollo."

12. 657 :

. . . . " mussat rex ipse Latinus,
quos generos vocet, aut quae sese ad foedera flectat."

And (4), because Statius's imitation, *Theb. 5. 29* (ed. Müller):

. . . . " immania vulnera, rector,
integrare iubes, Furias et Lemnon et atris
arma inserta toris debellatosque pudendo
ense mares,"

is plainly an imitation not of DOLOREM separated from the sequel by a period, but of DOLOREM explained by TROIANAS UT OPES—the " immania vulnera, rector, integrare iubes" of Statius corresponding as exactly as possible to Virgil's INFANDUM, REGINA, IUBES RENOVARE DOLOREM ; and the "Furias, et Lemnon et arctis arma inserta toris debellatosque pudendo ense mares" of Statius being his explanation of " immania vulnera," exactly as the TROIANAS UT OPES ET LAMENTABILE REGNUM ERUERINT DANAI, QUAEQUE IPSE MISERRIMA VIDI, ET QUORUM PARS MAGNA FUI of Virgil is his explanation of INFANDUM DOLOREM.

INFANDUM. The English and German translators (with the exception of Dryden and Sir J. Denham, who never even so much as attempt the true meaning of any of Virgil's words) agree in rendering INFANDUM, *ineffable, that cannot be told :* "untellyble" (Douglas) ; " cannot be told" (Surrey) ; " past utterance severe" (Beresford) ; " unaussprechlichen" (Voss). So also Forbiger, in his note on the passage : " Qui tantus est ut verbis exprimi non possit." Such, however, is not the meaning of the word, but, primarily, *that should not be told, that ought not to be told ; too horrible, too terrible, to be told ;* and, therefore, secondarily, *horrible, cruel, agonising.* Compare *Aen. 1. 255 :* " navibus (infandum !) amissis." 2. 132 : " iamque dies infanda aderat." 2. 84 : " insontem, infando indicio." 4. 85 : " infandum si fallere possit amorem." 4. 613 : " infandum caput." Nay, so little is infandus *ineffable* that it is even joined with memoratu by Apul. *Met. 10. 221 :* " Vocatoque uno et altero, ac deinde pluribus conservis, demonstrant *infan-*

dum memoratu hebetis iumenti gulam" [not, surely, ineffable to be told, but horrible to be told].

The Greeks—always so much less precise in their language than the Romans—seem to have used their αρρητος and αφατος in both senses, in that of *ineffabilis* no less than in that of *infandus*. Compare Soph. *Antig.* 555 (ed. Brunck):

> ΑΝΤ. συ μεν γαρ ειλου ζην· εγω δε, κατθανειν.
> ΙSΜ. αλλ' ουκ επ' αρρητοις γε τοις εμοις λογοις

(where αρρητος is simply *untold, unsaid*). Soph. *Ajax*, 773:

> τοτ' αντιφωνει δεινον αρρητον τ' επος.

Soph. *Oed. R. 464*: αρρητ' αρρητων φονιοις τελεσαντα χερσιν (in both which last instances αρρητος is *infandous*). Eurip. *Hec.* 705:

> αρρητ', ανωνομαστα, θαυματων περα,
> ουχ' οσια τ', ουδ' ανεκτα

(where it does not clearly appear in which of the two senses the word is used). Eurip. *Ion*, 782:

> πως φης; αφατον αφατον αναυδητον
> λογον εμοι θροεις.
>
> [quid ais? infandam infandam inauditam
> rem mihi narras].

Soph. *Oed. R. 1313*:

> ιω σκοτου
> νεφος εμον αποτροπον, επιπλομενον αφατον
> αδαματον τε και δυσουριστον.

Soph. *Oed. C. 1462*:

> ιδε μαλα μεγας ερειπεται
> κτυπος, οδ' αφατος
> Διοβολος

—in which three last places αφατος is no less ambiguous.

There are other Greek equivalents for infandus. (1), A less ambiguous one than either αρρητος or αφατος is απορρητυς (*forbidden, renounced;* therefore, *to be regarded with horror*), as Aristaen. 1. 16: Ερωτι περιπεσων απορρητω, κατ' εμαυτον εφασκον απορων. (2), Another is δυσωνυμος, as Apollon. Rhod. 2. 258

(Phineus assuring Jason that the gods will not be displeased at his expelling the Harpies):

> . . . ιστω δε δυσωνυμος, η μ' ελαχεν, κηρ,
> και τοδ' επ' οφθαλμων αλαον νεφος, οι θ' απενερθεν
> δαιμονες, οι μηδ' ωδε θανοντι περ ευμενεοιεν,
> ως ουτις θεοθεν χολος εσσεται εινεκ' αρωγης.

(**3**), Also δυσφραδης, αποφρας, and δυσφημος, as Eurip. *Hec.* 193 (ed. Porson), (Hecuba to Polyxena):

> αυδω, παι, δυσφημους φαμας,
> αγγελλουσ' Αργειων δοξαι
> ψηφω τας σας περι μοι ψυχας.

And, finally, (**4**), another is (for the Greek language is as endlessly rich and various as it is little precise) ουλομενος, as Hom. *Od. 11. 407:*

> αλλα μοι Αιγισθος, τευξας θανατον τε μορον τε,
> εκτα συν ουλομενη αλοχω, οικονδε καλεσσας,
> δειπνισσας,

with which compare Virgil, *Aen. 11. 266:*

> "ipse Mycenaeus magnorum ductor Achivum
> coniugis *infandae* prima inter lumina dextra
> oppetiit; devictam Asiam subsedit adulter,"

where our author himself has very plainly selected **infandus** as the most fitting representative of the ουλομενος of his prototype, thus furnishing the hint—not, so far as I know, yet taken by any Latin translator of the Iliad—to translate the ουλομενην of the second verse of that poem, not by **perniciosam**, but precisely by **infandam**.

The secondary meaning of **infandus**, viz., *horrible, abominable*, follows the word into the English, as Howell: "This *infandous* custom of swearing, I observe, reigns in England lately, more than anywhere else."

5-6.

QUAEQUE IPSE MISERRIMA VIDI
ET QUORUM PARS MAGNA FUI

QUAEQUE is epexegetic and limitative; the meaning of Aeneas being, not that he will describe the taking of Troy *and* the miseries he had himself witnessed, but that he will describe *so much* of the taking of Troy and its miseries *as* he had himself witnessed.

The view thus suggested by the grammatical structure of the introductory sentence is confirmed by the narrative itself; for Aeneas, having briefly mentioned the building of the wooden horse and the concealment of the Grecian navy at Tenedos, immediately proceeds to say that he was one of those who issued out of the gates rejoicing, as soon as the news of the departure of the Greeks was bruited abroad; that he saw the horse, and was present at the argument respecting what should be done with it; that he saw Laocoon fling his spear against it, and heard it sound hollow; that his attention was drawn off by the sudden appearance of Sinon, of the whole of whose story he was an ear-witness; that he was one of those who agreed to spare Sinon's life; that he saw the two serpents come across the sea, and destroy Laocoon and his two sons; that he assisted to break down the wall in order to admit the horse into the city; that Hector appeared to him in a dream, and informed him that the city was on fire and could not be saved—advised him to fly, and committed the Penates to his charge; that on awaking he saw, from the roof of the house, the city in flames; that, flying to arms, he met Pantheus, the priest of Apollo, escaping from the citadel, with his gods' images and the other sacred objects of his religion; that Pantheus informed him that armed men were pouring out of the horse, that Sinon was a traitor and had fired the city, and that the whole Grecian army was entering at the gates; that he united himself with a few friends whom he happened to meet, and, falling in with Androgeus and a party of Greeks, they slew them every one, and clothed themselves with their spoils; that, thus disguised, they for a while carried terror and death everywhere, but at length, in attempting to rescue Cassandra from a party who were dragging her from the temple, were discovered to be Trojans, and attacked by the Greeks, while the Trojans, taking them for Greeks, overwhelmed them with missiles from the top of the temple; that, the greater number of his party having thus perished, he with the small remainder was attracted by the tumult to Priam's palace, from the roof of which he beheld the door forced, the building set on fire, the women and the aged king driven for shelter to an altar in an interior court, and the king himself slain at the altar in the blood of his son; that, his companions having leaped in despair to the ground, or given themselves up to the flames, he was left alone; that, descending and happening to see Helen where she was hiding, he was about to sacrifice her to the Manes of his country, when his arm was stayed by Venus, who commanded him to seek out his aged parent and his wife and child, and with them fly instantly from Troy; and who, at the same time taking off the veil which clouded his mortal vision, showed him the gods actively and personally engaged in the destruction of the city; that, having returned to his father's house, he saw the encouraging omens of a tongue of fire on the head of Iulus, and a star shooting in the direction of Ida; that he escaped out of the city bearing his father on his shoulders, and leading Iulus by the hand; that Creusa, following behind, was lost on the road; that, returning to seek her, he found his father's house filled with Greeks, and on fire; that, extending his search everywhere, he returned to the citadel, and saw Phenix and Ulysses guarding captives and booty in the temple of Juno; that, as he called aloud upon Creusa through the streets and houses, her shade presented itself, and informing him that she was provided for by the mother of the gods, enjoined him to abandon all search for her, and proceed upon his divine mission to found a new empire in Hesperia, where another, and a royal, spouse awaited him; that accordingly he returned to the place where he had concealed his father and son and domestics, and found there a great number of fugitives from the burning city, collected and prepared to share his fortunes; and that with them and his father and son he bade adieu for ever to Troy, and made good his retreat to the mountains.

Nothing can be plainer than that this is a mere *personal* narrative of one of the principal sufferers; every circumstance related, with the single exception of the concealment of the Grecian fleet at Tenedos, having been witnessed by the relator, or heard by him on the spot from Pantheus or Sinon. This is, I think, a sufficient answer to those critics who have objected to Virgil's account of the taking of Troy, that it is by no means a full, complete, and strategical account of the taking of a great city; that many circumstances which may be supposed to have happened, and which indeed must have happened on such an occasion, have been either wholly omitted or left unexplained; and that, in short, Virgil in his second book of the Aeneid has evinced his infinite inferiority in strategical science to his great prototype and master, Homer. Many such objections have been urged from time to time by various critics; and, amongst others, by a celebrated personage whose opinion on any matter connected with military tactics must be received with the greatest deference—I mean the Emperor Napoleon, whose observations on this subject are to be found in a volume published after his death under the following title: "Précis des Guerres de César, par Napoléon, écrit par M. Marchand, à l'île Sainte Hélène, sous la dictée de l'Empereur; suivi de pleusieurs fragmens inédits": Paris, 1836; 1 vol. 8vo.

It is not my intention to enter into a detailed examination or refutation of all Napoleon's objections (although I shall probably in the course of these Remarks have occasion to refer specially to more than one of them), but simply to state that the whole of his critique is founded on the assumption that Virgil intended to give, or ought to have given, such a full and complete account of the taking of Troy as was given by Homer of the operations before its walls—such an account as might have been given by a historian, or laid before a directory by a commander-in-chief. On the contrary, it is to be borne carefully in mind that, Homer's subject being the misfortunes brought by the wrath of Achilles upon the army besieging Troy, that poet could scarcely have given too particular or strategical an account of all that happened before the Trojan walls; while, Virgil's subject being the adventures and fortunes of one man (as sufficiently evidenced by the very title and exordium of his work), the taking of Troy was to be treated of only so far as connected with the personal history of that hero. Virgil, therefore, with his usual judgment, introduces the taking of Troy, not as a part of the action of his poem, but as an episode; and—still more effectually to prevent the attention from being too much drawn away from his hero, and too much fixed upon that great and spirit-stirring event—puts the account of it into the mouth of the hero himself, whom, with the most wonderful art, he represents either as a spectator or actor in so many of the incidents of that memorable night that on the one hand the account of those incidents is the history of the adventures of his hero, and on the other, the adventures of his hero form a rapid *précis* of the taking of Troy.

Even if it had been otherwise consistent with the plan of the Aeneid to have given a full and complete account of the taking of Troy, and to have described, for instance (as required by Napoleon), how the other Trojan chiefs signalised in the Iliad were occupied during that fatal night, and how each defended his own quarter of the city with the troops under his command, such a full account must necessarily either have rendered Aeneas's narrative too long to have been delivered "inter mensas laticemque Lyaeum;" or, to make room for that additional matter, some part of the present story should have been left out; and then, I ask, which of the incidents would the reader be satisfied should have been omitted?—that of Laocoon, the unceasing theme and admiration of all ages, that shuddering picture of a religious prodigy?—that of Sinon, on which the whole plot hangs?—that of the vision, of the inimitable " tempus erat," the " moestissimus Hector "?—that of the Priamelan priestess, " ad caelum tendens ardentia lumina frustra (lumina, nam teneras arcebant vincula palmas)" ?—that of Neoptolemus blazing in burnished brass, "qualis ubi in lucem coluber"?—or Hecuba and her daughters flying to the sheltering altar, "praecipites atra ceu tempestate columbae"? —or the good old king, cased in the long-unused armour, and slipping and slain in his Polites' blood?—or Venus staying her son's hand, lifted in vengeance against the fatal spring of all these sorrows?—or the innoxious flame which, playing about the temples of Iulus, foreshowed him the father of a line of kings?—or the "ter frustra comprensa imago" of the for ever lost Creusa? Which of all these passages should have been omitted, to make room for the additional matter required by the imperial critic? What reader will consent to give up one, even one, of these most precious pearls, these conspicuous stars in, perhaps, the most brilliant coronet that ever graced a poet's brow? And even if the reader's assent were gained, if he were content with less of Aeneas and more of the other Homeric Trojans, with less of the romance and more of the art of war, would such an account have been equally interesting to the assembled guests and the love-caught queen? How coldly would a story in which Aeneas played a subordinate part have fallen upon Dido's ear? How would not her thought have wandered from the thing told to the teller? There was but one way to guard against the double danger that Dido would forget the story in thinking of Aeneas, and that the reader would forget Aeneas in thinking of the story ; and Virgil adopted that way. He made Aeneas speak of himself—QUAEQUE IPSE MISERRIMA VIDI, ET QUORUM PARS MAGNA FUI. With what effect he spoke, we learn in the beginning of the fourth book ("haerent infixi pectore vultus verbaque"), and Dido herself testifies—"heu, quibus ille iactatus fatis ! quae bella exhausta canebat!" Or, applying the words of another great master of the human heart (Shakespeare, *Othello, 1. 3*) :

> . . . "his story being done,
> she gave him for his pains a world of sighs :
> she swore—in faith, 'twas strange, 'twas passing strange ;
> 'twas pitiful, 'twas wondrous pitiful ;

> she wished she had not heard it; yet she wish'd
> that heaven had made her such a man; she thank'd him,
> and bade him, if he had a friend that lov'd her,
> he should but teach him how to tell his story,
> and that would woo her."

But let us suppose that the modern commander is right, and the great ancient poet and philosopher wrong; that the error lies not in Napoleon's total misconception, not only of Virgil's general scope and design, but of his meaning in the plainest passages (as, for instance, in the account of the situation of Anchises' house, and of the number of men contained in the horse); let us suppose, I say, that the error lies not in Napoleon's misconception of the poet, but in the poet's ignorance of heroic warfare; and that the episode does, indeed, sin against military tactique (but see Rem. on verse 608): yet where, in the whole compass of poetry, is there such another episode? so many heart-stirring incidents grouped together, representing in one vivid picture the fall of the most celebrated city in the world, and at the same time, and *pari passu*, the fortunes of one of the most famous heroes of all antiquity, the son of Venus, the ancestor of Augustus, the first founder of Imperial Rome? spoken, too, by the hero himself, at a magnificent banquet, and in presence not only of the princes of his own nation (the partners of his sufferings, and the witnesses of the truth of all he related), but of the whole Carthaginian court, and at the request of the young and artless queen, who, already admiring his godlike person and beauty, lost her heart more and more at every word he uttered—at every turn of griefs, which,

> . . . "so lively shown,
> made her think upon her own."

Alas, alas, for the cold-blooded criticism which could detect, or, having detected, could dwell upon, errors of military tactique in this flood of living poetry; which would chain the poet with the fetters of the historian; which, frigid and unmoved, would occupy itself with the observation of cracks and flaws in the scenic plaster, while the most magnificent drama ever presented to enraptured audience was being enacted!

6-9.

QUIS TALIA FANDO
MYRMIDONUM DOLOPUMVE AUT DURI MILES ULIXI
TEMPERET A LACRYMIS ET IAM NOX HUMIDA CAELO
PRAECIPITAT

QUIS TALIA FANDO . . . TEMPERET A LACRYMIS? Compare Eurip., Fragm. ex *Aeolo*, 23 :

τις αν κλυων τωνδ' ουκ αν εκβαλοι δακρυ ;

Eurip., *Hec. 296* (ed. Porson) :

τις εστιν ουτω στερρος ανθρωπου φυσις,
ητις γοων σων και μακρων οδυρματων
κλυουσα θρηνους, ουκ αν εκβαλοι δακρυ ;

Eurip., *Iph. in Aul. 791* (ed. Fix) :

τις αρα μ' ευπλοκαμους κομας
ρυμα δακρυοεν τανυσας
πατριδος ολλυμενας απολωτιει
δια σε, ταν κυκνου δολιχαυχενος γονον ;

Jacoponus, *Sequentia de septem doloribus Mariae Virginis* ("Stabat mater dolorosa") :

" quis est homo qui non fleret
matrem Christi si videret
   in tanto supplicio ?
quis non posset contristari,
piam matrem contemplari
   dolentem cum filio ?"

Metast., *Ciro, 1. 6:*

"chi potrebbe a que' detti
temperarsi dal pianto ?"

Also Sil. 2. 650, quoted in Rem. on 2. 3.

DURI ULIXI. Stubborn, hardened, and so indomitable. Compare 4. 247 : "Duri Atlantis," and 3. 94 : " Dardanidae duri."

ET IAM NOX HUMIDA CAELO PRAECIPITAT. "Nox descendit in oceanum, quasi cursu per medium caelum ab occidente ad orientem facto," Heyne. "Sol subit in oceanum occidentalem, nox ex eodem oceano occidentali oritur," Peerlkamp. No, no; that in the opinion of the ancients the night no less than the day rises in the east and sets in the west is placed beyond all manner of doubt by the reason assigned by Sol to Phaethon why he could delay no longer, but must forthwith proceed on his journey, Ovid, *Met. 2. 142* :

> " dum loquor, Hesperio positas in littore metas
> humida nox tetigit."

The picture presented by our text is therefore **not** that of the night setting in the east, in which case not only would there have been no flight of Nox before Sol, but there would on the contrary have been the very obvious danger of a collision between the chariots of the two deities—in plain terms you would have had day and night not succeeding each other, but meeting each other, and in the same place at the same time—**but** the picture is of the night setting in the west, the great hotel or sleeping quarters of day, night, Aurora, sun, and moon, and all the host of heaven. See Rem. on "ruit oceano nox," 2. 250.

PRAECIPITAT, *i. e.*, "fugit praeceps" (as explained by Virgil himself, 4. 565 :

> " non *fugis* hinc *praeceps* dum *praecipitare* potestas?"),

and equally applicable to day and to night. Compare Cic. *de Orat. 3. 55* : "His autem de rebus, sol me ille admonuit, ut brevior essem, qui ipse iam *praecipitans*, me quoque haec praecipitem paene evolvere coegit." Liv. 4. 9 : "*Praecipiti*que iam die curare corpora milites iubet" (see Rem. on 1. 749). Caes. *Bell. Civ. 3. 25* : "Multi iam menses transierant, et hiems iam *praecipitaverat*" [winter was already over].

While NOX PRAECIPITAT is "night *sets*," "nox ruit," 2. 250 (where see Rem.), and 6. 539, is "night *rises*." What a freakish thing is language! No two words can come much nearer to each other in general meaning, and yet they are used to express two things as directly opposed as white is to black, east to west, day to night! Stay ; have we not *altum mare* and *altum caelum?*

13.

INCIPIAM

Not *I will begin*, but *I will undertake*, or *take in hand;* **first**, because although it might, strictly speaking, be quite correct for Virgil—having just stated (verse 2) that Aeneas *began* to speak (ORSUS) with the words INFANDUM REGINA IUBES, &c.—to cause Aeneas almost instantly afterwards to say that he *began* his story with the words FRACTI BELLO, &c., yet it would be highly unpoetical, and evince a barrenness of thought and expression quite foreign to Virgil. **Secondly**, because it is evidently the intention of Aeneas not merely to *begin*, but briefly to tell the *whole* story, as it is no less evidently the intention of Pliny, where he writes to Tacitus in the very words of Aeneas, "quanquam animus meminisse horret, incipiam," not merely to begin, but to give a complete account from beginning to end of what he himself saw and suffered in the eruption of Vesuvius. **Thirdly**, because the very word *begin* involves the idea of a long story, and thus, however true in point of fact, contradicts the intention expressed by BREVITER (verse 11).

I, therefore, understand INCIPIAM to be here used (as in *Aen. 10. 876*) in its primary and etymological meaning of *undertaking, taking in hand (in-capio)*; so understood, it harmonises with ORSUS, with Aeneas's intention of telling the whole story, with BREVITER, and with the immediately preceding words, QUANQUAM ANIMUS MEMINISSE HORRET, &c. Compare Lucr. 1. 50 : "Disserere incipiam" [not *begin* or *commence*, but *undertake, take in hand, attempt, to discuss*]. Also Tibull. 4. 1. 1 :

   . . . " quanquam me cognita virtus
   terret, ut infirmae nequeant subsistere vires,
   incipiam tamen;"

and Hor. *Sat. 1. 1. 92* :

   " denique sit finis quaerendi; quoque habeas plus,
   pauperiem metuas minus, et finire laborem
   incipias, parto quod avebas"

[in which latter passage the difficulty pointed out by Mr. John Murray ("Original views of passages in the life and writings of the Poet-philosopher of Venusia:" Dublin, 1851) in the expression "incipias finire laborem parto"—hitherto somewhat absurdly understood to mean : "begin to end your labour now that you have gained your object"—is to be got rid of not by interpreting "finire" and "parto" in the manner proposed by Mr. Murray, but simply and at once by restricting "incipias" to its genuine and legitimate sense of *setting about, taking in hand*]. Compare also Virgil himself, *Aen.* 6. *493*:

> . . . . " *inceptus* clamor frustratur hiantes"

[not, *begins* with a shout and ends with a squeak, but *attempting* to shout, they only squeak]. *Ecl.* 5. *10:*

> Me. " *incipe,* Mopse prior, si quos aut Phyllidis ignes
> aut Alconis habes laudes aut iurgia Codri.
> *incipe ;* pascentes servabit Tityrus haedos.
> Mo. immo haec, in viridi nuper quae cortice fagi
> carmina descripsi et modulans alterna notavi,
> experiar"

(where we have not only in ci pere in the sense of undertake, but experiri used as a variation of or equivalent for incipere). Tacit. *Annal.* 13. 15 : "Britannico iussit exsurgeret, progressusque in medium, cantum aliquem *inciperet*" [*take in hand some song, undertake some song*]. Also Ter. *Andr.* 1. 3. 13 :

> " nam *inceptio* est amentium, haud amantium ;"

and Id. *ib.* 5. 1. 17 :

> " nuptiarum gratia haec sunt ficta atque *incepta* omnia ;"

and *3. 2. 12 :*

> . . . . " itane tandem idoneus
> tibi videor esse quem tam aperte fallere *incipias* dolis ?"

Val. Flacc. 6. 123 :

> " namque ubi iam viresque aliae, notosque refutat
> arcus, et *inceptus* iam lancea temnit heriles,
> magnanimis mos ductus avis, haud segnia morti-
> iura pati."

Coripp. Johann. 3. 52:

"praecipitur placidis Liberatus dicere verbis.
paruit ille celer, plena sic voce locutus:
'*Nitor*, summe ducum, caussas narrare malorum
et iussis parere tuis. dum dicere *tento*,
flamma nocens surgit, gelidus praecordia sanguis
turbat, et attentae vix prodit fabula linguae.'"

And, finally, Hom. *Il. 3. 99* (Menelaus speaking):

. . . επει κακα πολλα πεποσθε,
εινικ' εμης εριδος, και Αλεξανδρου ενεκ' αρχης

(where αρχης is *incepti*, in the sense of *undertaking*).

Almost exactly corresponding to ORSUS . . . INCIPIAM in the passage before us is "adorta . . . orsa," *Aen. 7. 386.*

That our own English *begin* had originally and primarily a similar signification, and meant not to *commence*, but to *undertake*, appears both from its German origin (viz., "beginnen," *to undertake*, as Schiller, *Die Piccolom. 1. 3:* .

"er würde freiheit mir und leben kosten,
und sein verwegenes *beginnen* nur
beschleunigen"),

and from the use made of the term, not only by the earliest English writers (as Robert of Gloucester:

"that Eneas *bigan* hys ofspring to Lumbardie first bring"),

but by Milton, no mean part of the excellence of whose poetry consists in the frequent employment of ordinary and current terms in primitive and obsolete, and therefore extraordinary meanings; see *Sams. Agonist. 274:*

. . . "if he aught *begin*,
how frequent to desert him, and at last
to heap ingratitude on worthiest deeds!"

INCIPIAM—first word of the verse to which it belongs, separated from the remainder of the verse by a complete pause, and constituting alone and by itself the apodosis referred to by the whole of the long preceding protasis SI . . . REFUGIT—is in the highest degree emphatic. See Rem. on 2. 246.

13-17.

FRACTI BELLO FATISQUE REPULSI
DUCTORES DANAUM TOT IAM LABENTIBUS ANNIS
INSTAR MONTIS EQUUM DIVINA PALLADIS ARTE
AEDIFICANT SECTAQUE INTEXUNT ABIETE COSTAS
VOTUM PRO REDITU SIMULANT EA FAMA VAGATUR

FRACTI BELLO FATISQUE REPULSI. "Cum verba FATIS RE-
PULSI alio modo idem quod FRACTI BELLO exprimere apertum
sit, quin intelligendae sint calamitates ac clades belli quibus
fatigati Danai tandem ad dolum confugerunt, dubium non est,"
Dietsch (*Theolog.*, p. 21). This is not the meaning. FATIS
REPULSI does not express in different terms the thought expressed by FRACTI BELLO (in other words, is not a variation of
a theme), but expresses the totally different, independent, and
additional thought that the repulses which the Greeks received
before Troy were the work of the fates; that the ill-success of
the Greeks was not owing to want of skill, or bravery, or
strength, but to the supreme ordinance of the fates.

FATIS REPULSI, a metonymy of the same kind as (5. 709)

. . . "quo fata trahunt retrahuntque, sequamur,"

and (5. 22)

. . . "superat quoniam fortuna, sequamur."

TOT IAM LABENTIBUS ANNIS. The translators refer LABENTI-
BUS to the dim and faded past, instead of the vivid and continuing present; for instance, Surrey :

. . . "all irked with the war,
wherein they wasted had so many years;"

Phaer :
"whan all in vaine so many yeeres had past ;"

and Alfieri :
. . . "da molti anni indarno
stringevan Troja i condottier de' Greci."

Yet the present and continuing force of LABENTIBUS is doubly evident; because the verb *labor* expresses a continuing action, and the present participle a continuing time. It is this continuing sense (observed by Wagner, *Quaest. Virg.* 29. 1) which constitutes the poetical beauty of the passage before us, as well as of Horace's exquisite

"eheu, fugaces, Postume, Postume,
labuntur anni."

Dryden, according to his custom, blinks the meaning altogether.

INSTAR MONTIS EQUUM. Even in more modern times, cities have been sometimes taken by a similar artifice; for instance, Breda in Holland, in the year 1590, by means of soldiers concealed under turf in a turf-boat, and so introduced into the city; and Luna in Italy, by means of soldiers performing the part of mourners, priests, &c., at the pretended funeral of Hasting. Compare Wace, *Roman de Rou*, 687 (ed. Pluquet):

"li mestre cler cante l'office,
. . . .
li Eveske canta la messe,
des Paenz fu la turbe espesse."

DIVINA PALLADIS ARTE. The commentators make Pallas a party in the Grecian stratagem, an accomplice of Epeus and Sinon. "PALLADIS ARTE, υποθημοσυνησι," Heyne, quoting *Od.* 8. 493: τον Επειος εποιησεν συν Αθηνη. "Pallas fabros in exstruendo equo consilio suo et praeceptis adiuvit," Forbiger, quoting, along with the same passage of the Odyssey, Eurip. *Troad.* 9:

. . . ο γαρ Παρνασιος
Φωκευς Επειος μηχαναισι Παλλαδος
εγκυμον' ιππον τευχεων συναρμοσας
πυργων επεμψεν εντος, ολεθριον βαρος.

"DIVINA, ergo non sua, sed ea quam dea Pallas iis monstraverat," Wagner (1861), quoting, along with the same passage of the Odyssey, *Il.* 15. 70:

. . . εις ο κ' Αχαιοι
Ιλιον αιπυ ελοιεν Αθηναιης δια βουλας.

Nothing could be further from the meaning of Virgil. Pallas has nothing whatsoever to do with the building of the horse. The leaders of the Danai are its builders (DUCTORES DANAUM AEDIFICANT), and built it DIVINA ARTE PALLADIS. Now, what is DIVINA ARTE PALLADIS? or rather, leaving out DIVINA as unessential, and taking ARTE PALLADIS by itself, what is ARTE PALLADIS? Ovid, *ex Ponto, 3. 8. 9*, uses the identical expression in the sense of *art of Pallas*, i. e., *Palladian art:*

"vellera dura ferunt pecudes, et *Palladis* uti
arte Tomitanae non didicere nurus,"

"the daughters of Tomi have not learned to use the Palladian art;" and so precisely our author: "the leaders of the Danai build with Palladian art." Not that the art of Pallas, the Palladian art, with which the leaders of the Danai build is the same art of Pallas, the same Palladian art, which the daughters of Tomi have not learned, but that—there being many arts of Pallas, many Palladian arts [Ovid, *Fast. 3. 833:* "mille dea est operum." Idem, *Art. Amat. 1. 691:*

"quid facis, Aeacida? non sunt tua munera lanae.
tu titulos alia Palladis arte petas]—

the one with which the DUCTORES DANAUM build is the building art, while the one which the daughters of Tomi have not learned is the weaving art. Compare (*a*), Propert. 3. 20. 7:

"est tibi [Cynthiae] forma potens, sunt castae *Palladis artes*,
splendidaque a docto fama refulget avo"

(where the "Palladis artes"—the Palladian arts—of which Cynthia was mistress are the art of weaving, exactly as in our text the PALLADIS ARTE—the Palladian art—with which the DUCTORES DANAUM AEDIFICANT is the art of building). (*b*), Eurip. *Troad. 9* (quoted above):

. . . ο γαρ Παρνασιος
Φωκευς Επειος μηχαναισι Παλλαδος
εγκυμον' ιππον τευχεων συναρμοσας
πυργων επεμψεν εντος, ολεθριον βαρος

(where μηχαναισι Παλλαδος is the Palladian art, the art invented and patronized by Pallas, with which Epeus constructed the horse, exactly as in our text PALLADIS ARTE is the Palladian art, the art invented and patronized by Pallas, with which the chiefs of the Danai build the horse). (*c*), *Aen. 9. 303* :

> . . . "ensem
> auratum, *mira* quem fecerat *arte* Lycaon
> Gnosius"

(where it is with " mira arte," wonderful art, Gnosian Lycaon had made the sword; exactly as in our text it is with DIVINA (PALLADIS) ARTE, divine (superexcellent : see below) art (Palladian), the DUCTORES DANAUM build the horse). (*d*), Juv. 14. 34 :

> . . . "quibus *arte benigna*
> et meliore luto finxit praecordia Titan"

(where it is with benign art Titan moulds the " praecordia," exactly as it is with divine (superexcellent) art (Palladian) the DUCTORES DANAUM build the horse). (*e*), Tibull. 1. 3. 47 :

> . . . " nec ensem
> *immiti* saevus duxerat *arte* faber."

And (*f*), Mart. 7. 55 :

> "astra polumque tua cepisti mente, Rabiri;
> Parrhasiam *mira* qui struis *arte* domum."

What, then? are the expressions Palladia ars and ars Palladis always and everywhere Palladian art used not by Pallas but by somebody else—here by the chiefs of the Danai, there by the women of Tomi, elsewhere by some other agent? Far from it. On the contrary, those expressions—occurring, as they occasionally occur, where there is no agent by whom Palladian art can be used—are to be understood not as signifying art invented and patronized by Pallas, but as signifying art used on the particular occasion by Pallas herself, *ex. gr.* Mart. 6. 13 :

> "quis te Phidiaco formatam, Iulia, caelo,
> vel quis *Palladiae* non putet *artis* opus?"

Stat. *Silv. 1. 1. 5* (to the equestrian statue of Domitian) :

> "an te *Palladiae* talem, Germanice, nobis
> effinxere *manus*?"

—the Palladian art (art of Pallas) of the former of which passages is as nearly as possible the Palladian hands (hands of

Pallas), of the latter. The mistake of the commentators consists in their confounding the "art of Pallas" (Palladian art) of Virgil, equivalent to art invented and patronized by Pallas, with the "Palladian art" (art of Pallas) of Martial, equivalent to art of Pallas's own hands. Instances, indeed, occur in which it is extremely difficult, if not impossible, to determine in which of these its two senses the expression Palladia ars or ars Palladis is to be understood, *ex. gr.* Propertius, 3. 9. 41 :

    "moenia cum Graio Neptunia pressit aratro
        victor *Palladiae* ligneus *artis* equus,"

where—there being on the one hand as total absence of agent to use art invented and patronized by Pallas, as there is on the other of indication that the art spoken of was used by Pallas herself—the "ars Palladia" spoken of is with equal probability art invented and patronized by Pallas, and art practised by Pallas herself on the particular occasion : an ambiguity which does not exist either in our text or in the parallel text of Euripides quoted above, in both which places the express mention of the agent by whom the Palladian art is used (DUCTORES DANAUM PALLADIS ARTE AEDIFICANT : Φωκευς Επειος μηχαναισι Παλλαδος συναρμοσας) as peremptorily forbids us to understand the Palladian art spoken of by those authors to be art employed by Pallas herself in the building of the horse, as (**1**) the συν Αθηνη of Homer ; (**2**) the

   . . . Αργειης ιππηλατον εργον Αθηνης

of Tryphiodorus (verse 2) ; (**3**) the

   χερσι μεν ανδρομεης, αυταρ βουλησιν Αθηνης

of the same author (verse 119) ; (**4**) the του Επειου τε και Αθηνας ιππον of Philostr. *Heroic.* (ed. Boisson.), p. 102 ; **and** (**5**) the του ιππον τον κοιλον, ου τεκτων μεν Επειος ξυν Αθηνα εγενετο of the same Philostr. *Heroic.* (ed. Boisson.), p. 166, **forbid** us to understand the Trojan horse of those authors to have been built without Pallas's personal assistance and co-operation ; **or**, as (**6**), the Αθηναιη ηρμοσε of Apollon. Rhod. 4. 582 :

    αυδηεν γλαφυρης νηος δορυ, το ρ' ανα μεσσην
    στειραν Αθηναιη Δωδωνιδος ηρμοσε φηγου·

(**7**) the καλεσσαμενη επετελλετο Τριτογενειη of Orpheus, *Argon.*
65 :

    και ρα καλεσσαμενη [Juno] επετελλετο Τριτογενειη,
    και οι φηγινεην πρωτον τεκτηνατο νηα,
    η και υπ' ειλατινοις ερετμοις αλιμυρεα βενθη
    πρωτη υπεξεπερησε·

and (**8**) the Αθηνα ενηρμοσεν of Apollodorus, 1. 9 : κατα δε την πρωραν ενηρμοσεν Αθηνα φωνηεν φηγου της Δωδωνιδος ξυλον, **forbid** us to understand the Argo of those authors to have been built without the personal presence and co-operation of the same goddess.

But, it will be said, this is to ignore Homer, who informs us, *Od. 8. 493* (quoted above), that the horse was made by Epeus συν Αθηνη ; and Homer is not to be ignored in the discussion of a Virgilian passage which treats of a subject already treated of by Homer. True : but however excellent a guide Homer may be to the meaning of Virgil's words in a case in which those words allow such meaning to be put on them and present no better of their own, Homer's guidance is none at all, or worse than none, in a case in which Virgil's words not only do not allow the Homeric meaning to be put on them, but, well considered, present a meaning more appropriate in the mouth of Virgil than the Homeric meaning had been—the very case we are considering, in which **not only** does PALLADIS ARTE, according to the use of the expression elsewhere (see above), not allow itself to be interpreted as it has been interpreted by various commentators—all taking their cue from the Homeric συν Αθηνη, either υποθημοσυνησι (Παλλαδος), or "consilio et praeceptis (Palladis)," or "ea [ARTE] quam dea Pallas iis monstraverat," **but** any of these meanings had been as little proper in the mouth of Virgil—writing for the highly cultivated, little romantic, almost sceptical, age and court of Augustus—as it was proper in the mouth of Homer, writing for an age so much less cultivated, more simple, and more ignorant. And Virgil—in not copying the Homeric myth to the uttermost letter, in bearing in mind the Horatian " nec deus intersit " and representing the horse as built by the chiefs of the Danai, not with the *assistance* of or by the hands of Pallas, but only with the *art* of Pallas, *i. e.*, with Palladian art—has only shown his usual preference of common sense to unnecessary, childish, and even absurd extravagance, and protected his Trojan horse from reproaches similar to those which have been so justly heaped (compare Claud. *de Bell. Get. 14:*

> . . . "licet omnia vates
> in maius celebrata ferant, ipsamque secandis
> Argois trabibus iactent sudasse Minervam;
> nec nemoris tantum iunxisse carentia sensu
> robora, sed, caeso Tmarii Iovis augure luco,
> arbore praesaga tabulas animasse loquaces")

upon the Argo of Orpheus, Apollonius Rhodius, and Apollodorus: the Argo, another myth in which another Roman poet almost coeval with our author, exercising a similar discretion, represents that still more wonderful structure, the first ship, as constructed neither by Pallas with her own hands nor by Argus with the personal assistance of Pallas, but by Argus "Palladio opere," as nearly as possible our author's DIVINA PALLADIS ARTE (Phaedr. 4. 6. 6):

> "utinam nec umquam Pelei nemoris iugo
> pinus bipenni concidisset Thessala,
> nec ad professae mortis audacem viam
> fabricasset Argus *opere Palladio* ratem."

If I am correct in these observations, artists skilled in arts communicated to mankind by the respective inventing gods were able under later polytheism to execute works which under primitive polytheism could not be executed without the personal presence and assistance of the respective inventing gods themselves; exactly as under modern monotheism men perform daily with God's mere will or God's mere providence—" Deo volente," or " providentia Dei"—acts which under primitive monotheism required the personal presence and co-operation either of the one God Himself or of the one God's special messenger: warrant for the sceptic dogma that the world as it advances in knowledge less and less either seeks or requires heaven's assistance; exemplifying so, in the collective, the truth of the proverb so true in the individual: "Help yourself and God will help you."

DIVINA. The meaning of PALLADIS ARTE remains the same whether we understand DIVINA literally or figuratively; whether as meaning *divine*, θεῖος, in the sense of derived from a god, as *Georg. 4. 220*:

> "esse apibus partem *divinae* mentis et haustus aetherios,"

or as meaning *divine*, θεῖος, in the sense of supremely excellent, as Cic. *Philipp. 12:* "Ipsa illa Martia, caelestis et *divina* legio, hoc nuntio languescet et mollietur." Compare the application by Cicero, *de Nat. Deor.* (ed. Lambin.), p. 227, of the same term in the same sense to the cognate and similarly wonderful piece of workmanship, the Argo: "Atque ille apud Attium pastor, qui navem nunquam ante vidisset, ut procul *divinum* et novum vehiculum Argonautarum e monte conspexit, primo admirans et perterritus hoc modo loquitur." Pallas, therefore, unless I greatly err, is no more personally present and helping here in the building of the wooden horse by the chiefs of the Danai DIVINA PALLADIS ARTE, than Phoebus is present and helping in the curing of the sick by physicians " Phoebea arte," Ovid, *Fast. 3. 827:*

> . . . . "Phoebea morbos qui pellitis arte."

Grave, however, as are these mistakes of modern commentators concerning our author's meaning in this place, the mistakes of the ancient commentators are graver still, Servius (ed. Lion) doubting whether ARTE (joined though it be with the highest term of praise it was possible to bestow) is not to be understood in its bad sense, viz. of *dolo* [" aut ingeniose aut dolose; ac si diceret ' consilio iratae deae, quae fuit inimica Troianis'"]; and Donatus (proh, pudor!) separating PALLADIS from ARTE and connecting it with EQUUM: "Ecce in bellum factum [*lege* "in bello fracti"]·verterunt se ad insidias, ut desperatam in aperto Marte victoriam adminiculo fraudis obtinere potuissent. Proinde ad INSTAR MONTIS EQUUM PALLADIS AEDIFICANT, et DIVINA ARTE COSTAS eius IN-

TEXUNT. Cur autem Palladis nomine aedificatus sit, datur color quo possent homines ab insidiarum suspicione transduci": a perverse interpretation, by whomsoever made—for it could hardly have been made by Donatus—and unparalleled in the long chronicle of perverse interpretations, unless, indeed, by our own Pope, of Homer's (*Il. 19. 126*):

by
αυτικα δ' ειλ' Ατην κεφαλης λιπαροπλοκαμοιο,

"from his ambrosial head, where perched she sate,
he snatched the fury-goddess of debate."

AEDIFICANT, theme; SECTAQUE INTEXUNT ABIETE COSTAS, variation; in other words, not two different acts are described, but only one, viz., the building of the horse; which, described as usual first in general terms (AEDIFICANT), is then described in particular (SECTAQUE INTEXUNT ABIETE COSTAS). Heyne therefore is right, and Turnebus wrong.

SECTAQUE INTEXUNT ABIETE COSTAS. It is a different tree in the almost repeated description, verse 112:

. . . . " cum iam hic trabibus contextus acernis
staret equus."

COSTAS. Not, by synecdoche, the sides, but literally the ribs of the horse, those strong timbers which we may suppose to have extended in an arched form transversely from the longitudinal spine, so as to surround the interior cavity and support the outer boarding; such timbers as in the ship are called "statumina" (Turnebus), Ital. *costole*, Fr. *les varangues*, Engl. *futtocks*, and which form the substantial framework of the ship, the skeleton, or as the Italians call it, the *ossatura*. TEXUNT expresses that these costae were not merely simple parallel ribs, but were supported by cross pieces so as to form a crates. The costae or internal framework of a ship are well distinguished from the tabulae or outside boarding by Corippus *de Laud. Justin. 4. 55*:

" protinus omnigeni caeduntur robora ligni,
quaeque suis aptanda locis. durissima *costas*,
mollia dant *tabulas*."

VOTUM. Not (with Servius) the verb, but the substantive, for we find in Petronius, 89 :

　　. . . "stipant graves
　　equi recessus Danai, et in ruto latent."

18-20.

HUC DELECTA VIRUM SORTITI CORPORA FURTIM
INCLUDUNT CAECO LATERI PENITUSQUE CAVERNAS
INGENTES UTERUMQUE ARMATO MILITE COMPLENT

Let not the too prosaic reader, interpreting this sentence according to its literal structure, suppose it to mean that, besides the DELECTA VIRUM CORPORA which were inclosed in the hollow sides of the horse, the vast caverns of its womb were filled with armed soldiers ; or that a considerable vacancy, remaining after the selected chiefs were inclosed, was filled up with a large body of common soldiers. On the contrary, the latter clause of the sentence is only explanatory of the former ; ARMATO MILITE informing us that the DELECTA VIRUM CORPORA were armed warriors; CAVERNAS INGENTES UTERUMQUE, that by CAECO LATERI was meant the whole interior cavity or chamber of the statue ; and COMPLENT, that the cavity was completely filled by the persons who were inclosed (INCLUDUNT)—in other words, HUC DELECTA VIRUM SORTITI CORPORA FURTIM INCLUDUNT CAECO LATERI is a theme of which PENITUSQUE CAVERNAS INGENTES UTERUMQUE ARMATO MILITE COMPLENT is the variation ; CAVERNAS INGENTES UTERUMQUE varying CAECO LATERI ; ARMATO MILITE varying DELECTA VIRUM CORPORA ; and PENITUS COMPLENT varying SORTITI FURTIM INCLUDUNT. That this is the true analysis and interpretation of the passage appears from the following considerations : (1), that it is according to our author's usual habit thus to present in the first clause of his sentence no more than the sketch or skeleton of his thought, and then in the subsequent clause to fill up and clothe with flesh and life such previous sketch or skeleton. (**2**), that, in the sequel, only DELECTA VIRUM CORPORA, viz., Thessander, Sthenelus, Ulysses, Acamas, Thoas, Neoptolemus, Machaon, Menelaus, and Epeus come out of the horse. (**3**), that even in the account given by Tryphiodorus, an author so much more likely than Virgil to disregard verisimilitude, we find (verses 152 *et seqq.*) the ambush consisting of no more than twenty-two individuals, every one of them named, and all of them collectively styled (verse 522) τευχηοται βασιληες, corresponding—βασιληες, to Virgil's DELECTA VIRUM CORPORA ; and τευχηοται, to Virgil's ARMATO MILITE. (**4**), that it is **as** plain from Cicero's (*Philipp. 2. 13*): " In huius me consilii societatem tanquam in equum Troianum cum principibus includis ?" that neither Cicero himself, nor the audience Cicero was addressing, viz., the Roman Senate, had any other notion of the ambush than that it consisted *solely* of " principes" (= DELECTA VIRUM CORPORA); **as** it is plain from a comparison of this same passage of Cicero with Cicero's still more remarkable (*de Orat. 2. 22*): " Exortus est Isocrates magister istorum omnium, cuius e ludo, tanquam ex equo Troiano, meri principes exierunt," that the selectness of the society inside the Trojan horse had become a proverb, at least with Cicero ; **and** (**5**), and lastly, that a satisfactory answer is thus afforded to the very obvious objection to the whole story as commonly understood (Napoleon, *ubi supra* (see Rem. on 2. 5-6), p. 228 : " En supposant que ce cheval contînt seulement cent guerriers, il devait être d'un poids énorme, et il n'est pas probable qu'il ait pu être mené du bord de la mer sous les murs d'Ilion en un jour, ayant surtout deux rivières à traverser"**)**, viz., that the horse, so far from containing one hundred individuals, did not even, the story being rightly understood, contain one-tenth of that number. Against all which if Mr. Conington's difficulty be urged, viz., that the expressions " armatos fundit equus" (verse 328) and " pars ingentem formidine turpi scandunt rursus equum" (verse 400) are indicative of multitude, I reply, first, that no conclusion as to number can be deduced from the word fundere—applied by Virgil himself, *Georg. 1. 12*, to the production of a single object:

> ... " cui prima frementem
> *fudit* equum tellus;"

and secondly, that even if fundere always implied either considerable number or considerable quantity (which the just-cited example proves it does not), still no conclusion as to the number of persons actually contained in the horse can be drawn from either of the passages cited by Mr. Coningtou—the expressions of Pantheus in the one being exaggerated by fear, and of Aeneas in the other by hatred.

DELECTA. Compare Cic. *Tusc. Quaest. 1. 20* (ed. Orelli): " ea [navis] quae est nominata Argo, quia ' Argivi in ea

> ... *delecti* viri,
> vecti, petebant pellem inauratam arietis.' "

CAVERNAS INGENTES UTERUMQUE = " cavernas ingentes uteri."

21-23.

EST IN CONSPECTU TENEDOS NOTISSIMA FAMA
INSULA DIVES OPUM PRIAMI DUM REGNA MANEBANT
NUNC TANTUM SINUS ET STATIO MALEFIDA CARINIS

EST IN CONSPECTU TENEDOS ... INSULA ... SINUS ET STATIO MALEFIDA CARINIS. Compare Aesch. *Pers. 445* (ed. Schütz):

> νησος τις εστι προσθε Σαλαμινος τοπων,
> βαια, δυσορμος ναυσιν.

Tenedos, as it was before the Greek invasion, viz., DIVES OPUM, is contrasted with Tenedos as it is now (NUNC), viz., a mere bay affording an unsafe roadstead for ships. The contrast serves the purpose of an explanation how it happened that the Greek fleet could ensconce itself in the STATIO or roadstead of Tenedos, without its coming to the knowledge of the Trojans that it was there, viz., because, the island having been deserted on the first appearance of the Greeks before Troy, there was now no one on it (NUNC TANTUM SINUS ET STATIO; HUC SE PROVECTI DESERTO IN LITTORE CONDUNT) to bring the intelligence to that city that the Greek fleet (supposed to have taken its departure for Greece) was actually riding at anchor in the roadstead of Tenedos. The contrast, therefore, of Tenedos DIVES OPUM with Tenedos TANTUM SINUS ET STATIO CARINIS is to be carefully distinguished from the contrast (Sil. 14. 201, ed. Rup.):

"et iusti quondam portus, nunc littore solo
    subsidium infidum fugientibus aequora, Mylae,"

of Mylae a port, and therefore affording (viz., by means of land on one side, and a mole or moles towards the sea) complete shelter, or shelter on every side, to ships, with Mylae no longer a port, but only (the mole or moles having been destroyed by storm or allowed to go to ruin) a mere statio or roadstead, and therefore affording shelter to ships on the land side only, *i. e.*, by means of the land or shore alone ("littore solo"). The latter contrast, or that of a regular port ("iusti portus," Sil.) with a mere statio or roadstead, has been repeated by Vell. Paterc. 2. 72: "exitialemque tempestatem fugientibus *statio* pro *portu* foret."

So far, then, is the information which our text gives us of the deserted state of the island of Tenedos, at the time the Greeks availed themselves of its roadstead, from being gratuitous and serving the mere purpose of ornament ["Ea vastities in insula facta, ut ea hoc uno nota sit, quod naves tempestate iactatae in littorum recessu, quem *sinum* appellat, *stationem*, etsi parum tutam, habeant," Heyne. "The island is said to be a SINUS, a bay forming a doubtful roadstead, being all for which it was then remarkable. . . . DESERTO IN LITTORE shows that the change in the fortunes of Tenedos had already begun," Conington], **that** it is precisely this piece of information which imparts to this part of the narrative verisimilitude and plausibility—a verisimilitude and plausibility so marvellously increased by the epithet by which the STATIO is characterized, viz., MALEFIDA; see next paragraph.

MALEFIDA = *infida*; faithless, unsafe. But why this character of the roadstead so especially put forward? Was not the faithlessness, the insecurity, of the roadstead the very reason why the Greek fleet, if it had any care for its own safety, should avoid it? On the contrary, the danger of an accident happening from the weather in the short interval for which the fleet was to be there was exceedingly small, while the danger of the Trojans learning they were there, had the STATIO been fida, and on that account, of course, a favourite resort for vessels, had been great. The STATIO was the very statio for the Greeks to choose above all others, **no less** on account of its convenient distance neither too near nor too far from Troy, and its position (if the information obtained by Heyne on the subject be correct: "Nunc autem per eos qui haec loca adierunt in compertis habeo, ex locis illis, quae Ilii vestigiis assignari solent (Bunarbaschi) Tenedum haud dubie prospici, et esse in eius littore australi stationem navium, quae earum conspectum oculis ex Ilio prospicientium eripiat") out of the view of that city, **than** on account of the loneliness of the shore (DESERTO IN LITTORE) and the small probable, perhaps even no, resort to a station so little in repute (MALEFIDA).

30–34.

CLASSIBUS HIC LOCUS HIC ACIES CERTARE SOLEBANT
PARS STUPET INNUPTAE DONUM EXITIALE MINERVAE
ET MOLEM MIRANTUR EQUI PRIMUSQUE THYMOETES
DUCI INTRA MUROS HORTATUR ET ARCE LOCARI
SIVE DOLO SEU IAM TROIAE SIC FATA FEREBANT

CLASSIBUS HIC LOCUS. In this passage Virgil, according to his custom (see Remm. on 1. 500; 2. 18 and 49), presents us first (verses 27 and 28) with the general idea, the deserted appearance of the places lately occupied by the Greeks; and then (verses 29 and 30) supplies the particulars, in the words of the Trojans pointing out to each other the various localities.

The reader, however, must not be misled by the words CLASSIBUS HIC LOCUS to suppose that there was a place set apart for the ships. Innumerable passages in the Iliad, and especially the account of the battle at the ships (*Il. 13*), render it perfectly clear that, the ships being drawn up on the shore, the tents were erected beside and amongst them; the ships and tents of one nation forming one group, those of another nation another group, and those of a third nation a third group; and so on, along the entire line of shore occupied by the encampment. CLASSIBUS means, therefore, not the ships, as contra-distinguished from the tents, but the ships taken together with their dependencies, the tents; or in other words, it means the Grecian encampment, called *classes* by Virgil, and αι νηες by Homer, from its most important and, especially from a distance, most conspicuous part, *the ships*.

Not only Dryden and such like translators, but even Alfieri ("Qui, fitte eran l'ancore lor") renders CLASSIBUS HIC LOCUS, "here the navy rode"—with what understanding of the Iliad, or of ancient naval expeditions (see *Aen. 3. 71; 9. 69, 70*), or of the Grecian encampment and mode of warfare at Troy, and especially of the battle at the ships, let the reader judge.

PARS STUPET INNUPTAE DONUM EXITIALE MINERVAE, theme; MOLEM MIRANTUR EQUI, variation. Both clauses together = " pars stupet admiratione ingentis equi, qui dono datus Minervae allaturus erat Troiae exitium." These words had not embarrassed and misled so many commentators, and myself among the number (" Twelve Years' Voyage," and " Advers. Virg."), had it been perceived that not only the words themselves but the entire passage is almost literally translated from Euripides, who in the person of the chorus, *Troad. 535* (ed. Dindorf), says:

> πασα δε γεννα Φρυγων
> προς πυλας ωρμαθη,
> πευκα εν ουρεια
> ξεστον λοχον Αργειων,
> και Δαρδανιας αταν
> θεα δωσων,
> χαριν αζυγος, αμβροτοπωλου.

where in χαριν αζυγος αμβροτοπωλου we have INNUPTAE DONUM

MINERVAE; in Δαρδανιας αταν, EXITIALE; in θεα δωσων, DUCI
INTRA MUROS ET ARCE LOCARI; in ξεστον λοχον Αργειων,
DANAUM INSIDIAS; in πευκα εν ουρεια, ABIETE; in προς πυλας
ωρμαθη, PANDUNTUR PORTAE, IUVAT IRE; and in πασα γεννα
Φρυγων, OMNIS TEUCRIA.

DONUM MINERVAE, *Minerva's present*, in the sense of *the
present made to Minerva*, not *the present made by Minerva*.
And so Servius, rightly: "Non quod ipsa dedit, sed quod ei
oblatum est." Exactly so, verse 189, of this same present to
Minerva: " si vestra manus violasset dona Minervae" [*Minerva's
present*, i. e., the present made to Minerva]; and 11. 566,
"donum Triviae" [*Trivia's present*, i. e., the present made to
Trivia]. Also Ovid, *Met. 13. 510* (Hecuba, of herself):

"nunc trahor exul, inops, tumulis avulsa meorum,
Penelopae munus"

[*a present for Penelope*]. Claud. *Epith. Pall. et Celer. 13*:

" scrutantur [Amores] nidos avium, vel roscida laeti
mala legunt, *donum Veneris*"

[*a present for Venus*]. Eurip. *Ion, 1427*:

CREUSA. δρακοντε μαρμαιροντε παγχρυσω γενυι.
ION. δωρημ' Αθανας, η τεκν' εντρεφειν λεγει;

[*a present for Minerva*]. Eurip. *Orest. 123*:

απανθ' υπισχνου νερτερων δωρηματα,

not *presents suitable to be received from*, but *suitable to be offered
to, the "inferi."* See Rem. on "ereptae virginis ira," 2. 413, and
compare Eurip. *Orest. 1434* (ed. Paley), of Helen:

σκυλων Φρυγιων επι τυμβον αγαλ-
ματα συστολισαι χρηζουσα λινω,
φαρεα πορφυρεα δωρα Κλυταιμνηστρα

[*offerings to Clytemnestra; funeral dress for corpse of Clytemnestra*]. Aesch. *Agam. 1385* (ed. Davies):

. . . και πεπτωκοτι
τριτην επενδιδωμι, του κατα χθονος
Διος νεκρων σωτηρος ευκταιαν χαριν.

Quint. Smyrn. 12. 235:

οι δ' αλλοι Τενεδοιο προς ιερον αστυ μολοντες,
μιμνετε, εισοκεν αμμε ποτι πτολιν ειρυσσωσι
δηιοι, ελπομενοι Τριτωνιδι δωρον αγεσθαι.

Epigr. Meleagri, *Anthol. Pal.* 7. *468* :

οικτροτατον ματηρ σε, Χαριξενε, δωρον ες Αδαν,
οκτωκαιδεκαταν εστολισεν χλαμυδι

[*present for Hades*]. Pind. *Nem.* 10. 66 (ed. Boeckh):

. . . τοι δ' αναντα σταθεν τυμβω πατρωιω σχεδον·
ενθεν αρπαξαντες αγαλμ' Αιδα, ξεστον πετρον,
εμβαλον στερνω Πολυδευκεως· αλλ' ου νιν φλασαν,
ουδ' ανεχασσαν·

(where Dissen: "donarium Plutonis, *h. e.* cippum cum arte dolatum Plutoni sacrum. Confer Διος τροπαια, Pausan. 5. 22, fin.; porro μελος Αιδα, *h. e.* θρηνος, querela Plutoni sacra, Eurip. *Electr. 143*; *Suppl.* 783, αδου μολπαι, et Αιδα γοος, Aristoph. *Thesmoph. 1050*"). Compare also the application by Homer of the term θελκτηριον θεων (*delenimentum deorum*) to the same wooden horse, *Od. 8. 509*:

η εααν μεγ' αγαλμα θεων θελκτηριον ειναι.

EXITIALE. Altogether by prolepsis, and expressive of the present feelings of the speaker. Compare verse 237, "fatalis machina," and verse 245, "monstrum infelix"—both of this very horse; also 1. 6, "Lavina littora," where D. Hieron. in *Ezech. 30*: "iuxta illud Virgilianum 'Lavinaque venit littora': non quo [*qu?* quod] eo tempore quando venit Aeneas in Latium Lavinia dicerentur, sed quae postea Lavinia nuncupata sunt."

Wagner (1861) reminds his reader that the DONUM was not a real but only a pretended donum ("per simulationem datum"), and Kappes (*Zur Erklärung von Virgil's Aeneide*: Constanz, 1863) finds Aeneas's words full of the bitterest irony: "Gerade darin liegt der schmerz und die ironie ausgedrückt, dass Aeneas das pferd nach des Sino angabe ein der Minerva dargebrachtes geschenk nennt, nachdem er es als die verderben bringende *machina* kennen gelernt hat." Aeneas's words are, on the contrary, a simple statement of the fact, without either allusion to the untruthfulness of the present, or irony. The horse is equally DONUM whether it contains an ambush inside or not (verse 49: "timeo Danaos et *dona* ferentes"). See Attius (quoted by Servius): "Minervae donum armipotenti Danai abeuntes dicant." Hyginus, *Fab. 108 :* " Danai Minervae dono dant." Petron. (ed. Hadrian, p. 325) :

> . . . " hoc titulus fero
> incisus, hoc ad fata compositus Sinon
> firmabat."

And how little irony enters into the feelings of Aeneas is clear both from the severe gravity and even sorrow of his expressions (as verses 54, 55, and 56), and from the circumstance that he was himself one of the principal persons imposed on, and one of the principal sufferers by the fraud (verses 105, 106). To be ironical Aeneas should have said not EXITIALE, but praeclarum, or egregium, should have described the gift not by its real character, but by the character in which it was viewed by himself and his friends at the time, by some character the very opposite of that which it merited.

Of the five places in which our author makes mention of the horse as a present, three (viz., verses 36, 44 and 49) expressly state who were the givers of the present, viz., the Danai; and two, viz., our text and verse 189, to whom the present was given, viz., to Minerva.

SIVE DOLO, SEU IAM TROIAE SIC FATA FEREBANT. " Sei's durch verrath, sei's weil schon nahete Ilions schicksal," Voss. TROIAE FATA is not " schicksal," the destiny (*i. e.*, final destiny) of Troy, but the series of fates appointed to Troy from the beginning ; and FEREBANT is not " nahete," *approached*, but *brought, occasioned, was the cause of.* Compare 2. 94 : " fors si qua tulisset ;" Ovid, *Met. 3. 174 :*

> " ecce! nepos Cadmi, dilata parte laborum,
> per nemus ignotum non certis passibus errans,
> pervenit in lucum: sic illum *fata ferebant.*"

35–44.

AT CAPYS—DANAUM

INSIDIAS, appropriation of the Homeric figure applied to this same horse, *Od. 4. 277*:

τρις δε περιστειξας κοιλον λοχον αμφαφοωσα.

Ibid. 8. 515:

ιππoθεν εκχυμενοι, κοιλον λοχον εκπρολιποντες.

Ibid. 11. 525:

ημεν ανακλιναι πυκινον λοχον ηδ' επιθειναι.

SUBIECTISQUE URERE FLAMMIS. The advice of Capys consists of two alternatives: either to destroy the horse (by fire or water as they might prefer), or to explore its contents. The copulative QUE is used to connect together the two parts of which the first alternative consists. The English language does not admit of a similar structure.

PRIMUS IBI ANTE OMNES . . . LAOCOON ARDENS SUMMA DECURRIT AB ARCE, ET PROCUL: O MISERI. Compare Liv. 1. 12: "Mettus Curtius . . . princeps ab arce decucurrerat . . . nec procul iam a porta Palatii erat, clamitans, 'vicimus . . . .'"

AUT ULLA PUTATIS DONA CARERE DOLIS DANAUM. Admirably translated by Schiller:

"ein Griechisches geschenk und kein betrug verborgen?"

Such masterly touches, promissory of the future splendour of Schiller's genius, occur every now and then in his "Freie Uebersetzung" of the second and fourth books of the Aeneid, which is, however, on the whole, an inferior production, evincing not merely immaturity of poetical power, but a considerable want of perception of the delicacies of Virgil's expressions, and even some ignorance of the Latin language.

49-53.

QUIDQUID ID EST TIMEO DANAOS ET DONA FERENTES
SIC FATUS VALIDIS INGENTEM VIRIBUS HASTAM
IN LATUS INQUE FERI CURVAM COMPAGIBUS ALVUM
CONTORSIT STETIT ILLA TREMENS UTEROQUE RECUSSO
INSONUERE CAVAE GEMITUMQUE DEDERE CAVERNAE

QUIDQUID ID EST, TIMEO. So Ovid, *Heroid. 19. 203* (of an ominous dream) : " quidquid id est, timeo."

TIMEO DANAOS ET DONA FERENTES. In this so oft-quoted sentiment there is nothing new except its application to the Danai: Εχθρων αδωρα δωρα κουκ ονησιμα was a proverb even in the days of Sophocles. See *Ajax*, 665.

VALIDIS INGENTEM VIRIBUS. The great size of the spear, and the force with which it is hurled, are not matters of indifference, but absolutely necessary to the production, on the huge mass of which the horse consisted, of the considerable effect described by the words

UTEROQUE RECUSSO
INSONUERE CAVAE GEMITUMQUE DEDERE CAVERNAE.

Of the five terms most frequently used by Virgil to express the casting of a spear, viz., iacio, coniicio, torqueo, intorqueo and contorqueo, the two first are the weakest and signify: iacio, simply *to throw*; coniicio, *to throw with the collected force of the individual*, which, however, need not be great, for the term is applied, 2. 544, to Priam throwing his " inbelle telum sine ictu." The three latter signify *to hurl*: torqueo, simply *to hurl*; intorqueo, *to hurl forcibly*; contorqueo, *with all the collected strength of a powerfully strong man*—con, when applied in composition to the act of *one*, being no less intensive than when applied to that of *a number of individuals*; in the former case indicating that the act is the result of *the whole collected power of the one*, in the latter that it is the

result of the *collected power of the several individuals concerned.*
See Rem. on "corripiunt spatium," 6. 634; and on "conclamat," 9. 375.

Impello, although interpreted by Heyne in his gloss on
Aen. 1. 86 intorqueo, immitto, is neither there nor anywhere else (except under the particular circumstances mentioned
in Rem. on *Aen. 1. 85*) used in that sense, but always in the
sense of *pushing*—either *physically pushing*, as *Aen. 1. 86*;
7. 621; 8. 239, &c.; or *metaphorically pushing*, as *Aen. 1. 15*;
2. 55, 520, &c.

IN LATUS INQUE FERI CURVAM COMPAGIBUS ALVUM.—IN ALVUM is not, as maintained by Thiel, and after him by Forbiger,
into the alvus; first, because there is much harshness in interpreting the IN before ALVUM so very differently from the IN before
LATUS, of which it is the mere repetition. Secondly, because
the word RECUSSO, verse 52, implies that the interior of the
horse was only *concussed*, not *perforated*. Thirdly, because the
expression FERRO FOEDARE, verse 55, almost expresses that the
interior had not been previously "foedata ferro." Fourthly,
because the words "tergo intorserit," verse 231, limit the lesion
made by the cuspis, verse 230, to the tergum, a term never
applied except to the exterior of the body. For all these reasons I reject Thiel's interpretation, and understanding (with
Wagner) QUE to be taken epexegetically (see Rem. on *Aen.
1. 500; 2. 18*) render the passage, *against that part of the side
which was the alvus or belly*. Thus the precise position of the
wound is determined to have been in the hinder part of the side,
corresponding to the cavity of the belly, not of the chest; and
in the lateral part of the belly, not the under part. Virgil
chooses this position for the wound with great propriety, because the portion of the horse's side corresponding to the belly,
being much larger than that corresponding to the chest, not
only afforded a better mark to Laocoon, but was precisely the
part where the enclosed persons were principally situated.
Compare *Aen. 7. 499*:

"perque uterum sonitu perque ilia venit arundo;"

through that part of the *uterus* (belly) which was the *ilia* (loin or flank).

CURVAM, bowed, bent outward; the opposite of cavam. Compare *Georg*. 1. 508 : " curvae falces." *Aen*. 6. 4 : " curvae puppes." 7. 184 : " curvae secures." 3. 564 :

"tollimur in caelum curvato gurgite." . . .

Silius, 6. 522 (ed. Ruperti) :

"ac legimus pontum, pinuque immane *carata*
aequor, et immersas *curva* trabe findimus undas,"

in which last we have the two opposite notions in contrast with each other—" cavata " expressing the hollow of the ship in which the passengers were safely lodged, and " curva " the exterior curved or bowed form (bow) which divided the water. There is a similar and even more striking opposition between *curved* or bowed and *concave* or hollowed out, in Synesius, *Ep*. 4 : ουτος [ventus] αφνω προσπεσων, το ιστιον εμπαλιν ωθησε, και τα κυρτα κοιλα πεποιηκεν (Lat. transl. : "quae *curva* erant, *cava* reddidit"); and we have only to put verse 53,

INSONUERE CAVAE GEMITUMQUE DEDERE CAVERNAE,

in apposition with our text, to have a similar contrast of our own making, between the convex exterior and concave interior of the belly of the wooden horse.

CURVAM COMPAGIBUS, put together (viz., with straight pieces of wood) so as to form a round, convex, or curve. The form was bowed or rounded, though the pieces of which it was put together were straight.

CURVAM COMPAGIBUS ALVUM = rounded belly.

INSONUERE CAVAE GEMITUMQUE DEDERE CAVERNAE. "Iunge: CAVAE INSONUERE, *i. e.*, cavum quid sonuere; s. ita ut res cavae solent," Wagner (1861). Certainly not. To express such sense it should have been not INSONUERE CAVAE, but *insonuere cavum*, as *Georg*. 4. 370 : " saxosumque sonans Hypanis;" Calpurn. 4. 119 :

. . . . "quae imparibus modo concinuistis avenis,
tam liquidum, tam *dulce sonant*, ut non ego malim," &c.

Nay, it should have been not even *insonuere carum*, but only *sonuere carum*, had the intention been as assumed by Wagner to express not the intensity, but the very opposite of intensity, the hollowness of the sound. No, no; CAVAE is the ordinary eke, of which Virgil here, as so often elsewhere, does not scruple to avail himself. Compare 10. 475:

"vaginaque *cava* fulgentem deripit ensem,"

where, all sheaths being necessarily hollow, "cava" adds nothing to the sense, and is added merely for the convenience of versification; exactly as in our text, all caverns being necessarily hollow, CAVAE adds nothing to the sense, and is added merely for the ease of versification. The kind of sound produced is expressed not by CAVAE, but according to our author's usual manner by the added clause, GEMITUM DEDERE; the loudness or intensity of the groaning sound, by the IN of INSONUERE—CAVAE CAVERNAE IN-SONUERE GEMITUMQUE DEDERE—as if he had said CAVAE CAVERNAE GEMITUM DEDERE.

CAVAE CAVERNAE, the CAVAS LATEBRAS of verse 38, and occupying it will be observed precisely the same position in the verse:

AUT TEREBRARE CAVAS UTERI ET TENTARE LATEBRAS.

GEMITUM, not at all the groan of any one inside, but the groan of the cavity itself, the resonance of the CAVAE CAVERNAE, as 3. 555: "gemitum ingentem pelagi;" 9. 709: "dat tellus gemitum." Compare Quint. Calab. 1. 615:

η ως τις στονοεντα βαλων εν ορεσσιν ακοντα
θηρητηρ ελαφοιο μεσην δια νηδυα κερση
εσσυμενως,

and our own "groaning axle."

FOEDARE, to spoil, to put out of its normal state; deformare, violare. See Rem. on 3. 241.

LATEBRAS. We have no corresponding word in English. The Italians have *nascondigli*.

56.

TROIAQUE NUNC STARES PRIAMIQUE ARX ALTA MANERES

VAR. LECT.

STARES*—MANERES **I** *Rom.*; *Pal.*; Pierius : " In antiquis omnibus codd. quotquot habui MANERES legi." **II** $\frac{11}{19}$. **III** Princ.; Mod.; Mil. 1475, 1492; Bresc.; P. Manut.; La Cerda; D. Heins.; N. Heins. (1670, 1671, 1676, 1704); Phil.; Heyn.; Brunck; Wakef.; Pott.; Dorph.; Lad.; Haupt.

STARET—MANERES **I** *Med.* (a T being placed over the S *a m. sec.*) **II** $\frac{2}{35}$. **III** Serv.; Ven. 1475 (Jenson); Voss; Wagn. (1832, 1841; *Lect. Virg.* and *Praest.*); Ribb.

STARET MANERET **II** $\frac{1}{35}$.

STARES MANERET **II** $\frac{4}{35}$. **III** Ven. 1470, 1471.

0 *Vat., Ver., St. Gall.*

STARES—MANERES, the reading of the great majority of the MSS., is to be preferred not only on account of the life which the sudden apostrophe throws into the passage, but on account of the apparent original from which our author drew, viz., Eurip. *Troad. 45*, where Neptune similarly apostrophizes Troy :

αλλ', ω ποτ' ευτυχουσα, χαιρε μοι, πολις,
ξεστον τε πυργωμ'. ει σε μη διωλεσε
Παλλας, Διος παις, ησθ' αν εν βαθροις ετι·

and of the apparent copy by later authors, as Silius, 10. 658 :

" haec tum Roma fuit, post te cui vertere mores
si stabat fatis, potius, Carthago, *maneres.*"

Id. 7. 563 :

" nullaque nunc *stares* terrarum vertice, Roma."

---

* Victorinus (*Ars Gram.*) gives this reading also, but does not cite the end of the verse.

TROIAQUE NUNC STARES, theme; PRIAMI ARX ALTA MANERES, variation.

In the same way as the Greeks used τυγχανειν and πεφυκεναι as varieties for ειναι—the former adding to the simple conception of existence that of chance or fortune, as the cause of such existence, and the latter that of nature or birth—so the Romans used stare and manere, the former adding to the simple conception that of uprightness of position, the latter that of continuance in respect of time. In either language, according to the particular circumstances of the case, it was sometimes the simple conception, sometimes the superadded, which predominated. In the case before us the superadded is strong: "thou Troy shouldst stand upright, and thou citadel of Priam shouldst *continue* in existence." Compare 6. 300: "stant lumina flamma," where "stant" is *stand fixed and wide open*, or, as we say, *stare*. At other times the superadded conception is wholly sunk and lost, as Manil. 1. 643 (Jacob):

"atque ubi se primis extollit Phoebus ab undis,
illis sexta *manet*, quos tum premit aureus orbis,"

where there is no notion of continuance at all, and "manet" is no more than *est*.

59-70.

QUI SE—ACCIPERE

HOC IPSUM UT STRUERET.—" Vel ut caperetur, vel quia Graeci simulabant," Servius. " Ut adduceretur ad regem," Heyne. By HOC IPSUM is not meant either merely " ut caperetur " or merely " ut ad regem adduceretur," but both together, viz., that he should be taken into custody and brought before the king, viz., as the first step or move towards his ultimate object— TROIAM aperire ACHIVIS.

Hoc IPSUM, this very thing which I have just presented to my readers, viz., MANUS POST TERGA REVINCTUM AD REGEM TRAHEBANT. Compare Ovid, *Met. 9. 723:*

"Iphis amat qua posse frui desperat, et auget
hoc ipsum flammas"

[this very thing, viz., that he loves one whom he despairs of ever enjoying]. Ovid, *Met. 11. 384:*

. . . "sed Alcyone coniux excita tumultu
prosilit, et, nondum totos ornata capillos,
disiicit *hos ipsos*"

[the very hair she had just been dressing].

ULTRO. Taking the initiative, doing what he need not have done.

TROIAMQUE APERIRET ACHIVIS. "And open Troyes gates unto the Greeks," Surrey. No; not literally *open the gates* of Troy, but *procure an entrance* for the Greeks into Troy; *make* Troy *accessible* to them. Compare *Aen. 10. 864:* "*aperit* si nulla viam vis." Statius, *Theb. 12. 293:*

"Theseos ad muros, ut Pallada flecteret, ibat,
supplicibusque piis faciles aperiret Athenas."

Sil. Ital. 13. 49:

. . . "caeleste reportat
Palladium, ac nostris *aperit* mala Pergama fatis."

Venant. Fortun. *Poemat. 1. 5. 3* (in cellulam S. Martini):

"exul enim terris, caeli incola, saepe solebat
clausus Martinus hinc *aperire* polos"

[open heaven, *i. e.*, guide to heaven, show the way by which heaven might be entered]. Iscan. *de bello Troiano, 1. 47:*

"hactenus haec; tuque, oro, tuo da, maxime, vati
ire iter inceptum, Troiamque *aperire* iacentem"

(in which latter the action of opening Troy is figuratively ascribed to the poet who describes it).

DANAUM INSIDIAS. These words are plainly repeated from Dido's request to Aeneas, *Aen. 1. 758.*

INERMIS. As arma means not merely *weapons, whether offensive or defensive*, but *all kinds and means of offence and defence*, so its compound inermis means not merely *without weapons*, but *without any means of offence or defence; helpless, defenceless*. The latter is the sense in which I think it is used in the passage before us; because, first, it is not to be supposed that Virgil, having told us that Sinon was a prisoner, with his hands bound behind his back, would think it necessary to inform us almost instantly afterwards that he was *unarmed* or *without weapons*. And, secondly, because even if Sinon had not been bound, weapons could have been of no avail to him against the AGMINA by whom he was surrounded, and therefore the want of them made no real difference in his condition, and could not have been assigned, even by poetical implication, as a reason for his emotion or conduct. It is in this strong sense of *utterly without means of offence or defence*, and not in its literal sense of *weaponless*, that "inermis" is to be understood also, *Aen. 1. 491:*

"tendentemque manus Priamum conspexit *inermes;*"

because, although it might have contributed to the pathos of the picture to have represented a *young* warrior's hands as stretched out *weaponless*, it could have had no such effect to have so represented the hands of Priam, who was so old as to be unable to wield weapons, and was equally "inermis" (*helpless and defenceless*) whether he had arms in his hands or not. See *Aen. 2. 509, 510, et seq.;* and compare Tacit. *Ann. 6. 31:* "Et senectutem Tiberii ut *inermem* despiciens." The same meaning follows *inermis* into the Italian, as *Gerus. Lib. 3. 11:*

"i semplici fanciulli, e i vecchi *inermi*,
e'l volgo delle donne sbigottite."

QUAE NUNC TELLUS ... ACCIPERE? Compare Quinctil. *Declam. 12. 28:* "Quomodo me a scelere meo divellerem? in quas ultimas terras, quae inhospitalia maria conderem?"

75.

QUIDVE FERAT MEMORET QUAE SIT FIDUCIA CAPTO

VAR. LECT.

QUIDVE FERAT · MEM. **I** *Pal.* **III** D. Heins.; N. Heins. (1670).
[*punct.*] CRETUS, QUIDVE FERAT; MEM. **III** Heyne; Wakef.; Wagn. (1832, 1841, 1861); Lad.; Haupt.
[*punct.*] CRETUS, QUIDVE FERAT, MEM. **III** P. Manut.; D. Heins.; N. Heins. (1670); Brunck; Voss ("Nach FERAT ein komma").
[*punct.*] CRETUS. QUIDVE FERAT MEMORET. **I** *Med.*
[*punct.*, &c.] CRETUS QUIVE FUAT, MEM. **III** Ribb.
O *Vat., Rom., Ver., St. Gall.*

QUIDVE FERAT. What news he brings, *i.e.*, what he has to say. Compare Metast. *La Clemenza di Tito, 1. 11:* "e ben, che rechi?" [what do you bring? *i.e.*, what news? what have you to say?]; Metast. *Achille, 3. 2:* "si turbato Arcade! che recasti?" [what news have you?]

QUAE SIT FIDUCIA CAPTO. "Qua fiducia se ipse captivitati obtulisset," Burmann, Forbiger, Kappes. "Quid illud sit quod illi fiduciam apud hostes capto pariat, ut putet a Troianis sibi esse parcendum," Servius; after much trifling, Wagner (1861). In both explanations both FIDUCIA and CAPTO are understood in a stronger sense than, as I think, has been intended by our author. CAPTO has just been used, and exactly in a similar position in the verse, in the simple sense of *the prisoner;* and, as it would seem, for no other reason than as a descriptive substitute for the pronoun (*ei*), always when possible avoided by poets. Why is its sense different, more special and emphatic, here only eleven lines later? Fiducia was the word commonly used by the Romans to express the confidence, expectation, view, object, which a person had on any occasion in his mind, or with which he went anywhere, or performed any, even the most trifling and indifferent act [compare Martial, 3. 38. 1 :

> " quae te causa trahit, vel quae *fiducia* Romam,
> Sexte ? quid aut speras, aut petis inde ? refer."

Ovid, *Met.* 9. 720 :

> . . . " sed erat *fiducia* dispar.
> coniugii pactaeque expectat tempora taedae,
> quamque virum putat esse, suum fore credit Ianthe.
> Iphis amat qua posse frui desperat, et auget
> hoc ipsum flammas ; ardetque in virgine virgo "].

What reason is there why its meaning here should be more emphatic and special ? The question, " what is the prisoner's case? what has he to say for himself, on what does he rely ?" [compare Tacit. *Annal.* 3. 11 : " Post quae reo [Pisoni] T. Arruntium, T. Vinicium, Asinium Gallum, Aeserninum Marcellum, Sext. Pompeium patronos petenti, iisque diversa excusantibus, M. Lepidus, et L. Piso, et Livineius Regulus adfuere, arrecta omni civitate, quanta fides amicis Germanici, *quae fiducia reo*], is perfectly appropriate ; and according to our author's custom, completes the meaning of the Trojans, not sufficiently fully expressed in the preceding questions: QUO SANGUINE CRETUS ? QUIDVE FERAT ? precisely as the self-same words ("quae fiducia ") in the passage just adduced from Martial complete the similar inquiry : " quae te causa trahit ?"

CAPTO, the captive. Compare Sil. 6. 492 (ed. Rup.) :

> . . . " quae [Poenorum cohors] moesta repulsa
> ac minitans *capto* [Regulo], patrias properabat ad oras."

76.

ILLE HAEC DEPOSITA TANDEM FORMIDINE FATUR

VAR. LECT.

ILLE—FATUR ||| P. Manut.; D. Heins.; Phil.; Pott.; Heyne; Wagn. (1832, 1841, and 1861); Haupt; Wilms.
ILLE—FATUR *OMITTED* I *Pal.; Med.* (but the verse written in red ink at bottom of page).
ILLE- FATUR *OMITTED OR STIGMATIZED* ||| N. Heins. (1670); Voss; Peerlk.; Ribb.
O *Vat., Rom., Ver., St. Gall.*

I cannot agree with the Leyden octavo edition of 1680, the younger Heinsius, and Burmann, in enclosing this verse between crotchets, and still less with Brunck in expunging it entirely, on the ground that it attributes *fear* to Sinon, whom Virgil but a few lines previously has represented as FIDENS ANIMI, ATQUE PARATUS, &c., and must therefore be supposititious. Neither do I plead in its defence, with Heyne and some other commentators, that Sinon first *pretends* to be agitated with fear (TURBATUS), and then *pretends* to lay his fear aside (" Fingit Sinon et hoc, quasi deposuerit formidinem," Heyne); on the contrary, I think that Virgil, having represented Sinon as entering upon the execution of his plot with boldness and confidence, represents him as *really* TURBATUS (*agitated and frightened*), when he comes to be actually confronted with the danger, and then as *really* recovering from his agitation when he finds that the immediate danger is over, and that the Trojans, instead of putting him to death instantly on the spot, are willing to hear what he has to say.

TURBATUS means *really* agitated, and DEPOSITA FORMIDINE, *really* recovering self-possession, because (I), if Virgil had intended to express by these words only simulated emotion, it can-

not be doubted that he would have afforded some clue by which
his intention might have been discovered; but he has not only
not afforded any such clue, but has actually assigned sufficient
cause for real emotion: Sinon is TURBATUS, because he stands
INERMIS in the midst of the PHRYGIA AGMINA; and DEPOSITA
FORMIDINE FATUR, because CONVERSI ANIMI, COMPRESSUS ET OMNIS
IMPETUS. (**2**), if the words mean only simulated emotion, then
Virgil represents Sinon as of such heroic constancy and resolu-
tion as to look upon instant violent death without blenching;
which is to hold him up, for so far at least, as an object of
respect and even of admiration to Aeneas's hearers as well as
to Virgil's readers, and thus to contradict the intention (evidenced by the terms DOLIS, ARTE, INSIDIIS, CRIMINE, SCELERUM
TANTORUM, PERIURI) of representing him as a mean-minded
man entering upon a dishonourable and dangerous enterprise,
with an audacious confidence (FIDENS ANIMI, ATQUE PARATUS,
&c.) in his own cunning and duplicity. (**3**), it is altogether
unlikely that Virgil should here employ to express *simulated*, the
very same words which he employs, *Aen. 3. 612*, in a similar
context and similar circumstances, to express *real*, emotion. (**4**,,
there is a perfect harmony between FIDENS ANIMI ATQUE PARA-
TUS, &c., and TURBATUS understood to mean *real* agitation, because a man may enter upon a dangerous undertaking with
confidence, and even with courage (which latter quality, however, it will be observed, is not expressed either by FIDENS
ANIMI, or PARATUS, &c.), and yet quail before the instant imminent danger, as exquisitely shown by Homer in his most
natural and touching account of Hector's flight before Achilles:
how much more, then, the wretch Sinon? (**5**,, TURBATUS means
real not *simulated* agitation, because *real* agitation was more
likely to move the Trojans to pity than any *simulation* of it.
Virgil, therefore, taking the most effectual method of moving
the hearts of the Trojans, and recollecting perhaps the advice of
his friend Horace,

    . . . " si vis me flere, dolendum est
   primum ipsi tibi,"

presents Sinon to them in a state of real agitation, pleading for his life with all the eloquence of unaffected fear. So Davus (Ter. *And. 4. 4*), instead of acquainting Mysis with his plot, and instructing her what answers she should give to Chremes, prefers to place her in such a situation that—speaking the truth, and in entire ignorance of his design—her answers must yet of necessity be the very answers which he desired ; and when Mysis afterwards inquires why he had not schooled her as to his intentions, replies :

" paullum interesse, censes, ex animo omnia
ut fert natura facias, an de industria ?"

It was inconsistent with Virgil's plot to make Sinon speak the truth, but he could with perfect consistency, and therefore did, represent him as actuated by real emotion ; which *real* emotion is in express terms contrasted with his *false* words at verse 107, PROSEQUITUR PAVITANS, ET FICTO PECTORE FATUR.

The reader will, however, observe that Virgil, always judicious, carefully avoids ascribing *extreme* fear or agitation to Sinon ; he is TURBATUS (*agitated*), PAVITANS (*in a flutter*), but he does not, like Dolon, his undoubted original, become χλωρος υπαι δειους, nor do his teeth chatter (αραβος δε δια στομα γινετ' οδοντων). Such extreme degree of terror, although beautifully consistent with the simple undisguised confession of Dolon, would have been wholly incompatible with the cunning and intricate web which Sinon, almost from the first moment he opens his mouth, begins to wrap round the Trojans. It is, therefore, with the strictest propriety and observance of nature that Virgil represents Sinon at first bold and confident ; then disconcerted and agitated at the prospect of immediate death ; then reassured by the encouragement he received ; then again, losing confidence when the Trojans manifest the vehement impatience expressed by the words TUM VERO ARDEMUS SCITARI, &c., and with renewed fear and trembling (PAVITANS) pursuing his feigned narrative ; and then, finally, when he had received an absolute promise of personal safety, going on, without further fear or hesitation, to reveal the pretended secret of his compatriots.

Throughout the whole story the reader must never forget

that, although it was Virgil's ultimate object to deceive the Trojans, by means of Sinon, with respect to the horse, yet he had another object also to effect (prior in point of time, and not less important than his ultimate object, because absolutely indispensable to the attainment of that ultimate object), viz., to save Sinon's life, or in other words, to assign to his reader sufficiently probable and natural reasons why the Trojans did actually spare his life, and did not, as might have been expected, execute such summary judgment upon him as Diomede and Ulysses executed upon Dolon under similar circumstances. Accordingly, the first words which he puts into the mouth of Sinon are a thrilling exclamation of despair, a piteous cry for mercy: HEU! QUAE NUNC TELLUS, &c. This has the effect of staying the uplifted sword, of averting the first and instant danger, COMPRESSUS ET OMNIS IMPETUS; they encourage him to speak, to tell who he is, and why he should not meet the captive's doom; Sinon respires, recovers his self-possession, and—endeavouring to make good his ground, and strengthen the favourable impression produced by his first words—says that he was the friend of that Palamedes of whose unjust condemnation and death they might have heard, and the principal cause of which was the opposition given by him to the undertaking of the war against Troy; and that he had not, like the other Greeks, come to the war out of hostility to the Trojans, or even voluntarily, but had, when a mere boy (and, therefore, irresponsible), been sent by his father, who was so poor as not otherwise to be able to provide for his son. He then enters upon an account of his quarrel with and persecution by Ulysses, their most dreaded and implacable enemy; but perceiving that they begin to take an interest in what he is saying, suddenly stops short, and artfully begs of them to put him out of pain at once, as he knew that, no matter how great or undeserved his sufferings had been, they could have no pity or forgiveness for one who was guilty of the crime of being a Greek. The Trojan curiosity is inflamed, and they insist to know the sequel. He proceeds PAVITANS (whether because he had not yet entirely recovered from his first alarm, or whether alarmed afresh by the vehemence and impatience of the

Trojans, or whether from both these causes conjointly), and relates how by the villanous concert of the priest Calchas with Ulysses he was selected to be offered up as a victim to appease the offended gods; how he escaped from the altar, and lay hid during the night (the preceding night) in a morass; and then lamenting that his escape from death by the hands of the Greeks had only led him to death by the hands of the Trojans, and that he was never more to see his country, home, or relatives, concludes with a pathetic adjuration, in the name of the gods above and of inviolable faith, that they would yet pity such unexampled, such undeserved misery, and spare his life. His tears, his agony of fear, the plausibility of his story, their sympathy with the object of the hatred and persecution of the Greeks and of Ulysses, prevail; they grant him his life; and so closes the first act of the interlude of Sinon.

In nothing is the admirable judgment of Virgil more remarkable than in the skill with which he has all this while kept the wooden horse, as it were in abeyance. No act has been done, no word uttered, which could excite in the Trojan mind, or in the mind of the reader, ignorant of the sequel, the slightest suspicion that Sinon has anything whatsoever to do with the horse, or the horse with Sinon. So careful is the poet to avoid every, even the slightest, ground for a suspicion, which would have been fatal to the entire plot, that it is from a distance, and by the agency of the Trojans themselves, he brings Sinon into the vicinage of the horse; and that, in the whole course of the long history which Sinon gives of himself, and which the reader will observe is now concluded, the horse is never so much as mentioned or even alluded to, except once, and then so artfully (as it were only for the purpose of fixing a date) that the mention which is made, while it stimulates the Trojans to question him on the subject, seems less remarkable than absolute silence would have been, inasmuch as it proves that Sinon does not *de industria* eschew all notice of an object which must have attracted his attention, and of the purport of which he could not but be supposed to have some knowledge.

In the second act of the interlude, or that part which commences with verse 152, we find Sinon totally changed; "now more bold, the tempter . . . new part puts on;" his life secure, guaranteed by the king himself, he is no longer the abject, cringing, hesitating, trembling wretch, but the successful and exulting villain. He loudly and boldly invokes the gods to witness his abjuration of the Greeks and acceptance of the Trojan covenant; and makes his revelation of the important secret which is to be the rich reward of the Trojan clemency, not, as he had pleaded for his life, in broken passages, leaving off at one place and commencing at another, but *uno tenore*—explaining in uninterrupted sequence the absence of the Greeks, their intended return, the object for which they built the horse, and why they built it of so large dimensions; the evil consequences to the Trojans if they offered it any injury, and to the Greeks if it were received into the city, &c. The impostor is fully credited; the generous, unwary, and fate-devoted Trojans are caught in the toils so delicately woven and so noiselessly drawn around them, and the curtain falls.

If the reader happen to be one of those critics who think the story of the wooden horse deficient in verisimilitude, he will receive with the greater favour an interpretation which tends to increase the verisimilitude, by representing the falsehood and cunning of Sinon as united, not with that quality with which falsehood and cunning are so inconsistent and so rarely united, heroic fortitude, but with their very compatible and nearly allied quality, audacity.

It is impossible to leave this subject without remarking how favourably to Trojan faith and generosity (as might be expected, Virgil being the *poeta* and Aeneas the narrator) the conduct of the Trojans towards Sinon contrasts with that of the Greeks towards Dolon. Ulysses and Diomede encourage Dolon, and tell him not to think of death, on which ambiguous pledge he tells the whole truth; they reward him by coolly cutting off his head, as the last word of his revelation passes his lips. Sinon tells the Trojans a tissue of lies, and not only has his life spared, but is treated with kindness and hospitality.

That most rigid and terrific of all the dispensers of the so-called divine retributive justice, Dante (see *Inferno, 30. 46, et sqq.*), punishes Sinon in hell with an eternal sweating fever, in company (according to the great poet's usual eccentric manner of grouping his characters) on the one side with Potiphar's wife, whom he punishes with a similar fever, and on the other with a famous coiner of base money at Brescia, whom he torments with a never-dying thirst and dropsy, and between whom and Sinon ensues a contention in none of the gentlest billingsgate, which of the two is the greater sinner.

77.

CUNCTA EQUIDEM TIBI REX FUERIT QUODCUNQUE FATEBOR

VAR. LECT.

FUERIT QUODCUNQUE **I** *Med.* **II** ⁶⁄₆. **III** Serv.; Venice, 1470, 1471, 1475 (Jenson); Modena; Brescia; Milan, 1492; G. Fabric.; D. Heins.; N. Heins.(3 eds.); Heyne; Wakef.; Pottier; Dorph.; Wagn. (1832, 1841, 1861); Haupt; Ribb.

FUERINT QUAECUNQUE **I** *Pal.* (thus: FUERINT, the N being, although very pale and almost indiscernible, apparently inserted by original hand. It is omitted by Ribb.) **II** ⁴⁄₈ (found by Pierius and N. Heins. in the greater number of their MSS., and by Burm. in almost all his). **III** Venice, 1472; P. Manut.; Philippe.

FUERIT QUAECUNQUE **III** Milan, 1475.

0 *Vat., Rom., Ver., St. Gall.*

FUERIT QUODCUNQUE. " Quicunque me sequatur eventus," Servius. " Quicquid evenerit, mihique exinde acciderit," Heyne. " QUODCUNQUE referendum ad CUNCTA," Wagner. Arguing against which interpretation of Wagner, and in favour of that of Servius and Heyne, Süpfle says (" Virgilii opera: mit anmerkungen zur Eneide versehen von Karl Fr. Süpfle: Karlsruhe, 1847") : "Auch haben schon die alten, wie Phaedrus im prologe zum dritten buche, die worte anders und wohl richtiger gefasst, nämlich : 'was auch daraus werden mag, wie es mir auch ergehen mag, wenn ich in allem euch die wahrheit sage.'"

I agree entirely with Wagner, and think the meaning is : "I will confess all whatever it may have been, whatever there may have been in it." The words are not less obscure in the quotation and application made of them by Phaedrus (see the two-column note on them in Schwabe's edition) than in Sinon's original use of them—a notable proof of the almost hopeless obscurity of the Latin language ; an obscurity arising from its brevity, and especially, as it seems to me, from its almost constant omission of pronouns and pronominal adjectives. I am, however, inclined to think that in Phaedrus's quotation of the words "quodcunque fuerit" stands in apposition to "librum exarabo tertium," and that the meaning of them there, as in Sinon's original use of them, is, *such as it is, good or bad, of whatever kind it may turn out to be.* It is as if Phaedrus had said : But now as to this third book of mine, ye shall, as Sinon told King Priam, hear the whole of it such as it is, be it good or be it bad. See Rem. on 1. 82.

CUNCTA . . . FUERIT QUODCUNQUE, FATEBOR. As we might say in English : I will tell you the whole of it, let it be how it will—meaning, not how it will be with me, but how it will be with the matter.

CUNCTA QUODCUNQUE, exactly (as well remarked by Wagner, *Praestab.*) the Greek παντα, ο τι. Compare 8. 427 : "Fulmen— Quae plurima." It may further be alleged in support of the above interpretation, and against the "quicunque me sequatur eventus" of Servius (an interpretation, however, not without the support of Corippus Johannes, 7. 510 :

"tunc Nasamon pinnatus ait: 'me cuncta fateri
iussio dura premit. mortem licet ipsa minentur
verba mihi meritam, narrans tamen omnia dicam'"),

that this third allusion to the danger of death with which Sinon was threatened seems to be a useless repetition of a fear of a danger already sufficiently often mentioned, viz., in almost

every line of the preceding account beginning with CERTAE
OCCUMBERE MORTI, verse 62, and ending with INFENSI POENAS
CUM SANGUINE POSCUNT, verse 72.

79-87.

HOC PRIMUM NEC SI MISERUM FORTUNA SINONEM
FINXIT VANUM ETIAM MENDACEMQUE IMPROBA FINGET
FANDO ALIQUOD SI FORTE TUAS PERVENIT AD AURES
BELIDAE NOMEN PALAMEDIS ET INCLYTA FAMA
GLORIA QUEM FALSA SUB PRODITIONE PELASGI
INSONTEM INFANDO INDICIO QUIA BELLA VETABAT
DEMISERE NECI NUNC CASSUM LUMINE LUGENT
ILLI ME COMITEM ET CONSANGUINITATE PROPINQUUM
PAUPER IN ARMA PATER PRIMIS HUC MISIT AB ANNIS

VANUM ETIAM MENDACEMQUE IMPROBA FINGET. VANUM, one
who asserts what is not the fact, from ignorance, folly, or mistake; Gr. ματαιον, ληρον (as Soph. *Aj.* 1161 (ed. Brunck):

   . . . καμοι γαρ αισχιστον κλυειν
   ανδρος ματαιου, φλαυρ' επη μυθουμενου.

Diog. Laert. 2. 140: Κατεφρονειτο [Menedemus] Κυων και
Ληρος υπο των Ερετριεων ακουων): MENDACEM, one who
asserts what is not the fact from a desire to deceive. In other
words, and less specially: VANUM, one who is deceived himself;
MENDACEM, one who desires to deceive others. Compare *Aen.*
1. 396:

   " ni frustra augurium *vani* docuere parentes"

(where "vani" is ill-informed on the subject, and therefore
teaching erroneous doctrine; teaching erroneous doctrine, but
believing what they taught to be the truth). Also, Liv. 6. 14:
" *Vera an vana* inceret"—things conformable to fact, or things
not conformable to fact, no matter whether he believed them

or not. Verus is an ambiguous word, sometimes meaning true in point of fact, *i. e.*, conformable to fact, and sometimes meaning true in the opinion of the speaker; on the contrary, there is no ambiguity either in vanus or mendax—vanus being always untrue in point of fact, *i. e.*, not conformable to fact, and mendax being always untrue in the opinion of the speaker, *i. e.*, not conformable to the opinion of the speaker.

Similar to the Latin use of vanus is the Italian use of its derivative *raneggiare*, as Metast. *La Clemenza di Tito*, 2. 7:

"cosi confuso io sono,
che non so se *raneggio* o se ragiono."

Metast. *Zenobia*, 3. 2:

"qual riposo aver poss' io,
se *raneggio* a tutte l' ore?"

FORTUNA ... FINXIT ... IMPROBA FINGET. See Rem. on *Aen.* 2. 552.

FANDO ALIQUOD SI, &c.—Not FANDO ALIQUOD, but FANDO, SI NOMEN ALIQUOD; FANDO being taken intransitively, as Ovid, *Met.* 15. 497:

"*fando, aliquem* Hippolytum vestras (puto) contigit aures,
credulitate patris, sceleratae fraude novercae
occubuisse neci."

Politian's Herodian (ed. Boecler), 1. 15: "neque unquam *fando* audiverant."

FANDO, *inter fandum, in conversation*, as Ausonius, *Epist.* 16. 36:

"quem nemo *fando* dixerit,
qui non prius laudaverit."

The report or rumour which so came *fando* was the φατις of Euripides, *Hippol.* 129 (ed. Stokes):

. . . οθεν μοι
πρωτα φατις ηλθε, δεσποιναν
τειρομεναν νοσερα
κοιτα, δεμας εντος εχειν
οικων,

where οθεν μοι φατις ηλθε is literally: from whom the first *saying* came to me, *i. e.*, from whom I first heard.

FALSA SUB PRODITIONE, "*h. e.* sub falso crimine proditionis," Servius; followed by Heyne, and all the other commentators and translators. To this interpretation I object: *Firstly*, that no authority has been adduced to show that proditio may be used for crimen proditionis; the *act* committed, for the *charge* founded upon the commission of the act. *Secondly*, that if Virgil had intended to say that the Pelasgi had condemned Palamedes, *on* or *by means of* a false charge of treason, he would more probably have used the words FALSA PRODITIONE in the same manner as INFANDO INDICIO, without a preposition. *Thirdly*, that this interpretation represents the whole Greek nation at Troy (PELASGI) as conspiring against Palamedes; which is (*a*) contrary to all verisimilitude; (*b*) deprives INFANDO INDICIO of its force, because, if all were conspiring against Palamedes, it was of small consequence how "infandous" the information or informer was, or, indeed, whether there were any information or informer at all; and (*c*) contradicts the statement (verse 90) that it was through the machinations of Ulysses that Palamedes' condemnation was accomplished.

Rejecting, for all these reasons, the received interpretation, I render FALSA SUB PRODITIONE, *during*, or *at the time of*, *a false or feigned treason;* i.e., when there was an alarm (whether of accidental or concerted origin it matters not) of treason in the Grecian camp. The words being so interpreted, the meaning of the passage is, not that the Pelasgi brought a *false* charge of treason against Palamedes, and condemned him, *although innocent;* but that the Pelasgi condemned Palamedes on an infandous information, which, being brought against him *at a time when there was an alarm of treason in the camp*, was on that account the more readily credited. In support of this interpretation, I beg to observe—(1), that it restores to PRODITIONE its simple grammatical signification. Compare Caes. *de Bell. Gall.* 7. *20:* "'Haec', inquit, 'a me, Vercingetorix, beneficia habetis, quem *proditionis* insimulatis'"; and (*ibid.*) "Vercingetorix—*proditionis* insimulatus—respondit." (2), that the use of *sub* in the sense of *during*, or *at the time of*, is familiar to every scholar; thus, sub nocte, sub somno, sub profectione, sub adventu, &c. Livy (26. 16) has even joined *sub* to the close cognate of proditio—deditio; only putting deditio in the accusative, because he wishes to express, not the *precise time*, but *about the time* of the deditio. (**3**, that, this interpretation being adopted, INSONTEM is no longer a tautology of FALSA; the latter expressing only the falsehood of the general rumour of treason, not of the particular charge brought against Palamedes. (**4**), that this interpretation represents the Pelasgi, not, unnaturally, in the triple character of conspirators, accusers, and judges, but naturally, in the single character of judges, prevailed upon partly by the prevalent alarm of treason, and partly by the offence they had taken against Palamedes, QUIA BELLA VETABAT, to give credit to an infamous information against him. (**5**), that a greater degree of verisimilitude is thus conferred on the words NUNC CASSUM LUMINE LUGENT, because it is more probable that the Pelasgi would lament Palamedes (as soon as experience had taught them the groundlessness of their dislike to him on account of his opposition to the war) if they had themselves been deluded into convicting him on an "infandum indicium," than that they would, under any circumstances, lament him, if their hatred to him had been so great as to induce them to convict him on a charge which they not only knew to be false, but of which they were themselves the concoctors. **And** (**6**), that Ovid draws an express and strong distinction between the party who *accused* and the party who *condemned* Palamedes (*Met. 13. 308*):

  . . . " an falso Palameden crimine turpe
accusasse mihi [*viz.* Ulyssi], vobis [*viz.* Pelasgis] *damnasse* decorum est ?"

FALSA PRODITIONE. Not only was Palamedes innocent of the crime laid to his charge, but the crime itself had no existence, had not been committed by any one; the "proditio" was "falsa," a mere concocted proditio, which had no existence whatever; just as, Tacitus, *Annal. 1. 39* ("Utque mos vulgo, quamvis *falsis* reum subdere, Munatium Plancum consulatu functum, principem legationis, auctorem senatus-consulti incusant"), the senatus-consultum which was laid to the charge of Munatius Plancus had no existence whatever, had never been passed at all, was a feigned (falsum) senatus-consultum. Compare also Ovid, *Met.* 15. 154:

> "quid Styga, quid tenebras, quid nomina vana timetis,
> materiem vatum, *fals*ique piacula mundi?"

[*a world which has no existence at all, a feigned world*].

QUEM (verse 83). This word (QUEM, and not *illum*) sufficiently shows that Sinon has not yet begun to give any new information to the Trojans, but is employed, as far as the word NECI, in recalling to their recollection facts with which he knew they were perfectly well acquainted ("incipit a veris," Servius). The words NUNC CASSUM LUMINE LUGENT (see below) are thrown in parenthetically between the exordium in which he thus reminds them of known facts and the new information which he begins to convey at verse 86, ILLI ME COMITEM, &c. Hence a plain reason why Sinon does not specify the precise charge made against Palamedes, his object being not to give a history of that individual, but merely to recal to the mind of the Trojans what they already knew respecting him.

NECI.—Nex, not merely death, but *death by violence*, and *of the unresisting*; slaughter, butchery, as *Georg.* 3. 478:

> "hic quondam morbo caeli miseranda coorta est
> tempestas, totoque autumni incanduit aestu,
> et genus omne *neci* pecudum dedit, omne ferarum,
> corrupitque lacus: infecit pabula tabo.
> nec via mortis erat simplex;"

therefore, in our text, NECI, *execution*; and, Liv. 34. 44 (quoted below), "necatus," *executed, put to death as a criminal*.

DEMISERE, *sent down*. DEMISERE NECI, *sent down to death by the hands of the executioner*. But why *down*? why the DE? Simply because nex is a form of death; and death, θανατος, Orcus, Pluto, Hades, the inferi, the umbrae, the manes, are all, in relation to this world, *down, below*. Accordingly, 5. 691:

> . . . "infesto fulmine *morti*,
> si mereor, *demitte*."

10. 664:

> "obvia multa virum *demittit* corpora *morti*."

2. 398: "multos Danaum demittimus Orco," and especially 12. 883:

> . . . "o quae satis ima dehiscat
> terra mihi, manesque deam *demittat ad imos*!"

(where we have the *down* force of the de twice intensified by imus). Also, Stat. *Theb.* 1. 658 (of Choroebus challenging Apollo to shoot him with his arrow):

> "proinde move pharetras, arcusque intende sonoros,
> insignemque animam *leto demitte*."

The same verb is used both by Sallust and Livy to express the letting down of a condemned prisoner into the "Robur" or underground dungeon in which he was to be executed—necatus [Sallust, *Bell. Catil.* 58: "Est locus in carcere, quod Tullianum appellatur, ubi paululum ascenderis ad laevam, circiter xii. pedes humi depressus. Eum muniunt undique parietes, atque insuper camera lapideis fornicibus vincta, sed inculta tenebris, odore foeda, atque terribilis eius facies. In eum locum postquam *demissus* est Lentulus, vindices rerum capitalium, . . . laqueo gulam fregere." Liv. 34. 44: "Pleminius in inferiorem *demissus* carcerem est, necatusque"]. In Rome I have myself visited this lower cell or "Robur," and a horrible place, indeed, it is—less horrible, however, at present than when it received unhappy Jugurtha or St. Peter; for it has now, for the convenience of visitors, a second opening (viz., a door on the level of the floor), and to enter it is no longer the same as never to leave it.

The notion of descent to Hades contained in DEMISERE NECI is repeated, verse 90, in SUPERIS CONCESSIT AB ORIS, where there seems to be a reference to the expression previously used. The ancient idea of descent in death—as expressed in the Latin demittere neci, demittere morti, demittere Orco, demittere leto,—seems early to have been lost, or, at least, mislaid and forgotten by the Italians; for we have in very old Italian the simple "missono a morte," *put to death*. See Leopardi's *Martirio de' Santi Padri*, cap. 2.

NUNC CASSUM LUMINE LUGENT, *they now* (viz., convinced by experience that it was unwise to have undertaken the war: see verso 108) *lament the loss of the prudent counsellor*, who BELLA VETABAT. But this is not the sole force of these words: they serve also to excite the Trojan sympathy, first and directly, for Palamedes (not only innocent, but lamented even by his executioners); and secondly and indirectly, for his friend and companion Sinon, AFFLICTUS (see verse 92, and Rem.) by his fall; like him, persecuted to the death by the same Ulysses; and (by implication) like him, innocent.

CASSUM LUMINE.—Literally *without light, dark;* compare Lucret. 5. 718:

"nec potis est cerni, quia *cassum lumine* fertur;"

and see Rem. on *Aen. 1. 550.* The use made of cassum by the Romans seems to correspond nearly with that made by us of the particle *less* in composition. Cassus lumine, *lightless*, i. e., *lifeless;* cassus sanguine (Cic. *de Divin. 2. 64*), *bloodless.*

PRIMIS AB ANNIS.—"*Ab initio belli*, bene Burm. post Servium," Heyne; and so Wunderlich, Wagner (1845, 1849), and Kappes. "Heyn. recte interpretatur: *ab initio belli.* Alii, velut Gossr. [and VOSS], *in iuventute prima* (quemadmodum *Aen. 8. 517*), cui tamen explicationi obstare videntur 'dulces nati' qui vers. 138 memorantur," Forbiger.

The opinion of Burmann, Heyne, Wunderlich, Wagner (1845, 1849), Forbiger, and Kappes (I do not say of Servius, Servius not seeming to have any opinion at all on the subject), that the "anni" here spoken of are the anni of the war, and not Sinon's own, is, I think, sufficiently disproved by *Aen. 8. 517*: "primis et te miretur ab annis," where the same word in a similar context can by no possibility mean anything else than the anni of Pallas. See also *Aen. 4. 30,* and compare Val. Flacc. 1. 22:

"Haemoniam *primis* Pelias frenabat *ab annis*."

Ovid, *ex Ponto, 2. 5. 45:*

"tu comes antiquus, tu *primis* iunctus *ab annis*"

(where observe that it is, as in our text, a comes who is spoken of). Ovid, *Met. 13. 595:*

. . . "qui [Memnon] fortia frustra
pro patruo tulit arma suo, *primisque sub annis*
occidit a forti (sic vos voluistis) Achille"

(where observe that it was to these very arma of which Sinon is speaking that Memnon went). And, finally, Ovid, *Fast.* 5. 517:

"quaeque puer [Hyrieus] quondam *primis* diffuderat *annis*,
prodit fumoso condita vina cado."

It is to be remarked, however, that the PRIMIS ANNIS spoken of are not the first years of Sinon's life (*i.e.*, Sinon's childhood), but the first years of Sinon's manhood (*i.e.*, his first adult years, his prime), because such, and no other, must be the meaning of the term in the just-quoted examples—Pallas not being a child but a grown man when he was sent in command of Evander's troops to assist and take example by Aeneas ; Pelias not being a child but a grown man when he ruled ("frenabat") Haemonia; Memnon not being a child but a grown man when he was killed at Troy by Achilles—nay, being expressly styled "vir fortis" by Ovid himself, verse 616 ; and Hyrieus not being a child but a grown man when he barreled the wine with which in his old age he entertained the three divine visitors, the explanation of the words being in Hyrieus's case given by no less an authority than Ovid himself, who at verse 525 informs us that Hyrieus had a wife who was the care of his "prima iuventa." If Hyrieus had a wife who was the care of his "prima iuventa" (= PRIMIS ANNIS), why might not Sinon also ? and, if a wife, why not children ? Compare also Ovid, *Fast. 4. 9* (of himself):

"quae decuit, *primis* sine crimine lusimus *annis*"

[the first years, certainly not of his life, but of his manhood ; the time when he was a young man (Virg. *Aen.* 7. 162:

. . . "pueri et primaevo flore iuventus"),

precisely of the age described by Sinon in our text]. Ovid, *Met. 12. 182* (Nestor speaking of himself) :

. . . "quamvis obstet mihi tarda vetustas,
multaque me fugiant *primis* spectata *sub annis*."

[observed in my early days, *i. e.*, in my youth]. Silius, 2. 68:

"hacc ignara viri, vacuoque assueta cubili,
venatu et silvis *primos* defenderat *annos*"

[certainly not her infancy, but her early years of maturity].
Cic. *ad Att.* 2. 3 (ed. Orelli):

"interea cursus, quos *prima a parte inreuntae*,
quosque adeo consul virtute animoque petisti,
hos retine atque auge famam laudesque bonorum."

Id. *ad Fam.* 6. 12 (ed. Orelli): "quod ego non mirabar, cum recordarer te et *a primis temporibus aetatis* in re publica esse versatum." Sil. 10. 13 (of Paullus):

"atque, ubi certamen *primi* ciet immemor *aevi*,
foetus Gradivo mentem Cato fertur in hostes."

And especially Sil. 6. 127:

"vix puerile mihi tempus confecerat aetas,
cum *primo* malas signabat Regulus *aevo*,"

where the time of boyhood, "puerile tempus," is directly contrasted with the first time, "primo aevo," *i. e.*, the beginning of manhood.

PRIMIS AB ANNIS is thus neither more nor less than the poetic equivalent for the prosaic *ab ineunte aetate*. Compare the inscription in honour of Stilicho, Gruter, p. 412: "Ab ineunte aetate per gradus clarissimae militiae ad columen gloriae sempiternae et regiae affinitatis evecto," where the context places it beyond doubt (as a similar context places it beyond doubt in Tacit. *Hist.* 2. 77: "duo iuvenes, capax iam imperii alter, et *primis* militiae *annis* apud Germanicos quoque exercitus clarus") that the age spoken of is the military age, the age at which the youth is first regarded as a man and fit for military duty. Compare also Pind. *Nem.* 9. 41 (ed. Boeckh):

. . . δεδορκεν
παιδι τουτ' Αγησιδαμου φεγγος εν αλικια πρωτα,

and our own Milton, *Par. Lost*, 11. 245:

"his starry helm unbuckled showed him prime
in manhood, where youth ended"

(where, however, youth is distinguished from manhood, not identified with it, as iuventus is by the Latin writers).

Such is the general notion expressed by primi anni, viz., "prima iuventa" (as Tacit. *Annal.* 4. 1 (of Ael. Sejanus): "Genitus Vulsiniis, patre Seio Strabone equite Romano, et prima iuventa C. Caesarem divi Augusti nepotem sectatus"), the age of commencing manhood, the age when the individual is regarded no longer as a child, but as a man, and is entitled to wear the toga virilis (Tac. *Ann.* 4. 4). Now, what was this age in the Roman polity? Of course, the age of puberty, *i. e.*, fourteen years complete. Up to this age the individual was not a man but a spes, and his death during this period was acerba, or immature, and celebrated neither by funeral procession nor panegyric. Compare *Aen.* 6. 426:

> "continuo auditae voces, vagitus et ingens,
> infantumque animae flentes, in limine primo,
> quos dulcis vitae exsortes et ab ubere raptos
> abstulit atra dies, et funere mersit *acerbo.*"

Tac. *Ann.* 13. 15: "Turbatus his Nero, et propinquo die, quo *quartum decimum* aetatis annum Britannicus explebat, volutare secum," &c. *Ibid.* 13. 17: "Festinationem exsequiarum edicto Caesar defendit, id a maioribus institutum referens, 'subtrahere oculis acerba funera, neque laudationibus aut pompa detinere.'"

This interpretation of PRIMIS AB ANNIS, and that which I have given of "Tu Marcellus eris," *Aen.* 6. 884, confirm each other. Sinon, who lives to be a man, reaches his primi anni and is sent to the war, becomes a soldier (PRIMIS AB ANNIS IN ARMA MISIT); but Marcellus, who dies in childhood without reaching his primi anni, does not become a soldier, does not fight, only *would* have become a soldier, *would* have fought ("tulisset," "iret," "foderet"), if he had lived to be a man, if he had reached his primi anni, if he had come to be Marcellus. We thus get rid, not only of Forbiger's (and my own former—see "Twelve Years' Voyage") objection to refer ANNIS to Sinon, but of Peerlkamp's proposed wholesale emendation.

The expression "primis ab annis" is preserved in the Italian, as Agnese di Merania, del Visconti di Arlincourt (traduzione di G. Paganucci) : " Il detto Olburgo è stato la sola guida dei di lui *primi anni.*" *Ibid. :* " Il barone di Valdsburgo si era imposto il più assoluto silenzio sugli *anni primi* della sua vita." Metast. *Regolo, 1. 1 :*

   . . . "ah! rammenta
  che del tuo genitore emulo antico
   fu da' prim' auni."

La Nazione, Firenze, 7 Aprile, 1862 : " Fino dai suoi *primi anni* mostrò grande propensione per la caccia, si esercitò nel maneggio dell' armi, con tanta attività, che acquistossi nel suo paese fama d'infallibile tiratore."

IN ARMA, "*h. e., ad bellum*," Heyne. I think the meaning is rather, *to the profession of arms, to seek a military fortune*. Compare Terent. *Heaut. 1. 1. 59 :*

  " sed in Asiam abii hine propter pauperiem, atque ibi
  simul rem et gloriam armis belli repperi."

88–89.

DUM STABAT REGNO INCOLUMIS REGUMQUE VIGEBAT CONSILIIS

VAR. LECT.

REGNUM I *Pal.* (REGNU, the M torn off; Ribb. has omitted the N); Pierius (" REGUM CONCILIIS ego nusquam in his veteribus legi exemplaribus "). III P. Manut. ; D. Heins. ; Philippe.

REGUM I *Med.* (REGVM), *Ver.* (very indistinct). III Donat. ; N. Heins. (1670) ; Heyne ; Brunck ; Wakef. ; Peerlk. ; Wagn. (1832, 1841, 1861) ; Lad. ; Haupt ; Ribb.

O *Vat., Rom., St. Gall.*

VAR. LECT.

CONSILIIS I *Ver.* (CONSILIIS, very indistinct, except the superscribed C); Pierius. III Rom., 1473; P. Manut. ; D. Heins. ; N. Heins. (1670); Philippe ; Wagn. (1841, 1845, 1861).

CONCILIIS **I** *Pal.*, *Med.* **II** cod. Canon. (Butler). **III** Heyne; Brunck; Wakef.; Pott.; Wagn. (1832); Peerlkp.; Lad.; Haupt; Ribb. O *Vat.*, *Rom.*, *St. Gall.*

Compare Herder, *Der Cid unter Ferd. d. grossen, 2:*

"in Asturiens gebirgen
zählet Gormatz tausend freunde,
er *in koenig's rath der erste*,
er der erste in der schlacht."

Also Claud. *Bell. Gild. 46* (personified Rome speaking):

"armato quondam populo, *patrumque vigebam
consiliis*."*

Dares Phryg. 18: "Dum Agamemnon consulit de tota re, ex Cormo advenit Nauplii filius Palamedes cum navibus triginta. Ille se excusavit; morbo affectum Athenas venire non potuisse; quo advenerit, quum primum potuerit. Gratias agunt, rogantque eum *in consilio* esse."

Query: should not the reading both in Claudian and Virgil be "conciliis?" Compare *Georg. 1. 24:*

"tuque adeo, quem mox quae sint habitura deorum
concilia incertum est."

AFFLICTUS (verse 92). Not *sorrowful*, for that meaning is contained in LUCTU; but *dashed to the ground, beaten down from his prosperity*, viz., by the death of his friend and patron. It is used in this its primitive sense on the only other occasion on which Virgil has used the word, *Aen. 1. 456*; also by Milton, *Par. Lost, 1. 186*, "afflicted powers;" and *2. 166*, "afflicting thunder."

---

* Bentley, ad Hor. *Od. 3. 6*, reads "conciliis" here:

"armatis quondam populi patrumque vigebam
conciliis."

96-99.

PROMISI ULTOREM ET VERBIS ODIA ASPERA MOVI
HINC MIHI PRIMA MALI LABES HINC SEMPER ULIXES
CRIMINIBUS TERRERE NOVIS HINC SPARGERE VOCES
IN VULGUM AMBIGUAS ET QUAERERE CONSCIUS ARMA

ET VERBIS ODIA ASPERA MOVI.—ET is epexegetic, and VERBIS the words in which " promisit se ultorem ;" as if Virgil had written : " et movi odia aspera verbis, quibus me promisi ultorem," or " me promittens ultorem."

CONSCIUS affords the key to the passage HINC . . . ARMA. Sinon having mentioned no names, but merely threatened the authors of Palamedes' ruin, Ulysses had no reason to believe himself to be the object of these threats, except his own consciousness that he was the guilty person. Moved by this consciousness (CONSCIUS), he met Sinon's threats by a recourse to arms (QUAERERE ARMA), viz., by making accusations against Sinon, by spreading ambiguous reports concerning him, and finally by procuring Calchas first to declare that a Greek life must be sacrificed to Apollo, and then that that life was Sinon's.

CONSCIUS means conscius sibi, as in Ovid, *Trist. 5. 4. 18:*

"nec fore perpetuam sperat sibi numinis iram,
conscius in culpa non scelus esse sua."

Also Tacit. *Annal. 13. 18* (of Nero) : " sceleris *sibi conscio*, et veniam sperante, si largitionibus validissimum quemque obstrinxisset," as if he had said : " veniam quaerente largitionibus."

The mistake of the commentators is twofold—first, the connecting of CONSCIUS not with the whole three clauses, but with the last only; and secondly, the confounding of QUAERERE CONSCIUS ARMA with quaerere conscia arma: " Quidam CONSCIUS ARMA hypallagen putant, pro *conscientia arma*, ut (5. 595): ' et quondam *patriis* ad Troiam missus in *armis*,' " Servius (ed. Lion)—an *aliter* of Servius which, like so many other of Servius's *aliters*, shows the extreme modesty of that critic, how very little confidence he had in that better judgment with which he had just interpreted CONSCIUS ("aut peracti sceleris et de nece Palamedis, aut dolorum suorum . . . aut certe sciens hunc meum animum"). "ARMA esse possunt consilia, quae agitabat Ulysses ad depellendum imminens sibi a Sinone periculum, sic CONSCIUS, sc. periculi imminentis; possunt etiam esse fraudes et insidiae quas in Sinonem parabat, CONSCIUS, tacite intra se; aut CONSCIUS est cum aliis, communicato scilicet cum aliis consilio. Hoc verum videtur, cum statim Calchantem consiliorum socium assumpsisse dicatur," Heyne. "Nempe illud QUAERERE ARMA vagum est et ambiguum h. l. nisi addatur aliquid, quo appareat, quam notionem his inesse voluerit poeta; adiectum est igitur CONSCIUS, quo indicetur communio quaedam; . . . CONSCIUS ARMA QUAERERE igitur poeta dixit, et cum Ulixis nomine adiectivum copulavit, quum, si metrum pateretur, nihil mutata sententia, etiam *quaerere conscios*, quae est communis ratio, dicere liceret," Wagner (1832), followed by Jacob, *Quaest. Epic.* p. 121. "Diese stelle machte von jeher grosse schwierigkeit. . . . Die zwei bedeutendsten, aber fast entgegengesetzten, erklärungen sind: 'er zieht noch andere in sein geheimniss, sucht vertraute, und mit diesen und durch diese die weiteren feindlichen mittel (ARMA) *gegen* Sinon;' oder, "Die waffen, die er heimlich im zelte des Palamedes tückisch versteckt hatte, sucht er nun mit mitwissern offen auf, um daraus die klage des verraths gegen denselben zu begründen, und so auch den Sinon zu verderben," Süpfle. "QUAERERE CONSCIUS ARMA, to seek allies as a conspirator—nearly equivalent to quaerere arma consciorum, or quaerere conscios, as Wagner gives it," Conington.

ARMA, *arms*, in the sense of *war*, as "arma virumque cano." QUAERERE ARMA, *seeks war*, *sets himself to make war*, viz., with me; *has recourse to war*. We have the precise expression, Tacit. *Hist.* 1. 51: "Tum adversus Vindicem contractae legiones, seque et Gallias expertae, quaerere rursus arma, novasque discordias; nec *socios*, ut olim, sed *hostes* et victos vocabant." Compare Ovid, *Amor.* 2. 9. 45:

"et modo blanditias dicat; modo iurgia quaerat"

[have recourse to reproaches]. Propert. 1. 7. 5 :

"nos, ut consuemus, nostros agitamus amores,
            atque aliquid duram quaerimus in dominam"

[I seek for something—some weapon—to turn against, to use against, my hard mistress]. Tacit. *Annal. 13. 18* (of Agrippina): "Nomina et virtutes nobilium, qui etiam tum supererant, in honore habere, quasi quaereret ducem et partes," viz., against Nero.

QUAERERE ARMA differs both from poscere arma and sumere arma; while poscere arma is to call for arms when you are ready and determined for the fight, and sumere arma, actually to take up arms, to arm—QUAERERE ARMA is to go in search of arms, to turn towards arms, to have recourse to arms.

QUAERERE CONSCIUS ARMA, conscious that he is the person whom I have threatened, has recourse to arms, *i. e.*, to war; makes war against me as the best means of defending himself, in self-defence begins hostilities.

101-103.

SED QUID EGO HAEC AUTEM NEQUIDQUAM INGRATA REVOLVO
QUIDVE MOROR SI OMNES UNO ORDINE HABETIS ACHIVOS
IDQUE AUDIRE SAT EST IAMDUDUM SUMITE POENAS

VAR. LECT.

[*punct.*] REVOLVO, QUIDVE MOROR ? SI OMNES UNO ORDINE HABETIS ACHIVOS, IDQUE AUDIRE SAT EST, IAMDUDUM SUMITE POENAS ; III Jahn (1825) ; Thiel.

[*punct.*] REVOLVO ? QUIDVE MOROR ? SI OMNES UNO ORDINE HABETIS ACHIVOS, IDQUE AUDIRE SAT EST ; IAMDUDUM SUMITE POENAS. III P. Manut. ; D. Heins. ; N. Heins. (1670) ; Heyne.

[*punct.*] REVOLVO ? QUIDVE MOROR, SI OMNES UNO ORDINE HABETIS ACHIVOS, IDQUE AUDIRE SAT EST ? IAMDUDUM SUMITE POENAS ; III Wagn. (1832, 1861) ; Forb. (1852) ; Coningt.

O *Vat., Rom., St. Gall.*

VAR. LECT. (vs. 103).

[*punct.*] IDQUE AUDIRE SAT EST. IAMDUDUM SUMITE POENAS. **III** Servius; Schol. in Palimps. Veron. (ap. Maium); P. Manut.; D. Heins.; N. Heins.; Gesner; Voss; Heyne; Wagn. (1832 and 1861); Ribbeck.

[*punct.*] IDQUE AUDIRE SAT EST IAMDUDUM. SUMITE POENAS. **III** Ancient interpreters cited in the following words by Schol. in Palimps. Veron. (ap. Maium): " Plerique tamen sic distinguunt : IDQUE AUDIRE SAT EST IAMDUDUM ;" also Donatus (" Professus sum iamdudum me vestrum esse inimicum, sumite de confesso supplicium "); Catrou.

I do not at all doubt that the construction is : " SI HABETIS UNO ORDINE OMNES ACHIVOS et (si) SAT EST vobis ad meam damnationem me AUDIRE Graecum (*i. e.*, me esse ex Graecis), SUMITE IAMDUDUM POENAS de me ;" and the meaning : " If ye put to death all Greeks without distinction, merely because they are Greeks, here, I am a Greek, put an end to me at once." In order to indicate this construction and meaning the punctuation of Jahn and Thiel should be adopted.

IDQUE AUDIRE = *idque me audire* = *Graecumque me audire* = *Graecumque me esse.* Compare Hor. *Epist. 1. 16. 17* :

" tu recte vivis, si curas esse *quod audis.*"

Ibid. 1. 7. 37 : " rexque paterque *audisti* coram." Diogen. Laert. 2. 140 : Κατεφρονειτο [Menedemus] Κυων και Ληρος υπο των Ερετριεων ακουων. Theocr. *Idyll. 16. 30* :

οφρα και ειν Αϊδαο κεκρυμμενος εσθλος ακουσης.

Philostr. *Heroic.* p. 8 (ed. Boisson.) : εκεινον λεγω τον της Λαοδαμειας· τουτι γαρ χαιρει ακουων. And especially, Dio Cassius, 72. 16 : ουτος ουν ο χρυσους, ουτος ο Ηρακλης, ουτος ο θεος (και γαρ τουτ' ηκουεν), where we have in τουτ' the very ID of our text.

I shall not take on me to say in what sense the passage was understood either by Servius or Heyne, the gloss of the former (" IDQUE AUDIRE, etc. : me Graecum esse") being as obscure on account of its brevity as that of the latter (viz., " Placet, AUDIRE ID, esse me unum ex Achivis ; et ad primam enuntiationis partem refero : SI SAT EST. Ad apodosin retulisse videtur Cerda, ut sit, vel haec audire satis est, nil ut amplius addam necesse. Sed ID et QUE et AUDIRE pro *audirisse* valde duram orationem efficerent. Manendum adeo in prima interpretatione, quam et Servius agnoscit ") is obscure, notwithstanding its length. Cynthius Cenetensis (" AUDIRE pro *audirisse*"), Ascensius ("Si sat .i. satis est vobis audire id .s. quod dixi"), Voss (" und das allein zu hören genügt"), Thiel ("aliquem ex numero Graecorum esse"), Wagner (1832), approved doubtingly by Forbiger ("Si ad cognoscenda principum Achivorum ingenia satis est, id, hanc unam rem, audire"), Süpfle (" IDQUE, nämlich, dass auch ich ein Achiver bin"), Gossrau (" IDQUE, sc. me Argivum esse"), Conington (" ID, that I am a Greek, v. 78"), **all** agree in understanding the structure to be IDQUE [VOS] AUDIRE SAT EST—Wagner alone correcting his error and interpreting (1861): " ID, h. e. Achivum ... AUDIRE, h. e. appellari;" and, of course, then at last understanding the accusative suppressed before AUDIRE to be not *vos*, but *me*.

QUIDVE MOROR? "Vestram, scilicet, festinationem; vel mortem," Servius. No; the verb is here intransitive, and the sense is: "What am I dallying about? why am I tedious? why am I talking here when there is no use in talking, you having already decided on punishing me with death?" Compare Ovid, *Met. 13. 516* (of Hecuba lamenting Polyxena):

> ... "quo ferrea resto?
> *quidve moror?* quo me servas, damnosa senectus?"

IDQUE AUDIRE SAT EST IAMDUDUM SUMITE POENAS.—"IAMDUDUM hic est quamprimum, ut: '*iamdudum* erumpere nubem ardebant,'" Schol. ad Palimps. Ver. (apud Maium); and so Servius, Ascensius, Heyne, Voss, Thiel, Wagn. (1861). IAMDUDUM is not quamprimum, but the very contrary; refers not to the future, but to the just past time, and is equivalent to the English *already, at last*, the German *schon*. Compare 4. 1:

> "At regina gravi *iamdudum* saucia cura"

[not quamprimum, but *now, for some time, already—schon*]. 5. 26:

> ... "equidem sic poscere ventos
> *iamdudum*, et frustra cerno te tendere contra."

5. 513 :

> "tum rapidus iamdudum arcu contenta parato
> tela tenens"

[*already*]. Also (the very passage quoted by Wagner (1861) as example of iamdudum used in the sense of quamprimum), Ovid, *Met. 11. 482 :*

> "'ardua' *iamdudum* 'demittite cornua' rector
> clamat, 'et antennis totum subnectite velum'"

(where the structure is not (with Wagner) "iamdudum demittite," and the meaning quamprimum demittite; but the structure is "iamdudum clamat," and the meaning, *already calls out*—the sense of the whole passage being : They are not more than half across the sea when the waves begin to swell and show white tops, and the captain *already* shouts out, &c.). Compare also *Georg. 1. 212 :*

> "nec non et lini segetem et Cereale papaver
> tempus humo tegere, et *iamdudum* incumbere aratris,
> dum sicca tellure licet, dum nubila pendent"

[*now at last* to press the plough]. Ovid, *Met. 13. 457 :*

> "'utere *iamdudum* generoso sanguine,' dixit;
> nulla mora est"

—a passage which is the exact counterpart of our text, and in which the meaning is not "shed my blood as fast as possible," but "now at last shed my blood; shed my blood already, my blood is ready to be shed."

Iamdudum, therefore, so far from being the equivalent of quamprimum, is almost the very opposite,—quamprimum looking forward and signifying *as soon as all difficulties shall have been removed*, iamdudum looking backward and signifying that all difficulties have been already removed, that all is ready ("nulla mora").

104-105.

HOC ITHACUS VELIT ET MAGNO MERCENTUR ATRIDAE
TUM VERO ARDEMUS SCITARI ET QUAERERE CAUSAS

Hoc ... ATRIDAE. Compare Ovid, *Her. 9.* ? (Dejanira to Hercules) :

"hoc velit Eurystheus, velit hoc germana Tonantis."

TUM VERO ARDEMUS SCITARI ET QUAERERE CAUSAS. The reader is left, as he is occasionally left elsewhere—*ex. gr.* 1. 86; 4. 663; 6. 77; 6. 529; 12. 603—to conclude the actual fact from the context. We have an exact parallel in Ariosto, *Orl. Fur. 4. 28* :

"la donna di saper ebbe desio,
che fosse il negromante, ed a che effetto
edificasse in quel luogo selvaggio
la rocca, e faccia a tutto 'l mondo oltraggio.

"'nè per maligna intenzione, ahi lasso,'
disse piangendo il vecchio incantatore,
'feci la bella rocca in cima al sasso,
nè per avidità son rubatore,' "

where the desire to ask the question is, without any question being asked, followed by the answer. Compare 9. 303, where the actual giving of the sword to Euryalus is omitted, and left to be deduced from the context ; and *Georg. 4. 459*, where the actual death of Eurydice, and *Aen. 12. 603*, where the actual death of Amata, is omitted, and left to be similarly deduced. The sentence seems to be both in structure and sense a very exact translation of Hom. *Od. 10. 249* (of Ulysses and his comrades full of anxiety and curiosity to hear some further account of their companions who had been turned into beasts by Circe) :

αλλ' οτε δη μιν παντες αγασσαμεθ' εξερεοντες,

where the text continues :

και τοτε των αλλων εταρων κατελεξεν ολεθρον.

and where αγασσαμεθα is interpreted by Heliodorus (see Apollon. Lexic., where, however, the reading is not αγασσαμεθα, but, by a manifest error, αγαπαζομεθα) αγαν προσεκειμεθα, exactly equivalent to Virgil's ARDEMUS. See Remarks on 1. 86; 6. 77, 529.

TUM VERO. "*Then indeed* we are all on fire." They were curious before to hear his history, see verse 74; but, having heard so far, are now doubly curious. See Rems. on 2. 228; 3. 47, and 4. 396, 449, 571.

ARDEMUS. The force of the verb ardere is infinitely more intense than that of its English derivatives; which, having first lost their literal, have at last, as a consequence, almost wholly lost even their metaphorical sense. The Latin word, on the contrary, where it is not literal, is fully metaphorical. Compare Cic. *de Orat*. 2. 45: "Tantum est flumen gravissimorum optimorumque verborum, tam integrae sententiae, tam verae, tam novae, tam sine pigmentis fucoque puerili, ut mihi non solum tu *incendere* iudicem, sed ipse *ardere* videaris." Argum. ad Terent. *Adelph*.: "tanta iracundia incitatus est, ut *arderet*."

107.

FICTO PECTORE.

"*Pectus* pro *verbis* posuit. Nam nunquam fingitur pectus," Servius (ed. Lion). "Ad fraudem composito animo, *h. e.* subdole et fraudulenter," Heyne. "Subdolo animo, *h. e.* subdole et fraudulenter. Contrarium est 'apertum pectus' apud Cic. *Lael*. 26. 97," Forbiger. "Subdole," Wagn. (1861). "Mit heuchelnder seele," Voss. According to this interpretation, PECTORE adds nothing to the sense, which, had the metre allowed it, had been fully expressed by "ficto fatur," – speaks with a feigned meaning, a feigned mind, a feigned purport, *i.e.*, falsely. Let us see whether this be not a mistake, and whether pectus—always elsewhere the breast, either literally or figuratively—have not here, too, its own proper and peculiar meaning; be not here, too, breast, either literally or figuratively. That it is not breast literally being perfectly plain, inasmuch as it is not with the literal physical breast, but with the mouth, we speak, our inquiry immediately limits itself to the question whether **pectus** be not here used in its usual figurative sense of emotion, feeling, heart, as we, using a similar metaphor, sometimes say (see 9. 275:

> "te vero, mea quem spatiis propioribus aetas
> insequitur, venerande puer, iam *pectore* toto
> accipio"

[receive you with my whole feeling, my whole heart]. Auctor *Dial. de Cl. Orat. 28:* "ut sincera et integra, et nullis pravitatibus detorta, uniuscuiusque natura toto statim *pectore* arriperet artes honestas" [take to itself with its whole heart]). And, **first**, the meaning: "speaks with feigned emotion, feigned feeling, feigned heart," is in perfect accordance with the fact that it is with feigned feeling, feigned emotion, feigned heart, Sinon speaks all through, as, verse 145:

> "his lacrymis vitam damus, et miserescimus ultro:"

verse 195:

> "talibus insidiis periurique arte Sinonis
> credita res, captique dolis lacrymisque coactis
> quos neque," &c.:

and, secondly, it is in this sense our author uses **pectus** in the precisely parallel passages, (***a***), 1. 525:

> "maximus Ilioneus placido sic *pectore* fatur"

[*not*, surely, with placid words or meaning, *but* with placid animus, placid feeling]. (***b***), 9. 740:

> "olli subridens sedato *pectore* Turnus"

[*not*, surely, with sedate words or meaning, *but* with sedate animus, sedate feeling, sedate heart]. And, especially, (***c***), 10. 555:

> . . . "truncumque tepentem
> provolvens super haec inimico *pectore* fatur:"

[*not* says these words with hostile meaning, *but* these words with hostile feeling, hostile heart, hostile animus]. Compare also (***d***), Ovid, *Trist.* 2. 561 (Ovid supplicating the clemency of Augustus):

"aspicias, quantum dederis mihi *pectoris* ipse:
quoque favore animi teque tuosque canam"

[with how much feeling, how much love, how much affection you have yourself inspired me]. (***e***), Ovid, *Amor.* 3. 3. 42:

"di quoque habent oculos; di quoque *pectus* habent.
si deus ipse forem, numen sine fraude liceret
foemina mendaci falleret ore meum"

(where "pectus" can be nothing else than feeling, susceptibility of the impression, made by beauty, of the passion of love). (***f***), Ovid, *Ep.* 16. 305 (Paris to Helen, of Menelaus):

"hunccine tu speres hominem sine *pectore* dotes
posse satis formae, Tyndari, nosse tuae?"

[man without feeling, without sensibility]. (***g***), Ovid, *Met.* 13. 290 (Ulysses, of Ajax): "rudis et sine *pectore* miles" [without feeling, without sensibility]. (***h***), Ovid, *ex Ponto,* 4. 1. 17:

"da mihi, si quid ea est, hebetantem *pectora* Lethen"

[Lethe, that dulls the feeling, the sensibility]. (***i***), Catull. *Epith. Pel. et Thet.* 68 (of Ariadne):

"sed neque tum mitrae, neque tum fluitantis amictus
illa vicem curans, toto ex te *pectore*, Theseu,
toto animo, tota pendebat perdita mente"

(where "pectore," being placed in the same category with "animo" and "mente," cannot be the literal breast, can only be feeling). (***j***), Hor. *Ep.* 1. 4. 6: "non tu corpus eras sine *pectore*" [a body without feeling, without sensibility]. (***k***), Lucan, 7. 701 (of Caesar, after the battle of Pharsalia):

". . . "quo *pectore* Romam
intrabit, factus campis felicior istis"

[with what feeling? with what emotion?] (***l***), Val. Flacc.

5. 533 (of Aeetes moulding the passion ("pectora") which Jason's demand of the fleece has excited in him) :

"interea quoniam belli pugnaeque propinquae
cura prior, fingit placidis fera *pectora* dictis"

[moulds his fierce feeling, his fierce passion]. (*m*), Claud. *4 Cons. Honor.*, p. 60 (of the unbought affection of the army for Honorius) :

"perdurat non empta fides, nec *pectora* merces
alligat. ipsa suo pro pignore castra laborant."

(*n*), Val. Flacc. 1. 642 (Neptune speaking of the Argo) :

. . . "'hanc [Argo] mihi Pallas
et soror hanc,' inquit, 'mulcens mea *pectora* fletu
abstulerint'"

[soothing, softening my feeling]. **And**, above all, (*o*), Quintil. *Inst. 10. 7. 15:* "Quare capiendae sunt illae, de quibus dixi, rerum imagines, quas vocari φαντασιας indicavimus, omniaque de quibus dicturi erimus, *personae*, *quaestiones*, *spes*, *metus*, habenda in oculis, in affectus recipienda ; *pectus* [feeling] est enim quod disertos facit, et vis mentis. Ideoque imperitis quoque, si modo sunt aliquo affectu concitati, verba non desunt." The commentators, therefore, are wrong in their interpretation, and FICTO PECTORE is not ficte, *i.e.*, verbis fictis, but ficto affectu, with feigned emotion, with an affectation of emotion.

But with what kind of feigned emotion, what kind of "fictum pectus," is it that Sinon speaks ? Are we left to conclude from the "his lacrymis" and "miserescimus" of verse 145, the " lacrymis coactis" of 196, and the kind words of comfort addressed to him by Priam, verses 148 and 149, that Sinon's feigned emotion is that of a heart-broken man, a man bowed to the ground with affliction and sorrow ? No, we are not. Our author is quite precise and particular. Sinon is PAVITANS, all over in a flutter of agitation and apprehension ; and this flutter not being real—for he is

. . . "fidens animi atque in utrumque paratus
seu versare dolos seu certae occumbere morti"—

FICTO PECTORE is added for the purpose of reminding us that

it is not: *he proceeds flurried, and speaks with feigned emotion;*
the feigned emotion with which he speaks being the flutter
(PAVITANS) with which he proceeds. Compare Ovid, *Heroid.*
19. 191 (Hero to Leander):

"sed mihi, caeruleas quoties obvertor ad undas,
nescio quae pavidum frigora pectus habent,"

where "pectus," directly and immediately connected with
"pavidum," is (although somewhat more literally *breast* than
the "pectus" of our text) still the sentient, feeling breast, not
at all the meaning, intending breast; not at all the thoughts,
sentiments, or ideas.

FICTO PECTORE is thus the complement of PAVITANS, and the
entire sense of the two sentences, PROSEQUITUR PAVITANS and
FICTO PECTORE FATUR, is prosequitur ficto pavore, or ficto
pavore fatur or prosequitur ficte pavitans, or ficte
pavitans fatur—the second verb contributing nothing to the
sense, and being added solely for the purpose of making up the
second of the two sentences into which the author has thought
proper for the sake of rhetorical effect and the more easy com-
pletion of his verse to divide the thought prosequitur ficto
pavore, or ficto pavore fatur, or prosequitur ficte
pavitans, or ficte pavitans fatur.

112—115.

CUM IAM HIC TRABIBUS CONTEXTUS ACERNIS
STARET EQUUS TOTO SONUERUNT AETHERE NIMBI
SUSPENSI EURYPYLUM SCITATUM ORACULA PHOEBI
MITTIMUS

VAR. LECT.

SCITATUM **I** *Med.* (thus SCITANTVM). **III** Mod.; P. Manut.; D. Heins.;
N. Heins. (1670); Philippe; Heyne; Brunck; Wakef.; Pott.

SCITANTEM **I** *Pal.* **II** "In Longobardico cod. SCITANTEM legimus," Pierius.
III Rob. Steph.; Wagn. (ed. Heyn., ed. 1861); Voss; Lad.; Haupt;
Ribb.

0 *Vat., Rom., Ver., St. Gall.*

The reading of the Mediceau, SCITATUM, is confirmed both by Liv. 5. 15: "Quidnam eo dii portenderent prodigio, missi sciscitatum oratores ad Delphicum oraculum;" and by Iscan. 4. 254:

> "hic patriae et propriis *scitatum* oracula regnis
> venerat."

STARET.—"STARET, esset," Heyne, Forbiger. This is neither to interpret Virgil, nor to understand poetry. Stare is, indeed, one of those verbs which are used in the Latin language in place of esse, but it does not on that account lose its own proper meaning. STARET places the horse before our eyes, not merely existing, but *standing* there, a remarkable, striking object. The object is the more striking, the picture the more vivid, not only on account of the position of STARET—first word in its own verse, and preceded by an introduction raising expectation, viz., TRABIBUS CONTEXTUS ACERNIS (see Rem. on 2. 247)—but on account of its being itself placed before its nominative. The same verb, in the selfsame position in the verse, preceded by a similar introduction, and preceding in the same manner its nominative, will be found applied to a real living horse, 4. 135:

> . . . "ostroque insignis et auro
> *stat sonipes*."

and with the same effect, that of placing before our eyes, if we only deign to use them, the horse, not merely being or existing, but standing there bodily; exactly as the same verb in the same position in the verse and similarly preceding its own nominative places so livelily before us the three hundred horses, not merely being or existing in the stables of Latinus, but standing there, 7. 275:

> "*stabant* ter centum nitidi in praesepibus altis."

It is in the same way the urn is said not to be or exist, but to stand, at 6. 22: "stat ductis sortibus urna;" the tower is said to stand, 6. 554: "stat ferrea turris ad auras;" the altars are said to stand, 4. 509: "stant arae circum;" the silex is said to stand, 8. 233: "stabat acuta silex;" and this very wooden horse itself is said to stand, Hom. Od. 8. 505: ως ο μεν εστηκει. And such, I believe, will invariably be found to be the use made by Virgil of stare, viz., to express either, as here, literal, or (as 2. 162:

"omnis spes Danaum et coepti fiducia belli
Palladis auxiliis semper stetit,"

where see Rem.) figurative standing, never to express mere existence or esse.

The use of stare in the sense assigned to it in our text by Heyne is happily not to be found either in Virgil, or, as far as my memory at this moment serves me, in other first-class Latin writers. To the great disgust of the Latin scholar, it is very frequent in Italian writers, even of the first class (as Dante, *Inferno*, 34. 13:

"altre *stanno* a giacere, altre *stanno* erte,
quella col capo, e quella con le piante",,

and in Italy jars on his ear many times every day in the ordinary salutation: "Come sta?" Then there is the Sp. *estar*.

SUSPENSI. "Solliciti, dubii quid facerent," Heyne. The latter part of the definition is nearer to the truth than the former. Suspensus is not sollicitus, anxious, uneasy, but suspended, at a loss what to do, and, because at a loss what to do, doing nothing; suspended, not merely mentally, but in act, at a nonplus, ἀπορίᾳ κεχρημένοι, as Euripides (*Iphig. Aul.* 89) says of the same persons in that precisely similar situation at Aulis which is referred to at verse 116. Compare (*a*), 4. 9: "quae me *suspensam* insomnia terrent?" [not sollicitam, but, as is plain from the context, irresolute, undecided, taking no step, suspended from action by the terrifying dreams ("insomnia terrent"), the effect of which upon her is so great that it is only after her sister has encouraged her—

"his dictis incensum animum inflammavit amore,
spemque dedit dubiae menti, solvitque pudorem"—

that she begins to act ("principio delubra adeunt," &c.)]. Also (*b*), 2. 728:

"nunc omnes terrent aurae, sonus excitat omnis
suspensum et pariter comitique onerique timentem"

[*not* anxious, *but* irresolute, undecided whether to go on or stop—otherwise the poet has failed to convey the full picture, and the words "omnes terrent aurae, sonus excitat omnis" are without their most ordinary and natural consequence]. **And** (*c*), Sil. 15. 460:

> "ille, ubi *suspensi* Patres, et curia vocem
> posceret, ut cantu ducebat corda Senatus"

[where the fathers were at a nonplus, did not know what step to take]. That suspensus is not sollicitus, but *suspended, hanging undetermined*, appears further from the marked distinction made by Cicero between the two terms, *ad Att.* 2. 18 (ed. Orelli): "intellexi, quam *suspenso* animo et *sollicito* scire averes, quid esset novi;" *de Leg. Agrar.* 1. 8 (ed. Orelli): "*sollicitam* mihi civitatem suspicione, *suspensam* metu, perturbatam vestris legibus et concionibus et seditionibus, tradidistis." Compare Manil. 1. 66:

> "nam rudis ante illos, nullo discrimine, vita
> in speciem conversa operum ratione carebat,
> et *stupefacta* novo *pendebat* lumine mundi,"

where "pendebat stupefacta," *hung stupefied*, is equivalent to: remained stupefied, not able or not knowing how to advance.

119-126.

ARGOLICA—RECUSAT

ARGOLICA, the emphatic word of the sentence. It was this word which filled the minds of the hearers with horror. No matter how much blood was to be shed, if it had not been *Argolic* blood there would have been no horror. To aid the effect of the word and point out the precise meaning and import, our author has placed it in the most emphatic position, viz., at the end of the sentence to which it belongs, and in the beginning of a new line, from the rest of which it is separated by an abrupt and complete pause. See Rem. on 2. 246.

CUI FATA PARENT, QUEM POSCAT APOLLO.—CUI FATA PARENT, theme ; QUEM POSCAT APOLLO, variation ; QUEM corresponding to CUI, POSCAT to PARENT, and APOLLO to FATA, as if he had said : who it is for whom the fates are preparing ruin ; who it is whom Apollo, the oracle of the fates, demands. That this is the true structure is placed beyond doubt by Stat. *Theb. 3. 700*:

"hic certe est, quem fata dabant, quem dixit Apollo,"

where we have not only the same fata and the same Apollo, but the same repeated relative, the same rhythm, and the same theme and variation, and where " fata " is the nominative. Who is there who, observing that the two relatives in the line of Statius have one and the same antecedent, does not at once conclude that the two relatives in the line of Virgil must have one and the same antecedent ; and that, therefore, the received reading CUI is not to be ejected to make room either for Peerlkamp's conjectural QUID, or for Dietsch's no less conjectural QUOD or QUAE, each of the three requiring an antecedent of its own ? Who is there who, observing that " fata " in Statius's line is the nominative to " dabant," and varied in " Apollo," does not immediately conclude that FATA in Virgil's line is the nominative to PARENT, and varied in APOLLO, and that the alteration proposed in the *Misc. Observ.*, p. 86, of PARENT into PARET is as little called for as it is little in accordance with Apollo's recognized office and mission—that of announcing, not at all that of ordering or disposing of, the future, as in 3. 251 :

"quae Phoebo pater omnipotens, mihi Phoebus Apollo
praedixit."

Thus, as I am fain to hope, is set at rest a question so long at issue among Virgilian students ; and not only the reading of the manuscripts justified, but the opinion of Servius and the majority of commentators, viz., that FATA is in the nominative, established as against that of Freudenberg (*Spicil. Vindic. Virg.*) and those who, quoting Ovid, *Met. 14. 213*:

"talia fingebam misero mihi *fata* parari,"

insist that FATA is the accusative, and the sense either CUI *illi* PARENT FATA (an interpretation to which there is the special objection that there was as yet no suspicion of foul play), or CUI EA VERBA (verses 116-119) PARENT FATA, to which there is the no less strong objection that the plural *ea verba* cannot consistently be supplied after the singular QUAE VOX immediately preceding.

The verb parare has been (*a*) repeatedly joined with the nominative fata by Lucan, as 2. 131 :

> " ille fuit vitae Mario modus, omnia passo,
> quae peior fortuna potest, atque omnibus uso,
> quae melior, mensoque, homini quid *fata pararent*,"

and 6. 783 :

> . . . "quid *fata pararent*
> hi[*hic*, Weber] fecere palam ;"

(*b*), once with the same nominative by Seneca, *Oedipus*, 28 :

> " iamiam aliquid in nos *fata* moliri *parant* ;"

(*c*), once with the nominative fortuna by Valerius Flaccus, 1. 326 : " siu aliud Fortuna parat ;" (*d*), once with the nominative superi by Silius, 1. 136 :

> "magna *parant superi*; tonat alti regia caeli,
> bellantemque Iovem cerno :"

and, (*e*), once by our author himself with the nominative "[vos, o] di patrii," 9. 247 :

> " di patrii, quorum semper sub numine Troia est,
> non tamen omnino Teucros delere *paratis*"

—instances to which might be added very numerous others, but slightly different in construction, in which either the fates or the gods are said parare, to prepare, whether good or evil, for men ; as Lucan, 2. 68 :

> " 'non alios,' inquit, 'motus tunc *fata parabant*
> quum,' " &c.

Ibid., 1. 642 :

> " ' aut hic errat,' ait, ' nulla cum lege per aevum
> mundus, et incerto discurrunt sidera motu ;
> aut, si *fata* movent, urbi generique *paratur*
> humano matura lues.' "

Ibid., 649 :

> " quod cladis genus, o *superi*, qua peste *paratis*
> saevitiam ?"

Ibid. 2. 4:

> . . . "rector Olympi,
> . . . .
> sit subitum, quodcunque paras."

Plaut., *Mil. Glor.* 725 (ed. Ritschl):

> . . . "aequum fuit
> deos pararisse, uno exemplo ne omnes vitam viverent."

Aen. 5. 14: "quidve, pater Neptune, paras?"

FATA PARENT, the fates may be preparing, as Cic. *ad Quint. fratr. 3. 9:* "Pompeius abest; Appius miscet; Hirrus parat" [Hirrus is preparing].

QUAE SINT EA NUMINA DIVUM, FLAGITAT. "Qui sint ii dii, scilicet, qui tam atrocia postulent, ut, quasi dubitans nec credens id fieri posse, quaerat Ulixes, num dii sint, qui talia postulare possint," Dietsch (*Theolog. Virg.*, p. 5). This is not the meaning. Ulysses merely demands an explanation of the NUMINA—will or pleasure of the gods as announced by the oracular response—first, because it is to give this explanation Calchas refuses:

> BIS QUINOS SILET ILLE DIES, TECTUSQUE RECUSAT
> PRODERE VOCE SUA QUEMQUAM, AUT OPPONERE MORTI;

and secondly, because the exactly corresponding expression, 3. 100: "cuncti quae sint ea moenia quaerunt," contains no reprobation of the "moenia" spoken of, but only the simple inquiry what those "moenia" are. Servius, therefore, is perfectly right in his gloss: "quaeritur modo non quid dicant (nam planum), sed quis debeat immolari."

NUMINA, the will or pleasure of the gods concealed under the mysterious oracular announcement. See Rem. on "perverso numine," 7. 584; and on "haud numine nostro," 2. 396.

ARTIFICIS SCELUS. Precisely the converse expression is used by Euripides, *Med. 410* (ed. Pors.):

> κακων δε παντων τεκτονες σοφωταται

TECTUS. That TECTUS is here used, not in its derived sense of *secret*, but in its literal and primitive sense of *covered*, i.e., *shut up*, or *closed up*, viz., *in his dwelling*, is sufficiently proved by Statius's imitation (*Theb. 3. 570*):

"ille nec aspectum vulgi, nec fida tyranni
colloquia, aut coetus procerum perferre, sed atra
sede tegi, et superum clausus negat acta fateri."

Compare also Stat. ibid. 621.; Aen. 7. 600 (of Latinus) :

"saepsit se tectis, rerumque reliquit habenas;"

7. 618 (also of Latinus) :

"abstinuit tactu pater aversusque refugit
foeda ministeria et caecis se condidit umbris;"

Soph. Oed. Tyr. 320 (Tiresias refusing to acquaint Oedipus with his guilt) : αφες μ' ες οικους.

129-137.

COMPOSITO—VIDENDI

RUMPIT VOCEM. Compare Div. Paul. ad Galat. 4. 27 : ρηξον και βοησον, η ουκ ωδινουσα, where Wakefield, with his usual rough vigour, "i.e., ρηξον βοην. Nos Angli pariter locutionem break de sonis [he should have said de flatu] usurpamus, sed illis quidem minime honestis et ab altera porta erumpentibus." He might have still more appositely quoted Shakesp. Com. of Errors, 3. 1:

"a man may break a word with you, sir, and words are but wind;
ay, and break it in your face, so he break it not behind."

CONVERSA TULERE. "Passi sunt verti"—"conversa passi sunt," say Ruaeus, Voss, Jahn, Forbiger, Kappes and Weidner. "Converterunt," say Heyne, Wagner, and Gossrau; while Conington hesitates between the former of these interpretations and that which I advocated in my "Twelve Years' Voyage," viz., "converterunt et tulerunt, turned and carried to," i.e., "not only turned to but carried to"—an interpretation which I now find to have been La Cerda's before it was mine, and before I adduced in support of it Aen. 4. 376: "furiis incensa feror,"

TULERE is after all so vague, and therefore so weak and insignificant a word, that too much fault is not to be found with those commentators who regard it as here serving merely to make out the verse and give the participle the force of a finite verb. On a similar occasion Livy (5. 47)—happily for himself not under the necessity of either measuring the length or counting the number of his syllables—has expressed, forcibly and without any ambiguity, the thought which our so much and often so justly vaunted author has here required two to express weakly, lamely, and ambiguously : " Tum vigiles eius loci, qua fefellerat ascendens hostis, citati ; et quum in omnes more militari se animadversurum Q. Sulpicius tribunus militum pronunciasset ; consentiente clamore militum, *in unum vigilem coniicientium culpam*, deterritus, a ceteris abstinuit : reum haud dubium eius noxae, approbantibus cunctis, de saxo deiecit."

ERIPUI, FATEOR, LETO ME ET VINCULA RUPI.—VINCULA, "quibus ligatus servabatur, et ad aram adducebatur," Heyne. No, Thiel is right : VINCULA is not to be taken too strictly. It is merely confinement, state of restraint, state of being a prisoner —VINCULA RUPI, I broke away, burst from among my guards, from the confinement in which I was held. Compare 1. 58 : "vinclis et carcere frenat," where the meaning is, as correctly explained by Heyne himself, not *with chains and a prison* (the winds not having been chained), but *with the restraint of a prison*. Compare also 8. 651 :

"et fluvium *vinclis* innaret Cloelia *ruptis*"

[*not* her chains being broken, *but* her confinement, or state of custody, being broken—" frustrata custodes," Liv. 2. 13]. Also 12. 29 :

"victus amore tui, cognato sanguine victus,
coniugis et maestae lacrymis, *vincla* omnia *rupi*,
promissam eripui genero, arma impia sumpsi."

Ovid, *Fast. 4. 602* :

"statque semel inucti *rumpere vincla* tori."

Ovid, *Amor. 3. 2. 5* :

"scilicet asserui iam me, *rupique catenas*;
et quae depuduit ferre, tulisse pudet"

—examples, the two former of the use of the expression rum-pere vincula, the latter of the use of the even more precise expression rumpere catenas, in a still less literal sense, the confinement or bondage spoken of being not even so much as physical, only moral. Sinon's chains had been already taken off, and he was standing at the altar with the sacred fillet round his head (verses 155 and 156), when he burst away from among the hands of his executioners ("vincula rupit et eripuit se leto"). See Rem. on "vinclis et carcere frenat," 1. 58.

Wagner (1861) does not know what VINCULA are here spoken of, but is quite sure they are not the same as those spoken of in verse 147: "Quae VINCULA? certe non ea quae, vers. 147, commemorantur"—a piece of information second in importance to none in his entire work, the VINCLA of verse 147 being those Trojan VINCLA with which Sinon is brought bound before Priam and from which Priam now orders him to be relieved (ATQUE ARCTA LEVARI VINCLA IUBET PRIAMUS); and the VINCULA of our text being those (Grecian) VINCULA from which he had previously broken loose (ERIPUI, FATEOR, LETO ME, ET VINCULA RUPI). In his next edition Wagner's doubt will have been cleared up, and he will be able to tell us all this.

DELITUI DUM VELA DARENT, SI FORTE DEDISSENT. I adhere to the received punctuation, and reject that of Heyne, which places the words DARENT SI FORTE between two commas so as to refer VELA not to DARENT, but to DEDISSENT. I am determined to this choice, not only by the reasons assigned by Wagner, but by the very remarkable parallel, verse 756:

"inde domum si forte pedem, si forte tulisset,
me refero."

PATRIAM ANTIQUAM.—ANTIQUAM, not merely *old* ("Pristinam, nihil amplius," Heyne), but, as occasionally elsewhere, *dear old* ("der heimath alte gefilde," Voss)—old, and because of its being old, and therefore associated with so many recollections, dear. This suggested meaning, if I may so call it, does not accompany the word into the English language, but is found in the Saxon derivative *old*, which therefore and not "ancient" is the word which corresponds with the ANTIQUAM of our text. Thus we never say in this sense "ancient England," or "ancient Ireland," but always "old England," and "old Ireland;" never "the good ancient times," but always "the good old times." Compare Soph. *Oed. Tyr.* 1394: τα πατρια λογω παλαια δωμαθ'.

141-143.

QUOD TE PER SUPEROS ET CONSCIA NUMINA VERI
PER SI QUA EST QUAE RESSTAT ADHUC MORTALIBUS USQUAM
INTEMERATA FIDES ORO

SUPEROS and NUMINA are not two distinct co-ordinate subjects joined together in the sense as they are joined together in the grammar by the copulative ET. There is in the sense but one subject, SUPEROS (*i. e.* the gods, appealed to by Sinon as conscios veri); but, it being a matter of difficulty for the author to connect conscios veri with that word and at the same time round his verse, NUMINA is had recourse to in order to supply the necessary dactyl in the fifth place, and so a word wholly superfluous to the sense, and both embarrassing to and deceptive of the reader, introduced—the sense being neither more nor less than superos conscios veri; and the reader being lured away in search of some difference in meaning between SUPEROS and NUMINA to account for the latter alone, and not the former, being conscious of truth. Such is the real nature of the epexegesis so much admired by those numerous readers who, to admire anything, require no more than to find it in Virgil. See Rem. on "Italiam Laviniaque littora," 1. 6-9, and concluding paragraph of Rem. on "molem et montes altos," 1. 65.

FIDES.—"FIDES quam hic inclamat est iusti rectique observantia, *h. l.*, iuris divini et humanitatis," Heyne; as if Sinon adjured Priam by his reverence for the gods on the one hand, and by his respect for right and justice on the other. This is not the meaning. There is neither a double adjuration, nor is *fides* ever " observantia iusti rectique." For (**1**), the adjuration is not double, but single and simple,—" I adjure thee by the gods and by INTEMERATA FIDES, if there is any among men," *i. e.* by the INTEMERATA FIDES of the gods, and men if, indeed, there is any such thing among men; plainly an adaptation to the epo of the "pro deum atque hominum fidem" of every-day life, and the genteel comedy. Compare 6. 458 (Aeneas addressing the shade of Dido):

. . . " per sidera iuro
per *superos*, et si qua *fides* tellure sub ima est."

'I swear by the gods above, and by whatever fides there is here in Hades," *i. e.*, " I swear by the fides both of the gods above, and of the Manes; **and** (**2**), FIDES is not " observantia iusti rectique, *i. e.* iuris divini et humanitatis," but, as *fides* is always and invariably *faith*, the keeping inviolate of one's word, promise, or pledge (as Cic. *de Off*. 1. 7: " Fundamentum est autem iustitiae *fides*; id est, dictorum conventorumque constantia et veritas"); in other words, fides is moral truth. Compare 11. 511:

. . . " ut fama *fidem* missique reportant
exploratores."

[as public rumour and the report of our scouts pledge us their faith, *i. e.* assure us]; 4. 597 : " en dextra *fides*que," [see how he has kept his pledged faith]; 4. 552 :

" non servata *fides*, cineri promissa Sychaeo."

And such, if I am not mistaken, will be found to be the meaning of *fides* wherever it occurs, and it is also the meaning of our English derivative and parallel, *Faith*, as Clarke, *Sermon*, 8. "The word faith always contains the notion of faithfulness or fidelity."

It being Sinon's first and principal object, failing which all he could say or do would be worse than useless, to convince his hearers of his moral truth, of his fides [Gr. το πιστον, It. *lealtà*, Fr. *loy*-

auté), nothing could be more proper than his adjuring Priam by the FIDES, *i. e.* moral truth, of gods and men, especially of the gods who knew the facts, the absolute truth (CONSCIA NUMINA VERI), and would themselves their own FIDES being INTEMERATA, testify truly. Into what court were ever more competent witnesses brought—unimpeachable themselves, and acquainted besides with all the facts? Never in any treatise of Ethics were the two so essentially different kinds of truth more accurately distinguished from each other: the verum, or the true in fact and independently of opinion; and the fides, or true in opinion independently of fact. In like manner, 6. 458, it being Aeneas's first and principal object to convince Dido of his fides, his moral truth and sincerity, his appeal is as before to the fides or moral truth and sincerity; but being no longer among men, his appeal is no longer to the same fides, the same moral truth and sincerity as before, viz., the fides of gods and men, but to the fides of the gods and of those among whom he now finds himself, viz., the Manes:

> . . . " per sidera iuro
> per superos, et si qua *fides* tellure sub ima est."

On the contrary, Aeneas's object in his first interview with Dido being not to inspire her with confidence in his words (entire confidence being already and beforehand placed in them by the guileless, generous, and candid queen), but to express his unbounded gratitude and everlasting obligation to her, his appeal is made not to fides, but to iustitia, that iustitia which, whether to be found in heaven or wherever else, would never leave unrewarded, such unexpected and unexampled benignity, generosity, and munificence:

> . . . " si qua pios respectant numina, si quid
> usquam *iustitia* est,"

with which appeal to iustitia, Heyne, followed, as I believe, by most commentators, has confounded the very different appeal in our text to FIDES. Again, and with similar propriety, 2. 535, it is neither to fides nor to iustitia, but to pietas, tenderheartedness, the tender-heartedness of heaven (see Rem. on 1. 14), that Priam appeals when he calls upon the gods to reward, as it deserves, the outrage inflicted by Pyrrhus on an affectionate tender-hearted parent:

> "'at tibi pro scelere' exclamat, 'pro talibus ausis.
> di, si qua est caelo pietas, quae talia curet,
> persolvant grates dignas et praemia reddant
> debita, qui nati coram me cernere letum,
> fecisti, et patrios foedasti funere vultus.'"

CONSCIA NUMINA VERI. Not NUMINA VERI, but CONSCIA VERI as, *Aen. 4. 519*:

> "testatur moritura deos et *conscia fati* sidera."

Manil. 1. 1:

> "carmine divinas artes et *conscia fati*
> sidera . . . .
> . . . . . . deducere mundo
> aggredior."

The two expressions *conscia fati* and *conscia veri* are, indeed, nearly identical, that which is fated being of course true, and that which is true being fated.

145.

MISERESCIMUS ULTRO

"ULTRO autem non est *sponte*, nam iam rogaverat, sed *insuper*," Servius (ed. Lion), followed by Wagner (1861), and Conington. "ULTRO est *libenter, facili promptoque animo*," Heyne, followed by Wagner, *Quaest. Virg.* "Non solum eius precibus et lacrymis impulsi, sed nostro etiam sensu commoti, facili promptoque animo," Forbiger. "Talibus LACRYMIS VITAM DAMUS, ET MISERESCIMUS *vel* ULTRO; nedum rogati, ut ab hoc nunc duri simus," Doederlein. Let us try to extricate ourselves out of this cloudy uncertainty and confusion, and in order to arrive at the meaning of ULTRO in our text, of ULTRO in connexion with MISERESCIMUS, inquire first what is the meaning of ultro elsewhere, what is the proper and usual meaning of the word ultro. The proper and usual meaning of ultro, like the proper and usual meaning of any other word, is only to be ascertained by induction. Compare, accordingly (*a*), Caelius Symposius, *Aenigm. 96* 'of Echo) :

"virgo modesta sacri legem bene servo pudoris:
ore procax non sum, nec sum temeraria lingua;
ultro nolo loqui, sed do responsa loquenti"

[here "ultro" is plainly neither "insuper," nor "facili promptoque animo," nor both together, but proprio motu; *i.e.* of myself, taking the initiative]. (*b*), Terent. *Eun. 4. 7. 42:*

... "novi ingenium mulierum:
nolunt, ubi velis; ubi nolis, cupiunt *ultro*"

[*i.e.* cupiunt proprio motu; of themselves, taking the initiative]. (*c*), Sen. *Hippol. 441:*

"at si quis *ultro* se malis offert volens,
seque ipse torquet, perdere est dignus bona,
queis nescit uti"

[*i.e.* proprio motu offert]. (*d*), Liv. 21. 1: "Romanis indignantibus, quod victoribus victi *ultro* inferrent arma; Poenis, quod superbe avareque crederent imperitatum victis esse" [*i.e.* proprio motu inferrent; of themselves, taking the initiative]. (*e*), Liv. 26. 17: "Ne iis quidem quae *ultro* dicta erant stabatur" [*i.e.* proprio motu dicta erant]. (*f*), *Aen. 2. 193:*

"*ultro* Asiam magno Pelopea ad moenia bello
venturam"

[where also "ultro" is proprio motu, of itself, taking the initiative]. (*g*), *Ibid. 9. 126:*

"at non audaci cessit fiducia Turno
ultro animos tollit dictis atque increpat *ultro*'

[where also "ultro" is proprio motu, of itself, taking the initiative]. (*h*), 10. 312:

"occiso Therone, virum qui maximus *ultro*
Aenean petit"

[where also "ultro" is proprio motu]. (*i*), 11. 471:
"multaque se incusat, qui non acceperit *ultro*
Dardanium Aenean"

[where also "ultro" is proprio motu]. (*j*), 9. 6:
"Turne, quod optanti divum promittere nemo
auderet, volvenda dies en attulit *ultro*"

[where also "ultro" is proprio motu]. And (*k*), 5. 446:
"Entellus vires in ventum effudit, et *ultro*
ipse gravis graviterque ad terram pondere vasto
concidit"

[where also (although we do not usually employ the expression proprio motu in such cases) "ultro" is really proprio motu, *of himself*, Entellus being himself the cause of his own fall]. Nor is there one single one either of the examples adduced by Tursellini to show that "ultro ex contrariis varias significationes accipit, nam cum *coacto* opponitur est *sponte*, cum *petenti* est *non petenti*," or of the still more numerous examples adduced by Wagner (*Quaest. Virg.*) to show that ultro is sometimes εις το περαν, sometimes περαιοθεν, in which ultro is not simply and without any *ambages* proprio motu, αυτοματως, αυτομολως, of one's self. See Rem. on 4. 304.

Let us now see what objection can be made to ULTRO understood here also in this its usual and proper sense: "To these tears we grant his life, and pity him proprio motu." There is, I am told, the objection put forward by Servius, viz., that ULTRO, so understood, is in contradiction to HIS LACRYMIS DAMUS. Their pity, I am told, cannot be proprio motu because Sinon had besought it ("iam rogaverat"); and not only had Sinon besought it, but the author taking up in HIS ... MISERESCIMUS Sinon's most pitiful MISERERE, MISERERE, had called our special attention to the fact that Sinon had besought it. The objection is not without weight so long as ULTRO is regarded as belonging no less to HIS LACRYMIS VITAM DAMUS than to MISERESCIMUS, for it is not easy to conceive the life which we have just heard was granted to tears to be granted proprio motu. But the moment we confine the operation of ULTRO to its own clause, the difficulty vanishes, and we have Sinon's life granted to his tears, and at the same time his hearers so softened that they pity him proprio motu. To be sure, this softening effect is, philosophically speaking, produced by Sinon's tears, nor is there any such thing in nature as motion without motor, any such thing as proprio motu at all; but it is not so felt by the Trojans, who regarded it as Aeneas describes it, viz., as a spontaneous uncaused proprio motu (ULTRO) operation of their own minds. We have a precisely similar apparently uncaused, but really caused, proprio motu of the mind of Turnus, expressed by the same ultro, in the beginning of the twelfth book, where Turnus, stimulated by the public impatience that he should come forward and redeem his pledge of meeting Aeneas in fight, not only comes forward, but

    ". . . *ultro* implacabilis ardet
 attollitque animos,"

i. e., proprio motu will not be appeased, but is on fire for the battle.

The second clause of the verse is thus a climax of the first — "not merely do we grant his life to his tears, but we pity him proprio motu also." Thus, also, the MISERESCIMUS of our text is really "insuper," but this meaning is not contained in, is only a deduction from, ULTRO.

To the suggestion of Gesner: "Malim tamen ULTRO ad sequentia referre : ULTRO IPSE VIRO PRIMUS MANICAS, &c., ut indicetur animus Priami mitis, qui *non rogatus, non monitus*, demi iubet Sinoni vincula." I object (*a*), That HIS LACRYMIS VITAM DAMUS ET MISERESCIMUS, "we grant him his life and pity him," is a bald, a much less fitting, response to Sinon's thrilling cry for pity :

    MISERERE LABORUM
  TANTORUM ; MISERERE ANIMI NON DIGNA FERENTIS.
  HIS LACRYMIS VITAM DAMUS ET MISERESCIMUS ULTRO,

"we grant his life and pity him proprio motu, *i. e.* by the impulse of our own hearts." (***b***), That IPSE PRIMUS IUBET gains nothing, whatever it may lose, by the addition of ULTRO—those words of themselves sufficiently expressing the alacrity of Priam, himself one of those who " miserescunt" ULTRO. (***c***), That the euphony of the verse forbids the separation of the sixth foot from the fifth by a period. (***d***), That such separation, if occurring at all in the Aeneid, is of the rarest; and (***e***), That misereri and ultro are not only joined together, but joined together at the end of a verse, and so as to afford the same sense as in our text, by Ovid, *Art. Amat. 3. 679 :*

" iamdudum persuasus erit, miserebitur *ultro*."

148-156.

QUISQUIS—FUGI

The elder Heinsius placed a semicolon at GRAIOS and a comma at ERIS. The younger Heinsius, and, after him, Emmenessius and Burmann, retain the semicolon at GRAIOS, but substitute a colon for the comma at ERIS—correctly, as I think; NOSTER ERIS being thrown in according to Virgil's usual manner (see Rems. on *Aen. 1. 4 ; 3. 571 ; 4. 484 ; 6. 84, 741* and *882*) parenthetically between the two connected verbs OBLIVISCERE and EDISSERE, and the sense running thus : " forget the Greeks (for thou shalt from henceforward be ours) and answer me truly these questions." Wagner in his edition of Heyne returns to the punctuation of the elder Heinsius, and observes in his note : " Comma post ERIS ponendum, et quae sequuntur hunc in modum accipienda : ac *proinde* EDISSERE ;" thus separating the two similar verbs, and connecting the two dissimilar. In his *Praestabilior*, however, the same critic, profiting *sub silentio* by the lessons read him in my " Twelve Years' Voyage" and " Advers. Virgil.," restores with his right hand the punctuation to the state from which he had removed it with his left.

NOSTER ERIS, *i. e.* shalt be Trojan, shalt be counted as one of us. Compare Ovid, *Fast.* 4. 272 (Attalus permitting the statue of Cybele to go to Rome) : " nostra eris," *thou shalt* [*still*] *be Phrygian*.

SIDERA, sky, as *Aen.* 5. 126, 628 ; and " astris," 5. 517.

IGNES, not, with Servius and Donatus, the fires of or in the sky, *i. e.* the sun, moon, and stars, but the sky itself considered as fire, the fiery ethereal sky. The sun, moon, and stars considered as fires in the sky cannot have a numen (NON VIOLABILE VESTRUM NUMEN), but the whole sky—sun, moon, and stars inclusive—considered as a unity, can. See Apuleius, *de Mundo*, quoted below.

NON VIOLABILE, not to be profaned, viz., by any nefas, such for instance as a false oath, as if he had said : by whom to swear falsely were a profanity requiring expiation. Compare Liv. 2. 38 : "An non sensistis triumphatum hodie de vobis esse ? vos omnibus civibus, peregrinis, tot finitimis populis spectaculo abeuntes fuisse ? vestras coniuges, vestros liberos, traductos per ora hominum ? Quid eos qui audivere vocem praeconis ? quid qui vos videre abeuntes ? quid eos qui huic ignominioso agmini fuere obvii, existimasse putatis ? nisi aliquod profecto nefas esse, quo si intersimus spectaculo, *violaturi* simus ludos, piaculumque merituri : ideo nos ab sede piorum, coetu concilioque abigi." Eurip. *Med.* 750 :

ομνυμι γαιαν, ηλιου θ' αγνον σεβας,
θεους τε παντας, εμμενειν α σου κλυω.

Apuleius, *de Mundo* (ed. Flor. p. 708) : "Caelum ipsum, stellaeque caeligenae, omnisque siderea compago aether vocatur: non, ut quidam putant, quod ignitus sit et incensus, sed quod cursibus rapidis semper rotetur : elementum, non unum ex quatuor quae nota sunt cunctis, sed longe aliud, numero quintum, ordine primum, genere divinum et *inviolabile*." Sil. 9. 168 :

" tum iuvenis, maestum attollens ad sidera vultum ;
'pollutae dextrae et facti Titania testis
infandi, quae nocturno mea lumine tela
dirigis in patrium corpus, non amplius,' inquit,
' his oculis et damnato *violabere* visu.' "

The sense assigned to the word by Servius (viz., αφθαρτον) belongs to a later latinity. Compare Flav. Vopisc. *Vita Divi Aureliani, 41 :* "Recte atque ordine consuluissent dii immortales, P. C., si boni ferro *inviolabiles* exstitissent, ut longiorem ducerent vitam : neque contra eos aliqua esset potestas iis qui neces infandas tristissima mente concipiunt. Viveret enim princeps noster Aurelianus quo neque utilior fuit quisquam."

VOS ARAE ENSESQUE NEFANDI QUOS FUGI. "Neque ullis adpetitus insidiis est, neque devotus hostiae; denique sic de omnibus iurat, ut per ea quae non fuerunt dans sacramentum, careat obiurgatore," Fragm. vet. interp. in Virg. ap. Maium, vol. 7, p. 272. See the similarly equivocating oath of Andromache, Senec. *Troad. 604.*

156-170.

VITTAEQUE—DANAUM

VAR. LECT.

[*punct.*] VITTAEQUE DEUM, QUAS **III** Servius; P. Manut. ; D. Heins.; N. Heins. ; Heyne ; Wagn. (*Praest.*); Ribb.

[*punct.*] VITTAEQUE, DEUM QUAS **III** "Multi hic distinguunt, et sic subiungunt : DEUM QUAS HOSTIA GESSI," Servius; Voss.

Not HOSTIA DEUM, but VITTAE DEUM, exactly as 11. 4 :

"*Vota deum* primo victor solvebat Eoo."

To make DEUM the commencing word of the clause is to throw an emphasis on it wholly foreign to the sense. On the contrary, it comes in easily and naturally after VITTAE, bringing with it, in that secondary position, no emphasis.

FAS MIHI. The subsequent TENEOR points out the structure ; FAS *est*, not FAS *sit ;* i. e. TESTOR FAS MIHI *esse* . . . *et me teneri.*

OMNIA FERRE SUB AURAS. Compare Timaeus, *Lex. Platon. :* Υπ' αυγας, υπο του ορθρον, η υπο του πεφωτισμενον αερα, where Hemsterhusius: "Usitata locutio ὑπ' αυγας αγειν in apertam lucem proferri."

SERVATAQUE SERVES. Compare Petron. (ed. Hadrian.), p. 155: "serva me, servabo te." Sil. 14. 172: "servas nondum servatus ab hoste."

STETIT (163).—"STETIT pro vulgari *posita fuit in*," Heyne. On the contrary, stare, in this the figurative use of the term, loses nothing of its sense of *standing*, and the hope and confidence of the Danai is said to stand—not *in*, but—*by* the assistance of Pallas, exactly as the Roman state is said to stand—not *in*, but—*by* military discipline, Liv. 8. 7 (T. Manlius Torquatus to his son): "Disciplinam militarem, *qua stetit* ad hanc diem Romana res, solvisti;" as the Latin state is said to stand—not *in*, but—*by* the guardianship of a woman, Liv. 1. 3: "Tantisper tutela muliebri (tanta indoles in Lavinia erat) res Latina et regnum avitum paternumque puero *stetit*;" as the Lacedaemonian state is said to have stood for so many years by the laws of Lycurgus, Liv. 39. 33: "ademptas, *quibus* ad eam diem civitas *stetisset*, Lycurgi leges;" as the Italian kingdom is said by Scipio Africanus the elder (Silius, 13. 654, ed. Rup.) to have stood—not *in*, but—*by* P. Corn. Scipio, his father:

"quis te, care pater, *quo stabant* Itala regna,
exosus Latium deus abstulit?"

as the Romans are said by Propertius (3. 22. 21) not merely to be, but to *stand* powerful:

"nam quantum ferro tantum pietate potentes
stamus : victrices temperat ira manus;"

and as Cicero, *ad Fam. 1.5.50*, informs Plancus that he (Plancus) knows by what men and men of what rank he (Cicero) stood, (held his erect position): "per quos homines ordinesque *steterim*, quibusque munitus fuerim, non ignoras." Compare also Propert. 4. 11. 1:

"desine, Paulle, meum lacrimis urgere sepulcrum :
panditur ad nullas ianua nigra preces.
cum semel infernas intrarunt funera leges,
non exorato *stant* adamante viae"

[the ways (*i. e.* the passages) stand (*i. e.* stand close) with adamant]. Compare also Ovid, *Fast.* 5. *383:* "saxo *stant* antra vetusto" [caves stand built of old rock]. *Aen. 4. 509:* "*stant arae circum*" [altars not merely are around, but *stand* around].

STETIT, so understood, is well opposed to FLUERE AC RETRO SUBLAPSA REFERRI, verse 169.

PALLADIUM.—The best account I know of the Trojan Palladium is in Procopius, *Bell. Gothic. 1. 15*, where he thus describes a representation of it, cut in stone, in these words: αυτη δε η εν τω λιθω εικων πολεμουση τε και το δορυ ανατεινουση ατε ες ξυμβολην εοικε. ποδηρη δε και ως τον χιτωνα . . . εχει, &c.

FLUERE AC RETRO SUBLAPSA REFERRI SPES DANAUM.— "FLUERE, delabi, et est των μεσων. Nam ideo addidit RETRO. Contra Sallustius: 'rebus supra vota fluentibus,'" Serv. (ed. Lion). That Servius is right, and the Latin fluere simply *to flow*, is still further placed beyond doubt by Cicero, *de Off. 1. 26:* "In rebus prosperis et ad voluntatem nostram *fluentibus*, superbiam magnopere, fastidium arrogantiamque, fugiamus" compared with Liv. 27. 17: "Hasdrubal, quum hostium res tantis augescere incrementis cerneret, suas imminui, ac fore ut, nisi audendo aliquid moveret, qua coepissent *fluerent*, dimicare quam primum statuit." As in each of these passages, no less than in the Sallustian, the further meaning of the word fluere, *i. e.* whether the flowing signified by that word is flowing in a good sense, or flowing in a bad, is determined by the context, so in our text whether the flowing spoken of is flowing in a good sense or in a bad, is to be determined by the context only; and fortunately the context is sufficiently decisive—RETRO SUBLAPSA REFERRI explaining as clearly and unmistakably as it is possible for words to explain, that the flowing is backward, or in a bad sense; in other words, FLUERE AC RETRO SUBLAPSA REFERRI SPES DANAUM is neither more nor less than the thought: *the hope of the Danai is ebbing*, expressed for the verse sake, by two theses instead of one, *flows* and *is carried back;* in one word, *ebbs*. Compare Lucret. 4. 699:

"quippe etenim *fluere* atque *recedere* corpora rebus
multa modis multis docui, sed plurima debent
ex animalibus iis quae sunt exercita motu,"

where "fluere" is the very FLUERE of our text, and where "fluere" and "recedere" make up jointly the notion of ebbing; exactly as in our text FLUERE and RETRO SUBLAPSA REFERRI make up jointly the same notion, viz., that of ebbing. Nothing is farther from Virgil's mind than the "*retro ferri, labi,*" of a "moles, quae in altum erat invecta" (Heyne), or of a "fragminis saxi quod vetustas subruit, vel ruina qualibet decidentis" (Wakefield), unless it be Conington's "man carried off from his standing-ground *in solido* by the reflux of a wave, and so borne back to sea."

Little objection will be made to the *ebb* of hope by anyone who happens to remember Edmund Burke's ebb and flow of monarchies (*On a regicide peace*): "Such, and often influenced by such causes, has commonly been the fate of monarchies of long duration. They have their ebbs and their flows. This has been eminently the fate of the monarchy of France."

178-179.

OMINA NI REPETANT ARGIS NUMENQUE REDUCANT
QUOD PELAGO ET CURVIS SECUM AVEXERE CARINIS

VAR. LECT.

AVEXERE **I** *Vat., Pal., Med.*; "In Mediceo cod. et aliquot aliis AVEXERE legitur," Pierius. **II** $\frac{13}{0}$. **III** N. Heins.; Phil.; Burm.; Heyne; Brunck; Pott.; Jaeck; Dorph.; Haupt; Wagn. (*Lect. Virg.* and *Praest.*); Ribb.; Kappes.

ADVEXERE **II** $\frac{1}{0}$. **III** Ven. 1470, 1471, 1472, 1475; Mil. 1475, 1492; Bresc.; P. Manut.; D. Heins.; La Cerda; Lad.; Bask.

VEXERE **II** $\frac{3}{70}$.

EVEXERE **II** $\frac{1}{70}$.

AUXERE **II** $\frac{1}{70}$. **III** Pr.

ADDUXERE **II** $\frac{3}{70}$.

DUXERE **II** $\frac{1}{70}$.

O *Rom., Ver., St. Gall.*

Numen reducant.—" Cum ipso Palladio avecto ut solennibus sacris restituatur in sedem suam revertendum," Heyne, Wagner, Kappes, and commentators generally. Erroneously, as I think; numen is not the Palladium, the statue of the goddess, nor is the Palladium to be restored. Numen is the approbation, the good will of the gods, the blessing of heaven (not by any means the blessing of Pallas in particular), that blessing of heaven with which the Greeks formerly sailed to Troy—

quod pelago et curvis secum avexere carinis.

This numen is rendered *ipso facto* void and null by their return; in other words, having been obtained only for the expedition, it ceases of itself, that expedition being concluded; and it becomes necessary to obtain a new numen for the new expedition. This is precisely the *rationale* of the superstition as it prevailed in Virgil's own time. Disappointed in his expedition, the consul, or other commander of the army, returned to Rome, in order to set out *de novo* on the new expedition to the same place with new auspices; and so precisely our text: numen reducant, go home with the numen; quod avexere carinis, with which they had set out; omina repetant, take new auspices (deos parant comites, obtain a new numen; pelagoque remenso aderunt, set out again and arrive afresh). Numen reducant is thus, not a totally independent action from omina repetant, but that previous action which was necessary and indispensable before omina repetant was possible—in other words, omina repetant and numen reducant, intimately bound together by the conjunction que, constitute one whole; and re-petant and re-ducant are but modifications of the same general idea of applying to heaven *de novo*.

Numen reducant, although expressive of an action which in point of time precedes, is yet placed after omina repetant, according to Virgil's usual custom (ὑστερον προτερον) of placing the principal or main action first, and that which was only subsidiary to the main action, after.

The Palladium is not to be restored, profaned and violated by bloodstained hands; it is now worth nothing, enters no more into the calculations either of the Trojans or Calchas, reappears no more upon the scene. Pallas is to be atoned not by the restoration of the old image, but by the presentation of the wooden horse, which, according to Sinon's story, has been made of so enormous size expressly in order that it might not be taken into the city, and serve the purpose of a new Palladium.

As to NUMEN see, further, Rem. on "numine laeso," 1. 12.

———

182-184.

ITA DIGERIT OMINA CALCHAS
HANC PRO PALLADIO MONITI PRO NUMINE LAESO
EFFIGIEM STATUERE NEFAS QUAE TRISTE PIARET

ITA DIGERIT OMINA CALCHAS.—What is the force of ITA? Of course, *thus, in hoc modo*—this is the way in which Calchas DIGERIT OMINA; or—this is Calchas's mode digerendi omina. But is this all? does Virgil indeed only mean to tell us that the way, which he has just informed us is the way in which Calchas DIGERIT OMINA, is the way in which Calchas DIGERIT OMINA? Impossible! There must be some further meaning in the words, or they are useless, this meaning having been previously expressed. The further meaning is, as I think: it is in this manner Calchas DIGERIT OMINA, *i. e.* this is the effect of Calchas's manner digerendi omina, viz., not to rid you of the Greeks, as you ignorantly suppose, but to bring the Greeks back upon you under new religious auspices, and with increased force (ARMA DEOSQUE PARANT COMITES, PELAGOQUE REMENSO IMPROVISI ADERUNT)—ITA, this is the way in which Calchas DIGERIT OMINA; this is the ultimate result of all this designing priest's manipulation of omens, viz., to bring greater danger on you than ever; it is not I alone who am ruined by them, but you also. No argument could be more powerful to enlist the sympathies of the Trojans on the side of Sinon than the argument that Calchas was their enemy no less than his, was using

all the means in his power to effect the ruin of both—ITA
DIGERIT.

DIGERIT, digests, *i. e.* analyses, calculates, solves the problem of, disposes of. Compare Ovid, *Met. 12. 21* (of the same Calchas similarly expounding portents):

"atque novem volucres in belli *digerit* annos."

Ovid, *Fast. 2. 625:*

"cui pater est vivax, qui matris *digerit* annos."

Ovid, *Met. 4. 469* (of Ajax Oileus):

"quam meruit solus poenam *digessit* in omnes"

[distributes and so gets rid of, disposes of]. Senec. *de Constantia Sapientis, 15:* "Domus haec sapientis angusta, sine cultu, sine strepitu, sine apparatu, nullis observatur ianitoribus, turbam venali fastidio *digerentibus*" [arranging and disposing of according to pleasure]. Senec. *Thyest. 822:*

. . . "non succedunt
astra, nec ullo micat igne polus:
nec Luna graves *digerit* umbras"

[clears up, dissipates, and so disposes of]. Senec. *Quaest. Nat. 7. 22:* "Nubes . . . modo congregantur, modo *digeruntur*" [cleared up, dissipated, and so disposed of]. Liv. 2. 21: "Nec quid quoque anno actum sit, in tanta vetustate, non rerum modo sed etiam auctorum, *digerere* possis."

Nor is this the whole force of the DIGERIT of our text; there is something offensive in it, not properly or essentially belonging to, but nevertheless occasionally to be found both in digerere itself and the synonyms of digerere in other languages. See Hom. *Il. 2. 236:*

. . . τονδε δ' εωμεν
αυτου ενι Τροιη γερα πεσσεμεν, οφρα ιδηται
η ρα τι οι χ' ημεις προσαμυνομεν, ηε και ουκι.

Pind. *Pyth. 4. 184* (ed. Dissen):

τον δε παμπειθη γλυκυν ημιθεοισι ποθον προσδαιεν Ηρα
ναος Αργους, μη τινα λειπομενον
ταν ακινδυνον παρα ματρι μενειν αιωνα πεσσοντ', αλλ' επι και θανατω
φαρμακον καλλιστον εας αρετας αλιξιν ευρεσθαι συν αλλοις.

NUMINE LAESO, *not* the violated image or Palladium, *but* the violated supreme will of the deity—violated, viz., by the carrying off of the Palladium. The latter part of the verse is the variation of the theme contained in the former part; and theme and variation taken together are equivalent to: for the violation of the supreme will (numen) of the goddess, by the carrying off of the Palladium. The words NUMINE LAESO are used, both of them, in the precise sense in which they are used, 1. 12, where see Rem.

193-200.

ULTRO—TURBAT

ULTRO ASIAM MAGNO PELOPEA AD MOENIA BELLO VENTURAM.— Compare Liv. 3. 8 (ed. Walk.): "iam satis valida civitate, ut non solum arcere bellum, sed ultro etiam inferre posset."

QUOS NEQUE ... CARINAE. Compare Luc. 6. 140:

> "quem non mille simul turmis, nec Caesare toto
> auferret Fortuna locum, victoribus unus
> eripuit, vetuitque capi."

HIC ALIUD MAIUS MISERIS MULTOQUE TREMENDUM OBIICITUR MAGIS ATQUE IMPROVIDA PECTORA TURBAT.—This prodigy is not merely *ominous*, but *typical*, of the destruction about to come upon Troy. The twin serpents prefigure the Grecian armament, which, like them, comes from Tenedos (where, as must not be forgotten, it is lying concealed at the very moment of the prodigy); like them, crosses the tranquil deep; like them, lands; and, going up straight (probably over the very same ground) to the city, slaughters the surprised and unresisting Trojans (prefigured by Laocoon's sons), and overturns the religion and drives out the gods (prefigured by the priest Laocoon). Even in the most minute particulars the type is perfect: the serpents come abreast towards the shore, like ships sailing together ("Argiva phalanx instructis navibus ibat . . . littora . . . potens"), with flaming eyes raised above the waves by the whole length of the neck and breast ("flammas quum regia puppis extulerat"), and with the hinder part floating and curling along on the surface of the water (the hinder vessels of the fleet following the lead of the foremost); and, when their work is done (the Trojans slaughtered, or, with their gods, driven out of the city), take possession of the citadel, under the protection of Pallas ("iam summas arces Tritonia, respice, Pallas insedit," &c.).

The Greek army besieging Troy is always typified by a serpent. Compare *Il. 2. 326:*

ως ουτος [δρακων] κατα τεκν' εφαγε στρουθοιο, και αυτην,
οκτω, αταρ μητηρ ενατη ην, η τεκε τεκνα·
ως ημεις [Αχαιοι] τοσσαυτ' ετεα πτολεμιζομεν αυθι,
τω δεκατω δε πολιν αιρησομεν ευρυαγυιαν.

Il. 12. 201 :

αιετος υψιπετης . . . .
φοινηεντα δρακοντα φερων ονυχεσσι πελωρον
. . . .
ως ημεις, &c.

Also the swarm of bees, 7. 69, not only ominous, but typical, of the arrival of Aeneas and his Trojans at Laurentum :

. . . "et partes petere agmen easdem
partibus ex isdem, et summa dominarier arce."

Also the serpent, which, issuing from the tumulus at Saguntum (Sil. 2. 592) and gliding through the middle of the town directly into the sea, typified the flight of the Manes of the dead from the city which was soon to be taken by storm by the enemy:

. . . "ceu prodita tecta
expulsi fugiant Manes, umbraequae recusent
captivo iacuisse solo."

Since the above commentary was written, I have found a confirmation of the opinion therein expressed, in Petronius's poem descriptive of the taking of Troy (see his *Satyr.*, ed. Hadrian., p. 328), in one part of which he informs us that the noise made by the serpents in their passage through the water was like that of vessels rowing and at the same time cutting their way through the sea—

" qualis silenti nocte remorum sonus
longe refertur, quum premunt classes mare,
pulsumque marmor abiete imposita gemit"—

and in another (two verses lower down on same page), that the necks and breasts of the serpents, as they came along through the water, resembled tall ships:

. . . "tumida quorum pectora,
rates ut altae, lateribus spumas agunt."

HIC ALIUD MAIUS, . . . MULTOQUE TREMENDUM. Compare Hom. *Od. 4*. 698:

αλλα πολυ μειζον τε και αργαλεωτερον αλλο.

IMPROVIDA PECTORA TURBAT.—"TURBAT PECTORA ita ut fierent IMPROVIDA; ita enim praecipites egit ea res Troianos, ut omissa omni cautione facerent quod Sinon optabat," Wagner. No; but IMPROVIDA TURBAT are to be taken as so connected together as to form one complex idea, viz., that expressed by the single English word *alarm*—TURBAT (*disturbs*) IMPROVIDA (*unforeseeing, not-expecting*), i. e. *alarms*. The Latin language being poor of words, is frequently thus constrained to describe or express by a phrase what in richer languages is expressed by a single word, as: "gelidus coit," *freezes;* "angusti claustra Pelori," *straits of Pelorus;* "aggredior dictis," *accost;* "expediam dictis," *explain;* "excussos laxare," *uncoil;* "vela damus," *sail;* "eques sternet," *ride over;* "aequare sequendo" (3. 671), *overtake,* &c. See Rem. on 6. 801.

203-213.

ECCE—PETUNT

HORRESCO REFERENS.—This interjection is not placed indifferently anywhere in the middle of the sentence, but in its most natural and effective position, after the words GEMINI A TENEDO

TRANQUILLA PER ALTA, excitatory of expectation; and immediately before IMMENSIS ORBIBUS ANGUES, expressive of the actual horrid object. The weaker effect which it would have had, if placed at a greater distance *before* IMMENSIS ORBIBUS ANGUES, is shown by Dryden's translation:

> " when, dreadful to behold, from sea we spied
> two serpents, ranked abreast, the seas divide,"

and the still weaker which it would have had if placed *after*, by Surrey's:

> " from Tenedon, behold, in circles great
> by the calm seas come fleeting adders twain;
> which plied towards the shore (I loathe to tell)
> with reared breast lift up above the seas."

Compare "Tritonia, respice, Pallas," verse 615, and Rem. PECTORA QUORUM, &c. Compare Milton, *Par. Lost, 1. 192:*

> " thus Satan, talking to his nearest mate,
> with head uplift above the wave, and eyes
> that sparkling blazed; his other parts besides
> prone on the flood, extended long and large,
> lay floating many a rood."

FIT SONITUS SPUMANTE SALO.—*The brine foams audibly.* Compare Quint. Smyrn. 12. 456 (ed. Heyn.), of the same serpents: επεσμαραγησε δε πυντυς νισσομενων· and Petr. 89 (of the same): "dat cauda sonitum."

Dryden's translation of the passage is marked by even more than Dryden's usual extravagance, recklessness, and ignorance of his author's meaning:

> " their speckled tails advance to steer their course,
> and, on the sounding shore, the flying billows force;"

with which mistranslation I know none, not Dryden's own, at all comparable, unless it be Pope's of Hom. *Il. 19. 126:*

> " from his ambrosial head, where perched she sate,
> he snatched the fury-goddess of debate."

ARVA.—There is no occasion to suppose, with Heyne, that ARVA is used "pro littore," because, interpreted literally, it affords a better meaning, viz., *the fields*, or *cultivated plain, inside the beach*, where it is probable the "solennis ara" stood, at such a distance from the actual shore as to be in no danger from the violence of the sea during stormy weather. Compare: "pelago premit arva sonanti," *Aen. 1. 250*, and Rem.

ILLI AGMINE CERTO LAOCOONTA PETUNT. Wagner (1861), followed by Conington, refers to "ille agmine longo" (5. 90), and "agmina caudae" (*Georg. 3. 423*), and interprets: "Intellige spiras ac volumina longumque eorum tractum"—confounding, as it seems to me, agmina caudae, the agmina of a serpent's tail (the joints of the serpent's tail, so numerous as to be called agmina, his troops), and the agmen, march, or course of a serpent. I agree, however, with Wagner in his other comparison, viz., that of "agmine longo" (5. 90) with our text, drawing, however, from it the very opposite conclusion, viz., that AGMINE CERTO in our text, means not "spiras ac volumina longumque eorum tractum," but "certum eorum cursum," their sure and certain march; exactly as "agmine longo" in the passage compared by Wagner means the long march of the serpent there spoken of, and as "leni agmine," 2. 782, means the mild march of the Tiber. See Rem. on 2. 782.

213-217.

ET PRIMUM PARVA DUORUM
CORPORA NATORUM SERPENS AMPLEXUS UTERQUE
IMPLICAT ET MISEROS MORSU DEPASCITUR ARTUS
POST IPSUM AUXILIO SUBEUNTEM AC TELA FERENTEM
CORRIPIUNT SPIRISQUE LIGANT INGENTIBUS

PRIMUM . . . POST.—There is a most material discrepancy between the account given by Virgil and the view presented by the sculptor, of the death of Laocoon and his two sons. According to the former, the serpents first (PRIMUM) kill the two sons,

and afterwards (POST) seize (CORRIPIUNT) the father, SUBEUNTEM
AC TELA FERENTEM, and kill him also; while, according to the
latter, the serpents are twined about and kill the father and the
two sons simultaneously. Virgil's is the more natural and
probable account, because it was more easy for the serpents to
conquer Laocoon's powerful strength (see verse 50) with the
whole of their united force and folds than with such part only
of their force and folds as was not employed upon the sons.
There is even some difficulty in understanding (nor does an
examination of the sculpture tend much to diminish the difficulty) how two serpents, already twined about and encumbered
with the bodies of two persons, even although those bodies
were small (PARVA), could seize and squeeze to death a third
person possessed of more than ordinary strength, and armed.

The sculptor, if he had had the choice, would, doubtless, no
less than the poet, have represented the killing of Laocoon to
have been subsequent to the killing of the sons; but his art
failed him; sculpture could not represent *successive acts;* the
chisel could fix no more than a single instant of fleeting time:
driven, therefore, by necessity, he places the three persons simultaneously in the folds of the serpents, and his so much admired
group becomes, in consequence, complicated and almost incom-
prehensible, and appears in the most disadvantageous contrast
with the simple and natural narrative of Virgil.

Such is the infinite inferiority of sculpture, and of painting,
to poetry. The sculptor, or painter, labours day and night, and
for years together, on one object; and, in the end, his work,
representing but an instant of time, fails to present to the mind
as many ideas as the poet supplies in half-a-dozen lines, the
work perhaps of half an hour.

PRIMUM . . . ARTUS.—Not AMPLEXUS CORPORA, IMPLICAT ET
DEPASCITUR ARTUS, but AMPLEXUS IMPLICAT CORPORA ET DEPAS-
CITUR ARTUS. In order that the structure may be shown by the
punctuation, the comma, placed by the older editors (the two
Heinsii and Heyne), and removed by Forbiger, Thiel, Wagner
(*Praest.*, and Ribbeck, should be restored.

IMPLICAT—winds round, twines round. See Rem. on 12. 743.

AMPLEXUS IMPLICAT: as verse 218, AMPLEXI SUPERANT; verse 290, "amplexae tenent."

DEPASCITUR—feeds *away* on. See Rem. on "desaevit," 4. 52.

SPIRIS.—Spirae are not merely *coils*, but *spiral coils*—tending upwards, like those of a corkscrew held point-upward. See *Georg. 2. 153 & 154*, where Virgil informs us, almost in express terms, that a snake is in *orbs* ("orbes"), while coiled upon the ground, but in *spires* ("spirae"), when he raised himself with a motion twisting upwards. The same distinction is observable in the passage before us, where the serpents are said to be in *orbs* while on the water, and in *spires* when folded round Laocoon. A right understanding of this word is the more necessary, because it is the only word in the description, except SUPERANT CAPITE ET CERVICIBUS ALTIS, which shows that the poet so far agrees with the sculptor as to represent Laocoon and the serpents twined about him as forming an *erect* group. With a similar correct precision, our own Milton applies the term *spires* to the coils of the serpent when *erect*, or *raised upright*. Compare his *Par. Lost, 9. 496*:

> . . . "not with indented wave,
> prone on the ground, as since, but on his rear,
> . . . .
> with burnished neck of verdant gold, erect
> amidst his circling spires."

Leopardi, therefore (Libr. Sec. del *En.*), is incorrect:

> . . . "e l' altra parte si strascina
> radendo l' acqua, e si contorce, *in spire*
> gli smisurati dorsi ripiegando."

223-231.

QUALIS MUGITUS FUGIT QUUM SAUCIUS ARAM
TAURUS ET INCERTAM EXCUSSIT CERVICE SECURIM
AT GEMINI LAPSU DELUBRA AD SUMMA DRACONES
EFFUGIUNT SAEVAEQUE PETUNT TRITONIDIS ARCEM
SUB PEDIBUSQUE DEAE CLIPEIQUE SUB ORBE TEGUNTUR
TUM VERO TREMEFACTA NOVUS PER PECTORA CUNCTIS
INSINUAT PAVOR ET SCELUS EXPENDISSE MERENTEM
LAOCOONTA FERUNT SACRUM QUI CUSPIDE ROBUR
LAESERIT ET TERGO SCELERATAM INTORSERIT HASTAM

QUALIS MUGITUS . . . SECURIM. Compare Dante, *Inferno., 12. ??:*

"qual è quel toro che si slaccia in quella
ch' ha ricevuto già 'l colpo mortale,
che gir non sa, ma qua e là saltella;
vid' io lo Minotauro far cotale;"

also Bocc., *in Filos.:*

"non altrimenti il toro va saltando
qualora il mortal colpo ha ricevuto,
e dentro la foresta alto mugghiando,
ricerca il cacciator che l' ha ferito."

QUALIS MUGITUS.—"QUALES, *i. e.* QUALES MUGITUS TOLLIT," Heyne, Wagner (*Praest.*), Thiel, Forbiger. I rather agree with Peerlkamp: "QUALIS est MUGITUS *tauri.*" Compare *Ecl. 8. 85:*

"talis amor Daphnim, qualis cum fessa iuvencum
per nemora atque altos quaerendo bucula lucos
propter aquae rivum viridi procumbit in ulva,"

quoted by Conington.

SUB PEDIBUS . . . TEGUNTUR. Compare Hygin. *Fab. 88:* "Ea compressione gladium de vagina ei extraxit Pelopia, et rediens in templum sub *acropodio Minervae* abscondit." [The awe in which the goddess was held rendered the place safe either as an asylum or as a place of concealment].

TUM VERO marks the production of the full effect. The story of Sinon had moved them, but it was only the punishment of Laocoon which decided them:

DUCENDUM AD SEDES SIMULACRUM, ORANDAQUE DIVAE
NUMINA CONCLAMANT.

See Remm. on *Aen.* 2. 105; 3. 47; 4. 396, 449, 571.

NOVUS PAVOR.—NOVUS, new, *i. e.* new in kind, strange, such as we had never before experienced; exactly as 5. 670, " novus furor;" 3. 181 (where see Rem.), " novo errore;" and 3. 591, " nova forma viri."

SCELUS EXPENDISSE MERENTEM.—" SCELUS, supplicium," Servius. " Merito Laocoontem punitum," La Cerda. "SCELUS: poenas meritas pro scelere," Heyne, Wagn. (ed. Heyn. and *Praest.*), Ladewig, Gesner. But how is it possible for the same word to have the two opposite meanings, of wickedness and punishment of wickedness? What kind of language was that in which two so opposite expressions as scelus expendere and scelerum poenas expendere are not only equivalents, but used as such by the same author in the course of the same work, the former in our text, the latter at 11. 258; nay, in which the one expression is cited by commentators as explanatory of the other? "Scelus expendere hat gleiche bedeutung mit dem, 11. 258, gebrauchten ausdruck," Ladewig. No; the SCELUS of our text is neither the wickedness of Laocoon, nor the punishment of the wickedness of Laocoon, but it is the wickedness of the punishment of Laocoon; not poenas sceleris, but the very point-blank opposite, scelus poenarum. The onlookers do not say that Laocoon had suffered (paid) punishment (expendisse poenas). Poenas, the word ordinarily applied to all manner of punishment—to the infliction of half-a-dozen lashes, of a week's imprisonment, no less than to banishment or death—had been too general, and therefore too weak a term feelingly to express what they had just seen befall Laocoon. It was not mere ordinary poenae they had seen him suffer; it was something far worse. They had seen him and his two sons devoured alive by two great sea serpents; that shocked and horrified them, and they applied to it the strongest term they had at command, the strongest term the author could put into his verse—they called it a SCELUS. Laocoon, they cried out, had deserved the SCELUS he suffered (SCELUS EXPENDISSE MERENTEM). It was a scelus, indeed, but well deserved by him .

SACRUM QUI CUSPIDE ROBUR
LAESERIT, ET TERGO SCELERATAM INTORSERIT HASTAM.

It was but right that he should suffer a scelus (EXPENDISSE SCELUS) who had himself committed a scelus (TERGO SCELERATAM INTORSERIT HASTAM). He who had with his "scelerata hasta" violated (LAESERIT), the SACRUM ROBUR had merited the SCELUS they had seen him suffer. And so exactly, 7. 307 :
"quod *scelus* aut Lapithas tantum aut Calydona *merentem*"

(where we have the same scelus and the same merentem; "scelus" is not poenas scelerum, but scelus poenarum; and, the cases of the Lapithae and Calydon being the reverse of that of Laocoon, neither the Lapithae nor Calydon having committed a scelus to justify the scelus of their punishment, a scelus to justify their scelestas poenas, the question is triumphantly asked: what so great scelus (poenarum) had they merited? what scelus had they committed to justify the "scelus" of their punishment?) Compare also Stat. *Silv.* 2. 1. 19:

"ipse etenim tecum nigrae solennia pompae,
spectatumque urbi *scelus*, et puerile feretrum
produxi, et saevos, damnati thuris acervos,
plorantemque animam supra sua funera vidi"

(where "scelus" is only the premature death of the innocent young man). How much more abominable, how much more detestable, how much more fitly termed SCELUS, the atrocious spectacle of Laocoon! of Laocoon the priest, along with his two sons devoured alive by serpents, while he was in the very act of sacrificing. It was, if there ever was, a scelus (Scott, *Lay of the last Minstrel*, 1. 4) :

"deadly to hear and deadly to tell;
Jesu! Maria! shield us well."

For another example of the application of the term scelus to an awful spectacle, see Stat. *Theb.* 10. 546 :

"lora excussa manu, retroque in terga volutus,
semianimos artus ocreis retinentibus haeret;
mirandum visu belli *scelus*! arma trahuntur,
fumantesque rotae tellurem, et tertius hastae
sulcus arant."

Compare also Val. Flacc. 2. 294 (Hypsipyle speaking) :

" solvimus heu! scrum Furiis *scelus*?"

[not poenas scelerum, but scelestas poenas]; and Stat. *Silv.* 2. 175 (of the funeral of the favourite of Melior) :

. . . . " plebs cuncta *nefas*, et praevia flerunt agmina,"

[the sin, the scelus, the nefas, that so young and amiable a person should have died]. See Remm. on 2. 576 ; 5. 793.

SACRUM . . . HASTAM. Compare Coleridge, *Anc. Mar.* :

" is it he ? quoth one. Is this the man ?
by him who died on cross,
with his cruel bow he laid full low
the harmless albatross."

SACRUM QUI CUSPIDE ROBUR LAESERIT, theme ; TERGO SCELE-RATAM INTORSERIT HASTAM, variation.

234-243.

DIVIDIMUS MUROS ET MOENIA PANDIMUS URBIS
ACCINGUNT OMNES OPERI PEDIBUSQUE ROTARUM
SUBIICIUNT LAPSUS ET STUPEA VINCULA COLLO
INTENDUNT SCANDIT FATALIS MACHINA MUROS
FOETA ARMIS PUERI CIRCUM INNUPTAEQUE PUELLAE
SACRA CANUNT FUNEMQUE MANU CONTINGERE GAUDENT
ILLA SUBIT MEDIAEQUE MINANS ILLABITUR URBI
O PATRIA O DIVUM DOMUS ILIUM ET INCLYTA BELLO
MOENIA DARDANIDUM QUATER IPSO IN LIMINE PORTAE
SUBSTITIT ATQUE UTERO SONITUM QUATER ARMA DEDERE

DIVIDIMUS MUROS, ET MOENIA PANDIMUS URBIS. In order to understand the picture here presented, it must be borne in mind that the gates of ancient cities were very small, little larger than our modern doors ; and that the walls, which were high, were carried across over the gates, so that there was no division of the wall, but only a hole or opening in the undivided wall, where the gate stood. By the expression DIVIDIMUS MUROS, therefore, we are to understand that the Trojans enlarged the gate so as to make a complete division of the wall, viz., by breaking down that part of the wall over the gate on which the continuity of the wall depended. It appears from Plaut. *Bacchid. 953* (ed. Ritschl), that the breaking down of the wall over the Scaean gate was one of the three " fata" of Troy :

"Ilio tria fuisse audivi *fata*, quae illi fuere exitio :
signum ex arce si perisset ; alterum autemst Troili mors ;
tertium, quum portae Phrygiae limen superum scinderetur."

It is, no doubt, in tacit reference to this prophecy that our author dwells so emphatically on the breaking down of the wall :

DIVIDIMUS MUROS, ET MOENIA PANDIMUS URBIS.

Compare the similar tacit reference to another (fourth) fatum of Troy, in the words (*Aen. 1. 476*) :

. . . "priusquam
pabula gustassent Troiae Xanthumque bibissent."

DIVIDIMUS MUROS and MOENIA PANDIMUS are not two distinct acts, but one act and its consequence—" we breach the walls, and by so doing open the fortifications of the city, leave the city unprotected and exposed to the enemy "—and this in a double sense, because not only is an opening made through which the enemy may enter, but the city is deprived of the charm or talisman which it had possessed in the continuity of its enclosure.

In Statius's account of the equestrian statue of Domitian (*Silv. 1. 7*), not only is this same fatum of Troy alluded to, but, in words which are a manifest copy of our author's, a similar stress is laid upon the *divisio* of the wall :

" hunc neque *divisis* cepissent Pergama muris."

ACCINGUNT . . . GAUDENT.—Man is essentially the same in all ages and countries. With this reception of, these divine honours paid to, the wooden horse, compare the account given by Anna Harriette Leonowens in her work, "The English

Governess at the Siamese Court" (Trübner and Company, London, 1870), ch. 16, of the conveyance of the sacred white elephant to Bangkok, the capital of Siam : " Thus in more than princely state he is floated down the river [Meinam] to a point within seventy miles of the capital, where the king and his court, all the chief personages of the kingdom, and a multitude of priests, both Buddhist and Brahmin, accompanied by troops of players and musicians, come out to meet him, and conduct him with all the honours to his stable-palace. A great number of cords and ropes of all qualities and lengths are attached to the raft, those in the centre being of fine silk. These are for the king and his noble retinue, who, with their own hands, make them fast to their gilded barges; the rest are secured to the great fleet of lesser boats, and so with shouts of joy, beating of drums, blare of trumpets, boom of cannon, a hallelujah of music, and various splendid revelry, the great Chang Phoouk [white elephant] is conducted in triumph to the capital."

ACCINGUNT OMNES OPERI, not, literally, *gird themselves up for the work*, but *set themselves to the work*. Compare 9. 74 :

" atque omnis facibus pubes *accingitur* atris"

[not, of course, *engirt with dark torches*, but *is furnished or armed with dark torches, having dark torches in their hands*].

STUPEA VINCULA COLLO INTENDUNT.—In order to tow it along as if it were a ship. Compare Eurip. *Troad. 538* (of this same drawing up of the horse with ropes into the citadel) :

κλωστοῦ δ᾽ ἀμφιβόλοις λίνοισι, ναὸς ὡσεὶ
σκάφος κελαινὸν, εἰς ἕδρανα
λαΐνα δάπεδα τε φόνια πατρίδι
Παλλάδος θέσαν θεᾶς.

Also Auson. *Mosell. 39* (apostrophizing the Moselle) :

" tu duplices sortite vias, et quum amne secundo
defluis, ut celeres feriant vada concita remi ;
et quum per ripas nusquam cessante remulco
intendunt collo malorum *vincula* nautae." *

---

* Query whether collo malorum, or collo nautarum? Lemaire understands it to be the latter, I the former.

Heyne, Forbiger, and Thiel inform us without doubt or hesitation, that INTENDUNT is here elegantly used ("exquisitius") in place of illigant, innectunt; and this is the meaning which has been adopted by all the translators, as well as by Forcellini in his Dictionary. I dissent, however, on two grounds: (*a*), because there is not only no instance of intendere being used in this sense, but no instance of its being used in any sense bordering on, or at all related to, this sense; and (*b*), because the strict interpretation of INTENDUNT (viz., *stretch* or *extend*) affords an unobjectionable meaning of the passage: *they stretch ropes to the neck;* prosaically, *throw ropes over the neck.* Compare 5. 136: "intentaque brachia remis," where see Rem. This meaning is not only unobjectionable in itself, but preferable to the former, inasmuch as it was easier to throw a rope over the neck than to tie or fasten it at so great a height.

The idea of stretching, or extension, will, I think, be found to enter into all the significations, whether literal or metaphorical, of intendere.

COLLO.—"In COLLO noli argutare; cum fune ex eo nexo trahi equus vix commode posset, intellige simpl. funem ex anteriore parte aptum," Heyne; who seems not to have perceived how useful the rope round the neck would be, not alone for steadying and preventing the horse from toppling over to one side, but for drawing it *up* into the city, viz., over the broken down fortifications (SCANDIT MUROS, verse 237). See Quint. Smyrn. 12. 422:

   . . . αγειρομενοι δ' αρα παντες,
  σειρην αμφεβαλοντο θοως περιμηκεῖ ιππω,
  δησαμενοι καθυπερθεν, επει ρα οι εσθλος Επειος
  ποσσιν υπο βριαροισιν εὐτροχα δουρατα θηκεν,
  οφρα κεν αιζηοισιν επι πτολιεθρον επηται,
  ελκομενος Τρωων υπο χειρεσιν·

where καθυπερθεν answers exactly to our author's COLLO.

ILLA SUBIT MEDIAEQUE MINANS ILLABITUR URBI.—" Placet etiam mens Donati haec: SUBIT [MACHINA] et ILLABITUR, et, nondum ingressa, adhuc etiam in porta *haerebat;* nam infra, QUATER IPSO IN LIMINE PORTAE SUBSTITIT; iam mediae urbi minari videbatur," Lemaire. This is all, and in every respect, erroneous: QUATER IPSO IN LIMINE PORTAE SUBSTITIT, although in position it comes after MINANS ILLABITUR, is previous to it in the order of time (see Rem.); and MEDIAE URBI depends, as rightly observed by Heyne, not on MINANS, but on ILLABITUR.

MINANS.—Servius's first explanation, " eminens" (high and towering), is correct. Servius's second explanation, " minitans"— especially as explained in some editions by the further gloss, " eventum aliquem malum ominans"—is incorrect. The horse, if "minitans" at all, was "minitans" only in the sense in which all tall towering objects are minitantia, viz., in the sense of *awe-inspiring* (see Remm. on 1. 166; 2. 628; 4. 88; 8. 668). Boileau's reprehension of our author therefore (*Reflex. Crit. 11:* " Il ne se contente pas de prêter de la colère à cet arbre [where has our author been guilty even of this minor offence?] mais il lui fait faire des menaces à ces laboureurs") falls to the ground harmless, or harming only the critic himself.

O PATRIA . . . DARDANIDUM.—" Versus Ennianus," Servius. On which comment of Servius, Heyne observes: "Scilicet in verbis: 'O pater, O patria, O Priami domus'!" The original of both apostrophes is no doubt that most touching apostrophe of Oedipus, Soph. *Oed. T. 1394:*

> ω Πολυβε και Κορινθε, και τα πατρια
> λογω παλαια δωμαθ', υιον αρ' εμε
> καλλος κακων υπουλον εξεθρεψατε!

the parental relationship of which passage to our text is declared and made plain not merely by the resemblance between the two apostrophes, but by the similarity of the reflections which gave rise to them—the reflection, in the case of Oedipus, that he was himself a καλλος κακων υπουλον to his country; in the case of Aeneas, that the wooden horse was a καλλος κακων υπουλον to Troy, a fair outside pregnant within with destruction:

> QUATER IPSO IN LIMINE PORTAE
> SUBSTITIT, ATQUE UTERO SONITUM QUATER ARMA DEDERE.

246-247.

TUNC ETIAM FATIS APERIT CASSANDRA FUTURIS
ORA DEI IUSSU NON UNQUAM CREDITA TEUCRIS

TUNC ETIAM.—ETIAM has been understood by some commentators to connect the sentence to which it belongs, viz., TUNC FATIS APERIT CASSANDRA FUTURIS, with the preceding context, so as to afford the sense: *besides all the warnings we had had not to do as we were doing, we had the additional warning of Cassandra; Cassandra also raised her warning voice.* " ETIAM : not, then as often before; but, besides our other warnings," says Conington. " Etiam ei vocabulo, quod ecferendum sit, postponi satis constat (Fabr. ad Liv. 21. 1. 5), sed apparet *h. l.* non tam tempus illud ecferendum esse quam vaticinia Cassandrae ad ea quae, versu 242, commemorata sunt omina accessisse, nec tamen magis quam illa Troianos ab temeraria laetitia ad sanam mentem traduxisse," says Dietsch (*Theolog.* p. 22)—**both** of them combating the opinion adopted by Heyne and Gossrau, as well as by Forbiger, from Servius, viz., that TUNC ETIAM is equivalent to etiam tunc (" TUNC ETIAM int. pro etiam tunc, alias languet," Heyne. " Sicut antehac saepius," Gossrau. " Sicut antea iam saepius," Forbiger)—an opinion as correct and well-founded as that of its impugners is ill-founded and incorrect. The vaticination of Cassandra is not an omen; is not, like the three sudden haltings of the horse in the Scaean gate, a warning not to proceed with their blind act: the act has been already accomplished; the omens—that of the hollow sound returned by the wood to the spear, that of the punishment of Laocoon, and that of the three haltings of the horse in the Scaean gate—have all alike failed to deter the Trojans from carrying their fatal determination into effect, and they have actually placed the horse in the citadel:

ET MONSTRUM INFELIX SACRATA SISTIMUS ARCE.

Omens are now too late; the act has been already done, and

Cassandra opens her mouth, TUNC ETIAM, then also (*i. e.* then, as so often before : "Sicut antehac saepius, nam Helena veniente praedixerat futura bella et mala," Servius (ed. Lion)), not to add an omen, or to increase the effects of the preceding omens, but to inform the Trojans in inspired, but as usual wholly disbelieved words, of their impending ruin, FATIS FUTURIS. It is as if our author had said : " We place the unlucky monster in the citadel, on which occasion, as on so many previous ones, Cassandra announces our impending ruin ; we nevertheless, who were never to see another day, put as little faith as ever in her words, and deck all our temples out with wreaths of rejoicing and thanksgiving."

If it be objected to the preceding interpretation that it leaves the sentence unconnected by any particle with the preceding, I ask, in reply, where is the particle which connects the succeeding sentence with this ?

ORA.—Let us see if there be anything in the position or circumstances of this word to raise a suspicion that it is of somewhat more weight than commonly supposed ; that it is something more than a mere supplement for the purpose of making up with APERIT the simple sense *breaks silence*, *speaks*. First, it is the *first* word in the line. Now, a word placed in this position is advantageously placed for the reception of an emphasis from the voice of the reader or reciter, **if** the line be the first line of the sentence, on account of the natural impetus with which the mind sets out on any undertaking ; **if** the line be not the first line, as in the present instance it is not, **then** on account of the rise in the voice which naturally follows the fall and accompanying pause at the close of the immediately preceding line. But ORA is not alone the first word of its own line ; it is also the last word of its own sentence, and separated from all the succeeding context by a pause. Both these circumstances render it still more marked. Being the last word of its own sentence, the preceding words of the sentence lead to it, prepare both the voice of the speaker and the mind of the hearer for it ; and, being separated from the succeeding context by a pause, the voice of the speaker and the attention of the hearer are prevented from hurrying off from it to the next word. We would expect *a priori* that a word placed in this situation should be an important word; and, on examining the words which Virgil has placed in similar situations, we find that they are always important— *ex. gr.*, 2. 13, "incipiam;" 5. 480, "arduus;" 5. 319, "emicat;" 8. 672, "aurea;" 12. 340, "sanguineos;" 1. 153, "seditio;" 8. 562, "stravi." In some instances—as, *ex. gr.*, the two last cited—it will even be found that the single word so placed has more weight and importance than the whole of the rest of the verse; nay, that this whole rest of the verse is a mere illustration (*erläuterung*) of that single word. Considered according to these principles, ORA should be an important word—not merely the supplement to APERIT, but the subject of the whole remainder of the line—CREDITA agreeing with it and not with CASSANDRA. The inference is confirmed by Ovid, *Met. 15. 74*:

> . . . "primus quoque talibus *ora* docta quidem solvit, sed non et *credita*, verbis."*

where, the person spoken of being masculine, "credita" must agree with "ora" even although the position of "ora" does not indicate such agreement. Compare also (*a*), *Aen. 10. 822*:

> "*ora* modis Anchisiades pallentia miris,"

the "ora pallentia" of which corresponds exactly with the ORA CREDITA of our text. (*b*), 9. 181:

> "*ora* puer prima signans intonsa iuventa,"

where not only do "ora" and "intonsa" occupy the precise po-

---

* Gossrau is no doubt at liberty—who shall cripple the commentator's liberty, or clip the free wings of thought?—to understand the "credita" of this passage, not as accusative plural and belonging to "ora," but as nominative singular belonging to some unspecified unknown feminine subject; nay, is at liberty to draw such argument as he can from the Ovidian passage so understood in favour of his (the received) interpretation of the Virgilian text, and to insist as much as he pleases, first that Ovid's "credita" is feminine and singular, and then that Virgil's CREDITA must therefore be feminine and singular; but he is not at liberty to leave out of his Ovidian parallel all that part of it which impugns and disproves his own statement, and establishes that of his adversary—is not at liberty to quote Ovid as saying:
> . . . "ora docta quidem solvit, sed non *est* credita verbis,"

sitions of ORA and CREDITA in our text, but where we have the entire line cast in the same mould as, and having the precise cadence of, our text. (*c*), Ovid, *Met.* 10. 209 : " vero . . . Apollinis ore." (*d*), Apul. *De deo Socrat.* 18 : " incredita vaticinia Cassandrae." Add to all which (*e*), the quotation by Nonius of the verse,

ORA DEI IUSSU NON UNQUAM CREDITA TEUCRIS,

without either CASSANDRA or other part of the preceding verse, is a more than sufficient balance for Iscanius's (6. 894) :

" at regina gemens, et nunquam credita Teucris,
Cemusium Cassandra petit."

In like manner, " Troia," 1. 253, considered according to these principles, is an important word embracing not merely the near "arma" but the distant "nomen" (see Rem. on 1. 253). "Troas" also, 1. 34, is an important word, the subject not merely of the preceding " iactatos aequore toto " but of the succeeding " reliquias Danaum atque immitis Achillei," as if Virgil had said: these famous Trojans, the subject not only of the Iliad, but of the whole of the following poem. Owing to this position, Africus, alone, 1. 90, has a weight equal to that of Eurus and Notus, in the preceding line, taken together. Compare 2. 418, where " Eurus equis," owing to its similar position, possesses a

while in point of fact what Ovid says is :

. . . "primus quoque talibus ora
docta quidem solvit, sed non et credita verbis."

The same commentator is at liberty to argue from the fact of the "credita" of Ovid's (*Fast.* 4. 307) " casta quidem sed non et credita" being nominative singular, that the CREDITA of Virgil is nominative singular also, and to show if he can that Ovid's " credita" is spoken of Cassandra; but he is not at liberty to omit from the Ovidian passage the words which show that the subject of Ovid's "credita" is not Cassandra, but Claudia Quinta :

" Claudia Quinta genus Clauso referebat ab alto ;
nec facies impar nobilitate fuit.
casta quidem, sed non et *credita*."

The following are the *ipsissima verba* of Gossrau-- not to be misunderstood by anyone : " Ita ' credor' dicunt pro ' mihi creditur' ; cf. Ovid, *Fast.* 4. 307, eadem Cassandra dicitur ' casta quidem sed non et credita ;' cf. *Met.* 15. 74 : ' ora docta quidem solvit, sed non est credita.'"

similar weight. Sarpedon, 1. 104, the son of Jove, has as honourable mention as Hector, though Hector is the first named; and the single "Spartanae," 1. 320, without further help or adjunct, is a balance for the " Threissa Harpalyce," though the latter is in possession of nearly two whole lines. So also the voice and sense delight to dwell *on* the long slow word " conspexere," 1. 156, for which the attention has been prepared by the preceding " pietate gravem ac meritis si forte virum quem ;" *on* "solabar," 1. 243; *on* "Teucrorum," 1. 252, correlative to " Troïa" in the next line, as if Virgil had said " of *his* (Antenor's) Teucri ;" *on* "prodimur," 1. 256, explained by the whole remainder of the line; *on* " vultu," 1. 259, also explained by the remainder of the line; *on* " Romanos," 1. 286, also explained by the whole remainder of the line ; *on* "iactemur," 1. 336, explained by remainder of the line and following line ; *on* " mudavit," 1. 360, explained by the whole remainder of the line ; *on* " thesauros," 1. 363, item ; *on* " suspirans," 1. 375, item ; *on* " regia," 8. 242, item ; also *on* " spiravere," 1. 408 ; " imminet," 1. 424 ; " condebat," 1. 451 ; " suppliciter," 1. 485 (does not the reader's ear rebel against the union of this word with "tristes" ?). And need I do more than point with the finger to " bellatrix," 1. 497 ; " incessit," 1. 501 ; "dispulerat," 1. 516 ; " ardebant," 1. 519 ; " oramus," 1. 529 ; " aetherea," 1. 551 ; " arvaque," 1. 554 ; " purpureum," 1. 595 ; " argentum," 1. 597 ; " Troianae," 1. 628 ; " iactatam," 1. 633 ; " munera," 1. 640 ; " instruitur," 1. 642 ; " consilia," 1. 662 ; " vocibus," 1. 675 ; " irrigat," 1. 696 ; " conveniunt," 1. 704 ; " expediunt," 1. 706 ; " convenere," 1. 712 ; " Phoenissa," 1. 718 ; " haeret," 1. 722 ; " incipit," 1. 725 ; " hiberni," 1. 750 ; " insidias," 1. 758 ?

It would be an affront to the reader's good sense to accompany him in this manner through the other books, but I must not pass by unnoticed the eminently emphatic position of " Argolica," 2. 119—*last word* both of the sentence to which it belongs and of the whole oracle ; prepared for as well by the repeated " sanguine" of the preceding verse as by the whole of that verse, especially by the awful words " animaque litandum :" while at the same time it is *first word* of its own verse, and separated from the sequel not merely by a full pause but by the change of the speaker. Nor is the whole of our author's art exhausted when he has placed the word in this emphatic position. He can render the word still more emphatic, double its emphasis, **either** by making it the repetition of a former word, as "lumina," 2. 406; "Crethea," 9. 775; "Misenum," 6. 164; "ora," 10. 822; "Parthus," 12. 858; "uni," 10. 692; "Gallo," *Ecl. 10. 72* (compare "ibimus," repeated with such extraordinary effect by Statius, *Silv. 2. 1. 219*), **or** by entirely cutting off its connexion with the subsequent context by means of a full and sudden stop, as "incipiam," 2. 13; "offera," 8. 6; "impulit," 8. 239; "horrisono," 9. 55; "terribilis," 12. 947; "dividit," 12. 45; "suscipiunt," 11. 806; "substiterat," 11. 609; "desiluit," 11. 500; "buccina," 11. 475; "devovi," 11. 442; "viximus," 10. 862; "Tydides," 10. 29; "femina," 4. 570; "respice," 4. 275; "debentur," 4. 276; "deseruere," 3. 618; and Hom. *Il. 1. 51:*

αυταρ επειτ' αυτοισι βελος εχεπευκες εφιεις,
βαλλ',

where βαλλ', being but one single syllable, is even more emphatic than any of the Virgilian examples. And who is there will dispute with me that it was not by mere accident, but by artistic design, that Euripides (*Hipp. 312*, ed. Stokes) placed precisely in this position—viz., last word of the nurse's long address, and at the same time first word of a new line, with every word of several preceding lines pointing directly to it—that fatal Ιππολυτον which, like the last turn of the torturer's vice, wrung from Phaedra her first groan of confession, that never enough to be admired οιμοι ?

NUTR. μα την ανασσαν ιππιαν Αμαζονα,
η σοις τεκνοισι δεσποτην εγεινατο
νοθον, φρονουντα γνησι', οισθα νιν καλως,
Ιππολυτον.
PHAED.   οιμοι.
NUTR.   θιγγανει σεθεν τοδε ;

Where even in our own Shakespeare is there an equal amount of dramatic effect within an equal compass, and how much of this effect is owing to the mere position of the word Ιππολυτον?

The reader will of himself understand that all that has just been said respecting single words is no less applicable to a word which is not absolutely the first in the line, but preceded by a short connecting link (see Rem. on " fugis," 4. 314), for instance, " et ferit," 12. 730 ; or to a phrase consisting of two or even three words intimately bound together, as " it lacrymans," " ossa tremor," " intemerata colit pelagi rupes" (where we have not only the position, but the reduplication), " voce vocat," " bella gero."

In Leopardi's translation of the passage:

"allor, *volente il Dio*, Cassandra il labbro
non mai creduta apre al futuro,"

there is not only the usual error, the connexion of CASSANDRA with CREDITA, but the still more unpardonable one, that of the junction of DEI IUSSU with APERIT.

ORA . . . CREDITA. Compare the somewhat similar application of " credula" to " ora" by Prudent. *Cathem. 3. 48:*

" piscis item sequitur calamum,
raptus acumine vulnifico,
credula saucius *ora* cibo;"

also the "ora nescia" of the same author, where the face is said *not to know*, by the same figure by which in our text the mouth is said *not to be believed (Met. 4. 329)* :

. . . " pueri rubor *ora* notavit
nescia quid sit amor."

The above interpretation, never entirely without advocates— **for** [first proposed by Servius as an alternative ("CREDITA : dubium a quo verbo veniat, et an femininum singulare sit participium an neutrum plurale"), and afterwards adopted by J. H. Voss in his translation,

" jetzo entschliesst auch Kassandra den mund annahendem schicksal,
der, auf des gottes gebot, nie sprach, das glaubten die Teucrer"]

it was three several times discussed by myself, and established not only on particular, but on general grounds—(see "Twelve Years' Voyage," 1853 ; "Jahrb. für Phil." 68, p. 509 ; and "Adversaria Virgiliana," Göttingen Philologus, bd. 11, 1856)— found, nevertheless, but slow and partial acceptance with Virgilian students, until by some happy chance not the interpretation only, but the very Ovidian parallel with which I had established, it made their appearance in Wagner's Virgil, *Carm.* ed. min. 1861 (no word of either in any of Wagner's previous editions) ; and being, as usual with the interpretations of that work— no, not put forward, God forbid ! but—mistaken for the editor's own, CREDITA came forthwith to be joined to ORA, at least in all the gymnasia in Germany.

FESTA VELAMUS FRONDE.—VELAMUS (very imperfectly rendered by Thiel, "ornamus"; by Surrey, "deck") means *to veil*, i. e., *to cover in such a manner, or to such an extent, as to hide from view;* and thus denotes *the profusion* of green boughs used. Compare *Aen. 3. 25 :* "ramis tegerem ut frondentibus aras."

250-255.

RUIT—LUNAE

Inasmuch as the ancients always represented night as following the course of the sun, *i. e.*, as rising in the east, traversing the sky, and descending or setting in the west (see Stat. *Theb. 2. 61 ;* Virg. *Aen. 2. 8,* and Remm. ; *3. 512*), the words RUIT OCEANO NOX, applied to the commencement of night, are to be understood, not as presenting us with the ordinary English image, of night *falling on the ocean*, but as presenting us with the directly reverse image, of personified night *rising* (rushing) *from the ocean.* So Dante (*Il Purgat. 2. 1*), philosophically, and following the ancient model :

" già era 'l sole all' orizzonte giunto,
lo cui meridian cerchio coverchia
Ierusalem col suo più alto punto:
e la notte ch' opposita a lui cerchia
uscìa di Gange fuor."

And Shelley (*Prometheus Unbound*, act 1, sc. 1):

" and yet to me welcome is day and night;
whether one breaks the hoarfrost of the morn,
or starry, dim, and slow the other *climbs*
the leaden-coloured east."

And Schiller (" Der abend"):

" an dem himmel *herauf* mit leisen schritten
kommt die duftende *nacht*."

If it be doubted that ruere can express motion upwards toward the sky, I beg to refer to *Georg. 2. 308:*

. . . " *ruit* atram
ad caelum picea crassus caligine nubem;"

and to *Aen.* 10. 256, where the rising of the day is described by the very same term:

. . . " revoluta *ruebat*
matura iam luce *dies* noctemque fugarat."

See also Rem. on *Aen.* 1. 749.

Leopardi has fallen into the vulgar error:

. . . " il ciel fra tanto
si cangia, e notte *a l' ocèan ruina*,
in grande ombra avvolgendo e terra e polo," &c.

FUSI PER MOENIA TEUCRI CONTICUERE. — " Dispersi per urbem," Forbiger. No; FUSI is not *dispersi*, but, as rightly interpreted by Forbiger himself at *Aen.* 1. 218, "prostrati, *hingestreckt*." Compare Stat. *Silv.* 1. 2. 59: " fusa iacet stratis," and see Rem. on *Aen.* 1. 218.

TACITAE PER AMICA SILENTIA LUNAE. The silence (*i. e.*, silent time) of the night was favourable to the descent of the Grecians, there being no one in the way to observe their motions. The moon is called *tacit*, because she does not tell—does not blab—says nothing about what she sees. In other words, and connecting the two terms SILENTIA and TACITAE, *nobody sees them but the moon, and she does not tell what she sees—does not betray.* Compare Tibull. (ed. Amst. 1708), 1. 7. 5:

>   . . . " iam Delia furtim
>   nescio quem *tacita* callida nocte fovet."

Also *Ibid.* 1. 2. 14:

>   " cardine nunc *tacito* vertere posse fores."

That SILENTIA LUNAE does not mean the interlunium, but the time when the moon was actually shining, appears from Stat. *Theb.* 2. 58:

>   " inde per Arcturum *medioeque silentia lunae*
>   arva super populosque meat."

TACITAE PER AMICA SILENTIA LUNAE belongs not to PETENS but to IBAT, and is, therefore, to be placed (with D. Heins., N. Heins., Heyne, and Ribbeck) between two commas, not (with Wagner, ed. Heyn. and *Praest.*) to be thrown by the expunction of the comma after LUNAE entirely to PETENS. To place the words before LITTORA NOTA PETENS as forming part of the same clause is to make them emphatic. Being unemphatic, and merely heightening and completing the picture, they come in with propriety only in the second place, *i.e.* after, not before, the word descriptive of action.

256-260.

FLAMMAS—EQUUS

FLAMMAS QUUM REGIA PUPPIS EXTULERAT.—" Intelligendum est . . . Agamemnonem signa Sinoni dedisse veniendi, sublata face." Servius, Voss, Wagn. (1861). " Fax sublata, signum profectionis, e nave praetoria," Heyne. It being usual, when a fleet was to sail by night, for a light to be hoisted on the admiral's ship, or whatever ship was to take the lead, as the signal for sailing (see Livy, 29. 25 : " Lumina in navibus singula rostratae, bina onerariae haberent: *in praetoria nave insigne nocturnum trium luminum fore.*" Stat. *Achill. 1. 33:*

"*ecce novam Priamo, facibus de puppe levatis,
fert Bellona nurum*),

and there being no mention at all of Sinon in our text, but only of the light hoisted on the admiral's ship, and the sailing of the fleet as soon as the light is hoisted, there seems no ground whatever for the assumption that the light was other than the usual signal for sailing. I therefore agree with Heyne against Servius, Voss, and Wagner, and find in the following words of Servius's as usual confused and contradictory gloss a confirmation of my opinion : " More militiae, ut (3. 519) ' dat clarum e puppi signum ' "—equivalent to saying: a signal for sailing.

EXTULERAT. — Efferre being the verb employed in Roman military tactics (see Liv. 10. 19; 40. 28) to express the raising of the standard, and the carrying it forward out of the camp against the enemy, there can, I think, be little doubt that there is here a tacit comparison of the personified REGIA PUPPIS raising its signal flame, and followed by the ARGIVA PHALANX INSTRUCTIS NAVIBUS, to the standard-bearer of an army raising the standard, and followed by the soldiers to battle.

The practice of the admiral's ship carrying a light by night for the guidance of the other vessels of the fleet, having come down to more modern times, is thus humorously alluded to by Shakespeare, *Henry 4*, part 1, act 3, sc. 3 (Falstaff to Bardolph) : " Thou art our admiral; thou bearest the lantern in the poop,— but 'tis in the nose of thee."

INCLUSOS ... SINON.—CLAUSTRA, not the closed doors or vents, but the enclosure itself, the *chiostri*.

PINEA CLAUSTRA repeats and explains UTERO, and is substantially a variation of that theme, although—there being only one verb for the two clauses—the form is less strictly that which I have so often designated theme and variation. The picture of the enclosure, the *chiostri*, presented in UTERO, and repeated in PINEA CLAUSTRA, is again repeated in the very next breath : ILLOS PATEFACTUS AD AURAS REDDIT EQUUS. Here EQUUS is substantially a variation of PINEA CLAUSTRA as PINEA CLAUSTRA has been of UTERO, and as CAVO ROBORE in the same verse is of EQUUS.

LAXAT . . . EQUUS.—Compare "Impulit in latus: ac venti," &c., Aen. 1. 86, and Rem. LAXAT is simply *opens :* as Stat. Theb. 10. 550 (of Ganymede's dogs):

>   . . . " frustraque sonantia *laxant*
>   ora canes umbramque petunt et nubila latrant."

Stat. Theb. 2. 128:

>   . . . " tigris
>   . . . .
>   bella cupit, *laxatque* genas, et temperat ungues."

263.

PRIMUSQUE MACHAON

"PRIMUS: aut princeps (inter primos, aut arte primus) aut numeri sui, nam per ternos divisit," Servius. "Qui primus aut inter primos egressus est," Heyne. "Molestum *h. l.* PRIMUS: interim amplector Heynii explicationem: 'qui primus aut inter primos egressus est;' quanquam fateor, ita nescio quid exile inferri orationi," Wagner (*Quaest. Virg. 28. 5,* and *Praest.*). I understand PRIMUS here to mean not who was the first to come out of the horse, but who took the principal part in the business, who regulated and directed the movement of the party, ο αριστευων, as if he had said: "and especially Machaon," or: "foremost, most prominent of them all, Machaon." Compare (*a*), Sil. 7. 85:

>   " nec non et proprio venerantur Pallada dono,
>   Phoebumque, armigerumque deum, *primamque* Dionem,"

where the meaning is not *Dione first in order,* or *they worshipped Dione first;* but *Dione of most and principal consequence, paid chief and special honour to Dione,* viz., as mother of Aeneas and best friend and protectress of Rome—" Aeneadum nutrix." (*b*), verse 32, above: "primusque Thymoetes"—Thymoetes, not the first in order, but the principal person, the person who takes the lead, management, or initiative—and observe how exactly parallel the two passages are in structure, in location in the line, even in the connecting particle que, no less than in the sense. Observe also how both passages stand in exactly similar relation to the horse, one of them referring to the party outside, and the other referring to the party coming out. Compare also (*e*), 8. 6: "ductores primi," where see Rem. (*d*), Lucr. 1. 85:

" Aulide quo pacto Triviai virginis aram
Iphianassaeo turparunt sanguine foede
ductores Danaum delectei *prima* virorum"

[principal among men, first and foremost among men]. (*e*), 2. 612:

. . . " hic Iuno Scaeas saevissima portas
prima tenet"

where "prima" can mean nothing else than principal person, taking chief part in the assault and occupation of the gate, directing the party). (*f*), 10. 241:

. . . " Aurora socios veniente vocari
primus in arma iube"

[taking the initiative, setting yourself at the head of the movement]. (*g*), Sil. 2. 579:

" fama dehinc gliscente sono iam sidera adibat,
iam maria et terras *primamque* intraverat urbem"

[the city more than all, the city specially]. Whoever last got into the horse was likely, from the necessity of position, to be the first to get out. Now, the last who got in was not Machaon, but Epeus (Tryphiodorus, 179):

. . . υστατος αυτε
τεχνης αγλαομητις εης επεβαινεν Επειος.

Epeus therefore, not Machaon, was likely to be the first who got out. Compare **also** (*h*), Capitolin. *Vita Maxim. Iunioris*, 1: "Literis et Graecis et Latinis imbutus ad *primam* disciplinam," where Salmasius: " ' Prima disciplina' hic non est quae pueris incipientibus traditur, sed praecipua. . . . Sic 'primam doctrinam' dixit supra Spartianus; sic 'primum amatorem' pro 'praecipuum et egregium amatorem'; sic etiam 'prime

Latinis' pro 'egregie': ut 'prime proba,' apud Naevium in *Acontizomeno:*

  ' Acontizomenus fabula est *prime* proba.'

Ita Plautus '*prime catam*' dixit in *Milite Glorioso:*

  Pa. ' At scietis. sed ecqua est ancilla illi ? Pe. Est *prime* cata.'

Ita fere Graeci πρωτον usurpant, ut πρωτον εἶδος, praecipua et primaria forma."

I have dwelt the longer on this passage, because primus is precisely, on account of the difficulty of determining whether it is to be understood in its literal or in its figurative sense, perhaps the most frequently ambiguous word in our author's whole poem. A similar ambiguity attends the synonyms of primus in other languages. An almost ludicrous example of this in our own language is read every day, if not with admiration at least without a smile, by the thousand English visitors of the eternal city : it is where the indispensable red book pronounces its judgment of a picture which to me, profane and uninitiated as I am, is as bad a specimen of pictorial composition as the sentence in which the judgment is couched is of verbal: " 'The Transfiguration,' the *last* and greatest oil picture of the immortal master, and justly considered as the *first* oil painting in the world." *

---

  * The above Rem. was written in 1865. Upon further consideration, I may add that—while still fully adhering to the view enunciated above, that primus is here not *first in order*, but *first in quality*—I am now rather inclined to think that the epithet is bestowed on Machaon in compliment to the usefulness of his art. Compare Hom. *Il.* 11. 514 :

   ιητρος γαρ ανηρ πολλων ανταξιος αλλων
   ιους τ' εκταμνειν, επι τ' ηπια φαρμακα πασσειν,

  The word is used in the same manner by Auson. *Idyll.* 2. 1 :

   " nomen ego Ausonius, non ultimus arte medendi,
   et mea si nosses tempora, *primus* eram,"

  where not only is "primus" first in merit, but the merit is that of a physician. And so the primus of our text has been understood by Cynthius Cenetensis (" Machaon filius Aesculapii, primus in arte medendi"), exercising his own judgment, not as usual echoing Servius, who leaves us uncertain between no less than three meanings: " Aut princeps (inter primos, aut arte primus) aut numeri sui, nam per ternos divisit."

268-269.

TEMPUS ERAT QUO PRIMA QUIES MORTALIBUS AEGRIS
INCIPIT ET DONO DIVUM GRATISSIMA SERPIT

Compare Spenser, *Visions of Bellay*, 1 :
 " It was the time when rest, soft sliding down
 from heaven's height into men's heavy eyes,
 in the forgetfulness of sleep doth drown
 the careful thoughts of mortal miseries."

"GRATISSIMA answers to PRIMA: ' PRIMA eademque GRATISSIMA,'" Conington. I think not. Sleep is always gratissima, no matter whether early or late (as Eurip. *Rhesus*, 555 :

θελγει δ' ομματος εδραν
υπνος· αδιστος γαρ εβα βλεφαροις προς αους);

and GRATISSIMA in our text belongs to QUIES only, not at all to PRIMA, the sense being the same as if Virgil had written: "Tempus erat quo primum quies," &c.

270-279.

IN SOMNIS ECCE ANTE OCULOS MOESTISSIMUS HECTOR
VISUS ADESSE MIHI LARGOSQUE EFFUNDERE FLETUS
RAPTATUS BIGIS UT QUONDAM ATERQUE CRUENTO
PULVERE PERQUE PEDES TRAIECTUS LORA TUMENTES
HEI MIHI QUALIS ERAT QUANTUM MUTATUS AB ILLO
HECTORE QUI REDIT EXUVIAS INDUTUS ACHILLI
VEL DANAUM PHRYGIOS IACULATUS PUPPIBUS IGNES
SQUALENTEM BARBAM ET CONCRETOS SANGUINE CRINES
VULNERAQUE ILLA GERENS QUAE CIRCUM PLURIMA MUROS
ACCEPIT PATRIOS

"VISUS est ADESSE MIHI talis QUALIS erat quum RAPTATUS esset," Wagner. No; this is entirely erroneous. The meaning is not:

appeared to be present to me in such condition as he had been when RAPTATUS BIGIS ATERQUE ; but : RAPTATUS BIGIS ATERQUE, appeared to be present to me and to shed floods of tears. The whole force and beauty of the picture consists in the positiveness of the predications concerning Hector, viz., that being (not appearing to be) MAESTISSIMUS, and RAPTATUS BIGIS, and ATER CRUENTO PULVERE, he appeared to be present to Aeneas, and to shed floods of tears. VISUS ADESSE MIHI LARGOSQUE EFFUNDERE FLETUS is placed immediately after the subject in order to satisfy the impatience of the reader. Instead of reserving his account of what the subject appeared to do, until after he had completed his account of the subject himself, our author informs you as speedily as possible that he appeared to stand before Aeneas and shed floods of tears. There is then time, without teazing the reader with uncertainty, to complete the description of the subject, commenced with MAESTISSIMUS and immediately broken off ; and the description is accordingly completed in the words RAPTATUS BIGIS, ATERQUE CRUENTO PULVERE, PERQUE PEDES TRAIECTUS LORA TUMENTES. We have thus, according to our author's usual manner, first (viz., from IN SOMNIS as far as FLETUS), a rapid sketch of the whole, and then (viz., from RAPTATUS as far as TUMENTES), the colouring and filling up of the details. The prosaic arrangement would be : HECTOR, MAESTISSIMUS, RAPTATUS BIGIS, ATERQUE CRUENTO PULVERE, PERQUE PEDES TRAIECTUS, VISUS ADESSE MIHI LARGOSQUE EFFUNDERE FLETUS. At TUMENTES the direct description of the plight of Hector in the dream is again interrupted, in order to place in pathetic contrast with it the appearance presented by the same Hector in the pride of strength and flush of victory on the battle-field before Troy, and so introduce with the greater effect the remainder of the description, the last finish of the picture (SQUALENTEM . . . PATRIOS), the beard and hair clotted with blood and dust, and the person gashed with wounds received in the defence of his country.

How comparatively dull and tedious had been the narrative, had the natural as it is called, or prosaic order, been preserved throughout—the description of Hector's plight first completed in every particular, then that plight contrasted with the appearance formerly presented by him on the field of battle, and only then at last the listening audience and the reader informed that this so described Hector appeared to stand beside Aeneas and shed floods of tears! So arranged, the passage would have run pretty much as follows:—HECTOR, MAESTISSIMUS, RAPTATUS BIGIS (UT QUONDAM [raptatus erat]), ATERQUE CRUENTO PULVERE, PERQUE PEDES TRAIECTUS LORA TUMENTES, SQUALENTEM BARBAM, ET CONCRETOS SANGUINE CRINES, VULNERAQUE ILLA GERENS QUAE CIRCUM PLURIMA MUROS ACCEPIT PATRIOS— HEI MIHI, QUALIS ERAT! QUANTUM MUTATUS AB ILLO HECTORE QUI REDIT EXUVIAS INDUTUS ACHILLI, VEL DANAUM PHRYGIOS IACULATUS PUPPIBUS IGNES!—IN SOMNIS ANTE OCULOS VISUS ADESSE MIHI LARGOSQUE EFFUNDERE FLETUS.

Gronovius (*Diatrib. Stat. 22*)—removing the comma from after BIGIS, and placing a comma instead of a period at TUMENTES, and a comma before as well as after ERAT—connects ERAT with RAPTATUS, ATER, and TRAIECTUS, and thus observes:—"Distinctio huius loci, quae omnes editiones occupavit, arguit nemini hactenus cum satis intellectum. Intricatior constructio est sic evolvenda: VISUS MIHI, UT QUONDAM ERAT RAPTATUS BIGIS, ATERQUE PULVERE CRUENTO, ET PER PEDES LORA TRAIECTUS (HEI MIHI!) QUALIS? QUANTUM MUTATUS, &c. Imitatio Val. Flacc. hoc satis docet (4. 397):

> 'Inachias errore etiam defertur ad undas,
> qualis? et a prima quantum mutata invenea?'"

But how very much simpler, more natural, and more pathetic is the passage considered as consisting of four paragraphs, each grammatically complete and independent, and all four constituting so many intimately connected and mutually supporting links of thought, each preceding one of which as it passes through the mind draws the other after it, the first link terminating at FLETUS, the second at TUMENTES, the third at IGNES, and the fourth at PATRIOS!

UT QUONDAM.—These words are thrown in parenthetically in order to connect the appearance presented by the ghost of Hector in the dream with the appearance the real Hector presented at Troy after he had been dragged at Achilles' chariot wheels. Hector presented in Aeneas's dream exactly the appearance he had presented on that fatal day at Troy. The comma therefore, placed after BIGIS by the more correct judgment of the older editors, and removed by Wakefield, Heyne, and Wagner, should be replaced.

I need scarcely point out to the reader that the words UT QUONDAM, although intended only to illustrate the meaning of RAPTATUS BIGIS, present us also with a natural and philosophical explanation why Aeneas, in his dream, saw Hector *quasi* RAPTATUS BIGIS; viz., because of the strong impression made upon his mind by the sight of Hector after he had been actually dragged by the bigae of Achilles.

CRUENTO PULVERE = $\lambda v \theta \rho \omega$, Hom. *Il.* 11. 169 ; 20. 503 ; *Od.* 22. 402 ; 23. 48.

TUMENTES.—Dead limbs do not swell in consequence of violence : either, therefore, Virgil means that the swelling of Hector's feet was the result of putrefaction, or he applies the adjunct TUMENTES in ignorance of the physiological truth ; or, aware of the truth, falsely, for the sake of effect ; or else he means that both the swelling and the violence which produced it were anterior to death.

It is highly improbable that he means that the swelling was the consequence of putrefaction ; because, although he might not have felt himself bound by the authority of Homer, who expressly states (*Iliad*, books 23 and 24) that Apollo prevented putrefaction from taking place in the corpse of Hector, yet no poetical advantage was to be gained by suggesting the idea of putrefaction, inasmuch as that idea was not only revolting in itself, but, by removing our thought so much the further from the living sentient Hector, directly tended to diminish that sympathy with him which it was the sole object of the description to excite.

It is still less likely that Virgil, aware of the physiological truth, applied the term falsely, for the sake of effect ; the unworthy supposition is contradicted by everything which is known, or has even been heard, of Virgil.

The conclusion, therefore, is inevitable, either that Virgil applied the term TUMENTES in ignorance of the physiological truth, that violence inflicted on dead limbs will not cause them to swell; or that the non-Homeric narrative (see Heyne, *Excurs. 18 ad Aen. 1*), which he certainly must have followed, when describing Hector as having been dragged round the walls of Troy (and not, as in the Iliad, from Troy to the Grecian tents, and round the tomb of Patroclus), represented Achilles as having bored Hector's feet and dragged him after his chariot before he was yet dead. Nor let the reader, living in times when man has some bowels of compassion for brother man, reject with horror the imputation to Achilles of so atrocious cruelty; let him rather call to mind the boring of the feet of Oedipus, of the feet and hands of malefactors on the cross, the slitting of noses and cropping of ears, the burnings at the stake and breakings on the wheel, not so very long since discontinued in Christian countries. This latter explanation of the difficulty involved in the word TUMENTES derives no small confirmation from the words in which Virgil (*Aen. 1. 487*) has described the dragging of Hector round the walls of Troy :

"ter circum Iliacos raptaverat Hectora muros,
exanimumque auro corpus vendebat Achilles."

There must be some good reason (see Rem. on verse 552) why in these lines "exanimum corpus" is not applied, as might have been expected, to "raptaverat," but solely to "vendebat;" and such good reason is at once suggested by the explanation just given of the word TUMENTES. Achilles drags round the Ilian walls *Hector* (not Hector's " exanimum corpus," Hector being yet alive), and having thus deprived him of life, sells his *corpse* (" exanimum corpus") for gold. Compare :

ητις σφαγας μεν Εκτορος τροχηλατους
κατειδον, οικτρως τ' Ιλιον πυρουμενον,

quoted by Hesselius ex Graeca *Andromache* in his note on the following verses of the *Andromache* of Ennius :

" vidi, videoque passa sum aegerrime,
curru Hectorem quadriiugo raptarier."

Also Ovid, *Met. 13. 435* (of Polydorus):

> " ut cecidit fortuna Phrygum, capit impius ensem
> rex Thracum, iuguloque sui defigit alumni;
> et tanquam tolli cum corpore crimina possent,
> exanimem e scopulo subiectas misit in undas."

If its discrepancy from the Homeric narrative raise any considerable obstacle in the mind of the reader against the reception of this explanation, I beg to refer him for a discrepancy, not merely with an isolated passage, but with a very large and important part of the story of the Iliad, to Euripides's Helen, who never even so much as saw Troy.*

HEI MIHI, QUALIS ERAT!—Here again, as at verse 270, the even tenor of the narrative, which should be HEI MIHI, QUALIS ERAT! SQUALENTEM BARBAM ET CONCRETOS CRINES VULNERAQUE ILLA GERENS, is broken off at QUALIS ERAT, in order to follow

---

* Since the above Comment was written and published (in "The first two books of the Aeneis rendered into English blank iambic," Lond. 1845), I have fallen accidentally upon the following passage in the *Ajax* of Sophocles, verse 1030 (ed. Eton. 1786):

> Εκτωρ μεν, ω δη τουδ' εδωρηθη παρα
> ζωστηρι πρισθεις ιππικων εξ αντυγων,
> εκναπτετ' αιεν εστ' απεψυξεν βιον.

Although these lines, proving the existence of an account of Hector's having been dragged alive after Achilles' chariot, convert almost into certainty the argument which in that Comment I have presented only as a probability, I have yet allowed the Comment to remain unaltered, in order to exemplify the importance and necessity of a closer examination than is usual of the apparently trivial or supposed well-understood expressions of our author.

Still more lately (January, 1853), I have found the following additional evidence that some writers did describe Hector as having been dragged alive after the chariot of Achilles. It is in the account given by Q. Curtius (4. 28) of Alexander the Great having caused Betis to be fastened alive to a chariot, and so dragged to death: "Per talos enim *spirantis* lora traiecta sunt, religatumque ad currum traxere circa urbem equi; gloriante rege, Achillem, a quo genus ipse deduceret, imitatum se esse poena in hostem capienda."

I can hardly sufficiently praise the docility—slow, albeit, and almost too late—of my venerable pupil, Wagner. Compare the total darkness in which he leaves this passage, not only in his edition of Heyne's Virgil (1832), but in his own *Virgils* of 1845 and 1849, with the marvellous light which, translating, and as usual without acknowledgment, from my "Twelve Years' Voyage" (1853), he throws on it in his edition of 1861: "Viva membra tument sic mu'cata, non mortua. Vivum raptatum esse Hectorem etiam Soph. refert, *Aj. 1030, sqq.*, Curt. 4. 28."

out and enlarge upon (in the words QUANTUM MUTATUS . . . IGNES)
the thought QUALIS ERAT!

HEI MIHI, QUALIS ERAT!—Compare that most touching lamentation in that most pathetic perhaps of all the ancient dramas, the *Electra* of Sophocles, verse 1126 : ω φιλτατου μνημειον, &c. Classical scholars, so called, delight to quote Shakespeare's certainly neither very correct nor very apt reference to this passage, *King Henry 4*, part 2, act 1, sc. 1 :

> NORTH. " Even such a man, so faint, so spiritless,
> so dull, so dead in look, so woe-begone,
> drew Priam's curtain in the dead of night,
> and would have told him half his Troy was burnt,
> but Priam found the fire ere he his tongue,"

as one of a thousand proofs of the great imperfection of Shakespeare's scholastic acquirements. The proof is a cogent one perhaps, and even if it were not, it could be spared, for there is no lack of others to which no exception can be taken. But scholars will excuse me if I ask in the name of those who admire Shakespeare only the more because he is so little of a classical scholar, so little of a Milton or Ben Jonson, which of the two is the more ridiculous—Shakespeare, who puts Priam in the place of Aeneas ; or that Coryphaeus of classical scholars, Bentley, who bids us put "Ucalegon" in place of "so woe-begone" in Shakespeare's line, and instead of

> " so dull, so dead in look, so *woe-begone*,"

read
> " so dull, so dead in look, *Ucalegon ?* "

The whole passage HEI MIHI, QUALIS ERAT ! . . . ACCEPIT PATRIOS has been taken by Silius, 10. 508, and applied almost *verbatim* to Paullus :

> " heu, quis erat ! quam non similis modo Punica telis
> agmina turbanti! vel cum Taulantia regna
> vertit, et Illyrico sunt addita vincla tyranno !
> pulvere canities atro, arentique cruore
> squalebat barba, et perfracti turbine dentes
> muralis saxi, tum toto corpore vulnus."

Chateaubriand (*Génie du Christianisme*, part 2, livre 5, c. 11), instituting a parallel between this dream of Aeneas and that in which Athalie (Racine, *Athalie*, 2. 5) sees her mother Jesabel, observes: "Quel Hector paraît au premier moment devant Enée, tel il se montre à la fin. Mais la pompe, mais l'éclat emprunté de Jesabel, 'pour réparer des ans l'irréparable outrage,' suivi tout à coup, non d'une forme entière, mais

. . . ' de lambeaux affreux
que des chiens dévorans se disputaient entr' eux,'

est une sorte de changement d'état, de péripétie, qui donne au songe de Racine une beauté qui manque à celui de Virgile. Enfin cette ombre d'une mère qui se baisse vers le lit de sa fille, comme pour s'y cacher, et qui se transforme tout à coup ' en os et en chairs meurtris,' est une de ces beautés vagues, de ces circonstances terribles, de la vraie nature du fantôme." In reply to which criticism I shall perhaps be permitted to observe: **first**, that the absence from Aeneas's dream of a "péripétie" similar to that which has been so much and so justly admired in the dream of Athalie, so far from being a defect, is rather new evidence of that superior poetical judgment which informed Virgil that the proper place for such a "péripétie" was not in the warning, exhorting, encouraging dream of Aeneas, but exactly where the poet has placed it, in the horrifying dream of Turnus (*Aen*. 7. *445*):

" talibus Alecto dictis exarsit in iras," &c.

It was **with** this similar dream of Turnus—with that Calybe changing into the furious Alecto hissing with all her hydras; **or** with the similar dream of Eteocles—with that Tiresias converted into the ominous Laïus baring his divided throat, and deluging his grandson's sleep with blood ("undanti perfundit vulnere somnum," Stat. *Theb*. 2. *124*), **not** with the totally dissimilar Hector of the totally dissimilar dream of Aeneas, that Chateaubriand might have correctly compared the Jesabel of Athalie. But lest it should be imagined that I use this plea of dissimilarity as a mere pretext for eschewing a comparison from which my favourite Virgil might perhaps issue with tarnished laurels, I beg to add, **secondly**, that I prefer Aeneas's dream to Athalie's, (*a*), on account of its greater simplicity—the former consisting of a single view or scene, with but a single actor; while the latter is complicated of two scenes, each with its separate actor, and those scenes so far distinct and independent of each other, that Chateaubriand in his parallel has (whether disingenuously or through mere error I will not pretend to say) assumed and treated one of them as the whole dream, and compared Aeneas's dream with that one, without making any, even the least, reference or allusion to the other. (*b*), Because the *rôle* assigned to Hector (viz., that of announcing to Aeneas the capture of the city and his own immediate personal danger; of urging, and thereby justifying, his flight; of conveying to him the first information that it was he who was to take charge of the "sacra" of Troy, and establish for them a new and great settlement beyond the sea—that settlement no less than the beginning of that Roman empire whose foundation was the subject and key of the whole poem—and finally of actually committing those "sacra" into his hands) confers upon Hector the dignity and importance of a real character—of one of the poet's actual *dramatis personae*; while Jesabel, whose part rises little, if at all, beyond the production of a certain amount of terror, is a mere phantom, subsidiary to and making way for the child Joas; who, as that personage of the dream on which the whole plot and future incidents of the drama hinge, mainly attracts and fixes on himself the interest. **Finally**, Aeneas's dream is to be preferred to Athalie's, because the former is interwoven with and forms part of the narrative; the latter stands separate from it, and is only explanatory, or, at the most, casual. The sailing of the ambushed fleet from Tenedos, Sinon's opening the CLAUSTRA of the wooden horse, the descent of the chiefs into the city, the throwing wide the gates to the whole Grecian army, Aeneas's seeing Hector in a dream, receiving from him the "sacra" of Troy, waking and hearing the tumult, taking arms, &c., are so many mutually dependent and connected parts of the same history, related in one even uninterrupted tenor by the same narrator, and received by the audience with the same undoubting faith; while on the other hand even Athalie herself does not credit her own dream until she has dreamt it twice over, and even then, when she comes to relate it, thinks it necessary to warn her hearers, in verbiage sufficiently French and tedious, against taking so bizarre an assemblage of objects of different kinds for the work of chance:

> " de tant d'objets divers le bizarre assemblage
> peut-être du hasard vous paraît un ouvrage;
> moi-même quelque temps, honteuse de ma peur,
> je l'ai pris pour l'effet d'une sombre vapeur.
> Mais de ce souvenir mon âme possédée
> a deux fois en dormant revu la même idée ;
> deux fois mes tristes yeux se sont vu retracer."

I should not perhaps have so long dwelt on this comparison, if Racine had not been put forward, not merely by Chateaubriand but by so many other French critics, and by the French nation generally, as the French Virgil—in his other performances equal, in *Athalie* superior, to the Mantuan. Alas for that superiority which even here, in this selected passage of this selected work, is guilty, I will not say of a mere inaccuracy of expression, but of a downright confusion of ideas; inasmuch as, Athalie having made no mention of the real Jesabel but only of that Jesabel which appeared to her in the dream, the "*son ombre*" intended by Racine to refer to the real Jesabel must of necessity be referred by the audience or reader to the Jesabel of the dream, and be understood as meaning the shade of that apparition; or, in other words, although Racine undoubtedly wished his audience to understand that the figure which stooped down to embrace Athalie was no other than the apparition which had just spoken to her; yet as the only correlative in the whole context for the word "son" is the preceding "elle," the sense which he has actually expressed is, that the figure which stooped down to embrace Athalie was not that figure which had just spoken to her, but only the shade of that figure, *i.e.*, the shade of a shade—a confusion of ideas, or, to use the milder term, an inaccuracy of expression, for which we in vain seek a parallel even in the least correct of the Latin authors.

279-287.

FLENS—MORATUR

FLENS IPSE.—"Non minus quam ille," Forbiger, correctly. Compare Ovid, *ex Ponto*, 1. 4. 53:

"et narrare meos *flenti flens ipse* labores."

O LUX DARDANIAE. Compare Cic. *ad Fam*. 14. 5: "Si tu et Tullia, *lux nostra*, valetis, ego et suavissimus Cicero valemus." Pind. *Ol*. 2. 9 (ed. Dissen): Σικελιας τ' εσαν οφθαλμος. *Ibid.* 6. 16:

... ποθεω στρατιας οφθαλμον εμας,
αμφοτερον μαντιν τ' αγαθον και δουρι μαρνασθαι.

EXSPECTATE: not *expected*; but *longed for, desired, desiderated*, as Cic. *pro domo* (ed. Lamb.), 406: "Cum illo die minus valerem, in senatum nominatim vocabar. Veni *exspectatus* ... meae valetudinis ratio non habebatur." Ter. *Adelph*. 5. 4. 20:

"illum, ut vivat, optant; meam autem mortem *exspectant*."

EXSPECTATE VENIS. Compare Cicero, just quoted: "Veni exspectatus."

UT TE ... DEFESSI ASPICIMUS! &c.—UT belongs not to DEFESSI (Voss, Wagner), but, as sufficiently shown by the exactly corresponding (*Aen*. 8. 154):

... "*ut* te, fortissime Teucrûm,
accipio agnoscoque libens! *Ut* verba parentis
et vocem Anchisae magni vultumque *recordor*,

to ASPICIMUS, the force of which is increased by DEFESSI, as in the passage just quoted that of "accipio" and "agnosco" is increased by "libens." Translate therefore: "How we behold you! *i. e.*, with what pleasure we behold you!" exactly as in the first clause of the just quoted parallel (even without attending at all to the "libens"): "How I receive and recognise you! *i.e.*, how gladly I receive and recognise you!" and in the second it is

"Ut recordor," "how I remember! *i. e.*, how well I remember!" Conington coincides with this interpretation.

TE POST URBIS LABORES ASPICIMUS! Query, is there a tacit reference here to the expression of the Greeks, προσωπον πολεως?

ILLE NIHIL. Not, *he does not say anything,* for, as immediately appears, he says a great deal, but, taken together with the complement, NEC ME QUAERENTEM VANA MORATUR, *he does not say anything in reply, nor mind my vain inquiries,* i. e., *he does not say anything in reply to my vain inquiries.*

NEC ME QUAERENTEM VANA MORATUR. Not, as I have rendered it in my "Adversaria Virgiliana," *does not delay me* (i. e., my instant flight) *by answering my idle inquiries,* but, *does not mind me asking idle questions,* i. e., does not mind my idle questions. Compare 5. 400 : "nec dona moror" [nor do I mind, *i. e.,* care for, pay attention to, the presents]. Leopardi, so often astray in his translation, is right in this instance: "nè di mie vane inchieste cura." *

---

* As remarked above, I formerly entertained a different opinion on the text. I may add that in favour of this other view I had noted the following passages : --
Aen. 1. 674 :

"hunc Phoenissa tenet Dido blandisque *moratur* vocibus."

Lucr. 6. 245 (quoted by Conington) :

" expediam neque te in promissis plura *morabor.*'

Hor. *Ep. 2. 1. 4 :*

" si longo sermone *morer* tua tempora, Caesar."

Georg. 2. 45 :

. . . " non hic te carmine ficto atque per ambages et longa exorsa *tenebo.*"

290-301.

HOSTIS—SONITUS

VAR. LECT.

ALTA A CULMINE **III** Wakef.; Lad.; Haupt; Wagn. (*Lect. Virg.* and *Praest.*)

ALTO A CULMINE **I** *Vat.* (ALTO^CULMINE, the A in original ink); *Pal.*; *Med.* (a point in the middle of the added A has been omitted by Foggini); *Ver.* **III** Pierius; P. Manut.; La Cerda; D. Heins.; N. Heins. (1670); Philippe; Heyne; Brunck; Wagn. (ed. Heyn.); Ribbeck.

O *Rom., St. Gall.*

VAR. LECT.

[*punct.*] QUAERE: MAGNA PERERRATO **III** P. Manut.; D. Heins.; N. Heins. (1670).

[*punct.*] QUAERE MAGNA, PERERRATO **III** Servius; Voss.

[*punct.*] QUAERE, MAGNA PERERRATO **III** "Multi QUAERE distinguunt, et sic subiungunt: MAGNA PERERRATO," Servius; Heyne; Brunck; Wakef.; Wagn. (ed. Heyn. and *Praest.*); Lad.; Ribb.

RUIT ALTO A CULMINE TROIA. Compare Hom. *Il.* 11. 117:

ος δη πολλαων πολιων κατελυσε καρηνα,
ηδ' ετι και λυσει.

FATORUM COMITES, literally, *companions of your fates*, but, in sense, *your companions in your fates;* i.e., to share your fates, to partake of the same good or evil which befalls you. Hector performs only the one act, viz., that described in the words MANIBUS . . . IGNEM, and this act is accompanied with the words HOS CAPE FATORUM COMITES. This is undoubtedly the meaning, whether we understand the word PENATES to mean several statuettes, which are represented at verse 296 by the most considerable of them, VESTA; or whether we consider the PENATES of verse 293 and the VESTA of verse 296 to mean one and the same thing, viz., the statuette of Vesta alone.

It has also been thought that the visioned Hector actually puts the real objects into the hands of Aeneas, not merely seems to put them—an opinion which certainly derives general countenance from the fashion of visions to perform (let him explain it who can) real and substantial acts (as, for instance, Venus in a dream puts into the hands of Polyxo a real sword, Stat. *Theb.* 5. 139:

"'ipsa faces alias, melioraque foedera iungam,'
dixit, et hoc ferrum stratis, hoc 'credite) ferrum,
imposuit"),

but to which there seems to me to be this strong objection, that it is little likely our author would have made so remarkable a statement without some historical or mythical authority for it; and if there had been any such, some notice of or reference to it would have been found somewhere among the ancient writers; whereas so far is such reference from being to be found, that there is not to be found even so much as a repetition of the statement on the authority of Virgil.

MAGNA (verse 295). Not QUAE STATUES MAGNA, but MOENIA MAGNA, QUAE STATUES: (**1**), On account of the much greater emphasis thus thrown on MAGNA (see Rem. on 2. 246). (**2**), Because, according to my sense at least, the line reads so much better broken than wholly unbroken—not to say that it is so much according to our author's manner so to break his lines by a pause after the first or second word, thus at one and the same time better connecting the lines in respect of sense, and better preventing that sing-song which inevitably results from the conclusion of the separate thoughts within an equal number of separate lines, the beauty of short poems, but the great damning defect of long, especially of the long Latin poems of the early churchmen, and, with perhaps the single brilliant exception of the *Paradise Lost* and *Regained*, of all the long poems of modern languages. **And** (**3**), Because such is the structure in the repetition of the injunction, 3. 159:

>   ... " tu moenia magnis
>   magna para, longumque fugae ne linque laborem."

ET MANIBUS ... IGNEM.—It has been thought (Conington *ad locum*) that the act here described is separate from and independent of an act with which Hector's ghost accompanied the words HOS CAPE, verses 294 *et seq*. In other words, it has been thought that the ghost while uttering the words HOS CAPE, &c., put the Penates into the hands of Aeneas, and only now, after he has ceased to speak, brings Vesta out of the penetralia and puts her also into his hands. This is the usual error of understanding our author's words too literally. The fact is, the ghost does it not really, but only in appearance. Compare Val. Flacc. 5. 242 (of Phrixus, in the vision, appearing to put the golden fleece into Jason's hands):

>   " dixit et admota pariter fatalia *visus*
>   tradere terga manu."

DIVERSO LUCTU.—Diversus indicates difference, not of kind or quality, but of situation. " Diversus luctus": *woe in a quarter of the city at some distance from the house of Anchises*. By this single word thus happily placed at the commencement of the new action, not only is the reader carried at once out of the retired house in which Aeneas is sleeping, into the midst of the sacking and burning of the city, but time allowed for the numerous events described by Pantheus (verses 325 *et seqq*.) to occur before Aeneas is awakened by the noise.

QUAMQUAM SECRETA PARENTIS ANCHISAE DOMUS ARBORIBUSQUE OBTECTA RECESSIT.—One of the objections made by Napoleon (see his " Note sur le deuxième livre de l'Énéide," quoted in Rem. on verse 5) to Virgil's account of the taking of Troy is, that it was impossible for Aeneas, " dans ce peu d'heures et malgré les combats," to have made numerous journeys (" plusieurs voyages") to the house of Anchises, situated " dans un bois à une demi-lieue de Troyes [*sic*]." This criticism is doubly erroneous; first, because the house of Anchises was not half a league's distance, nor any distance, from Troy, but in Troy itself, as evidenced by the account (verses 730, 753) of Aeneas's flight from Anchises' house, *out of* Troy, *through* the gate of the city; and, secondly, because Aeneas visits the house only twice, and on one of these occasions (as if Virgil had been careful to guard against any demur being made to so many as even two visits to a house situated, as he here informs us, in a remote part of the town) is miraculously expedited by a goddess.

I know not whether it will be regarded as an extenuation, and not rather as an aggravation, of Napoleon's error, that he has here (as in the other parts of his critique) depended wholly on Delille's very incorrect translation:

"déjà le bruit affreux (quoique *loin de la ville* mon père eût sa demeure *au fond d'un bois* tranquille), &c."

It was incumbent on him, before he sent forward to the world, under the sanction of his illustrious name, a condemnation of the second book of the Aeneid both in the general and in the detail, to have taken, at least, ordinary pains to ascertain Virgil's true meaning; and to have assured himself that he was not fulminating his condemnation against errors the greater part of which had no existence except in the false medium through which alone (as sufficiently evidenced both by his own words and his quotations) he had any acquaintance with Virgil.

302–312.

SUMMI—UCALEGON

FASTIGIA TECTI, i. e., *tectum fastigatum;* a sloping or ridged roof, such as is commonly used throughout Europe at the present day. That this is the meaning of the term is placed beyond doubt by the passage in which Livy describes the testudo (44. 9): "Scutis super capita densatis, stantibus primis, secundis submissioribus, tertiis magis et quartis, postremis etiam genu nisis, *fastigatam sicut tecta aedificiorum sunt* testudinem faciebant."

TUM VERO MANIFESTA FIDES, DANAUMQUE PATESCUNT IN-

SIDIAE.—TUM VERO marks as usual the acme, the extreme degree. He had first heard the noise, increasing continually in nearness and clearness (ET MAGIS ATQUE MAGIS . . . CLARESCUNT SONITUS, ARMORUMQUE INGRUIT HORROR), but now from the top of the house (TUM VERO) all is plain.

MANIFESTA FIDES.—"Non somnii, ut quidam volunt, sed fraudis Graecorum," Servius, La Cerda. But the " fraus Graecorum" being the very thing of which the dream had told, the " FIDES fraudis Graecorum," *i.e.*, the truth of the Grecian fraud, comes to be the truth of the dream—TUM VERO MANIFESTA FIDES, *then indeed the truth of what the dream had told was plain;* DANAUMQUE PATESCUNT INSIDIAE, *and the* INSIDIAE *of the Danai are open to my senses.* I cannot at all agree with Conington, that " it matters little whether MANIFESTA be taken as a predicate, or FIDES constructed with PATESCUNT." The two distinct predications, FIDES [est] MANIFESTA and INSIDIAE PATESCUNT, have double the force and energy of the single predication, MANIFESTA FIDES INSIDIAEQUE PATESCUNT, and Virgil prefers wherever he can to make distinct separate sentences—the making one verb serve two clauses being with him the exception, not the rule, unless where some advantage is to be gained by the contrary proceeding. Even taking the words as they occur in Livy, 6. 13 (" manifesta fides, publica ope Volscos hostes adiutos"), to guide us in our analysis of the Virgilian sentence, we have still the double predication:—Then indeed (there is) clear proof, clear evidence (in other words: the truth is clear); and the INSIDIAE of the Danai are exposed, lie wide open. The second clause is, as so often elsewhere, explanatory of the first. The Latin f i d es is here, as always, precisely the Greek πιστις.

I do not at all doubt but that there is a direct reference in the words to the words of the chorus in Aesch. *Sept. c. Theb.* 846 (ed. Blomf.). The chorus who have *heard* from the αγγελος the account of the death of the two brothers by each other's hands *sees* the two dead bodies brought in on the stage and says:

    . . . ηλθε δ' αι-
ακτα πηματ' ου λογω.
ταδ' αυτοδηλα· προυπτος αγγελου λογος.

manifesta fides was a current expression among the Romans. Our text affords one instance of its use. A second instance occurs in Livy as above quoted; a third in Lucan, 1. 522; and I doubt not there are many others. The precise expression in the precise sense has descended into the Italian. Compare Biagioli, on Dante, *Inferno*, 2. 98: "In prova della prima parte si può addurre . . . queste parole del Convito, che ne fanno *manifesta fede*."

IAM PROXIMUS ARDET UCALEGON.—The prosopopoeia is plain and unobjectionable: Ucalegon for *Ucalegon's house*. It is seldom our author uses the figure so happily, only too often he introduces with it confusion into a picture otherwise faultless, *ex. gr.* (***a***), *Aen.* 5. 203:

    "namque furens animi dum proram ad saxa suburguet
      interior spatioque subit *Sergestus* iniquo
      infelix saxis in procurrentibus *haesit*;"

where it is the real bodily Sergestus who is "furens" and "infelix," and who "suburguet," while it is only the figured Sergestus, *i.e.*, the ship of Sergestus which "subit" and "haesit." Also (***b***), 5. 270:

    "cum saevo e scopulo multa vix arte *revulsus*,
      amissis remis atque ordine *debilis* uno,
      irrisam sine honore ratem *Sergestus* agebat;"

where it is the real bodily Sergestus who "agebat ratem," while it is only the figured Sergestus, *i.e.*, the rates itself which is "revulsus" and "debilis"; **and** (***c***), 10. 207:

    "it *gravis Aulestes*, centenaque arbore fluctum
      verberat assurgens: . . . .
      hunc vehit immanis Triton,"

where, if we understand Aulestes to be a prosopopoeia of the ship, *i.e.*, to mean the ship itself, we have the ship carried by itself the ship on board the ship ("hunc vehit immanis Triton"); and if we understand Aulestes to be the veritable captain Aulestes himself, we have the veritable captain Aulestes himself not only heavy ("gravis") but, notwithstanding his heaviness, rising to and lashing the sea with a hundred oars, a piece of confusion worthy of Bavius or Maevius.

Instances of this sort of confusion, this intermixture, direct and figurative, are unhappily of so frequent occurrence in our author, that I have sometimes been disposed to explain "illum expirantem" (where see Rem.) in a similar manner, and to understand "illum" literally in respect of "expirantem transfixo pectore flammas," and figuratively, or as a prosopopoeia of the ship, in respect of "turbine corripuit scopuloque infixit acuto": an explication which I have however been prevented from ultimately adopting, first, by its too great aberration from the Homeric myth; and secondly, by the too great lameness and commonplace of the picture it presents.

320-327.

SACRA MANU VICTOSQUE DEOS PARVUMQUE NEPOTEM
IPSE TRAHIT CURSUQUE AMENS AD LIMINA TENDIT
QUO RES SUMMA LOCO PANTHU QUAM PRENDIMUS ARCEM
VIX EA FATUS ERAM GEMITU CUM TALIA REDDIT
VENIT SUMMA DIES ET INELUCTABILE TEMPUS
DARDANIAE FUIMUS TROES FUIT ILIUM ET INGENS
GLORIA TEUCRORUM FERUS OMNIA IUPITER ARGOS
TRANSTULIT

SACRA ... TRAHIT. Compare Callim. *Lavacr. Pallad. 38* (of Eumedes, priest of Minerva):

ος ποκα βουλευτον γνους επι οι θανατον
δαμον ετοιμαζοντα, φυγα τεον ιρον αγαλμα
ωχετ' εχων, Κρειον δ' εις ορος ωκισατο.

DEOS is the explanation of SACRA, and the meaning is, not *the sacred objects and the gods' images*, but *the sacred images of the gods*, first because Pantheus would be too much encumbered by three different objects—sacred things, gods' images, and his grandson; and secondly, because we find sacra, by itself and without any explanation, meaning *sacred images*, or *images of the gods*, as Ovid, *Met*. 10. 696: "sacra retorserunt oculos." *Ibid*. 624:

> . . . " *sacra* et, sacra altera, patrem,
> fert humeris, venerabile onus, Cythereius heros."

Ovid, *Fast*. 1. 527:

> " iam pius Aeneas *sacra* et, sacra altera, patrem,
> afferet. Iliacos excipe, Vesta, deos."

Ovid, *Heroid*. 7. 157 (Dido to Aeneas):

> " tu modo per matrem fraternaque tela, sagittas,
> perque fugae comites, Dardana *sacra*, deos."

This use of sacra to signify, κατ' ἐξοχην, the images of the gods exactly corresponds to the use of iusta to signify funeral, of *tithes* to signify the special tenths which are the church's dues, &c.

QUO RES SUMMA LOCO, PANTHU, QUAM PRENDIMUS ARCEM?— The meaning of this passage, so much and to so little purpose disputed by the commentators, is placed beyond all doubt, no less by Silius's imitation, 1. 598:

> " o patria, o Fidei domus inclyta, quo tua nunc sunt
> fata loco ? sacraene manent in collibus arces ?"

the first clause of which is the first, and the second clause of which is the second clause of Virgil's sentence expressed in different words, than by Plautus's prototype, *Mercat*. 986 (ed. Ritschl):

> " ubi loci siet res summa publica ?"

QUO LOCO, not, *where?* but *in what condition?* Compare Senec. *Hippol*. 358:

> CHOR. " altrix, profare; quid feras? quonam in *loco* est
> regina? saevis ecquis est flammis modus?"

[not, *where is*, but *in what condition is the queen?* as shown by "saevis," &c., and by the answer "spes nulla," &c.]. Lucan, 8. 557:

> . . . " nescis, puer improbe, nescis,
> quo tua sit fortuna *loco*."

[*in what condition thy fortune is*]. Terent. *Adelph. 3. 2. 46*:

"peiore res loco non potis est esse, quam in hoc, quo nunc sita est."

QUO RES SUMMA LOCO? *In what condition is the State?* RES SUMMA, *our all, the main chance, that on which everything hinges,* by consequence, *the State,* "salus suprema publica." See *Aen. 11. 302*; Ovid, *Heroid. 7. 12*; C. Nepos, *Eumen. 9. 2*; Liv. *33. 7* and *8*; *Hist. Rom.* Parth. App. tributa: φοβω δε περι του συμπαντος, αμα και ποθω του παιδος. Procop. *de Bello Gothico, 3. 13*: Βελισαριος δε περι τε τη Ρωμη και τοις ολ πραγμασι δεισας. *La Riforma* [newspaper], Firenze, 4 Gen. 1868: "Vedendo la persistenza del conte Menabrea [primo minister] a voler tenere in mano *la somma* della cose italiane." Milton, *Par. Lost, 6. 671*:

"had not the Almighty Father, where he sits
shrined in his sanctuary of heaven secure,
consulting on the *sum of things*, foreseen
this tumult, and permitted all, advised;"

and again, verse 697:

. . . "which makes
wild work in heaven, and dangerous to *the main*."

QUAM PRENDIMUS ARCEM?—*If we throw ourselves into the "arx," what kind of an arx shall we find it to be? is the "arx" any longer defensible?* Compare Cic. *ad Fam. 14. 5*: "Etsi in quam rempublicam veniamus intelligo." PRENDIMUS is nearly as in Caesar, *Bell. Civ. 3. 112*: "Pharon prehendit, atque ibi praesidium posuit." Aeneas uses the present tense because he is actually (see verse 315) on his way to the "arx" at the moment when he meets Pantheus coming from it, verse 319.

The questions QUO RES SUMMA LOCO? and QUAM PRENDIMUS ARCEM? are not to be considered as two distinct independent questions, but the second as supplementary to the first, the RES SUMMA being lost if the "arx" was lost. Compare Aristeas, *Hist. 72 interpretum* (Gallandi, vol. ii., p. 784), of the arx which stood beside the temple of Jerusalem: του δη ιερου την πασαν ειναι φυλακην την ακραν. The second clause of the verse is thus a variety of the first, and sets before the reader in the concrete form that which the first presents merely in the abstract. See also Sil. Ital., as above, where precisely the same two questions stand in precisely the same relation to each other.

INELUCTABILE TEMPUS.—Not *inevitable*, but *out of which there is no possibility of escaping by any exertion*; therefore, *final, that shall finish and utterly destroy us*, as Stat. *Theb.* 5. 45 (of the Nemean forest):

"quippe obtenta comis, et *ineluctabilis* umbra"

[so dense, intricate, and large, that no exertion would get you out of it]. Senec. *Nat. Quaest.* 6. 7: "*Ineluctabiles* navigio paludes, nec ipsis quidem inter se pervias quibus incoluntur." *Ibid.* 6. 8: "Pervenimus ad immensas paludes, quarum exitum nec incolae noverant nec sperare quisquam potest, ita implicitae aquis herbae sunt; et aquae nec pediti *eluctabiles*, nec navigio, quod, nisi parvum et unius capax, limosa et obsita palus non ferat." Compare our author's use of the similar verb at *Georg.* 2. 243: "aqua eluctabitur omnis" [the whole of the water will make its way out]. Δυσπαλαιστος seems to be used in the same sense by Euripides, *Alcest.* 889 (ed. Fix.): τυχα, τυχα δυσπαλαιστος ηκει [fatum, fatum ineluctabile venit]; and αφυκτος by the same author, one hundred lines farther on in the same play:

και σ' εν αφυκτοισι χερων ειλε θεα δεσμοις.

FUIMUS TROES, FUIT ILIUM.—The full force of these expressions will be perceived by those readers only who bear in mind that among the Romans the death of an individual was, not unfrequently, announced to his friends by the word fuit; see, in Wernsdorf's *Poetae Latini Minores*, "Elegia incerti auctoris de Maecenat. morib.":

"mollibus ex oculis aliquis tibi procidet humor,
cum dicar subita voce, *fuisse*, tibi."

So also Plautus, *Truc.* 1. 2. 93:

"horresco misera, mentio quoties fit partionis;
ita paene tibi *fuit* Phronesium;"

and *Pseud.* 246 (ed. Ritschl):

. . . "BA. Quis est, qui moram mi obcupato molestam optulit?
PS. Qui tibi sospitalis fuit. BA. Mortuost, qui *fuit*: qui est, is vivost."

(where there is a play upon this meaning of the word). *Ibid. Mostell. 820* (ed. Ritschl) Simo (selling his house):

> . . . "Pol mihi
> eo pretio empti fuerant olim. TRAN. Audin '*Fuerant*' dicere?
> vix videtur continere lacrumas"

(where there is a similar play upon the word "fuerant"). Compare also Cicero's announcement of the execution of the Catilinarian conspirators, "vixerunt;" and Schiller, *Mar. Stuart*, act 4, sc. 11:

> . . . "jene *hat gelebt*,
> wenn ich dies blatt aus meinen handen gebe."

Charlotte Corday in her letter to Barbaroux, written on the eve of her execution, and preserved in Lamartine's *Histoire des Girondins* (44. 30), refers to this Roman mode of expression: "C'est demain à huit heures que l'on me juge. Probablement à midi *j'aurai vécu*, pour parler le langage Romain." So also Manzoni, *Il Cinque Maggio* (of Napoleon):

> "*ei fu*: siccome immobile
> dato il mortal sospiro
> stette la spoglia immemore
> orba di tanto spiro,
> cosi percossa, attonita
> la terra al nunzio sta."

Accordingly the meaning of our text is not: *We were Trojans*, but *we Trojans no longer exist, Ilium no longer exists, all is past*: exactly as *Aen.* 7. *413*: "sed fortuna fuit" [its fortune is past and gone]. From the Latin fuit, used in the above sense, come both the Italian *fu* and the French *feu*, *defunct*, as is placed beyond all doubt by the plural *furent*—"Les notaires de quelques provinces disent encore, au pluriel, *furent*, en parlant, de deux personnes conjointes et décédées," Trevoux; and to the same effect, Furetiere. Corresponding to this use of the past tenses of the verb sum, emphatically, to express *death*, i. e., the cessation of existence, was the use of its present tenses to express *life*, i. e., the continuance of existence (as Stat. *Silv.* 1. *4*. 1:

> "*estis*, io Superi, nec inexorabile Clotho
> volvit opus."

Matth. 2. 18: "Rachel weeping for her children, and would

not be comforted, because they are not (ουκ εισι)." Soph. *Antig.* 567 :

αλλ' ηδε μεντοι μη λεγ'. ου γαρ εστ' ετι)

and of its future tense, to express *future* existence, *i. e.*, existence after death, as Cic. *ad Fam.* 6. 3: "Nec enim, dum *ero*, angar ulla re, cum omni vacem culpa : et si non *ero*, sensu omnino carebo."

ET INGENS GLORIA TEUCRORUM.—Heyne need not have doubted that these words are a translation of Euripides, *Troad.* 581 :

ANDROM. πριν ποτ' ημεν.
HEC. βεβακ' ολβος· βεβακε Τροια.
ANDROM. τλαμων.

The similarity is far too great to be accidental.

TRANSTULIT ARGOS. Compare Lucan, 2. 136 :

"tunc cum paene caput mundi, rerumque potestas
mutavit *translata* locum " &c.

330–335.

PORTIS ALII BIPATENTIBUS ADSUNT
MILLIA QUOT MAGNIS UNQUAM VENERE MYCENIS
OBSEDERE ALII TELIS ANGUSTA VIARUM
OPPOSITI STAT FERRI ACIES MUCRONE CORUSCO
STRICTA PARATA NECI VIX PRIMI PRAELIA TENTANT
PORTARUM VIGILES ET CAECO MARTE RESISTUNT

VAR. LECT.

NUNQUAM [or NUMQUAM] **II** ⅔⅙. **III** Princ.; Ven. 1472, 1475; Mil. 1475, 1492; Bresc.; P. Manut.; D. Heins.; Bersm.

UNQUAM [or UMQUAM] **I** *Pal.*, *Med.* **II** ⅔⅜ ; ood. Camer.(Bersm.); cod. Canon. (Butler). **III** Auson. in perioch. *20. Iliad. ;* Ven. 1470, 1471 ; N. Heins. (1671, 1676, 1704) ; Heyn. ; Brunck ; Wakef. ; Pott.; Wagn. (ed. Heyn., ed. 1861) ; Thiel ; Süpfle ; Forb. ; Lad. ; Haupt ; Ribb. ; Coningt.
() *Vat., Rom., Ver., St. Gall.*

PORTIS BIPATENTIBUS.—"Variatum pro simplici : patentes, apertae," Heyne. " Intelligemus portas duarum valvarum," Wagner (ed. Heyn.). The gate was two-valved, *bifores*, otherwise there would be no BI- ; it was also open, otherwise there would be no PATENTIBUS : and so Wagner (1861). Compare *La Nazione* (newspaper), Giugno 3 e 4, 1867 : " Questa ospitalità che apre a due battenti le porte," and see Rem. on 10. 5.

MILLIA QUOT MAGNIS UNQUAM VENERE MYCENIS.—" Totum versum abesse malim, quot enim ex illis millibus per decem annos caesos esse putare licet!"—Heyne, mistaking a mere exaggeration, very natural and proper in the mouth of the terrified speaker, for the positive matter-of-fact enunciation of an historian. Heyne's error has been pointed out by Voss, and, a rare thing for that critic, without any bitterness towards a man whose deserts in respect of Virgil were at least not inferior to his own. He contents himself with quoting Heyne's explanation, and adding : " Melius, augendi gratia, cum Servio." Servius's explanation is even better, more full and explicit, than it has been represented by Voss. His words are : " Ita vel augendi gratia, vel perturbatus, dicit tantos esse Graecos quanti olim venerint, quasi nemo perierit decennali bello." The only defect in this explanation is that two things are separated which should be united. The explanation should have been : " perturbatus (metu) auget." In similar circumstances now-a-days one would say : all Greece is at the gates. The expression, without however the exaggeration, is Homeric: see *Il. 2. 248:*

ου γαρ εγω σεο φημι χερειοτερον βροτον αλλον
εμμεναι, οσσοι αμ' Ατρειδησ' υπο Ιλιον ηλθον.

VIX PRIMI PRAELIA TENTANT PORTARUM VIGILES. " Vel in

primo introitu collocati, vel periculo primi," Servius (ed. Leon), followed by Thiel, Forbiger, Wagner (ed. 1861 and *Quaest. Virgil.*), and Conington. " Die posten der ersten nachtwache," Ladewig, Gossrau. I agree entirely with Servius and Wagner. Compare Sil. 6. 1 :

> "iam, Tartessiaco quos solverat aequore, Titan,
> . . . . equos iungebat Eois
> littoribus, *primi*que novo Phaethonte retecti
> *Seres* lanigeris repetebant vellera lucis,"

where "primi" and "Seres" occupy, respectively, the same positions in the verse as the PRIMI and PORTARUM VIGILES of our text, and where the meaning is, *nearest to the sun, the first to be touched by the rays of the sun;* as in our text the meaning is, *nearest to the enemy, the first to come in the way of the enemy.* PRIMI PORTARUM VIGILES may, therefore, be looked upon as the translation of the Greek προφυλακες (our *pickets*)—VIGILES, as φυλακες, expressing the function, and PRIMI, as προ, the forward or foremost position, the position towards the enemy. Compare (*a*), Aeneas, *Poliorc. 22:* εγρηγορεναι τε ως πλειστους αμεινον εν τοις κινδυνοις, και παντα φυλαξαι εν τη νυκτι, ιν' ως πλειστοι καθ' εκαστην φυλακην προ-φυλασσωσι. (*b*), Aeneas, *ib.:* προφυλασσοιεν τ' αν εκ των επι τω τειχει φυλακων προφυλακες ωδε. (*c*), *Ibid. 26:* . . . φωνουντας τι πορρωθεν, οπως αν εγερθη εαν καθευδη ο προ-φυλαξ, και παρασκευασηται αποκρινεσθαι το ερωτωμενον. (*d*), Xenophon, *Anab.* 2 (ed. Hutchins. p. 120): Οι δ' επει ηλθον προς τους προφυλακας, εζητουν τους αρχοντας, translated : hi cum ad primos excubitores venissent, ubi duces essent quae-rebant. Compare also, (*e*), *Aen. 12. 577:*

> "discurrunt alii ad portas *primos*que trucidant,",

where "primos" (not here termed vigiles because it was not night) must be the same προφυλακες, or *pickets*. **And** (*f*), *Aen. 12. 659*, where we have a picture precisely the parallel of that before us :

> . . . "soli *pro portis* Messapus et acer Atinas
> sustentant aciem," &c.

341-357.

CHOROEBUS—RABIES

CHOROEBUS.—Choroebus is the Othryoneus of Homer, *Il. 13. 361 :*

ενθα, μεσαιπολιος περ εων, Δαναοισι κελευσας,
Ιδομενευς Τρωεσσι μεταλμενος εν φοβον ωρσεν.
πεφνε γαρ Οθρυονηα, Καβησοθεν ενδον εοντα,
ος ρα νεον πολεμοιο μετα κλεος ειληλουθει·
ητεε δε Πριαμοιο θυγατρων ειδος αριστην,
Κασσανδρην, αναεδνον· υπεσχετο δε μεγα εργον,
εκ Τροιης αεκοντας απωσεμεν υιας Αχαιων.

INSANO CASSANDRAE INCENSUS AMORE.—Commentators are divided between two opinions concerning the word INSANO, whether it means that it was insanity of Choroebus to love Cassandra at all, or at least to love her under the circumstances of the war ("INSANO, quia belli tempore amabat," Servius's *aliter*. "INSANO, because it hurried him to his ruin," Conington. "Denn ihn brannt' unsinnige lieb' um Kassandra," Voss), or whether it is to be taken as the ordinary epithet of love—"aut perpetuum epitheton amoris est," Servius's first interpretation, adopted by Thiel and Forbiger, and with which I entirely agree. INSANO, as here used, is not at all *insane*, in our sense of the word, but *insane* in the sense in which everything is insane which is violent or passionate, as Hor. *Od. 1. 16. 15 :*

. . . "*insani* leonis
vim stomacho apposuisse nostro."

Ovid, *Heroid. 7. 53 :*

"quid? si nescieris *insana* quid aequora possint."

It is neither madness nor foolishness in Choroebus to be in love with Cassandra, but he is in love with her to madness, passionately in love with her, or, as we commonly say, desperately in love with her. Compare Plaut. *Curc. 1. 3. 20 :*

"nam bonum est pauxillum amare sane; *insane* non bonum est" [it is not good to love passionately] ; and especially Ovid, *Art. Amat.* 1. 371 :

> "tum de te narret, tuua persuadentia verba
> addat, et *insano* iuret amore mori,"

where "insano," being recommendatory of the love ("persuadentia verba"), can by no possibility signify the love's irrationality, can only signify its intensity.

Understood in this sense, the epithet raises our respect not only for Choroebus but for Cassandra, in the same degree as, understood in the former sense, it lowers it; and most readers will, I think, agree with me that that interpretation which tends to elevate both characters in our estimation accords better with the drift of the whole passage than that which tends to depreciate both.

ET GENER . . . FEREBAT.—Supplementary to VENERAT, as "peplumque ferebant," 1. 484, is to "ibant."

INFELIX.—As "suppliciter," 1. 485, belongs both to "ibant" and "ferebant," but principally to "ibant," so here INFELIX belongs both to VENERAT and FEREBAT, but principally to VENERAT. Wagner has done well to remove the Heynian period after FEREBAT.

SUPER HIS.—"His verbis; SUPER, autem, insuper," Servius, correctly (compare 1. 33: "his accensa super"), and correctly followed by Weickert, Forbiger, and Wilms. Heyne, explaining SUPER HIS "posthaec, inde," and Wagner (1861), explaining HIS, "ad hos," have missed the true sense.

IUVENES . . . RUAMUS.—The elder Heinsius incloses all the words from SI, the younger all from QUAE SIT, as far as STETERAT inclusive, in a parenthesis. Both are wrong, and Wagner is right. There is no parenthesis; the train of thought runs on uninterrupted : SI VOBIS CUPIDO . . . VIDETIS . . . EXCESSERE, with its climax, SUCCURRITIS . . . RUAMUS . . . MORIAMUR.

MORIAMUR ET IN MEDIA ARMA RUAMUS, a υστερον προτερον of which we have an exact parallel in Eurip. *Hec.* 266 :

> κεινη [Helen] γαρ ωλεσεν νιν [Achilles], ες Τροιαν τ' αγει·

also, *Aen. 11. 593*:

> " post ego nube cava miserandae corpus et arma
> inspoliata feram tumulo, patriaeque reponam ;"

Ibid. 3. 639:

> " sed fugite, o miseri, fugite, atque a littore funem
> rumpite."

EXCESSERE OMNES, ADYTIS ARISQUE RELICTIS, DI QUIBUS IMPE-RIUM HOC STETERAT.—Macrobius says (*Sat. 5. 22*) : " Hoc unde Virgilius dixerit, nullus inquirit; sed constat, illum de Euripide traxisse qui in fabula *Troadibus* [23] inducit Apollinem, cum Troia capienda esset, ista dicentem:

> εγω δε, νικωμαι γαρ Αργειας θεου
> Ηρας Αθανας θ', αι συνεξειλον Φρυγας,
> λειπω το κλεινον Ιλιον βωμους τ' εμους·
> ερημια γαρ πολιν οταν λαβη κακη,
> νοσει τα των θεων ουδε τιμασθαι θελει.

Let not Christians mock a touching and picturesque superstition which still (how few are aware of it!) exists among themselves, handed down to them by the piety of their pagan forefathers. See Ruga e Parrisit, ed. Rom., 1845, quoted by Camarda, appendice al " Saggio di Grammatologia comparata sulla lingua Albanese," Prato, 1866, p. 16: " Calezoime pra si ka kjilue t' ieunit Zoies e Shkodres, e massannei mennoime me *dobii* te shpirtite si me e sbutte per me passe miscirier. Njate Shcodres ashte nji kjishe tash e remmome, ne te tsilen ishte 'nne rue nji figure e bukure sheitnushmes Meri. Pos masi forti i fort Shkanderbek dikj, Shkodra ran 'nner duore turkjevet e kje vume 'nnen *charace*. Ate chere bani *rakji*, e tash kan shkueme tre kjinte e shtate dhete e tete viete kji Zoia e beecueme tui ike prei assai kjishe, sheoi afer Rhomes 'nne nji te vottser eatune kji thochete Genazzano: atie kje, edhe ashte 'nneerue prei gjith populite, perse ka bame, e ban deri sote shume mereculi. Te lumete ato di *konakje* Gjergjite e Sklavis, kji pas kan [*sic*] *najakje* me pertsiele (persiel) figureu e mreeuluoshme Zoies e beeeueme, prume prei nji shtule ziermite naten, e prei nji shtule ereiete diten! Por te shemete in, o te kershtenete emii, kji 'mmeteni pa nannen e dashtnushme! . . . E pse o nana dashtnushmeia, pse *braktise ietimite* e tuu, pa 'nnime cundra anmikjevet, pse s' kee *serap* per birte tui, kji kjain, kji gjimoin tash gadi per katter scekule pa tii ? Ah ! me dukete, kji zoia beccueme m' pergjegje : ah ! une ika prei Shkodres per mecatete ; e s' iam njite *allaa* perse s' kan pushueme *allaa* mecatete ; t' pushoin mecatete, e une kame per me njite prape ! . . . ''—thus translated by Camarda : " Narriamo dunque come è accaduta la fuga della Signora (Madonna) di Scodra, e quindi pensiamo con vantaggio dell' anima come placarla per ottenerne misericordia. Vicino Scodra è una chiesa ora diruta, nella quale era onorata un' immagine (figura) bella di Maria santissima. Dopo che il forte trai forti Scandergh morì, Scodra cadde nelle mani dei Turchi, e fu posta sotto tributo. In quel tempo fece davvero (*positivo*), ed ora sono passati trecento settant' otto anni che la Signora benedetta partendo (fuggendo) da quella chiesa, passò vicino a Roma in un piccolo paese, che si domanda Genazzano : ivi fu ed è anche ora onorata da tutto il popolo, perchè ha fatto e fa sino ad oggi molti miracoli. Beate quelle due famiglie di Giorgio e Sclavi che hanno avuta la fortuna di seguitare l'immagine miracolosa della Signora benedetta portata da una colonna di fuoco la notte, e da una colonna di nuvola il giorno ! Ma disgraziati voi, O Cristiani miei, che siete rimasti senza la mamma amorosa ! . . . E perchè, O madre amorosa, perchè hai abbandonato gli orfani tuoi senza ajuto contro i nemici ; perchè non hai pietà dei figli tuoi, che piangono, che gemono, ora *son* vicini quattrocento anni, senza di te ? Ah ! mi pare che la Signora benedetta mi responda : ' ah ! io mi partii da Scodra pei peccati ; e non sono ritornata (riaccostata) ancora (?) perchè non sono cessati ancora i peccati ; che cessino i peccati, ed io ritornerò indietro ! ' ''

UNA SALUS VICTIS, &c.—Compare Ammian. 16. 2 : " Ut solet abrupta saepe discrimina salutis ultima desperatio propulsare." Trog. Pomp. 20. 3 : " Dum honeste mori quaerunt, feliciter vicerunt ; nec alia causa victoriae fuit, quam quod desperaverunt."

SALUS.—Not safety, but preservation of life (Gr. σωτηρια). We cannot express the meaning by a single word in English.

We come nearest to it in the words *life* and *salvation*: "the only chance we have of life (of saving our lives, of salvation) is to despair of life (of saving our lives, of salvation)." How pregnant of meaning the expression is, is shown by its repetition in the same line—SALUS, SALUTEM. We have an example of this use of salus in Ammian's translation of the reply of Alexander the Great to his mother, when, like another Herod's wife, she pressed him to put a certain person to death in compliment to her (14. 11) : "Aliam, parens optima, posce mercedem ; hominis enim *salus* beneficio nullo pensatur." Compare also Turnus to Drances, *Aen. 11. 399:* "nulla salus bello" [*not* there is no safety in war, *but* there is no salvation for us in war; war will not save our lives and liberties].

ADDITUS (verse 355) refers back to SUPER, verse 348.

IMPROBA VENTRIS... RABIES.—IMPROBA : "magna," Heyne. "Magna insatiabilis voracitas, et fames crucians," Forbiger. "Avidus, insatiabilis, et ob id audax et perstans," Forcellini—**all** utterly mistaking our author's meaning, no less than Wagner, who refers us to *Georg. 1. 119*, where he observes on "improbus anser": "Improbus commune nocentium et rapacium bestiarum epitheton, avidam voracitatem indicans, ut *Aen. 9. 62 ; 12. 250;* omnino improbus est quisquis modum non servat proptereaque improbari potest—cornix assidue crocitans, versu 388 ; mons vehementissime incitatus, *Aen. 12. 687.* Tum idem epitheton in laudem versum laborem imprimis acrem indicat, infra vers. 146 ; de pervicaci studio insidiantis Arruntis, *Aen. 11. 767.* Intelliges autem feros anseres, non domesticos." Nothing can be plainer than that all these so various and even contradictory meanings have been assigned to the word im-probus without the least regard to the proper signification of the word itself, and merely because the meaning so assigned was consistent or at least not inconsistent with the context; merely because in each case, the word being understood in the arbitrary sense assigned to it, the passage satisfied the *à priori* expectation of the commentator. "Improbus mons" was "mons vehementissime incitatus" because a mountain which fell at all could not but fall very rapidly ; "improbus" applied to "labor" was a term of as great praise as, applied to a goose, it was a term of great dispraise, for no other reason than that labour was in itself praiseworthy, while a goose, and especially a wild one, was worthy of all reprobation for its destructiveness to the grass; and in our text, IMPROBA VENTRIS RABIES was *magna* VENTRIS RABIES, because nothing could be more natural than that the wolves should have a most voracious appetite. But improbus does not signify either "magnus," or "avidus," or "insatiabilis;" neither is improbus ever a laudatory term. Improbus is always a term of reprobation, always means simply *wicked*. The falling mountain is "improbus" (wicked), on account of the ruin it brings on everything which comes in its way; the goose is "improbus" (wicked), on account of the harm it does to the grass and crops; labour is "improbus" (wicked), because it is painful, because it is labour; and for the same reason, viz., because it is painful, the VENTRIS RABIES of the wolves in our text is IMPROBA (wicked). The commentators here, as so often elsewhere, have not been able to discern the poetry; have been completely puzzled and defeated by the ascription of moral delinquency, not merely to brute animals but to objects incapable of all feeling; have forgotten the λαας αναιδης of Homer (*Il. 4. 521; Od. 11. 597*), and the "villanous saltpetre" of the English dramatist (*King Henry 4*, first part, 1. 4):

> "and that it was great pity, so it was,
> this *villanous saltpetre* should be digged
> out of the bowels of the harmless earth,
> which many a good tall fellow had destroyed
> so cowardly."

360.

NOX ATRA CAVA CIRCUMVOLAT UMBRA

"Hic accipere possumus perseverasse quidem lunam, sed fumo obscuratum eius lumen, qui ex magno civitatis incendio movebatur," Donat. "Hinc apparet occidisse iam lunam," Servius. "Nox CIRCUMVOLAT, quippe alata," Heyne, comparing 8. 369:

"nox ruit et fuscis tellurem amplectitur alis,"

personifying night and perceiving no difficulty. "Allerdings erhellt der mond die nacht, aber er wird . . . zeitweise durch wolken verhüllt," Ladewig. "Die nacht hat auch wenn sie vom hellen mondlicht beleuchtet ist etwas düsteres, ein ihr eigenthümliches helldünkel; in diesem erscheinen die dunkeln gehaltlosen schatten, und erhöhen gerade durch ihr dünkel die unheimlichkeit der nacht, durch diese hohlen schatten zeigt sich gerade richt in dem mondscheine die schwarze natur der nacht, die schwarze nacht," Kappes, *Progr. des Lyceums zu Constanz*, Constanz, 1863. "Nox . . . UMBRA aliunde assuta esse, conl. 340, coniecit Ortuinus, cui adsentiri mavult Peerlkampus quam, ex Hor. *Serm.* 2. 1. 58, NOX in *mors* mutare; et legit NOX Servius: nobis tibicen sane, sed is Vergilianus videtur, cf. 397, 420, 621," Ribbeck.

At the bottom of all these glosses lies that great and fundamental error which I have so often had occasion to point out in the course of these remarks, viz., that of taking figurative and poetic for literal and prosaic: an error scarcely less fatal to the exposition and understanding of Virgil than of Holy Writ, although—happy chance for Virgil's commentators no less than for the world!—not to be arbitrated by the same arbitrament. It is not literal night which CIRCUMVOLAT, *flits about*, Aeneas and his companions; it is the night of the tomb, the darkness of the grave, the shadow of death. Compare 6. 866:

"sed nox atra caput tristi circumvolat umbra."

The words are almost identical, yet no one dreams or ever dreamt that it was real literal night which Aeneas and the Sibyl saw flitting about the head of Marcellus. As surely as it is the gloom of death, the shadow of a premature tomb which flits about the head of Marcellus, so surely is it the shadow of a premature death which flits about Aeneas and his companions—VADIMUS HAUD DUBIAM IN MORTEM, the theme (see Rem. on 1. 550), of which our text is the variation. In both places—here, as in the sixth book—it is *figurative* not *real* night which is spoken of, exactly as it is *figurative* not *real* night, the darkness of death, the darkness of the grave, which is spoken of in the Homeric original (*Od. 20. 351*), where the destruction which is about to overtake Penelope's suitors is spoken of under the same allegory under which the destruction impending over Aeneas and his party is spoken of in our text:

a δειλοι, τι κακον τοδε πασχετε ; νυκτι μεν υμεων
ειλυαται κεφαλαι τε, προσωπα τε, νερθε τε γουνα·
οιμωγη δε δεδηε, δεδακρυνται δε παρειαι·
αιματι δ' ερραδαται τοιχοι καλαι τε μεσοδμαι·
ειδωλων δε πλεον προθυρον, πλειη δε και αυλη,
ιεμενων Ερεβοσδε υπο ζοφον· ηελιος δε
ουρανου εξαπολωλε κακη δ' επιδεδρομεν αχλυς.

Compare also (*a*), Quint. Smyrn. 12. 540 (Cassandra warning the Trojans):

a δειλοι, νυν εβημεν υπο ζοφον· αμφι γαρ ημιν
εμπλειον πυρος αστυ και αιματος, ηδε και οιτου
λευγαλεον· παντη δε τεραατα δακρυοεντα
αθανατοι φαινουσι, και εν ποσι κειμεθ' ολεθρου.

(*b*), Sil. 9. 44 (Aemilius Paullus adjuring Varro not to expose his soldiers, "has animas," to certain destruction by immediately engaging in battle with Hannibal—adjuring them too, not in the night, but in the broad daylight):

" ' per toties,' inquit, ' concussae moenia Romae,
perque has, *nox* Stygia quas iam *circumvolat umbra*,
insontes animas, cladi parce obvius ire.' "

(*c*), and the less figurative, less mistakeable, language of Horace, *Sat. 2. 1. 58:* "Mors atris circumvolat alis," where we have not only the circumvolare but the very ater of our text applied to death under his own proper name. (*d*), and of Falisc. *Cyneget.* 347 :

"stat fatum supra, totumque avidissimus *Orcus*
pascitur, et nigris orbem circumsonat alis,"

where we have death again ("Orcus") preying like a greedy vulture on the world, and swooping round it on his black noisy wings. Also (*e*), Stat. *Theb. 1. 46* :

"impia iam merita scrutatus lumina dextra
merserat aeterna damnatum nocte pudorem
Oedipodes, longaque animam sub morte tenebat.
illum indulgentem tenebris imaeque recessu
sedis, inaspectos caelo radiisque penates
servantem, tamen assiduis circumvolat alis
saeva *dies* animi, scelerumque in pectore Dirae,"

where consciousness, the figurative day or light of life, flits "assiduis alis" about Oedipus, exactly as in our text death, the figurative night of life, flits CAVA UMBRA about Aeneas and his companions. (*f*), Stat. *Silv. 5. 1. 216* (of Abascantius mourning at his wife's funeral) :

". . . "sed toto spectatur in agmine coniux
solus ; in hunc magnae flectuntur lumina Romae,
ceu iuvenes natos suprema ad busta ferentem :
is dolor in vultu ; tantum crinesque genaeque
noctis habent"

[*there is so much of night*, i. e., *the night* (*the darkness*) *of Hades* (*of death, of the grave*), *about them*]. (*g*), Lucan, 7. 177 (of the omens preceding the battle of Pharsalia) :

"inque vicem vultus tenebris mirantur apertos,
et pallere diem, galeisque incumbere *noctem*,
defunctosque patres, et cunctas sanguinis umbras*
ante oculos volitare suos"

[*their faces are covered with darkness ; the day loses its colour, and night* (i. e., *the gloom of death*) *broods on their helmets*].

As lux is life (see Rem. on 6. 721), life considered as light, so

---

* This reading makes better sense than the *aliter* :

"defunctos ululare patres, et sanguinis umbras,"

nox is death, death considered as darkness, Hades, *i. e.*, αιδης, *ubi non est videre*, as (*h*), *Aen. 6. 828* :

> "concordes animae nunc, et dum *nocte* premuntur,
> heu, quantum inter se bellum, si lumina vitae
> attigerint, quantas acies stragemque ciebunt !"

Compare, in addition to the above (*i*), Hor. *Carm. 1. 4. 16* :
"Iam te premet *nox*, fabulaeque manes" (in both which examples nox, the night of death, *i. e.*, death, not *circumvolat*, flits about ready to alight on you, but actually alights and oppresses *premit*). (*j*), Hor. *Od. 1. 28. 15* :

> . . . "omnes una manet *nox*,
> et calcanda semel via leti"

(in which example "nox" (death) neither oppresses nor flits round threatening to oppress, but awaits at a distance. We have thus the three degrees: *manet*, at a distance ; *circumvolat*, close at hand ; *premit*, actually on you : to which may be added a fourth degree, more than *circumvolat* and less than *premit*, viz., *circumdat*, entirely surrounds and encloses; as, *Georg. 4. 497* (Eurydice speaking) :

> . . . "feror ingenti circumdata *nocte*,
> invalidasque tibi tendens, heu ! non tua, palmas").

Compare also (*k*), Eurip. *Ion, 1465* (Creusa, who has just found her son Ion alive, whom she believed to have perished when he was exposed at his birth) :

> ανηβα δ' Ερεχθευς,
> ο τε γηγενετας δομος ουκετι νυκτα δερκεται,
> αελιου αναβλεπει λαμπασιν

(where we again have in the one sentence both figures : *seeing night* equivalent to *dead*, and *seeing the light* equivalent to *living* ; as we have also both figures (*l*), Senec. *Theb. 247* (Oedipus speaking) :

> . . . "protinus quosdam editos
> *nox* occupavit, et novae luci abstulit").

(*m*), Aesch. *Choeph. 51* (ed. Ahrens) :

> ανηλιοι, βροτοστυγεις
> δνοφοι καλυπτουσι δομους
> δεσποτων θανατοισι

[*sunless, hateful, darkness covers the house with deaths* (i. e., *the darkness of death covers the house*)]. (*n*), Soph. *Oed. Colon.* 1680 (Antigone after the death of Oedipus):

> τι γαρ, οτω μητ' Αρης
> μητε ποντος αντεκυρσεν,
> ασκοποι δε πλακες εμαρψαν
> εν αφανει τινι μορω φερομενον ;
> ταλαινα· νων δ' ολεθρια
> νυξ επ' ομμασιν βεβακε,
> πως γαρ η τιν' απιαν γαν
> ποντιον κλυδων' αλωμεναι βιου
> δυσοιστον εξομεν τροφαν;

[*night* (i. e., *the shadow, the darkness, of death) hath come over my eyes* : " Quid enim ? utpote in quem nec Mars nec pontus irruit ; sed quae oculos fugiunt, inferorum loca eum ablatum absorpserunt incomperto leti genere"]. (*o*), Hom. *Il.* 16. 567 (of Jupiter bringing, not real night, but the darkness of death, νυκτ' ολοην, over those who were combating for the corpse of Sarpedon) :

> Ζευς δ' επι νυκτ' ολοην τανυσε κρατερη υσμινη,
> οφρα φιλω περι παιδι μαχης ουλοος πονος ειη.

(*p*), Ovid, *Met.* 1. 721 (apostrophizing Argus, whom Mercury has just killed) :

> " Arge, iaces . . . .
> . . . centumque oculos *nox* occupat una"

[*one darkness of death*]. (*q*), Ovid, *Met.* 5. 70 :

> . . . . " at ille
> iam moriens, oculis sub *nocte* natantibus atra,
> circumspexit Athin"

[*the approach of dark night* (i. e., *of death*)]. (*r*), Claud. *Rapt. Pros.* 2. 221 (Proserpine to Dis) :

> " *nocte* tua contentus abi ; quid viva sepultis
> admisces ? nostrum quid proteris advena mundum ?"

[*content with thine own night* (i. e., *the night of Hades*)]. (*s*), Claud. *Rapt. Pros.* 3, p. 220 : " *nox* sua prosequitur currum" [*his own night (the darkness of Hades) accompanies the chariot* (of Dis)]. (*t*), Claud. *Rapt. Pros. 3*, p. 80 :

> "sed tunc ipsa, sui iam non ambagibus ullis
> nuntia, materno facies ingesta sopori.
> namque videbatur tenebroso obtecta recessu
> carceris, et saevis Proserpina vincta catenis,
> non qualem Siculis olim mandaverat arvis,
> nec qualem roscis nuper convallibus Aetnae
> suspexere deae. squalebat, pulchrior auro,
> caesaries, et *nox* oculorum infecerat ignes,
> exhaustusque gelu pallet rubor. ille superbi
> flammeus oris honos, et non cessura pruinis
> membra colorantur picei caligine regni."

(*u*), Sil. 8. 100 :

> "heu sacri vatum errores! dum numina *noctis*
> eliciunt, spondentque novis medicamina curis,
> quod vidi decepta nefas?"

(*v*), Sil. 13. 707 (the shade of Paullus to Scipio) :

> "lux Italum, cuius spectavi Martia facta,
> multum uno maiora viro, descendere *nocti*,
> atque habitanda semel subigit quis visere regna?"

(*w*), Sil. 5. 241 :

> . . . "nisi quem Deus ima colentum
> damnasset Stygiae *nocti*."

(.*x*), Sen. *Herc. Fur.* 279 (Megara calling on Hercules, who is in Hades, to return) :

> "emerge, coniux, atque dispulsas manu
> abrumpe tenebras; nulla si retro via,
> iterque clausum est, orbe diducto redi;
> et quidquid atra *nocte* possessum latet,
> emitte tecum,"

where "tenebras" is the darkness of Hades, and "atra nocte" the dark night of Hades. (*y*), Sil. 13. 270 : "dum copia noctis" [*whilst we have the power to die, whilst we may die if we please*]. (*z*), Sil. 13. 126 :

> "haec [cerva], aevi vitaque tenax, felixque senectam
> mille indefessos viridem duxisse per annos,
> seclorum numero Troianis condita tecta
> aequabat; sed enim longo *nox* venerat aevo."*

---

* Upon this passage Ernesti remarks: "Meo sensu voc. *noctis* nude positum nunc, praesertim de cerva, aliquid duri habet, quamvis mortis notioni significandae

Compare also, (*a'*), our own Shakespeare, *Julius Caesar*, act 5, sc. 8 (Brutus after the battle of Philippi) :

"*night* hangs upon mine eyes : my bones would rest,
that have but laboured to attain this hour."

To all these instances we may, perhaps, add, **finally** (*b'*), Sil. 2. 574, where the true reading is very probably not "morte obita," but, with the Oxford and Cologne MSS., "nocte obita."

As nox is, figuratively, *death* (the darkness of death), so it is also sometimes figuratively *sleep* (the darkness of sleep), *ex. gr.* 4. 529 :

    . . . "neque unquam
solvitur in somnos, oculisve aut pectore noctem
accipit,"

where the second clause is a mere variation of the first, and "noctem" (the darkness of sleep) is used instead of "somnos" (sleep itself), in order that the identical word may not be repeated.

With the use of nox for mors compare the use of lux (and φαος in Greek) for salus (Germ. *heil*, Eng. *salvation*), as *Aen.* 2. 281 :

"o *lux* Dardaniae, spes o fidissima Teucrum."

and Hom. *Il. 17. 615* :

και τω μεν φαος ηλθεν, αμυνε δε νηλεες ημαρ,

where φαος is so entirely *salus*, and the original meaning so entirely out of view, that φαος is opposed to ημαρ, exactly as in our text NOX is so entirely *death* and the original meaning so entirely out of view, that our author is not prevented from using the expression ILLIUS NOCTIS in the very next line by any apprehension that the reader might understand the NOCTIS of that line to be the NOX of the preceding, and to have ILLIUS added to it

---

passim adhibuerunt summi poetae. Ita et infra vs. 270 ; 8. 141 (' Di longae noctis'); Ovid, *Heroid. 10. 112 :* ' aeterna nox.' " These observations Ernesti would hardly have made if he had been aware of the word having been equally "nude positum" in the same sense no less than twice by Virgil, and of the constant use made both by his own author and Virgil, and others, of lux without any explanatory adjunct, in the sense of life.

for the express purpose of fixing it to be so, and o preventing the reader from mistaking it for any other (see Rem. on 2. 586). Compare Eurip. *Electr. 866* (ed. Fix) (Electra exulting in Orestes' murder of Aegisthus):

> ω φεγγος, ω τεθριππον ηλιου σελας,
> ω γαια και νυξ, ην εδερκομην παρος,
> νυν ομμα τουμον αμπτυχαι τ' ελευθεροι,
> επει πατρος πεπτωκεν Αιγισθος φονευς

(where the φεγγος and τεθριππον ηλιου σελας are not the real light of day and splendour of the four-in-hand sun, but spiritual light, the light of the soul, *i. e.*, joy and rejoicing; and γαια and νυξ, not earth and night, but, as we would say, the mortal gloom or darkness of the soul, *i. e.*, sorrow and mourning). Compare also Eurip. *Med. 827* (ed. Fix):

> . . . αει δια λαμπροτατου
> βαινοντες αβρως αιθερος. . .

Quint. Calab. 11. 507 (of the combat between Memnon and Achilles, in which Memnon is killed):

> και νυ κε δη μακαρεσσιν αμειλιχος εμπεσε δηρις,
> ει μη υπ' εννεσιησι Διος μεγαλοβρεμεταο
> δοιαι αρ' αμφοτεροισι θοως εκατερθε παρεσταν
> Κηρες· ερεμναιη μεν εβη ποτι Μεμνονος ητορ,
> φαιδρη δ' αμφ' Αχιληα δαιφρονα·

See Rem. on "morte resignat," 4. 244.

CIRCUMVOLAT, περιπετεται, περιποταται, flits about like a rapacious bird—a hawk, or kite, or eagle—ready to pounce upon its prey. Compare Ovid, *Met. 2. 716:*

> "ut volucris visis rapidissima miluus extis,
> dum timet, et densi circumstant sacra ministri,
> flectitur in gyrum, nec longius audet abire,
> spemque suam motis avidus *circumvolat* alis."

Oed. Tyr. 481 (Chor., of guilty Oedipus):

> . . . τα δ' αει
> ζωντα περιποταται

[the Delphic oracles *fly about* him always no matter where he goes].

Independently of all argument drawn from the parallels afforded both by Virgil himself and other writers, this word alone is sufficient to show that the night spoken of can by no possibility be natural night, the night time, inasmuch as natural night, the night time, whether literal or personified, never flits about (CIRCUMVOLAT), ready to alight, but not alighting, but on the contrary is always either present or absent, or if neither, is coming, or going, never flits about without alighting. Therefore *nox silet, incubat, praecipitat, ruit, est, aufert, subit, operit, tenet, torquet, contingit, invertit, abit, adest, agitur, incipit, renit, transit,* but so far as I know never *circumvolat.* It follows that the NOX of our text is neither literal night, the night time, nor the literal night personified, the goddess *Nox,* but figurative night, the night or darkness of death or the grave. If it is the real literal night which CIRCUMVOLAT about Aeneas and his party, they must be in the day, and only occasionally shadowed by the night, which is absurd. If it is the goddess Night which CIRCUMVOLAT about Aeneas and his party, why does she only flit about and not alight? why does she only *circumvolare* about those whom night, no matter whether physical or personified, has already involved—

"vertitur interea caelum, et ruit oceano nox,
involvens umbra magna terramque polumque
Myrmidonumque dolos."

How is this picture to be reconciled with the alleged picture in our text, whether of real literal night or the goddess Night only flitting about, not already alighted on, Aeneas and his comrades?

NOX ATRA CAVA CIRCUMVOLAT UMBRA once rightly understood, a new light breaks in on the whole context, and the etiology of the description stands clear before us. Death, death, death, everywhere, before, behind, around, is the picture the poet has in his mind, and which he presents to his reader in every variety of form and colour. Death has been suggested to Aeneas in his dream by the vision of the mangled Hector. Death is his first thought, as, roused from his sleep, he rushes out of his house, "pulchrumque mori succurrit in armis." Death is the first word of the first person he meets—"Fuimus Troes:" *we are all lost, all dead and gone.* Death is his own first word to the little band which gathers round him (MORIAMUR ET IN MEDIA ARMA RUAMUS). It is to death he goes with them (VADIMUS HAUD DUBIAM IN MORTEM); it is death, the darkness of death, which flits about them as they go (NOX ATRA CAVA CIRCUMVOLAT UMBRA). "Who," he exclaims, "shall tell the deaths of that fatal night?"—

> QUIS CLADEM ILLIUS NOCTIS, QUIS FUNERA FANDO
> EXPLICET?

It is death in its concretest form which is on every side of them, in the streets, in the houses, in the very temples of the gods—

> PLURIMA PERQUE VIAS STERNUNTUR INERTIA PASSIM
> CORPORA, PERQUE DOMOS ET RELIGIOSA DEORUM
> LIMINA.

His very enemies are dying beside him (VICTORESQUE CADUNT DANAI), and everything is one picture of mourning, fright, and death—

> . . . . CRUDELIS UBIQUE
> LUCTUS, UBIQUE PAVOR, ET PLURIMA MORTIS IMAGO.

To the objection that Aeneas does not die—on the contrary, escapes and lives to tell the story—the answer is supplied by Aeneas himself. The whole of the little band except three, viz., Iphitus, Pelias, and Aeneas himself, perishes. Choroebus falls, Ripheus falls, Hypanis falls, Dymas falls, Pantheus falls, and if Aeneas himself does not fall, it is because the fates do not allow it, not because he was not every moment in danger of falling:

> "Iliaci cineres et flamma extrema meorum,
> testor in occasu vestro nec tela nec ullas
> vitavisse vices Danaum, et, si fata fuissent
> ut caderem, meruisse manu."

Similar to the indication of death, whether present or near at hand, by darkness, but of less frequent occurrence among writers and infinitely more striking, is its indication by mouldiness, as *Ballata di Garentina* (Camarda, appendice, p. 98) (Garentina addressing the ghost of Constantine, which she takes for Constantine himself):

> Κοσταντινε, ιμε βελα,
> vje σεγγε τε κεκje ου σσοχε [ms. σσογε],
> κραχετε [ms. κραγ] του [ms. τ' ενδε ? τε] γjερι τε
> jave τε μουγουλουαμι τε [μουχουλουαμι τε].
>
> Γαρεντινε, μοτρα ιμε,
> καμνοι σκουπεταβετ
> κραχετε [ms. κραγετε] με μουγουλοι [μουχουλοι];

thus translated by Camarda:

> "Costantino, fratel mio,
> un segno funesto io veggo,
> le spalle tue spaziose
> sono ammuffate.
>
> "Garentina, sorella mia,
> il fumo dei moschetti
> le spalle mi covrì di muffa [mi fece ammuffire]."

CAVA.—Heyne is right ("Quatenus ipsi ea circumdantur"), and Conington well quotes 1. 520, "nube cava... amicti." The English expressions *under cover of the night*, *under cover of the darkness*, are analogous. Compare also Sil. 13. 254:

> "et, ni caeca sinu terras nox conderet atro,"

where the same notion, viz., of embracing, containing, or enveloping, is expressed by "sinu," as is expressed by CAVA in our text.

It is, however, questionable whether CAVA should not be regarded as equivalent to *inane*, Germ. *leer*, Engl. *empty*.

361-369.

QUIS CLADEM ILLIUS NOCTIS QUIS FUNERA FANDO
EXPLICET AUT POSSIT LACRYMIS AEQUARE LABORES*
URBS ANTIQUA RUIT MULTOS DOMINATA PER ANNOS
PLURIMA PERQUE VIAS STERNUNTUR† INERTIA PASSIM
CORPORA PERQUE DOMOS ET RELIGIOSA DEORUM
LIMINA NEC SOLI POENAS DANT SANGUINE TEUCRI
QUONDAM ETIAM VICTIS REDIT IN PRAECORDIA VIRTUS
VICTORESQUE CADUNT DANAI CRUDELIS UBIQUE
LUCTUS UBIQUE PAVOR ET PLURIMA MORTIS IMAGO

ILLIUS NOCTIS.—Not referring at all to the NOX of the immediately preceding verse (which, as we have just seen, is not the real literal night, or night time, the figurative night of death), but to the night which he has been for some time describing, and which has not been specially mentioned since verse 250:

"vertitur interea caelum et ruit oceano nox,
involvens umbra magna terramque polumque
Myrmidonumque dolos."

Therefore the ILLIUS, *that night, that fatal night, the last of Troy*. The only excuse which occurs to me for this so deceptive use of the same word in one verse in a figurative, and in the very next in a literal, sense, is that the passages to which the two verses belong may have been written at different times, and afterwards put together without sufficient circumspection. The excuse would be more valid if it did not unfortunately happen that we find a similar confusion of expression occurring so often elsewhere, and even where no such excuse is possible, viz., within the limits of a single sentence: *ex. gr.*, 12. 684, "montis" is literal, and means a mountain, and in the same sentence,

---

* LABORES, *Med.*; om. in the other first-class MSS.; so also Ed. Princ.; P. Manut.; D. Heins.; N. Heins.; Philippe; Pottier; Haupt; Ribbeck.

† STERNUNTUR, *Pal.* and *Med.*; om. in the other first-class MSS.; so also Ed. Princ., and the editions of P. Manutius, D. Heinsius, N. Heinsius (1670). Philippe, Pottier, Haupt, and Ribbeck.

verse 687, "mons" is figurative, and means a great stone which has fallen from the top of the mountain ("montis")—a confusion of literal and figurative inexcusable even in an Eton ode. See Rem. on "sequor," 4. 384, and compare the similarly inconsiderate application by Lucan (4. 452) of "moles," in one verse to a ship, and in the next verse but two, to a rock:

> . . . " nec prima, neque illa,
> quae sequitur, tardata ratis ; sed tertia *moles*
> haesit, et ad cautes adducto fune secuta est.
> impendent cava saxa mari ; ruituraque semper
> stat (mirum!) *moles* ; et silvis aequor inumbrat."

INERTIA. — "Imbellia, ut senum, infantum, feminarum," Heyne, Voss, Wagner, Thiel. I think not, but *which had offered no resistance, which had died inertly*, as was to be judged by their being found lying there, *ex. gr.*, killed without either arms in their hands, or arms on their persons, without any signs of struggle or battle, and without any dead bodies of the enemy being mixed up among their own. Compare Ovid, *Met.* 7. 542 (of the war-horse dying by disease, in his stall):

> . . . " veterumque oblitus honorum,
> ad praesepe gemit, leto moriturus *inerti*."

Ibid., 12. 361 (of the pine trunk which Demoleon had thrown at Theseus without hitting him):

> " non tamen arbor *iners* cecidit : nam Crantoris alti
> abscindit iugulo pectusque humerumque sinistrum."

That it is not terrified or wounded, and still alive and breathing bodies which lie prostrate (STERNUNTUR), but dead bodies, is shown by the immediately succeeding NEC SOLI POENAS DANT SANGUINE TEUCRI, . . . VICTORES CADUNT DANAI, informing us that Greeks have in some instances fallen also, viz., in those instances in which the Trojans have mustered up sufficient courage to resist and attack the aggressors in their turn:

QUONDAM ETIAM VICTIS REDIT IN PRAECORDIA VIRTUS.

And that the bodies so lying dead and prostrate are not merely the bodies of old men, women, and children (" imbellia corpora,"

Heyne, Voss, Wagner, Thiel), but the bodies of unresisting persons (INERTIA CORPORA), is shown by

QUONDAM ETIAM VICTIS REDIT IN PRAECORDIA VIRTUS,

informing us that in some instances resistance has actually been made, and the aggressors too have fallen. Thus PLURIMA CORPORA has its tally in QUONDAM VICTORES DANAI; STERNUNTUR, its tally in CADUNT; and INERTIA, its tally in VICTIS REDIT IN PRAECORDIA VIRTUS.

The word so wholly misunderstood by modern commentators has been more or less nearly guessed at by some of the ancient. Thus, while Servius hesitates between "non repugnantia," "INERTIA dum occiduntur," and "per somnum INERTIA," Cynthius Cenetensis accepts the first of the three guesses, and adds: "ut inquit Dictys Cretensis, vice pecudum interficiebantur Troiani."

DOMOS.—In my "Adversaria Virgiliana" I connected DOMOS and RELIGIOSA DEORUM LIMINA intimately together, so as to make the sense *domos religiosas deorum*. I have been induced to change my opinion and to consider DOMOS as affording a separate view from RELIGIOSA DEORUM LIMINA, first, because the picture gains thereby in richness, not only the streets and temples being filled with dead bodies, but the palaces also; and, secondly, because in the precisely similar picture presented by Sallust, *Bell. Catil.* 50: "Fana atque *domos* exspoliari; eaedem, incendia fieri; postremo armis, cadaveribus, cruore, atque luctu, omnia compleri," as well as in the not very dissimilar picture presented by Tacitus, *Hist. 3. 33*: "Quas [faces], ubi praedam egesserant, in vacuas *domos* et inania templa, per lasciviam iaculabantur," there is no room for doubt that "domos" is not *temples of the gods*, but *the dwellings of the richer citizens, the palaces*, as there is also no doubt in the following passages: Ovid, *Met. 2. 76* (Phoebus to Phaethon):

"forsitan et lucos illic urbesque *domosque*
concipias animo, delubraque ditia donis
esse."

Lucan, 7. 716: "pandunt templa, *domos*." Stat. *Theb.* 10. 881:

. . . "et truncas rupes in templa *domosque*
praecipitat, frangitque suis iam moenibus urbem."

Aristides, *Rhodiaca*, θανατοι κατ' οικιας, εν ιεροις, εν θυραις, εν πυλαις. And our author himself, 11. 882:

>   . . . "inter tuta *domorum*
>   confixi expirant animas."

Domos, the houses *par excellence*, i. e., the great houses, the palaces, Fr. *hôtels*, the common houses being "tecta." Compare Tacit. *Annal. 13. 18:* "nec defuere qui arguerent viros gravitatem adseverantes, quod *domos*, villas [sciz. Britannici], id temporis, quasi praedam divisissent." *Ibid. 13. 4:* "Discretam *domum* et rempublicam" [*the royal palace and the republic should be kept distinct*]. Stock, ad Tacit. *Annal. 15. 41:* "Totâ in urbe, iuxta Victorem, fuere insulae 26602, *domus* 780."

From this use of domus to signify a great house or palace, a house standing by itself, flows naturally its use for a temple, a temple being *par excellence* the house, not only on account of its great size and splendour, but on account of its being consecrated to a superior being; and accordingly, we find even at the present day the principal church in a city called *il duomo*. The same use of οικος is common in Greek. Compare Procop. *de Aedif. 1. 10:* μεχρι ες τον Αρεος καλουμενον οικον. Aesch. *Sept. c. Theb. 279* (ed. Schutz):

>   θησειν τροπαια, πολεμιων δ' εσθηματα
>   λαφυρα δαιων δουριπληχθ' αγνοις δομοις.

Religiosa: "religiosa sunt quae non vulgo ac temere, sed cum castitate ceremoniaque adeunda et reverenda et reformidanda sunt magis quam invulganda," Aul. Gellius, 4. 9. 9.

Victoresque cadunt Danai. Compare *Il. 17. 361:*

>   . . . τοι δ' αγχιστινοι επιπτον
>   νεκροι ομου Τρωων και υπερμενεων επικουρων,
>   και Δαναων. ουδ' οι γαρ αναιμωτι γ' εμαχοντο.

Plurima mortis imago.—"Aut definitio timoris est, aut varietas mortis ostenditur, *i.e.*, gladio, igni, ruina. Aut frequentissima, aut praesentissima," Servius. "Plurima mortis imago, *h. e.*, ubique caedes facta cernitur; passim caesorum cadavera proiecta. Magis hoc accommodatum antecedentibus, quam varias caedis formas et genera intelligere," Heyne.

"IMAGO; forma, genus," Wagner (1861), quoting Tacit. *Hist. J. 28*: "Integri cum sauciis, semineces cum exspirantibus volvuntur varia pereuntium forma, et *omni imagine mortium*." "IMAGO MORTIS est, credo, quod Valerius Flaccus, 6. 419, dixit —*forma necis*," Peerlkamp.

PLURIMA MORTIS IMAGO is not "ubique caedes facta cernitur," because we have had "ubique caedes facta cernitur" already, viz., verse 364:

PLURIMA PERQUE VIAS STERNUNTUR INERTIA PASSIM
CORPORA, PERQUE DOMOS ET RELIGIOSA DEORUM
LIMINA,

and although such repetition were very usual and allowable in the form of variation to a theme, it had been intolerable here, as the winding up and peroration of a long passage already containing the identical thought. Neither is PLURIMA MORTIS IMAGO "variae formae et genera caedis," because although, as shown by Wagner's quotation from Tacitus, the words might, under different circumstances, viz., where such meaning was, as in Wagner's quotation, pointed out by the context, or even where such meaning was consistent with the context, be so interpreted, they cannot be so interpreted here, where such meaning is not only not pointed out by the context, but is inconsistent with the context, since to say that the slaughter was of different kinds affords a peroration so weak and unimpressive as to be scarcely less unsuitable than that afforded by the interpretation proposed by Heyne. What, then, is PLURIMA MORTIS IMAGO? I reply: a very great picture of death, a very great likeness or appearance of death—death appeared everywhere around and about, everything which was to be seen spoke of death, suggested the idea of death; the very sense in which the word imago is used (*a*), by Servius, at 12. 606: "Moris fuit apud veteres, ut ante rogos regum humanus sanguis effunderetur, vel captivorum vel gladiatorum; quorum si copia forte non fuisset, laniantes genas suum effundebant cruorem, ut rogis illa *imago* restitueretur" [viz., the appearance, show, of human blood]. (*b*), by Virgil himself, 8. 557:

. . . . "maior Martis iam apparet *imago*"

[the picture of war, the appearance of war, is greater than it was before; there is a greater appearance of war than previously; war appears more imminent, more immediate than ever]. (*c*), by Val. Flacc. 2. 640 (Cyzicus addressing Jason and his band of Aemathian chiefs):

> . . . "o terris nunc primum cognita nostris
> Aemathiae manus, et fama mihi maior *imago*"

["O image, picture, greater than your fame," *i.e.*, "O greater than the image, picture, which fame had presented of you." The objects which Aeneas and his party saw and heard (viz., the dead, dying, wounded, the lamentation and terror) were the very picture or image of death; the objects which Cyzicus saw, viz., Jason and his companions, were greater than the image or picture which fame had presented of them]. (*d*), by Ovid, *Met. 12. 233* (of the battle of the Centaurs and Lapithae):

> "raptaturque comis per vim nova nupta prehensis.
> Eurytus Hippodamen, alii, quam quisque probarant,
> aut poterant, rapiunt, captaeque erat urbis *imago*.
> femineo clamore sonat domus"

[there was the image or picture of a captive city, the scene that presented itself was the picture of a captive city, viz., because the women were treated with violence, as on the taking of a city, everyone carrying off by force her who pleased him best]. (*e*), by Claudian, *in Rufin. 2. 236 :* "en iterum belli civilis *imago!*" [the picture of civil war]. (*f*), by Ovid, *Met. 1. 238* (of the wolf into which Lycaon was metamorphosed):

> "canities eadem est, eadem violentia vultu,
> idem oculi lucent, eadem feritatis *imago*"

[the same picture of savageness was presented by the wolf as had previously been presented by Lycaon, the wolf's picture of savageness consisting of the particulars previously enumerated, viz., the grisliness, the fierce countenance, and the glaring eyes, exactly as in our text the picture of death consisted in the dead bodies which lay everywhere scattered about, the CRUDELIS LUCTUS and the PAVOR]. (*g*), by Cicero, *pro Sext. 19 :* "Alter, o Dii boni! quam teter incedebat! quam truculentus, quam terribilis aspectu ! Unum aliquem te ex barbatis illis, exemplum imperii veteris, *imaginem* antiquitatis, columen reipublicae, diceres intueri" [picture of old times]. (***h***), by Ovid, *Met. 11. 550:* "duplicataque noctis *imago* est" [the image of night (viz., that already produced in the mind by the usual signs of night) is doubled by the unusual darkness produced by the thick clouds]. (***i***), by Silius, 14. 616 (ed. Rup.) :

. . . " communis ubique
ira deum, atque eadem lethi versatur *imago*"

[as plainly as possible, Silius's usual appropriation of the Virgilian text]. **And** (***k***), by Tacitus, *Annal., 2. 53:* "Igitur paucos dies insumpsit [Germanicus] reficiendae classi : simul sinus Actiaca victoria inclitos, et sacratas ab Augusto manubias, castraque Antonii, cum recordatione maiorum suorum adiit ; namque ei, ut memoravi, avunculus Augustus, avus Antonius erant, magnaque illic *imago* tristium laetorumque" [a great picture both of sad and joyful events].

In all these passages, as in our text, certain objects, which resemble another object so much that the sight of them suggests that other object to the mind, are stated to be the "imago," image, or picture, of that other object, the comparison or likeness between being entirely of objects;—**in** our text, *of* the sights and sounds which struck the senses of Aeneas and his party, *to* death ; **in** the passage of Servius, *of* worship offered to the gods by worshippers with bleeding faces, *to* worship offered to the gods with bleeding victims ; **in** *Aen. 8. 557, of* the actual appearance of the Arcadian cavalry marching forth, *to* their reputation ; **in** Valerius Flaccus, *of* the real Jason and his band, *to* the representation given of Jason and his band by report ; **in** Ovid, *Met. 12. 223, of* the violence and tumult at the feast of the Centaurs and Lapithae, *to* the violence and tumult which take place when a city is taken by storm ; **in** Cicero, *of* a man of the modern times, *to* the man of ancient times ; **in** Ovid, *Met. 11. 550, of* the darkness produced by clouds in the night-time, *to* a doubling of night. In all these instances the resemblance expressed by *imago* is of one thing to another thing, exactly as in the case of a statue or picture, the resemblance expressed by *imago* is of the statue or picture to the original. Parallel expressions in English are:—That child is the very picture of health. That face is the very picture of happiness. That day is the very picture of winter. That corn-field is the very picture of plenty. That poor beggar is the very picture of want. That condemned culprit is the very picture of despair.

There is an entirely different use of imago, 9. 294:

" atque animum strinxit patriae pietatis *imago*."

and 10. 824:

" et mentem patriae subiit pietatis *imago*."

In both these places " imago " expresses the resemblance not of two objects to each other, but of one single object to our perception of it. There is, indeed, the same resemblance as in our text, in 8. 557, in the passage of Servius, and in the passage of Valerius Flaccus; but that resemblance is not of two different objects existing outside the mind and compared together, but of one object to the impression which that object makes on the mind. " Imago " in these last-adduced passages is the picture, image, εἴδωλον, idea, in the mind—in the one case in the mind of Iulus, in the other case in the mind of Aeneas. In both cases it is the "imago," εἴδωλον, or idea of paternal affection (" patriae pietatis "); and this " imago," εἴδωλον, or idea of paternal affection is excited, produced, or called up, in the mind by objects presented to the senses, between which objects and " patria pietas " there is no resemblance whatever, those objects suggesting or calling up the "imago," εἴδωλον, or idea, only by association. Therefore the lines close the accounts to which they belong, respectively; and in the one case Iulus, in the other case Aeneas, is left reflecting on this new thought, viz., that of " patria pietas " (the affection of a father for a child), suggested to him, called up in his mind (" animum strinxit," " animum subiit "), by the objects which have just been presented to his senses, of which objects the new thought is not the image, but only suggested by association, exactly as, 2. 560, " subiit cari genitoris imago," the picture which presents itself to the mind of Aeneas is not the image or resemblance of anything presented to his senses, but an image which the objects presented to his senses suggest to his mind, call up in his mind by the way of association.

PLURIMA, very great, very much, very strong, as *Georg. 3. 52;* " cui turpe caput, cui plurima cervix ; " Ovid, *Met. 14. 53 :*

    . . . " medio cum *plurimus* orbe
 sol erat."

See Remm. on " maior Martis iam apparet imago," 8. 557, and on " pietatis imago," 9. 294 ; 10. 824.

370–383.

PRIMUS—ARMIS

VAR. LECT.

[*punct.*] PRIMUS SE, DANAUM MAGNA COMITANTE CATERVA ||| D. Heins. ; N. Heins. ; Heyne ; Wagner (ed. Heyn.)

[*punct.*] PRIMUS SE DANAUM, MAGNA COMITANTE CATERVA ||| Voss ; Wagner (*Praest.*) ; Nauck.

[*punct.*] PRIMUS SE DANAUM MAGNA COMITANTE CATERVA ||| P. Manut. ; Ribbeck.

VAR. LECT.

[*punct.*] IRRUIMUS, DENSIS ||| P. Manut. ; D. Heins. ; N. Heins. ; Heyne ; Wagner (ed. Heyn. and *Praest.*).

[*punct.*] IRRUIMUS DENSIS ||| Voss ; Ribbeck.

PRIMUS SE DANAUM, MAGNA COMITANTE CATERVA, &c.—The structure is undoubtedly PRIMUS DANAUM, not CATERVA DANAUM— first, on account of the so much better cadence of the line, when divided at DANAUM than when divided at SE ; and secondly, on account of the exact parallelism of verse 40 :

"primus ibi ante omnes, magna comitante caterva,"

where the division of the line is just before "magna comitante caterva," and cannot possibly be anywhere else. If it be alleged that verse 501 of the first book,

"incessit, magna iuvenum stipante caterva,"

is divided exactly where our text is divided by the Heinsii and Heyne, and has a genitive ("iuvenum") exactly corresponding to the DANAUM of our text and depending on the very same "caterva," I put in the double demurrer; **first**, that the division after "incessit"—although at first sight a division after the same number of syllables as the division after PRIMUS SE—is yet a division of an essentially different kind, partakes not at all of the awkwardness of that division, on the contrary is full of grace and eloquence, being in fact a division not after the commencement of a sentence, not after the three syllables *in-ces-sit*, but after the ending of a sentence, after the long protasis "regina ad templum forma pulcherrima Dido incessit;" while the division after PRIMUS SE is a division not merely at the very beginning after the first three syllables of a paragraph, but immediately succeeding a monosyllable consisting only of two letters, a situation than which it is hardly possible to imagine one more ungraceful, unless in altogether peculiar circumstances, for a division. **And secondly**, that whereas verse 501 of the first book after the division at "incessit" runs on "magna iuvenum," not "iuvenum magna"—the emphasis being thrown (see Rem. on 2. 246), not on the troop's consisting of young men, but on the greatness of the troop—our text after the division at SE would run on, not "magna Danaum," the emphasis being thrown, as it should be thrown, on the greatness of the troop, but DANAUM MAGNA, the emphasis being thrown exactly where it should not be thrown, on the circumstance that the persons accompanying Androgeos were Danai.

IRRUIMUS, DENSIS ET CIRCUMFUNDIMUR ARMIS.—The structure is not, DENSIS ARMIS IRRUIMUS ET CIRCUMFUNDIMUR, but

IRRUIMUS, ET DENSIS ARMIS CIRCUMFUNDIMUR, and the comma therefore required ; first, because it is Virgil's habit so to divide his lines after the first or second word ; and secondly, on account of the division immediately following this word in the same position in the verse, 9. 554 :

> " haud aliter iuvenis medios moriturus in hostes
> *irruit*, et qua tela videt densissima, tendit."

The structure is similar, and the comma for the same reason required after the same word, 10. 579 :

> " *irruit*, adversaque ingens apparuit hasta"

[not " adversa hasta irruit apparuitque," but " irruit, adversaque hasta apparuit"] ; and 6. 294 :

> " *irruat*, et frustra ferro diverberet umbras"

[not " ferro irruat et diverberet," but " irruat, et ferro diverberet"].

390-393.

DOLUS AN VIRTUS QUIS IN HOSTE REQUIRAT
ARMA DABUNT IPSI SIC FATUS DEINDE COMANTEM
ANDROGEI GALEAM CLIPEIQUE INSIGNE DECORUM
INDUITUR

DOLUS AN VIRTUS.—Compare Werner, *die Söhne des Thales*, th. 2, akt 1, sc. 6 :

> " das ist das beste, was zum ziele führt ;
> und was gelungen ist auch rechtlich."

Casti, *Anim. Parl. 11. 4* :

> " vincasi per *virtude*, ovver per *frode*,
> è sempre il vincitor degno di lode."

The doctrine is cast up to the Romans by Sapor, Ammian. 17.

5: "Illud apud nos nunquam acceptum fuit, quod adseritis vos exultantes, *nullo discrimine virtutis ac doli*, prosperos omnes laudari debere bellorum eventus." Innocent Sapor! how little he knew about virtus or dolus! that never man lived who had not one virtus, as one dolus, for his friends, and another virtus, as another dolus, for his enemies; one virtus, as one dolus, under one set of circumstances, and another virtus, as another dolus, under another set of circumstances; and that if it were not so, there could be neither war nor politics, neither friend nor foe, neither acquaintance nor stranger, no relationship either of country, or of society, or of family, not even of lover and sweetheart, of man and wife, of parent and child, in the whole world. Hirtius, *de Bell. Afric.*, ascribes to the Gauls the simplicity of Sapor : " Contra Gallos, homines apertos, minimeque insidiosos, qui per *virtutem*, non per *dolum*, dimicare consueverunt." How different Gauls from the Gauls of to-day, or any people with whom the Gauls of to-day have to do!

ARMA DABUNT IPSI.—If, as hitherto supposed, IPSI mean *the persons whom Choroebus and his party are despoiling of their arms* (" die todten werden waffen geben," Schiller), the sentence ARMA DABUNT IPSI is a mere tautology, the same meaning being contained in the preceding MUTEMUS CLIPEOS, &c.; for, *let us exchange arms with these persons* and *these persons shall supply us with arms* are plainly but different ways of saying the same thing. I therefore refer IPSI to the Danai, the enemy generally: and understand Choroebus's meaning to run thus : " Let us change shields, &c., with these dead fellows here, and by so doing compel the Danai, the invaders themselves (IPSI), to furnish us with arms." The passage being so interpreted, there is, first, no tautology; and secondly, IPSI has its proper emphatic force.

It was not until after the above interpretation had been published in my "Twelve Years' Voyage" I observed that " ipsorum" in the not very unlike passage, 11. 195 :

   . . . . " pars munera nota,
   ipsorum clipeos et non felicia tela,"

means the dead, the actual persons to whom the arms belonged.

The parallelism, however, is not so perfect as to induce me to surrender an interpretation which fills ARMA DABUNT IPSI with point and spirit, for one which leaves that clause a mere dull tautology.*

The expression ARMA DABUNT IPSI is the stronger, arma dare being the usual and recognised phrase for supplying with arms, arming, as Ovid, *Ep. 13. 140* (Laodamia to Protesilaus):

"imponet galeam, barbaraque *arma dabit.*
arma dabit; dumque *arma dabit,* simul oscula sumet."

Also Virg. *Ecl. 6. 19:*

.... "iniiciunt ipsis ex vincula sertis."

The sentiment contained in ARMA DABUNT IPSI is familiar to us in the English proverbial expression, *furnish a rod to whip himself.*

CLIPEI INSIGNE, the ensign or device on the shield. Compare Aesch. *Sept. c. Theb. 383* (ed. Blomfield) σημ' επ' ασπιδος. Also *Aen. 7. 657:*

.... "*clipeoque insigne* paternum
centum angues cinctamque gerit serpentibus Hydram."

Aen. 7. 789:

"at levem *clipeum* sublatis cornibus Io
auro *insignibat,* iam setis obsita, iam bos,
argumentum ingens, et custos virginis Argus,
caelataque amnem fundens pater Inachus urna."

---

* As stated above, I argued in my "Twelve Years' Voyage" that IPSI could not mean the dead bodies which they were stripping, but the Danai generally, and that the gist of the passage was not *these dead fellows here,* but *the Danai, our enemies, shall supply us with arms,* and I quoted in illustration the familiar English proverb, "Furnish a rod to whip himself." This interpretation is sufficiently plausible, and has been accepted by Mr. Conington. I fear, however, it is more plausible than precisely and mathematically correct. At the time I wrote that comment I had neither remarked of how very frequent occurrence in Virgil is an almost tautologous repetition of the same thought (see Rem. on 1. 550), nor observed that in the very parallel passage, 11. 195, quoted above, "ipsorum" is the actual dead bodies, the actual owners of the arms. I am, therefore, bound to give Schiller the credit of having understood the passage correctly, and am only sorry the, as I still think, better thought appears not to have been the thought of Virgil.

Aen. 8. 625 : " clipei non enarrabile textum." Prudent. *contr. Symm. 1. 487:*

"Christus purpureum, gemmanti textus in auro,
signabat labarum; *clipeorum insignia* Christus
scripserat."

CLIPEI INSIGNE DECORUM; as if Virgil had said insigni ornatum clipeum, or clipeum insignitum.

396.

HAUD NUMINE NOSTRO

VAR. LECT.

NUMINE **I** *Pal., Med.* **II** ⁴⁺⁵⁄₆. **III** Venice, 1471, 1472, 1475; Milan, 1475, 1492; P. Manut.; D. Heins.; N. Heins. (1670); Philippe; Heyne; Pott.; Haupt; Ribb.

NOMINE **II** ₃⁲⁄₆.

O *Vat., Rom., Ver., St. Gall.*

"Aut diis contrariis, aut quia in scutis Graecorum Neptunus, in Troianorum fuerat Minerva depicta," Servius. "Averso nobis, non propitio," Heyne, Forbiger, Wagner. " Unbegleitet von gottheit," Voss—**all** equally erroneous and wide of the mark. Numen is used here in its primary sense, viz., that of will and pleasure, not in its secondary sense of deity or divinity (will and pleasure *par excellence ;* see Rem. on "quo numine laeso," 1.12; and "numen Iunonis," 1. 52); and NUMINE NOSTRO is not "our own or tutelary deity," but "our own proper will and pleasure:" "we go mixed with the Danai, and therefore HAUD NUMINE NOSTRO, not according to our own will and pleasure, but according to the will and pleasure of the Danai; in other words, follow the lead and guidance of the Danai, not the lead and guidance of our own will;" exactly as (*a*), verse 336 :

" talibus Othryadae dictis et *numine* divum
in flammas et in arma feror, quo tristis Erinnys
quo fremitus vocat et sublatus ad aethera clamor"

(where " numine divum" is not the deity or divinity of the gods
(which had been mere tautology, and equivalent to gods, gods,
or deity, deity), but the will and pleasure of the gods; and
where Aeneas follows the guidance not of his own free choice,
his own free will and pleasure, but of the gods, exactly as in our
text he follows the guidance not of his own free choice, his own
free will and pleasure, but the guidance of the Danai). (*b*),
6. 266 :

. . . " sit *numine* vestro
pandere res alta terra et caligine mersas"

(where " numine vestro "—*not* with your godhead, *but* with
your will and pleasure—corresponds precisely in every respect,
even in its very position in the verse, with the NUMINE NOSTRO
of our text). (*c*), *Eclog. 4. 47 :*

" concordes stabili fatorum *numine* Parcae"

[*not* with the steadfast god-head or deity of the fates, *but* with
the steadfast irresponsible will and pleasure of the fates]. (*d*),
1. 137 : "meo sine *numine* " [*not* without my god-head, *but*
without my will and pleasure]. (*e*), 2. 777 :

. . . " non haec sine *numine* divum
eveniunt "

[*not* without the god-head of the gods, *but* without the will and
pleasure of the gods]. (*f*), 10. 31 :

" si sine pace tua atque invito *numine* Troes
Italiam petiere"

[*not* thy deity being unwilling, *but* thy free will and pleasure
being unwilling; that quality of thy mind which assents or
dissents being unwilling: in other words, against thy will].
(*g*), 4. 269 :

. . . " caelum et terras qui *numine* torquet"

[*not* turns with his god-head, *but* turns with his will and pleasure—his free, irresponsible, absolute will and pleasure]. (*h*),

2. 703 : "vestroque in *numine* Troia est" (where "vestro numine" corresponds exactly to NUMINE NOSTRO of our text, and the sense is : Troy is in your pleasure, *i. e.*, is at your disposal, is in your hands to do with it as it seems to you proper). (*i*), Manil. 4. 56 :

"quis tantum mutare potest sine *numine* fati?"

not without the deity or divinity of fate, *but* without the will and pleasure of fate]. (*j*), and especially Ovid, *Met*. 10. 689 Venus relating the story of Hippomenes and Atalanta):

"illic concubitus intempestiva cupido
occupat Hippomenen, a *numine* concita nostro"

where we have the identical expression of our text, and where the meaning can only be *our will and pleasure*). (*k*), 7. 583 :

. . . "cuncti contra omina bellum,
contra fata deum, perverso *numine* poscunt"

(where the commentators, making the same mistake as in our text, understand "numine" to mean the deity, the godhead, but where it is all the while the will and pleasure of the "cuncti," and where the sense is not with Wagner (1861) : "quasi pervertentes, susque deque habentes, imperium deorum," but *perverso arbitrio*, with a perverse will and pleasure of their own). (*l*), 9. 661 :

. . . "avidum pugnae dictis et *numine* Phoebi
Ascanium prohibent"

[*not* with the deity of Phoebus, *but* with the will and pleasure of Phoebus—represent to Ascanius, that it is Phoebus's will and pleasure that he should not fight]. (*m*), 9. 247 :

"dii patrii quorum semper sub *numine* Troia est"

[under whose will and pleasure Troy always is, *i. e.*, to whose will and pleasure Troy always submits, by whose will and pleasure Troy is always guided]. (*n*), 2. 123 : "quae sint ea *numina* divum flagitat" [*not* what divinities of gods are those? *but* what will and pleasure of the gods is that? what is the meaning of that declaration of the gods' will and pleasure?]. (*o*), 3. 362 :

> . . . " namque omnem cursum mihi prospera dixit
> religio, et cuncti suaserunt *numine* divi
> Italiam petere"

[*not* the gods persuaded with their divinity, *but* the gods persuaded with their will and pleasure, *i. e.*, by the expression of their will and pleasure—the latter clause being a variation of the first, and the meaning of the two clauses together being : the gods declared by their omens and oracles it was their will and pleasure I should undertake this journey, and promised it should be prosperous]. (***p***), 3. 359 :

> . . . " qui *numina* Phoebi
> qui tripodas, Clarii laurus, qui sidera sentis"

[who understands, *not* the divinity of Phoebus, *but* the will and pleasure of Phoebus]. (***q***), 8. 78 :

> " adsis o tandem, et propius tua *numina* firmes"

[confirm, *not* thy godhead, *but* thy will and pleasure, *i. e.*, this expression of thy will and pleasure]. (***r***), 11. 901 : " saeva Iovis sic *numina* poscunt" [*not* the stern divinity of Jove, *but* the stern will and pleasure of Jove]. (***s***), Lucr. 5. 307 :

> " denique, non lapides quoque vinci cernis ab aevo ?
> non altas turres ruere, et putrescere saxa ?
> non delubra deum simulacraque fessa fatisci ?
> nec sanctum *numen* fati protollere fineis
> posse, neque adversus naturae foedera niti"

(where the material " delubra" and " simulacra" of the gods (" deum") are distinguished from the immaterial " numen" of the gods ; and where the meaning is not that the deity of the gods could not shove forward the limits fixed by fate, but that the willing faculty of the gods could not, however much it might desire). (***t***), Lucr. 2. 611 :

> " hanc [Terram] variae gentes, antiquo more sacrorum,
> Idaeam vocitant Matrem ; Phrygiasque catervas
> dant comites, quia primum ex illis finibus edunt
> per terrarum orbeis fruges coepisse creari.
> Gallos attribuunt ; quia *numen* quei violarint
> matris et ingratei genitoribus inventei sint
> significare volunt indignos esse putandos,
> vivam progeniem quei in oras luminis edant"

[*not* the divinity of their mother, *but* the will and pleasure of their mother, that will and pleasure entitled to so much respect]. (***u***), Cic. *de Nat. Deor.* 1. ? : "Haec enim omnia pure atque caste tribuenda deorum *numini* ita sunt, si animadvertuntur [taken notice of, noticed] ab his, et si est aliquid a diis immortalibus hominum generi tributum" [*not* to the deity of the gods, *but* to the self-originating will and pleasure of the gods]. (***v***), Cic. *Orat. de. Harusp. Responsis*, 9 : "quis est tam vecors, qui . . . quum deos esse intellexerit, non intelligat, eorum *numine* hoc tantum imperium esse natum, et auctum, et retentum?" [*not* by their deity, *but* by their self-originating absolute will and pleasure]. (***w***), Manil. 1. 483:

" ac mihi tam praesens ratio non ulla videtur,
qua pateat mundum divino *numine* verti
atque ipsum esse deum, nec forte coisse magistra"

[*not* the world moves with a divine deity, and is god, *but* moves with a divine will and pleasure, and is god]. (***x***), Manil. 1. 531 :

" non casus opus est, magni sed *numinis* ordo"

[*surely not*, is not the work of chance, but the arrangement of a great divinity (for the doctrine of the creation of the world by a divinity was not the doctrine of Manilius who was an Epicurean), *but* is not a work of chance, but an order or system instinct with a great will and pleasure: precisely the Epicurean doctrine, and the doctrine of Manilius—see preceding quotation]. **And** (***y***), Hygin. *Fab. 187 :* " Quem [Hippothoum] iterum equa nutriebat pastores iterum inventum infantem sustulerunt, sentientes eum deorum *numine* educari, atque nutrierunt" [by the high will, sanction, pleasure, ordinance, *placitum*, of the gods].

It is no m an recommendation of this interpretation of our text that it is not liable to the objection which has been very reasonably urged to every other interpretation of the passage yet offered, viz., that it forestalls and thereby weakens

HEU, NIHIL INVITIS FAS QUEMQUAM FIDERE DIVIS!

which comes better on the reader suddenly and by surprise. Besides all which, the going of the Trojans not under the direction of their own will, or to a determinate point, but at random as it were, and wherever the Greeks happened to go, harmonizes as well with CAECAM CONGRESSI PER NOCTEM in the next line (*meeting by chance in the darkness of the night*) as it contrasts well with verse 437 :

"protinus ad sedes Priami clamore vocati."

See Rem. on 1. 12 (*a*).

398-419.

MULTOS—FUNDO

MULTOS DANAUM DEMITTIMUS ORCO.—*Down* being an essential inseparable part of the notion expressed by demittere, the likeness between our author's DEMITTIMUS ORCO and Homer's Ἄϊδι προΐαψεν with which it has been compared by Heyne (followed by Wagner on 8. 566) is sufficiently distant. On this occasion, at least, our author has chosen better than to imitate, the notion of *down* expressed by his DE being much more graphic than that of *forward* or *before* expressed by Homer's προ. Had Virgil aimed to imitate he could very easily have said praemittimus, though he could not have said promittimus, being prevented by the special Latin signification of that word.

CONDUNTUR.—Condere is (strictly) not merely *to hide*, but, the force of dare being preserved in its compound (see Rem. on *Aen. 1. 56), to put or plunge into a place so as to hide*. Hence it is sometimes even joined with a preposition governing the accusative, as *Georg. 1. 438 :*

"sol quoque et exoriens, et cum se condet in undas."

Senec. *Ep. 7 :* "Ista, mi Lucili, *condenda* in animum sunt, ut contemnas voluptatem ex plurium assensione venientem."

HEU.—Wagner commences a new paragraph with this word, Heyne with ECCE in the next line, both I think erroneously, this line being intimately connected both with the preceding and succeeding. The train is : "but all this success was soon to end, the gods being against us; for see where Cassandra," &c.

INVITIS DIVIS = the Homeric θεων αεκητι.

LUMINA, NAM TENERAS ARCEBANT VINCULA PALMAS.—Heyne says: "Ovidiano lusui propior est; Ovidius tamen castior nunc ipso Virgilio, *Met. 13. 410 :*

   . . . ' tractata comis antistita Phoebi
   non profecturas tendebat ad aethera palmas.' "

How different the judgments of men! To me, Virgil is here not only quite as chaste as Ovid, but twice as graphic: Ovid omitting that all-important part in a picture, the countenance: Virgil painting both the supplicating eyes, strained towards heaven, and the hands prevented by bonds from joining in the supplication. There is or should be more or less "lusus" in all poetry. If it be true that Ovid's has too much of it, it is no less true that Virgil's has hardly enough. Virgil is, perhaps, as much too severe as Ovid is too playful. Who shall hit the just mean ? Of all charges levity is the last that should be brought against Virgil. In the present instance, if he be light, he has the levity of Euripides to countenance him, *Androm. 573 :*

αλλ' αντιαζω σ', ω γερον, των σων παρος
πιτνουσα γονατων, χειρι δ' ουκ εξεστι μοι
της σης λαβεσθαι φιλτατης γενειαδος,

as well as that of St. Jerome in his marvellous "Mulier septies percussa" (*Epist. 1, ad Innocent.* § 3) : " Oculis, quos tantum tortor alligare non poterat, suspexit ad caelum "—an expression of the thought, by-the-by, as incorrect as Virgil's is correct, for nothing was easier for the executioner than to bind the culprit's eyes, viz., with a bandage. Nor if Ovid abstained from the "lusus" in the case of Cassandra, did he always abstain from it. He would not have been Ovid if he had—the happy, gay, playful, captivating Ovid of the *Metamorphoses* and the *Amores*. It was quite too tempting, and he yielded to the temptation—let Heyne frown and shake his head as he will, I only clap my hands the harder, and cry " bravo !" the louder—yielded to the temptation once, twice, three times, for aught I know to the contrary; once, at all events, in the case of Io (*Met. 1. 731*):

"quos potuit solos tollens ad sidera vultus;"

and a second time in that of Andromeda (*Ibid. 4. 681*) :

. . . "manibusque modestos
celasset vultus, si non religata fuisset.
lumina, quod potuit, lacrimis implevit obortis"

—examples which have not failed to draw their imitators after them. See Victor Hugo, *Notre Dame de Paris*, 8. 6 (of Esmeralda): "'Phoebus'! s'ecria-t-elle, 'mon Phoebus!' Et elle voulut tendre vers lui ses bras tremblants d' amour et de ravissement, mais *ils étaient attachés.*"

ARCEBANT VINCULA.—The translators understand these words to be equivalent to "vincula ligabant," and to mean no more than that *chains bound her hands :*

"her eyes, for fast her tender wrists were bound." Surrey.

"rude fetters bound her tender hands." Beresford.

"che indegni lacci alla regal donzella
ambe avvincon le mani." Alfieri.

On the contrary, the idea of binding does not extend beyond the word VINCULA; and ARCEBANT has its own proper force of *hindering, keeping away :* bonds (VINCULA) *hindered, kept off* (ARCEBANT) her hands, viz., so that she could not extend them towards heaven.

DENSIS INCURRIMUS ARMIS.—"Κατασκευη : merito superati sunt a pluribus," Servius. "*Vel* ipsi densis ordinibus, denso agmine, *vel* irruimus in hostium densum agmen," Heyne. "DENSIS quia ipsi densi conferti, vs. 347, incurrunt," Wagner (*Praest.*). "Sie drängen sich in die den Coroebus bereits dicht umgebenden waffen," Kappes. How are we to decide the case. Servius and Kappes on one side, Voss and Wagner on the other. Heyne divided between, and grammar for both? By the context, and very easily. The words are in the ablative, the *dense arms* those of Aeneas and his party, first, because the party has been already twice described as dense—verse 346 :

"quos ubi *confertos* audere in praelia vidi;"

verse 383 :

" irruimus, *densis* et circumfundimur armis"—

the latter being manifestly our text in a very slightly changed form, and permitting, no doubt, of its " densis armis" being the ablative case and the arms of Aeneas and his party. Secondly, on account of the not very dissimilar " irruimus ferro" of 3. 322, where there can be no doubt of " ferro " being in the ablative. And, finally, on account of the CONSEQUIMUR CUNCTI of the beginning of the verse, words which set before us a numerous united body (see Rem. on " contorsit," 2. 52), and prepare us for DENSIS ARMIS, the arms of Aeneas's party who could not be CUNCTI and con-sequentes unless they were dense.

TUM DANAI GEMITU ATQUE EREPTAE VIRGINIS IRA.—Heyne's interpretation, " IRA propter ereptam virginem," is proved to be correct, **not only** by the appropriate sense which it affords, and our author's use elsewhere of a similar structure, *ex. gr.*, " mortis fraternae ira," *Aen.* 9. 736; " ira irritata deorum," *Aen. 4. 178;* GRAIARUM ERRORE IUBARUM, verse 412, above; " veterum errore locorum," 3. 181 ; " ereptae amore coniugis," 3.330 ; also " lacrymae rerum," 1.466; and " lacrymas Creusae," 2. 784; **but** by Livy's (5. 33) exactly parallel : " Aruntem Clusinum ira corruptae uxoris ab Lucumone," and (1. 5) " ob iram praedae amissae," and (8. 24) " ultra humanarum irarum fidem." Compare, also, Ovid, *Met. 9. 101* (of the passion of Nessus for Dejanira) : " eiusdem virginis ardor." Silius, 5. 344 :

" advolat interea *fraterni vulneris ira*
turbatus Libyae ductor."

Also the title by which Langland's poem is generally known, viz., *Piers Plowman's Vision,* or *Vision of Piers Plowman*, equivalent not to " Vision seen by Piers Plowman," but " Vision concerning Piers Plowman, Vision in which Piers Plowman appeared."

GEMITU.—" Dolore," Heyne. No, but *a loud roar*, or *groan*. Compare *Aen. 2. 53 ; 3. 555;* and especially 7. 15, where gemi- tus and ira are again united (" gemitus iraeque " : that angry roaring, that loud groaning or roaring which is the consequence of anger).

ADVERSI ... FUNDO (vv. 416-419). Compare Aesch. *Prom.
Vinct. 1080*, ed. Blomfield (Prometheus speaking):

> . . . αιθηρ δ'
> ερεθιζεσθω βροντη σφακελω τ'
> αγριων ανεμων· χθονα δ' εκ πυθμενων
> αυταις ριζαις πνευμα κραδαινοι,
> κυμα δε ποντου τραχει ροθιω
> ξυγχωσειεν, των τ' ουρανιων
> αστρων διοδους.

Dante, *Inferno*, 5. 29:

> "che mugghia, come fa mar per tempesta,
> se da contrari venti e combattuto."

Also Sir Walter Scott, in his fine lyric the "Pibroch of Donald Dhu:"

> "come as the winds come
> when forests are rended,
> come as the waves come
> when navies are stranded."

LAETUS EOIS EURUS EQUIS.—Wagner (1861) says: "equos tribuunt ventis etiam Hor. *Od. 4. 4. 44*

> [' ceu flamma per taedas, vel Eurus
> per Siculas *equitavit* undas'].

et Val. Flacc. 1. 608

> [' dixerat [Boreas]; at cuncti fremere intus et aequora venti
> poscere: tum valido contortam turbine portam
> impulit Hippotades: fundunt se carcere laeti
> Thraces *equi*, Zephyrusque, et nocti concolor alas
> nimborum cum prole Notus, crinemque procellis
> hispidus, et multa flavus caput Eurus arena:
> induxere hiemem; raucoque ad littora tractu
> unanimi freta curva ferunt, nec soli tridentis
> regna movent; vasto pariter ruit igneus aether
> cum tonitru, piceoque premit nox omnia caelo']."

This is to take our author, as usual, too literally, and not merely our author, but Horace, and Valerius Flaccus. Neither our author nor Horace means that Eurus actually rides over the sea, gallops over the sea on horseback; both Virgil's EOIS LAETUS EQUIS, and Horace's "equitavit," and Valerius Flaccus's "fundunt se carcere laeti Thraces equi," are but various translations of the Greek ιππευειν applied by Greek poets to the winds, and meaning not *ride*, but *gallop like a horse, go galloping*. Compare Eurip. *Phoen.* 210:

> . . . περιρρυτων
> υπερ ακαρπιστων πεδιων
> Σικελιας Ζεφυρου πνοαις
> ιππευσαντος εν ουρανω
> καλλιστον κελαδημα,

where the scholiast: Ζεφυρου σφοδρως πνευσαντος.

SAEVITQUE TRIDENTI SPUMEUS ATQUE IMO NEREUS CIET AEQUORA FUNDO.—The structure is not SPUMEUS NEREUS SAEVIT TRIDENTI, but NEREUS SAEVIT TRIDENTI SPUMEUS; and the meaning is, *produces a great deal of froth in the operation of stirring up the sea from the bottom with his trident*. Compare *Aen.* 11. 624:

> " qualis ubi alterno procurrens gurgite pontus
> nunc ruit ad terras, scopulosque superiacit undam
> *spumeus*, extremamque sinu perfundit arenam ;"

where, as in our text, "spumeus" is placed in the emphatic position, and separated, by a pause, from the sequel. See Rem. on 2. 247.

SAEVIT TRIDENTI.—The trident was used for stirring up the sea, and was laid aside when the waves were to be calmed, Ovid, *Met.* 1. 330:

> . . . " positoque tricuspide telo
> mulcet aquas rector pelagi."

422-425.

ILLI ETIAM SI QUOS OBSCURA NOCTE PER UMBRAM
FUDIMUS INSIDIIS TOTAQUE AGITAVIMUS URBE
APPARENT PRIMI CLIPEOS MENTITAQUE TELA
AGNOSCUNT ATQUE ORA SONO DISCORDIA SIGNANT

VAR. LECT.

PRIAMI CL. **I** *Pal.* (the A very indistinct and hardly traceable, still however traceable, not as marked by Ribbeck wholly untraceable, and only to be guessed). The actual reading of the MS. is RIAMI, the P and all the preceding part of the line having been torn or eaten away. **III** Ribb.

[*punct.*] APPARENT &c., without punct. **III** Ven. 1475.

[*punct.*] APPARENT PRIMI . CL. **I** "In codd. aliquot antiquis, eodem membro legas ADPARENT PRIMI disiunctim ; inde, CLIPEOS MENTITAQUE TELA ADNOSCUNT," Pierius. **III** Ven. 1471.

[*punct.*] APPARENT . PRIMI CL. **I** *Med.* **III** Donat.; P. Manut.; D. Heins.; N. Heins.; Philippe; Haupt; Wagner (*Praest.*).

[*punct.*] APPARENT; PRIAMI CL. **III** Ribb.

Donatus is right. PRIMI belongs to AGNOSCUNT not to APPARENT (1), because APPARENT must not lose its emphasis (see Rem. on 2. 247); and (2), because (as shown by ETIAM, verse 420), not the ILLI QUOS, &c., but the DANAI (verse 413), were the first to show themselves.

APPARENT, *show themselves, let themselves be seen, no longer hide.* Compare Ammian. 29. 5: "excubiasque agens cura pervigili, barbarorum aliquos ausos, cum *adparere* non possent, post occasum lunae castra sua tentare, fudit, vel irruentes audentius cepit." Apparere is exactly the Greek φαινεσθαι, to appear, show one's self, present one's self, as Hom. *Il. 10. 235* (Agamemnon exhorting Tydides to choose the best comrade, not the noblest):

τον μεν δη εταρον γ' αιρησεαι, ον κ' εθελησθα,
φαινομενων τον αριστον, επει μεμαασι γε πολλοι

[the best man of those who present themselves].

11*

CLIPEOS MENTITAQUE TELA AGNOSCUNT.—Not *recognise our shields and weapons to be false*, but *recognise our (false) shields and weapons to be the shields and weapons of their friends*. Agnoscere is always *to recognise, to acknowledge as an old acquaintance*. The discovery that the shields and weapons are false, *i.e.*, carried by Trojans, is made only on observing that the voices of those who bear the weapons are not Greek.

CLIPEOS MENTITAQUE TELA = mentitos clipeos et mentita tela. MENTITA = false, *i.e.*, which professed to be carried by Greeks, but were in reality carried by Trojans, as *Epit. Iliados, 830* (of Patroclus clad in the armour of Achilles):

   . . . " donec Troianus Apollo
   mentitos vultus simulati pandit Achillis,
   denudatque virum."

ORA SONO DISCORDIA.—*Our mouths in sound*, i.e., *the sound of our mouths, our voices or accent, disagreeing with our assumed weapons*. Heyne's gloss, "discrepantiam sermonis," is erroneous, and Wunderlich's whole disquisition, "Troianorum linguam a lingua Graecorum diversam," &c., to no purpose. The Greeks do not hear the language spoken by the disguised Trojans, only their sonus oris, *the sound of their mouth*, and that sound of their mouth (sonus oris, *voice*) does not agree with their appearance—"klingt fremd." Os is the mouth (*i.e.*, the speech, sermo, lingua, as, 12. 837, "omnes uno ore Latinos"); sonus, the sound of that mouth, the voice, as Ovid, *Fast. 4. 57:*

   " carmina mortali non referenda *sono*."

Compare, also, Sen. *Oed. 1019* (Oedipus hearing his mother's voice):

   . " quis frui et tenebris vetat ?
   quis reddit oculos ? matris, heu, matris *sonus*."

Sen. *Herc. Oet. 1130:* "est, est Herculeus *sonus*" [it is the voice of Hercules]. Ovid, *Met. 12. 203* (of Caenis undergoing metamorphosis):

   . . . " graviore novissima dixit
   verba *sono;* poteratque viri vox illa videri ;
   sicut erat."

Ovid, *Trist. 5. 7. 51:*

"in paucis remanent Graiae vestigia linguae;
haec quoque iam Getico barbara facta *sono*"

[the Greek language rendered barbarous by the Getic accent, voice, or sound of the speakers]. And especially Ennius (ed. Hessel), p. 40:

"ollei respondet suavis *sonus* Egeriai"

[the sweet sound of Egeria, *i.e.*, the sweet sound of Egeria's voice, Egeria's sweet voice].

Exactly as in our text ORA is the mouth and SONO the sound of the mouth, "os sonaturum," Hor. *Sat. 1. 4. 43,* is the mouth about to sound:

"ingenium cui sit, cui mens divinior atque os
magna *sonaturum*, des nominis huius honorem."

431-437.

ILIACI CINERES ET FLAMMA EXTREMA MEORUM
TESTOR IN OCCASU VESTRO NEC TELA NEC ULLAS
VITAVISSE VICES DANAUM ET SI FATA FUISSENT
UT CADEREM MERUISSE MANU DIVELLIMUR INDE
IPHITUS ET PELIAS MECUM QUORUM IPHITUS AEVO
IAM GRAVIOR PELIAS ET VULNERE TARDUS ULIXI
PROTINUS AD SEDES PRIAMI CLAMORE VOCATI

VAR. LECT.

[*punct.*] VICES DANAUM **I** *Med.* **III** P. Manut.; D. Heins.; N. Heins. (1670); Philippe; Heyne; Brunck; Wakef.; Wagner (ed. Heyn., *Lect. Virg.*, ed. 1861).

[*punct.*] VICES; DANAUM **III** Dietsch (*Theolog*, p. 22); Heyne (in nota); Peerlkamp; Ladewig; Haupt; Ribb.

VAR. LECT.

[*punct.*]   DIVELLIMUR INDE
IPHITUS, ET PELIAS MECUM : QUORUM IPHITUS AEVO
IAM GRAVIOR, PELIAS ET VULNERE TARDUS ULYSSI.

III P. Manut.

[*punct.*]   DIVELLIMUR INDE,
IPHITUS ET PELIAS MECUM (QUORUM . . .
, ... ULYSSI)
PROTINUS . . . . VOCATI.

III Heumann; Burmann; Voss.

[*punct.*]   DIVELLIMUR INDE
IPHITUS ET PELIAS MECUM (QUORUM IPHITUS AEVO
. . . . ULIXI),
PROTINUS . . . . VOCATI.

III Ribbeck.

[*punct.*]   DIVELLIMUR INDE
IPHITUS, ET PELIAS MECUM ; QUORUM IPHITUS AEVO
IAM GRAVIOR, PELIAS ET VULNERE TARDUS ULYSSEI ;
PROTINUS . . . . VOCATI.

III D. Heins.; N. Heins. (omitting however the comma after IPHITUS).

[*punct.*]   DIVELLIMUR INDE:
IPHITUS ET PELIAS MECUM ; QUORUM IPHITUS AEVO
IAM GRAVIOR, PELIAS ET VULNERE TARDUS ULIXI ;
PROTINUS . . . . VOCATI.

III Heyne; Wagner (ed. Heyn., and ed. 1861).

"ILIACI CINERES ex loquendi usu ad Ilium in cineres versum ducunt: tum: ' et vos, *o mei,* quibus incendium urbis pro rogo fuit ' . . . est tamen usui magis consentaneum *flammam extremam meorum* de rogo et funere, seu morte, accipere . . . Testatur igitur funus patriae et funera suorum," Heyne. But which of our author's readers will readily agree that of CINERES and FLAMMA occurring in one and the same verse, not only in immediate propinquity to each other, but actually connected together by the copulative ET (CINERES ET FLAMMA), the CINERES has nothing at all to do with the FLAMMA, the FLAMMA nothing at all to do with the CINERES? Who is there does not see—should not, at a single glance, see—that CINERES and FLAMMA belong to the same fire? So La Cerda saw, and interpreted " extinctam patriam testatur, conversamque in cineres; tum etiam exitialem illam flammam, qua Troia arsit," taking no notice of MEORUM, of which Ladewig, Weidner, Kappes, and Conington, taking insufficient notice, understand CINERES to be the ashes of Ilium, FLAMMA the flame which not only produced those ashes, but served at the same time as the pyre-flame (FLAMMA EXTREMA) of Aeneas's friends and companions in arms MEORUM) ["Da *ignis supremus* und *tori supremi* vom scheiterhaufen, *suprema officia, supremi tituli, supremi honores* von der bestattung gebraucht wurde, EXTREMA FLAMMA an unserer stelle gewiss für *suprema flamma* steht; so hat Ladewig wohl recht, wenn er erklärt: 'Es deuten diese worte auf den brand Troia's hin, insofern er den leichen die stelle des scheiterhaufens vertreten musste,'" Weidner. "In der engen verbindung mit ILIACI CINERES wird die EXTREMA FLAMMA auf den brand der stadt zu beziehen sein, welcher gleichsam 'pro rogo' war," Kappes. "FLAMMA EXTREMA MEORUM is parallel to ILIACI CINERES, as the flames of Troy were the funeral flames of Aeneas's countrymen and friends," Conington]—an analysis **which,** although so much more conformable than either Heyne's or La Cerda's to the usual structure of our author's verses, although presenting Troy to us under the so familiar aspect of grave of its own children (compare Catull. 68. 93:

"Troia (nefas!), commune *sepulchrum* Asiae Europaeque;
Troia, virum et virtutum omnium acerba cinis."

Senec. *Troad.* 55 :

" caret *sepulchro* Priamus et flamma indiget
ardente Troia."

Senec. *Agam.* 741 (Cassandra apostrophizing the ghosts of her slaughtered relatives):

" quid me vocatis sospitem solam e meis,
umbrae meorum? te sequor, tota pater
Troia *sepulte*."

Sen. *Troad. 28* (Hecuba speaking):

" testor deorum numen aversum mihi,
patriaeque cineres teque rectorem Phrygum
quem Troia toto *conditum* regno *tegit*,
tuosque manes."

Manil. 4. 64:

" inque rogo Croesum, Priamumque in littore truncum,
cui nec Troia *rogus*"),

is still not the true analysis, lays quite too little stress on MEORUM, the index to the whole passage, the key of the lock. It is not the FLAMMA EXTREMA only which belongs to Aeneas's " mei "; the CINERES also are theirs, not indeed in the grammar but in the sense, the MEORUM of the second clause being the ILIACI of the first, the ILIACI of the first the MEORUM of the second, and ILIACI CINERES ET FLAMMA EXTREMA MEORUM being the exact equivalent of *meorum cineres et flamma extrema Iliacorum* or *cineres et flamma extrema meorum Iliacorum*; all mere expansions—the original one, for the sake of filling up the verse (see below)—of the rudimental thought: dead companions in arms. It is as if Aeneas had said: " O ye Ilian companions in arms who are now but dust and ashes, I swear by you and by the flame of your funeral pyres, that when ye fell (IN OCCASU VESTRO) I shunned not," &c. There is thus but one flame spoken of, the flame of the funeral pyre; but one ashes spoken of, the ashes of Aeneas's fallen companions in arms; and instead of the connexion by the copula ET of the two incongruous conceptions *ashes of Ilium, pyre-flame of friends*, we have the blending by means of that copula of the two cognate conceptions, *ashes of Ilian citizens, pyre-flame of friends*, into the single conception, *pyre of Ilian friends*.

This analysis and interpretation is borne out (**1**), by our author's habit of dividing a compound thesis into two or more simple theses (see Rem. on " quem si fata virum servant," 1. 550, and on " progeniem sed enim," 1. 23–26). (**2**), by the immediately preceding context. Aeneas has just been narrating the deaths of his comrades one after the other. Choroebus, Ripheus, Hypanis, Dymas, Pantheus, have all fallen; with what adjuration could he so well satisfy his hearers that his own survival was not due to a cowardly flight as by that of the only witnesses of his fallen companions in arms? Was not such adjuration both much nearer and much more solemn than any adjuration of the burnt city? Was it not precisely to their fallen companions in arms both the Maeon of Statius and Silius's son of Regulus—each a sole survivor when all his companions in arms had fallen—appealed for testimony that they had courted death no less than those who fell, and that if they survived they survived only because the fates had decreed their survival? [Stat. *Theb. 3. 62:*

> . . . . " vix credo et nuntius, omnes
> procubuere, omnes : noctis vaga lumina testor,
> et *socium Manes*, et te mala protinus ales
> qua redeo, non hanc lacrymis meruisse, nec astu
> crudelem veniam, atque inhonorae munera lucis.
> sed mihi iussa deum, placitoque ignara moveri
> Atropos, atque olim non haec data ianua leti,
> eripuere necem."

Sil. 6. 113 :

> . . . . " testor mea numina, *Manes*,
> dignam me poenao tum nobilitate paternae
> strage hostis quaesisse necem, ni tristia letum,
> ut quondam patri, nobis quoque fata negassent,"

with which compare Quinct. *Decl. 12. 2:* " ignoscite tamen, violati *manes meorum*"]. And what reason can be assigned why Virgil, intending Aeneas to apostrophize in the first clause of the passage not his deceased friends and companions in arms but the burnt city, should use the—to say the least of it in so close connexion with FLAMMA EXTREMA MEORUM—very ambiguous term CINERES, and not the equally obvious, even more parallel to FLAMMA, wholly unambiguous, *ignes?* The above view is also supported (**3**), by the so frequent application of the terms cinis and cineres (*dust* and *ashes*) not merely to dead persons whose bodies have been actually reduced whether by fire or slow decay to dust and ashes, but to persons recently dead and who are only figuratively dust and ashes, as 6. 212 :

> " nec minus interea Misenum in littore Teucri
> flebant, et *cineri* ingrato suprema ferebant."

Sil. 13. 469 (ed. Rup.):

> . . . " variatque iacentum
> exequias tumuli et *cinerum* sententia discors"

[*of the tumulus and the dead*]. (**4**), by the no less frequent use of Iliacus to express belonging or in any way appertaining to Ilium, than to express forming an integrant part of or resulting from Ilium, as Sil. 15. 281:

> . . . " tibi barbara soli
> sanctius *Iliaca* servata est Phoebade virgo"

[*Ilian priestess of Apollo*]. Stat. Silv. 4. 2. 10:

> . . . " mediis videor discumbere in astris
> cum Iove, et *Iliaca* porrectum sumere dextra
> immortale merum"

[*Ilian right hand*]. (**5**), by the so much easier, simpler, and more natural reference in VESTRO to the single category of witnesses, Aeneas's fallen companions in arms, than to the dissimilar categories, the burnt city, and Aeneas's fallen companions in arms. **And** (**6**), by the application of occasus to person no less than to thing, as Cicero, *Acad. post.* 8 (ed. Orelli): "post L. Aelii nostri occasum."

To this analysis and interpretation, if anyone object with Voss: " Wer denn gab den gefallenen ein ordentliches leichenbegängniss?" I beg to refer to 6. 505, where Aeneas informs the shade of Deiphobus that after that fatal night he had searched in vain for the body of Deiphobus in order to bestow on it the usual funeral honours, and being unable to find it had erected a cenotaph to the memory of the deceased, and where the shade of Deiphobus replies:

> . . . " nil o tibi, amice, relictum ;
> omnia Deiphobo solvisti, et funeris umbris."

And, indeed, Aeneas and the other surviving Trojans having, after the burning of the city, remained long enough in the neighbourhood to build and man and equip a fleet (3. 5:

> . . . " classemque sub ipsa
> Antandro, et Phrygiae molimur montibus Idae ;
> . . . .
> contrahimusque viros")

what difficulty was there in the way of their performing that duty which in the ancient systems of morals and religion held a place second only to that of returning thanks to the gods for personal safety and preservation, viz., the duty of decently disposing of the remains of less fortunate friends and relatives ? (see 11. 1 :

> " Aeneas, quanquam et sociis dare tempus humandis
> praecipitant curae, turbataque funere mens est,
> vota deum primo victor solvebat Eoo").

What can be more certain than that after respects paid to the gods—respects which, on an occasion on which the gods had done so very little for and so very much against them (2. 610-618 , need not, one would think, have been either very cumbrous or very formal—their next and most pressing care was to perform that duty ? what more probable than that that duty was, as far as the circumstances of the case allowed, piously and scrupulously performed ? what more natural than that the very person on whom that duty had principally devolved, the very person who was so celebrated for his pious performance of such duties, " pious " Aeneas, should in a *résumé*—years after and in a foreign country, and before an audience of strangers—of all that had occurred, let it plainly appear, that neither had that so indispensable, so imperative, duty been neglected? And finally, how was it possible to make less parade of the due discharge of the incumbent obligation than is made of it in the apostrophe to the friends who had perished, and whose bodies he had burned on the funeral pyre, to testify for him that if he was still alive it was not that he had not exposed himself to danger as they had, but solely because it was the will of fate to preserve him ?

For the illustration of the text see also at verse 587 of this book the immediate connexion of " cineres " and " meorum " in the identical sense (viz., that of *dead friends*) afforded by the same two words so widely separated and without any immediate connexion in our text.

VESTRO (verse 432), *your*; referring back, past FLAMMA EXTREMA MEORUM, to ILIACI CINERES : " O ye fallen companions in arms, who are now but Ilian dust and ashes, I call you to

witness that when ye fell I would have fallen too, had the fates
permitted," &c., FLAMMA EXTREMA MEORUM being but a dilatation of, a dwelling on, the thought ILIACI CINERES: "Ye friends
of mine (MEORUM) who have been reduced to ashes (ILIACI
CINERES) on your funeral pyres (FLAMMA EXTREMA)," exactly
as in Anna's address to Aeneas, Sil. 8. 81 :

> " nate dea, solus regni lucisque fuisti
> germanae tu causa meae; mors testis, et ille—
> heu, cur non idem mihi tunc!—rogus,"

" ille rogus," is but a dilatation of, a dwelling on, the thought
"mors" (equivalent to mortua Dido, and corresponding precisely to the ILIACI CINERES or *dead companions in arms* of our
text), and along with that theme-thought is invoked to testify
(" testis," the TESTOR of our text) that Aeneas was the sole
cause of Dido's death.

Awkward and perverse as is this construction, more awkward
and more perverse is the construction adopted by Heyne: "ashes
of Ilium ['asche der Ilierstadt,' Voss], pyre-flame of my friends"
(whether regarded as together forming the notion, *ashes of Ilium
and my friends*, or regarded as two separate and independent
notions, *ashes of Ilium, flame of the funeral pyre of my friends*),
for what fall (VESTRO OCCASU) had ever, or could by possibility
ever have had, either the ashes of Ilium or the flame of Aeneas's
friends' funeral pyre? More awkward and more perverse also
is La Cerda's "extinctam patriam testatur, conversamque in
cineres, tum etiam exitialem illam flammam qua Troia arsit,"
for what fall had ever, or could by possibility ever have had,
the conflagration which reduced Troy to ashes? Only in MEORUM
(see above) and the double sense of CINERES, a word equally
capable of signifying burnt ashes and the dead, is a clue to be
found to our author's meaning in this most awkward, perplexed,
and obscure passage—*O ye Ilian dead and reduced to ashes on the
pyre!*

ILIACI.—According to the above analysis the sense had
been not only fully but clearly and unequivocally expressed in
the words CINERES ET FLAMMA EXTREMA MEORUM (pyre-flame and
ashes of my friends = friends reduced to ashes on the pyre).

What occasion, then, for ILIACI? Were not the CINERES of
Aeneas's friends necessarily ILIACI CINERES? Certainly: and just
because they were, and because CINERES was meagre and bald
without a descriptive adjective to balance EXTREMA, the descriptive adjective of FLAMMA; and because the measure of the verse
was incomplete without, and complete with, the addition; and
because the sentiment expressed in CINERES ET FLAMMA EXTREMA
MEORUM, however pathetic, was pathetic only, not at all patriotic;
and because ILIACI as first word of the verse was both graphic
and fine-sounding, ILIACI was prefixed to CINERES with the un-
perceived, or, if perceived, disregarded effect of separating that
word from its explanatory MEORUM, and so leaving the reader
with the information, indeed, that the CINERES spoken of were
Ilian cineres, but without any information what kind of Ilian
cineres they were, whether ashes of Ilium ("asche der Ilierstadt," Voss), or ashes of Ilian men. Compare (3. 366) the
similar ornamental *ad captum vulgi* use made of the same
word, happily, however, without a similar ill effect:

" Pergamaque *Iliaca*mque iugis hanc addidit arcem,"

where "Iliacamque" is as supererogatory following "Pergama-
que," as ILIACI in our text is supererogatory preceding CINERES
ET FLAMMA EXTREMA MEORUM; and contrast Statius, *Theb.* 5. 454
(Hypsipyle speaking):

   . . . " *cinerem* furiasque meorum
testor, ut externas non sponte aut crimine taedas
attigerim,"

where " cinerem," not having been, like the CINERES of our text,
separated from its explanatory " meorum " in order to be joined
to an adjective and so form a clause of its own, is in no danger
either of being misunderstood itself or of leading to a misunder-
standing of " furias."

To make my meaning clearer I shall repeat in other words
the view I have just taken of the etiology of this verse. Had
Aeneas, like Macon and the son of Regulus, used the usual
apostrophe and addressed his deceased friends' Manes, there had
been no difficulty. But this is not what Virgil has chosen his
hero should do. He has chosen rather that Aeneas should in-

voke his deceased friends' CINERES and FLAMMA EXTREMA. Now, it was not Aeneas's deceased friends alone who had cineres and a flamma extrema; Ilium had them also, and it therefore became incumbent on Virgil well to distinguish which cineres and which flamma extrema he meant. This care was not taken; for, although MEORUM places it beyond doubt that the FLAMMA EXTREMA is the flamma not of the city but of the funeral pyres, yet MEORUM only comes to the rescue after the harm has been done, and the incautious reader has already understood ILIACI CINERES to be the ashes of Ilium, a meaning which until he comes to the word MEORUM he has as indisputable a right (and La Cerda and Heyne exercise the right even in defiance of MEORUM) to assign to the words, as that other meaning in which Virgil without, however, sufficiently indicating his intention, intended them to be taken. To be more explicit still: CINERES ET FLAMMA EXTREMA MEORUM had been subject to no ambiguity, had been clear as daylight, but had been, at the same time, too simple and inartificial a form of expression for our author, ambitious as he was to write Latin in a style in which Latin was never before written by anyone. The verse, besides, was incomplete, and required to be filled up and rounded. A clause, therefore, is, according to the author's usual fashion, made out of CINERES by the addition of ILIACI, and so the verse not merely completed, but rendered thoroughly Virgilian and rhetorical, each separate half balancing its pendant or opposite part, and even the words of which each separate half consists balancing those of the pendant or opposite part— ILIACI CINERES balancing both in sense and rhythm FLAMMA EXTREMA MEORUM; and FLAMMA EXTREMA MEORUM, in like manner, ILIACI CINERES; while even the separate word ILIACI balances MEORUM, and the separate word CINERES balances FLAMMA EXTREMA. The addition of the word ILIACI conciliating for the build of the verse these certainly not despicable advantages, and the word being in itself by no means trite or vulgar, but rather of the *élite*, and sounding sweetly besides, and so helping to take something from the ill effect of the three "literae latrantes" which follow ILIACI,—we need not be surprised to find an author, so little solicitous about perspicuity and so very solicitous about harmony and effect as our author on all occasions shows himself to be, assigning not merely a place in his verse, but the most honourable place of all, to a word which not only adds nothing to the sense—for who does not know without being told that the CINERES of Aeneas's MEORUM are Ilian? —but introduces so much ambiguity into the verse as to lead even La Cerda and Heyne astray, nay, so far astray that each of those commentators assigns to the verse a meaning as widely different from the meaning assigned to it by the other as it is from the right one. See Rem. on "sequar," 4. 384; and on " illius noctis," 361, *supra*.

NEC TELA NEC ULLAS VITAVISSE VICES DANAUM : " I did not shun to do, was not shy of doing, anything I could against the Danai through fear of anything the Danai might do to me in return." In other words: "I used my weapons, all my art, skill, and strength against the Danai, without regard to the consequences to myself; I did my worst against the Danai, not fearing their worst." That this is the precise and at the same time the full and complete meaning of the passage is shown by Silius's only too undisguised, too palpable imitation (6. 113):

    ". . . " testor, mea numina, Manes,
dignam me poenae tum nobilitate paternae
strage hostis quaesisse necem, ni tristia letum,
ut quondam patri, nobis quoque fata negassent,"

where " testor Manes me strage hostis quaesisse necem " is precisely the sentiment expressed in our text, viz., " TESTOR VOS ILIACI CINERES me non VITAVISSE sed MANU MERUISSE mortem." The parallelism of the two passages is perfect in every particular. Aeneas invokes the friends who had fallen beside him, to witness that he had not consulted his own safety, but on the contrary had dared and provoked the enemy to the utmost, and was only saved by its being the will of fate that he should not then die. Silius's hero invokes the Manes to witness that he had by slaughter of the enemy provoked an honourable death, and would certainly have perished had the fates not denied him that favour. It is impossible for parallel to be more perfect, or meaning more certain in both places. TESTOR corresponds to "testor;" ILIACI CINERES ET FLAMMA EXTREMA MEORUM, to "mea numina, Manes;" NON VITAVISSE, to "quaesisse;" TELA and ULLAS VICES DANAUM, to "neceem;" MERUISSE MANU, to "strage hostis;" SI FATA FUISSENT, to "ni fata negassent;" and CADEREM, to "letum."

The sentiment to which Aeneas gives utterance is exactly that which was to be expected from him under the circumstances. How was he to account for his own escape, for his being there alive, well and unhurt to tell the whole story to Dido at a great entertainment, over the bottle, as we say in English? The stratagem of putting on the armour of the Greeks slain by him and his little party had failed, and they were overwhelmed by infuriated numbers. Choroebus, Ripheus, Hypanis, Dymas, and Pantheus had just fallen at his side; how did he escape himself? Dido's eyes asked, and the eyes of the assembled company, did he run for it? He could not but explain, and what other explanation, unless he had brought his mother to his help, and she had to be reserved for a still more urgent, more extreme peril to come by-and-by? What other explanation was possible than that the fates would not permit it? On the one hand, there must be no hiding, no shrinking from danger on his part; there must, on the contrary, be daring, daring even to the death, to desperation : on the other hand, there must be no boasting, no "twenty men in buckram killed with his own hand." How was it possible to hit the *juste milieu* more precisely than with this solemn invocation of his deceased friends to bear witness that if he was still alive it was by no fault of his; that if he survived that fatal hour, it was not because he had shrunk from doing his duty, but because the fates had willed that he should not then die, had preserved him from the consequences of his reckless desperation, from the reprisals (VICES) of an enemy whom he had provoked to the last and utmost? Compare the case of Caesar—so far as meriting death (albeit in a different manner) the same as Aeneas's, but directly opposite to Aeneas's in so far as Caesar was awarded by the fates the death he merited—Lucan, 7. 594:

> ". . . 'humanum culmen, quo cuncta premuntur,
> egressus, meruit fatis tam nobile letum.'"

VICES.—Vicis, vicem, vice (to speak first of the word in the singular) is *part* (in the sense of *rôle*), *move*, *turn* (in the sense of the French *tour*). Compare (*a*), Ovid, *Art. Amat. 1. 370*:

> "ut puto, non poteris ipsa referre *vicem*"

["you will not be able of yourself to return him his move, to play the same part towards him which he has played to you"— the notion of reciprocity, retribution, or *talio* being wholly absent from "vicem" and contained solely in "referre"]. (*b*), Ovid, *ex Ponto, 2. 10. 49*:

> "hic es, et ignoras; et ades celeberrimus absens;
> inque Getas media visus ab Urbe venis.
> redde *vicem*; et quoniam regio felicior ista est,
> illic me memori pectore semper habe"

["return me my move, play the part towards me which I have played towards you"—the notion of reciprocity being contained not at all in "vicem" but wholly and solely in "redde"]. (*c*), Auson. *Gratiarum actio*, in initio: "Ago tibi gratias, Imperator Auguste; si possem, etiam referrem. Sed nec tua fortuna desiderat remunerandi *vicem*, nec nostra suggerit restituendi facultatem" (where again "vicem" is simply *turn*, *move*, *rôle*, or *part*, the notion of reciprocity or repayment being confined to "referrem," "remunerandi," and "restituendi"). (*d*), Catull. *Epith. Pel. et Thetid. 68* (of Ariadne):

> "sed neque tum mitrae, neque tum fluitantis amictus
> illa *vicem* curans, toto ex te pectore, Theseu,
> toto animo, tota pendebat perdita mente"

[not caring what "turn" might befal her cap and loose-flowing robe, *i.e.*, not caring what might happen to, what might become of, her cap and loose-flowing robe]. (*e*), Ovid, *Art. Amat. 3. 665*:

> "nec nimium vobis formosa ancilla ministret;
> saepe *vicem* dominae praestitit illa mihi"

[performed to me the *part* or *rôle* of the mistress]. (*f*), Cic.

ad Fam. 4. 5: "At illius [Tulliae] *vicem,* credo, doles" [the turn which awaits her, the turn she has to undergo]. (***g***), *Ibid. 11. 18:* "Valde et meam et vestram *vicem* timeam necesse est" [the turn both you and I have to undergo]—**the last three** being examples in which, notwithstanding the presence of "vicem" as in the preceding examples, there is yet, on account of the total absence from them of the "referre" and "reddere" of those examples, no notion not even the least of reciprocity, retribution, or *talio.*

As with the singular so with the plural term. As long as reddere, referre, or equivalent, is absent from the sentence, the notion of reciprocity, retribution, or *talio,* is no less absent, no matter how much vices may be present. Compare (***h***), Ovid, *Met. 1. 625:*

"centum luminibus cinctum caput Argus habebat:
inde suis *vicibus* capiebant bina quietem,
cetera servabant, atque in statione manebant"

["rested in their turns, each pair in its turn"—no notion of reciprocity, retribution, or *talio,* there being no reddere, referre, or equivalent]. (***i***), Ovid, *Met. 15. 237:*

"haec quoque non perstant quae nos elementa vocamus:
quasque *vices* peragant (animos adhibete) docebo"

["what parts they perform"—no notion of reciprocity, retribution, or equivalent]. (***j***), *Culex, 208:*

. . . . "quis meritis, ad quae delatus acerbas
cogor adire *vices*"

["to accost bitter parts, to address myself to bitter performances, actions, roles, moves"—still no reciprocity, no retribution, no *talio*]. (***k***), Quint. Curt. 5. 24: "nec immerito mitiores *vices* eius [Fortunae] expecto" [milder turns of Fortune than her previous]. (***l***), Stat. *Silv. 5. 2. 152:*

"felix, qui viridi fi.lens coeptaque iuventa
durabis quascunque *vices*"

[will endure any turns whatever], **while** the notion of reciprocity, the reciprocal or retributive "turn" makes its appearance the moment **referre**, **reddere**, or equivalent, enters into the composition of the sentence, as (***m***), Ovid, *Met. 14. 35 :*

> . . . " spernentem sperne ; sequenti
> *redde vices*"

[serve your pursuer with similar turn, *i. e.*, pursue her who pursues you]. (***n***), Prop. 4. 4. 57 (ed. Hertzb.) :

> " si minus, at raptae ne sint impune Sabinae :
> me rape, et alterna lege *repende vices*"

[repay turns according to the *lex talionis*]. (***o***), Claud. *Rapt. Pros. 1.* p. 198 (the fates addressing Dis) :

> . . . " qui finem cunctis et semina praebes,
> nascendique *vices* alterna morte *rependis*"

[" repayest or balancest the turn of birth by the turn of death, balancest birth by death "—the notion of returning or paying being contained not in the " vices," but in the " alterna " and " rependis"]. (***p***), Petron. cap. 89 (of the sons of Laocoon) :

> . . . " neuter auxilio sibi,
> uterque fratri, *transtulit* pietas *vices*.
> uterque fratri *transtulit* pias *vices*."

(***q***), Sil. 9. p. 137 :

> " iamque inter varias Fortuna utrinque virorum
> alternata *vices*, incerto cluserat iras
> eventu"

[" alternating among the various turns "—the alternation being expressed by " alternata " and " varias," and the turns only by " vices"].

The **first** conclusion deducible from this long array of examples is, as has been already pointed out, that **vices**, whether in the singular or plural, involves no notion of reciprocity, retribution, or *talio*—[**not** that the word, whether in the singular or plural, has not always necessarily a reference to a previous or future **vix** or **vices**, exactly as our corresponding word *turn* has always, and of necessity, a reference to a previous or future state, bout, or turn (or some state or bout or turn must have preceded, as some state or bout or turn must also follow), **but** that this reference is general and inherent in the word itself, and by no means points to any special and particular vix or state or bout or turn which has preceded or is to follow, as, for instance, (**1**), 6. 535:

" hac *vice* sermonum roseis Aurora quadrigis
iam medium aetherio cursu traiecerat axem"

[*not* with this interchange of talk, or alternate speaking, or dialogue of Aeneas and Deiphobus, *but* with this bout of talk, this turn of talk, viz., both of Aeneas and Deiphobus—the " vice " not meaning any reciprocity, or alternation, from Aeneas to Deiphobus, and from Deiphobus in return to Aeneas, but meaning that the talk of the two persons was a turn or bout as contrasted with the preceding turn or bout of silence]. (**2**). *Georg.* 3. 188:

. . . " inque *vicem* det mollibus ora capistris"

[give his mouth to the muzzle for a turn]. **And (3),** *Aen.* 12. 501:

. . . " quos aequore toto
inque *vicem* nunc Turnus agit, nunc Troius heros"

[*not* whom Turnus and Aeneas alternately drive, *but* whom Turnus drives for a turn and Aeneas drives for a turn—the alternation being contained not in the " in vicem," but in the " nunc," as appears at once on striking out " nunc Troius heros," when it will be found that " in vicem nunc Turnus agit " can by no possibility signify: " now Turnus alternately drives," can only signify: " now Turnus drives for a turn"]. The **second,** that vices, whether singular or plural, is a *medium vocabulum* of grammarians, and takes its colour of good, bad, or indifferent from the surrounding text—is good, Ovid, *ex Ponto,* 2. 10. 49; Auson. *Grat. Act.* in initio; Curt. 5. 24; bad, Cic. *ad Fam.* 4. 5, and *11. 18; Culex, 208;* Stat. *Silv.* 5. 2; indifferent, Ovid, *Met.* 1. 625; 15. 237. Compare also the expression *vice-versa,* and the modern *vice-roy, vice-gerent, vice-chancellor, vice-president, vice-admiral,* &c. **And** the **third,** that vices is according to the context either active or passive, expresses *either* the *tour,* turn, part or move which one

person or thing performs towards another (as Ovid, *Art. Amat*
1. *370*; Id., *ex Ponto*, 2. 10. 49; Auson. *Grat. Act.* in init.; Ovid,
Art. Amat. 3. 665, Met. 1. 625, 15. 23, and *14. 35*; Prop. 4. 4.
57), *or* the *tour*, turn, part or move which person or thing suffers,
of which person or thing is the object (as Catull. *Epith. Pel. et
Theti 1. 60*; Cic. *ad Fam. 4. 5*, and *11. 18*; *Culex, 208*; Stat.
Silv. 5. 2).

Applying to our text these conclusions as established principles, we perceive at once that VICES is **neither** with Servius,
Heyne, and Mitscherlich, "pugnas, quia per vicissitudinem pug-
nabatur" (Serv. ed. Lion), "fortunae, casus, et quidem *h. l.*
pugnae, quae ut vidimus modo secunda, modo adversa fuerat"
(Heyne), "pugnam" (Mitscherlich, ad Hor. *Carm. 4. 14. 15*,
where he says: "copiam ipsis feci eaedem a me factam ulcis-
cendi; *pugnam* haud defugiendo, obtuli me ipsorum ultioni")
[for how can that be vices which has, not merely and according to Servius himself "vicissitudines," but according to Claud.
6 Cons. Honor. 282:

...."hoc aspera fati
sors tulerit, Martisque *vices*"

[the turns of Mars, *i. e.* of battle]; Sil. 3. 12 (ed. Rup.):

"hinc omen coeptis, et casus scire futuros
ante diem, bellique *vices* novisse petebat,"

even vices? How can that *be* vices which *has* vices? a thing,
one of its own characters?] **nor** with Burmann, ad Prop. 1. 13.
10, "poenas," so to explain VICES being neither more nor less than
to assign to it a notion (viz., that of retribution) which we have
just seen is foreign to the word; **nor** with Thiel and Conington, "cominus pugnare," as opposed to TELA ("eminus pugnare") ["Vielleicht bezeichnet TELA das *eminus*, VICES das
cominus pugnare," Thiel. "I can scarcely doubt that Thiel is
right in distinguishing VICES from TELA, as hand-to-hand en-
counters, *cominus*, from missiles," Conington], for cominus
pugnare is only a species of pugna, and we have just seen
that vices is not, cannot be, pugna.

What then is VICES here in our text, if it is neither "pugnae," nor "poenae," nor "cominus pugnare?" Why, what it is everywhere, *turns;* and there being two kinds of vices (active and passive, as there are two kinds of turns, active and passive), the VICES which Aeneas assures his hearers he did not shun are active VICES; and—the sole subject treated of, the sole picture before us being that of Aeneas on the one side and the enemy on the other—the active VICES, the active turns, which Aeneas did not shun are those of the enemy, the manoeuvres, no matter of what kind (ULLAS), directed against him by the enemy, the Danai; the turns the enemy, the Danai, might serve him, VICES DANAUM, ULLAS VICES DANAUM; exactly as, verse 572, " poenas Danaum . . . praemetuens," where not only is the structure the same as in our text ("praemetuens poenas Danaum" the same as VITAVISSE VICES DANAUM, "Danaum" being in both the same causal genitive as it is called), but "praemetuens" is as near as may be identical in sense with VITAVISSE, " Danaum" absolutely identical with DANAUM, and "poenas," except that it implies retribution, the exact representative of VICES, nay, so exact a representative of VICES as to be the very term by which that word is commonly interpreted; and where, still further and as if to complete the parallelism, the object of the verb, the object of the fearing, is double, divided into " poenas Danaum" and its explanation, " coniugis iras," as in our text the object of the verb, the object of the shunning, is double, divided into TELA and its explanatory VICES DANAUM.

But what need of this or other more or less imperfect parallel to illustrate a text when we have a little further on Aeneas's own exposition? Let us hear Aeneas himself, verse 726:

" et me, quem dudum non ulla iniecta movebant
tela, neque adverso glomerati ex agmine Graii,
nunc omnes terrent aurae, sonus excitat omnis,
suspensum et pariter comitique onerique timentem,"

"and me whom a short while ago no weapons of any kind flung against me, no bands, no detachments of the opposite host, moved at all, now every breath of air terrifies, every sound excites;" as if he had said : " me who so lately shunned neither weapons nor any turns the Danai might serve me, me who but for the fates had died the death my daring merited, every breath of air now terrifies, every sound excites"—the second passage being as plainly as possible a recast of the first, a recast in which the subjects "non ulla iniecta tela" and " neque adverso glomerati ex agmine Graii" represent the objects NEC TELA NEC ULLAS VICES DANAUM of the first, and in which the object "me" is the identical subject me *subauditum* of the first, and the verb "movebant" the reciprocal or correlative of the VITAVISSE of the first.

Right, I am told, all right; with the single exception that "adverso glomerati ex agmine Graii" represents VICES understood in its particular sense of ex cubiae, who are relieved per vices or keep guard vicibus, much more exactly than it represents VICES in its general sense of *turns, changes,* or *parts,* an objection to which my reply is (**1**), that VICES in the sense of the men themselves is quite too technical and special, fitter for prose than poetry. (**2**), That VICES in the sense of the men themselves limits too much the daring of Aeneas, confines it to men who are rather on the defensive than on the offensive, falls far short of the "adverso glomerati ex agmine Graii," *the bands of Graii*, of the correlative passage. (**3**), That the expression where used by our author elsewhere is always used in its general, never in its technical and special sense, not even where the subject-matter in hand is excubiae, as 9. 174:

"omnis per muros legio, sortita periclum,
excubat, exercetque *vices* quod cuique tuendum est;"

9. 221:

. . . "vigiles simul excitat; illi
succedunt servantque *vices;*"

9. 164:

"discurrunt, variantque *vices*, fusique per herbam
indulgent vino, et vertunt crateras ahenos;"

in not one of which examples is there any ambiguity, nor can "vices" be understood to mean the guards themselves. (**4**), That Alcimus Avitus in a passage very apparently imitated from our text, a passage in which we have not only vices but vices contra-distinguished as in our text from tela, uses the word not in its technical and special, but unequivocally in its general sense,

Trans. Mar. Rubr. (Poem. 5. 542):

" plebs trepidat conclusa loco, finemque sequenti
expectat pavefacta die, non *tela* nec ullas
bellorum molita *vices*, sed voce levata
vatibus insistens."

And lastly (**5**), that however usual at the gates are excubiae or bands of men keeping guard vicibus, or per vices, and therefore sometimes curtly denominated vices, such vices are not to be thought of here in the middle of the city—see verse 359 : "mediaeque tenemus urbis iter."

VICES DANAUM, as "poenas Danaum," 2. 572 (see above) ; "reliquias Danaum," 1. 34. A writer less ambitious of strength and novelty of expression would no doubt have used, with Alcimus Avitus just quoted, the ordinary expression, vices belli.

The construction is VICES DANAUM, not DANAUM MANU, because this latter construction leaves VICES altogether without specification, without so much as the slightest intimation what kind of VICES is meant, an omission which not even the advocates themselves of that most perverse construction have attempted by any explanation to supply : Peerlkamp—although discussing at some length the respective merits of CADEREM MANU and MERUISSE MANU, and treating at full of VICES DA-NAUM—saying no word at all of his widowed and lonely VICES ; Ladewig, Weidner, and Ribbeck treating her with no less disrespect ("Es ist zu construiren : ET, SI FATA FUISSENT, UT DANAUM MANU CADEREM, MERUISSE *me*, ut eorum manu caderem," Weidner. "MANU est mit CADEREM zu verbinden ; die construction ist : ET MERUISSE, UT MANU DANAUM CADEREM, SI FATA FUISSENT (nämlich, *ut caderem*)," Ladewig, 1867. " DA-NAUM ad MANU pertinere vidit Peerlkampus," Ribbeck**)**. DA-NAUM belonging as we have just seen to VICES, not to MANU, UT CADEREM of course belongs to SI FATA FUISSENT, not to MERUISSE, and the punctuation is : VITAVISSE VICES DANAUM ET—SI FATA FUISSENT UT CADEREM—MERUISSE MANU (viz. *ut caderem*).

VITAVISSE VICES, *avoided turns*, in the sense of *tours*, *evil turns*, as *Aen. 3. 367 :* " pericula vito" [*avoid dangers*].

MERUISSE MANU is expletory of NEC TELA NEC UL. VIT. VIC. DAN., *not only did not avoid, but even braved death*. MERUISSE (*subaud. id ipsum*), viz., UT CADEREM, in other words, MERUISSE necem, caedem: compare Luc. 2. 108 (of children butchered):

"crimine quo parvi *caedem* potuere *mereri?*"

MANU, *with my hand*, i. e. *with my sword;* MERUISSE MANU, *earned my death with my sword*, i. e. by fighting; exactly as, 2. 645: "manu mortem inveniam," *find death with my hand*, i. e. with my sword = by fighting; 6. 434: "letum peperere manu," *procured death for themselves with their own hand*, i. e. with their swords; Sil. 2. 705: "optabit [Hannibal] cecidisse manu," *to have fallen by the sword*, to have died fighting. In like manner, Sil. 7. 323 (ed. Rup.):

"inter equos, interque viros, interque iacebat
capta *manu* spolia et rorantia caede Maraxes,"

spoils taken by fighting, by the sword. Sil. 1. 160 (ed. Rup.):

"primus inire *manu*, postremus ponere Martem,"

the first to enter the battle with his sword, i. e. fighting.

TARDUS, *lame, limping*. Compare Propert. 2. 1. 59:

"*tardo* Philoctetae sanavit crura Machaon."

Catull. 36. 3:

"nam sanctae Veneri Cupidinique
vovit . . . .
electissima pessimi poetae
scripta *tardipedi* deo daturam
infelicibus ustulanda lignis."

VOCATI belongs to DIVELLIMUR, the direct thread of the narrative being interrupted at INDE, in order to explain (in the two intercalary lines IPHITUS . . . ULIXI: see Rem. on 5. 704; 6. 743, 880) who the people are to whom the word DIVELLIMUR applies.

442–458.

PÓSTESQUE—CULMINIS

VAR. LECT.

TECTA (vs. 445) **III** Servius; P. Manut.; D. Heins.; N. Heins. (1670); Heyne; Brunck; Wakef.; Wagn. (ed Heyn. and *Praest.*); Lad.

TOTA **III** Voss; Ribbeck.

POSTESQUE SUB IPSOS NITUNTUR GRADIBUS.—"Cum SCALAE memoratae sint, 'gradus' vix alii esse possunt quam scalarum," Heyne, Conington, Kappes, erroneously, as I think. *First*, because particular mention of the steps or rounds of the ladders was unnecessary, the ladders themselves being flights of steps; particular mention of the steps leading up to the door was necessary in order to prevent the entrance from being conceived to be on the level of the ground. *Secondly*, because it is not at the door the scaling ladders would be applied, but on the contrary an attempt would be made by some to break in the door (as we find was actually done, verses 469 *et seqq.*), while others were scaling the walls. *And thirdly*, because a double contest is plainly described, *one* at the door, in the words OBSESSUMQUE ACTA TESTUDINE LIMEN; POSTESQUE SUB IPSOS NITUNTUR GRADIBUS; ALII STRICTIS MUCRONIBUS IMAS OBSEDERE FORES, HAS SERVANT AGMINE DENSO; *the other*, that of the party scaling the walls, in the words HAERENT PARIETIBUS SCALAE; CLIPEOSQUE AD TELA SINISTRIS PROTECTI OBIICIUNT, PRENSANT FASTIGIA DEXTRIS. By the alternate mention of the fight at the door and of the attack of the scaling party, and then again of the fight at the door and the attack of the scaling party, the attention of Aeneas's audience and Virgil's readers is kept divided between the two combats which are going on at the same time and in the same field of view, not fixed on one to the exclusion of the other. The effect is most happy, except so far as marred by the inaptitude of the reader. But where is the fine writer, where ever was the fine writer, who has not suffered from the fault of his reader? Where ever was the superior mind which could either elevate the minds of bystanders to its own level, or debase itself to theirs?

NITUNTUR GRADIBUS: literally, *ascend, go upward by the steps;* less literally, *mount the steps.* NITUNTUR does not express any struggle with those defending the palace, or any other exertion than that of mounting the steps. Compare Tacit. *Hist. 3. 71:* "Hic ambigitur, ignem tectis oppugnatores iniecerint, an obsessi, quae crebrior fama est, quo *nitentes* ac progressos depellerent," where "nitentes" is *those who were ascending, going upwards, mounting.*

GRADIBUS, the flight of steps leading up to the door, as 1. 452: " aerea cui *gradibus* surgebant limina."

TURRES AC TECTA DOMORUM, &c. "TECTA; CULMINA. TECTA participium est; aut eandem rem bis dixit," Servius. "Docte pro ipso tecto iisque rebus quibus superior domus pars tegitur, *h. e.* tegulis," Heyne. I look upon TURRES AC TECTA as the proper object of CONVELLUNT, and DOMORUM CULMINA as the explanation of TURRES AC TECTA, as if he had said, "the TURRES and TECTA which are the tops of the palace, the TURRES and TECTA which together constitute the CULMINA of the palace." See verse 466, where one of these turres is again found in company with tecta:

> " *turrim* in praecipiti stantem summisque sub astra
> eductam *tectis.*"

AURATASQUE TRABES, &c., DEVOLVUNT. Compare Tacit. *Hist. 3. 71:* "ambustasque Capitolii fores penetrassent, ni Sabinus revulsas undique *statuas, decora maiorum,* in ipso aditu, vice muri, obiecisset."

HAS SERVANT AGMINE DENSO.—Not *guard* (which were custodiunt), but *remain beside, keep post beside, keep station beside;* exactly as 2. 711: "longe *servet* vestigia coniux" [not at all *guard* in the sense of *protect,* but *keep in*]; 2. 567:

> . . . " quum limina Vestae
> *servantem,* et tacitam secreta in sede latentem
> Tyndarida"

[not at all *guarding,* but *keeping close to, not stirring from*].

The Greek φυλασσω is used in the same manner, as Hom. *Od. 10. 434:*

οι κεν οι μεγα δωμα φυλασσοιμεν και αναγκη

[not, with Clarke and Damm, *custodiamus*, but (Anglicè) *keep* (*the house*), i. e. *remain in* (*the house*)]; *Od. 5. 208:*

ενθαδε αυθι μενων συν εμοι τοδε δωμα φυλασσοις

[not, with Clarke and Damm, *custodires*, but *keep* (*the house*), *remain inside* (*the house*)].

LIMEN ERAT . . . A TERGO.—The structure is: A TERGO ERAT LIMEN, CAECAEQUE FORES, ET PERVIUS USUS TECTORUM INTER SE PRIAMI, POSTESQUE RELICTI; and the meaning: at the rere [of the building] was an entrance through an abandoned secret door of communication between the besieged building and the other buildings of which Priam's palace consisted. Compare Sil. 11. 316:

"postquam posse datum meditata aperire, novosque
pandere conatus, et liber parte relicta
tectorum a tergo patuit locus"

["after a place opened to him in a deserted part of the building behind (*i. e.* in a deserted part of the rere of the building), where he might freely explain his purpose"]. The true structure seems never even so much as once to have crossed the mind either of Heyne, or Wunderlich, or Thiel, or Peerlkamp, or Conington, all of whom join A TERGO with RELICTI, and the second of whom is so little satisfied with the best he can make out of the words as to wish them at—"vellem abessent."

A TERGO, *at the rere.* Compare Plin. *Ep. 2. 17. 5:* "A tergo cavaedium, porticum, aream." *Ibid. 15:* "cingitur diaetis duabus a tergo." *Ibid. 21:* "A pedibus mare, a tergo villae, a capite silvae."

POSTES RELICTI, an abandoned door, *i. e.*, out of use. Compare Claud. *Rapt. Pros. 3. 146:*

. . . "domus excubiis incustodita remotis,
et resupinati *neglecto* cardine *postes.*" .

Tacit. *Annal. 13. 19:* "statim relictum Agrippinae limen; nemo solari, nemo adire." *Aen. 3. 123:* "sedes relictas." *Georg. 4. 127:* "cui pauca relicti ingera ruris erant" (where Servius: "deserti atque contempti"). And—exactly parallel to our text, both in sense, syllables, and position in the verse— 5. 612: "classemque relictam;" 4. 82: "stratisque relictis;" 2. 28: "littusque relictum."

PERVIUS USUS, a passage not merely into, but through, the building, as Liv. 10. 1: "in eam speluncam penetratum cum signis est; et ex eo loco obscuro multa vulnera accepta, maximeque lapidum ictu; donec, altero specus eius ore (nam *pervius* erat) invento, utraeque fauces congestis lignis accensae."

EVADO AD SUMMI FASTIGIA CULMINIS.—Evado (e-vado), *go the whole way through, pass over the entire space* (whether *upward, downward,* or *on the level*), *so as to pass out on the far side:* and that **whether** physically, as in the passage before us, and 12. 907:

"nec spatium *evasit* totum, neque pertulit ictum;"

4. 685: "sic fata gradus *evaserat* altos" [had mounted the topmost step]; and 2. 531:

"ut tandem ante oculos *evasit* et ora parentum"

(where "evasit" is *came the whole way*—viz., the whole way just described "per tela, per hostes, porticibus longis fugit, vacua atria lustrat"—into the very presence of his parents—see Rem. *ad locum*), **or** metaphorically, as in Terent. *Adelph. 3. 4. 63:*

. . . "verum nimia illaec licentia
profecto *evadet* in aliquod magnum malum;"

and *Andr. 1. 1. 100:* "quam timeo quorsum evadas," in both which passages the reference is to the ultimate event, the upshot. The corresponding Greek word is εκβαινω, as Eurip. *Med. 55:*

εγω γαρ εις τουτ' εκβεβηκ' αλγηδονος
ωσθ' ιμερος μ' υπηλθε γη τε κοιρανω
λεξαι, μολουσαν δευρο, δεσποινης τυχας.

Burmann, in his commentary on this passage, and Forcellini, in his dictionary, interpreting evado by *ascendo*, transfer to this verb a meaning wholly foreign to it, and contained only (incidentally) in the context.

460–465.

TURRIM IN PRAECIPITI STANTEM SUMMISQUE SUB ASTRA
EDUCTAM TECTIS UNDE OMNIS TROIA VIDERI
ET DANAUM SOLITAE NAVES ET ACHAIA CASTRA
AGGRESSI FERRO CIRCUM QUA SUMMA LABANTES
IUNCTURAS TABULATA DABANT CONVELLIMUS ALTIS
SEDIBUS IMPULIMUSQUE

IN PRAECIPITI STANTEM.—Previously to an oral communication I made to Forbiger in Leipzig, in 1851, and the publication in 1853 of my "Twelve Years' Voyage," these words were understood by commentators to mean *in a high situation* ("In alto, unde quis potest praeceps dari," Serv. (ed. Lion). "In editiore loco positam," Heyne. "In alto," Wagner. "In alto positam," Forbiger). I objected first, that IN PRAECIPITI—according to the use made of the word praeceps by Latin writers (viz., to signify not *high*, but *steep*, *perpendicular*, from whence a headlong fall might easily occur)—was not *in a high position*, but *on the edge of a precipice;* and secondly, that it was as unlikely that Virgil would inform his readers that a tower SUMMIS SUB ASTRA EDUCTAM TECTIS was on a high situation, as it was likely he would inform them that it was (where it must have been or it could not have fallen on the heads of the besiegers) on the edge of the roof, perpendicularly over the front wall. Since the period referred to, I have had no occasion to change my opinion, on the contrary, am confirmed in it, **first,** by the conversion to it of the two surviving of the above-mentioned critics, viz., Forbiger, who with his usual honourable candour observes in his edition of 1852: "IN PRAECIPITI STANTEM prius interpretatus sum *in alto positam,* coll. Iuv. 1. 149, 'omne in praecipiti vitium stetit,' *i. e.*, summum gradum assecutum est ; nunc cum Henrico explico *in extremo margine tecti stantem,* ut facile impelli posset in hostium capita," &c. ; and Wagner, who—reticent, as usual, not only of the cause of his change of opinion, but of the source whence his new light is derived—contents himself with the laconic gloss: "in crepidine tecti, unde praecipitari poterat in subeuntes;" **and secondly**, by the confirmation which my opinion receives *no less from* the very passage of Juvenal rightly understood, on which, wrongly understood, Forbiger had founded his previous wrong opinion—the " omne in praecipiti vitium stetit" of Juvenal meaning not "summum gradum assecutum est" [*had arrived at the top step and could go no higher*] but " ad crepidinem ventum est" [*had arrived at the edge of a precipice, and could go no farther*]—*than from* the plain meaning of the same expression where it is figuratively used by Celsus, 2. 6 (" *in praecipiti* iam esse [aegrum] denuntiat [alvus] quae liquida eademque vel nigra vel pallida vel pinguis est," in which passage "in praecipiti" is, and can only be, *on a precipice*), and of "ex praecipiti" where it is figuratively used by Horace, *Sat. 2. 3. 292:*

>   . . . " casus medicusve levarit
> aegrum *ex praecipiti*,"

in which passage " ex praecipiti" is and can only be *from the precipice*.

Conington's translation " with sheer descent, a turret high" is not English, conveys no notion at all to the English, scarcely any even to the Latin, scholar.

QUA SUMMA LABANTES IUNCTURAS TABULATA DABANT: *where the turret was connected with, and easily separable from, the terrace on the top of the palace.* Heyne and Wagner understand SUMMA TABULATA to mean the highest storey of the turret; but, admitting that the turret had a number of storeys, the Trojans could not have attacked round about with iron the highest storey of a turret EDUCTAM SUB ASTRA, without ascending the turret; and having ascended, it seems impossible to comprehend how they could precipitate it on the Greeks, without precipitating themselves along with it; or indeed, how, being in or on it, they could precipitate it at all. The words CONVELLIMUS and IMPULIMUS are, of themselves, sufficient to show that the Trojans stood on the roof of the palace, while they *tore up* the turret ALTIS SEDIBUS *from its high seat*, viz., on the roof of the palace, and *pushed* it forward, so as to cause it to fall on the besiegers. SUMMA TABULATA, therefore, is the flat or terrace (*solarium*— see "Palais de Scaurus," 15) forming the roof of the palace, on which the turret stood. This flat or terrace being a floor (*tafel-werk*, Germ.) is called TABULATA, and being on the top of the house is called SUMMA.

IUNCTURAS, the connection or jointings of the tower to the flat terrace on which it stood.

The relative positions and relationship of the turris and the tabulata are clearly set forth by Servius, ad *Aen. 8. 693*, where speaking of ship-towers he says: " Agrippa primus hoc genus turrium invenit, ut de tabulatis subito erigerentur." Add to this that the "turris" on the roof of Priam's palace stood perpendicularly (IN PRAECIPITI) over the front wall of the palace, and the whole picture is placed before the mind as distinctly as it is possible for words to place it. A tower on the roof, serving as a look-out, watch-tower, or specula was a characteristic of the ancient *schloss*, or palace; and villas, especially when they were on the sea-shore, were furnished with them for the sake of the prospect—see Ovid, *Met. 1. 288* (of Deucalion's deluge):

" si qua domus mansit, potuitque resistere tanto
  indeiecta malo, culmen tamen altior huius
  unda tegit, pressaeque labant sub gurgite *turres*."

Plin. *Ep. 2. 17* (of his villa near Ostia): " Hinc *turris* erigitur, sub qua diaetae duae; totidem in ipsa; praeterea coenatio, quae latissimum mare, longissimum littus, amoenissimas villas prospicit." Such towers are to be seen even at present on the top of royal palaces, *ex. gr.*, of the *schloss* in Dresden and of the *Palazzo Vecchio* in Florence, the tower in the latter instance being very striking and remarkable, inasmuch as it is not only exceedingly high—commanding a prospect over the whole city and neighbouring country, and forming a conspicuous object in the view of Florence taken from whatever quarter—but is built like the tower of Priam's palace perpendicularly over the front wall of the edifice. More remarkable for such towers than perhaps any other European city is the city of Cadiz: see *Allgemeine Familien-Zeitung*, Stuttgart, 1869, p. 296: " Die schnurgeraden strassen [viz., of Cadiz] sind mit marmor gepflastert, und um die verschiedenen prächtigen plätze, welche zu promenaden angelegt sind, erheben sich viele palastähnliche gebäude als zeugen des wohlstandes und reichthums der bewohner. Diese häuser haben alle flache dächer und jedes derselben ein eigenthümliches *thürmchen zur umschau*, mirador genannt; von wo aus man eine entzückende aussicht auf land und see hat." Ford, *Handbook for Spain* (of Cadiz): "Ascend the *Torre della Vigia;* below lies the smokeless whitened city, with its *miradores* and *azoteas*, its look-out towers and flat roofs, from whence the merchants formerly signalized the arrival of their galleons." It is most probably in such a tower on the roof of Agamemnon's palace the watchman is placed, who so strikingly opens Aeschylus's drama, the Agamemnon:

> θεους μεν αιτω τωνδ' απαλλαγην πονων,
> φρουρας ετειας μηχος, ην κοιμωμενος
> στεγης Ατρειδων αγκαθεν, κυνος δικην,
> αστρων κατοιδα νυκτερων ομηγυριν.

Compare also Hom. *Od. 4. 524:*

> τον δ' αρ' απο σκοπιης ειδε σκοπος, ον ρα καθεισεν
> Αιγισθος δολομητις αγων.

IMPULIMUS, not merely *pushed*, but *pushed so that it fell over, forward.* See Rem. on 8. 233.

469-475.

VESTIBULUM ANTE IPSUM PRIMOQUE IN LIMINE PYRRHUS
EXULTAT TELIS ET LUCE CORUSCUS AENA
QUALIS UBI IN LUCEM COLUBER MALA GRAMINA PASTUS
FRIGIDA SUB TERRA TUMIDUM QUEM BRUMA TEGEBAT
NUNC POSITIS NOVUS EXUVIIS NITIDUSQUE IUVENTA
LUBRICA CONVOLVIT SUBLATO PECTORE TERGA
ARDUUS AD SOLEM ET LINGUIS MICAT ORE TRISULCIS

VAR. LECT.

[*punct.*] TEGEBAT, NUNC **III** P. Manut.; D. Heins.; N. Heins. (1670);
Brunck; Wagn. (ed. Heyn. and *Praest.*); Lad.; Ribb.

[*punct.*] TEGEBAT; NUNC **III** Heyne; Wakef.

VAR. LECT.

[*punct.*] TERGA ARDUUS **III** P. Manut.; D. Heins.; N. Heins. (1670);
Heyne; Brunck; Wagn. (ed. 1861); Lad.

[*punct.*] TERGA, ARDUUS **III** Wakef.; Wagn. (ed. Heyn.); Voss; Ribbeck (ARDUOS).

VESTIBULUM.—The vestibule was under the roof, but outside the door of the house, as appears from the history which Statius gives of Tydeus and Polynices both taking shelter from the storm in the vestibule of the palace of Adrastus and yet outside the door and not discovered there until the doors of the palace were opened (*Theb. 1. 386, 435*, ed. Müller):

> . . . "actutum regia cernit [Polynices]
> vestibula; hic artus imbri ventoque rigentes
> proiicit ignotaeque acclinis postibus aulae
> invitat tenues ad dura cubilia somnos."
>
> . . . .
> " isque [Adrastus] ubi progrediens numerosa luce per alta
> atria dimotis adverso limine claustris
> terribilem dictu faciem, lacera ora putresque
> sanguineo videt imbre genas," &c.

QUALIS UBI IN LUCEM COLUBER, &c.—I doubt if the almost dazzling beauty of this simile considered as a separate and independent picture is more to be admired than its perfect suitableness and correspondence in every particular to the object which it illustrates. The serpent has lain underground inert and comatose, all winter: Pyrrhus, hitherto in abeyance, has not until this moment appeared before Troy. The serpent, newly born in the spring, fresh and vigorous and agile, lifts his head and breast erect towards the sun, coils his folds, and plays at *mora* (i. e. *micatura*) with his three-forked tongue: Pyrrhus, no less in his spring, fresh and vigorous and agile, exults and sparkles and flashes in the brazen light of his brandished weapons.

That the comparison is of Pyrrhus hitherto concealed and now at long and last appearing is evident not only from the emphatic position of the word NUNC (see Rem. on verse 246), but from Sil. Ital. 12. 6, where the precisely same comparison is applied to Hannibal, all the winter shut up in Capua and taking the field again in summer:

> . . . "ceu condita bruma,
> dum Rhipaea rigent Aquilonis flamina, tandem
> evolvit serpens arcano membra cubili,
> et splendente die novus emicat, atque coruscum
> fert caput, et saniem sublatis faucibus efflat."

The structure of the whole passage is of the very simplest. The sentence begun at QUALIS being broken off abruptly at TEGEBAT, and a new sentence begun with NUNC; and IN LUCEM depending neither on the preceding EXULTAT, nor the subsequent CONVOLVIT, but on the verb which was to have followed, if the author had carried on to the end the sentence which he has left unfinished at TEGEBAT—a dash should be placed after TEGEBAT in order to indicate that such is the structure. See Rem. on *Aen. 1. 240*.

The punctuation adopted by Brunck and Wagner converts the passage from one of the simplest into one of the most awkward and perplexed imaginable ("Post TERGA distingui debuit commate. Iungenda enim sunt IN LUCEM CONVOLVIT TERGA," Brunck. "Post TEGEBAT commate tantum interpunxi;

distinxi, Brunckium et cod. Medic. secutus, etiam post TERGA; IN LUCEM autem, eodem Brunckio auctore, iungo cum verbo CONVOLVIT," Wagner (V. L. ad edit. Heyn.)). Heyne, though punctuating better, makes by his interpretation a similar hodgepodge of the passage (" IN LUCEM trahendum aut ad EXULTAT aut ad CONVOLVIT; utrumque parum commode ").

TUMIDUM.—"TUMIDUM appellat serpentem, non quia graminibus tumet, nam hyeme non edunt, et V. illud momentum describit quo ex terra, POSITIS EXUVIIS, quasi ad novam vitam redit . . . vides talem serpentem non posse dici *cibo tumidum*. Fame potius laborant, ac propterea magis timendi sunt. TUMIDUM ergo appellat, quia ipsa terra sub qua serpens latet est tumida, ex quo tumore simul serpentis magnitudo intelligitur. Ad terram retulit Horat. *Epod. 16:* 'nec intumescit alta viperis humus,' " Peerlkamp. This is all, as I think, erroneous. Tumidus is the *epitheton constans* of serpents. See Ovid, *Met. 1. 460* (Apollo speaking):

" stravimus innumeris *tumidum* Pythona sagittis."

Ibid. 10. 313: " tumidisque afflavit echidnis," with which compare *Georg. 3. 421:*

" tollentemque minas et caerula colla *tumentem*
deiice."

Aen. 2. 381:

" attollentem iras et caerula colla *tumentem*."

It is, therefore, not necessary in order to account for the TUMIDUM of our text, to have recourse to MALA GRAMINA PASTUS; nor indeed is the serpent tumidus (or tumens) with grass at all, but with poison, as Ovid says, *Met. 3. 33* (of the Cadmean serpent): " corpus tumet omne veneno." That TUMIDUM is the ordinary epithet of serpents, and equivalent to tumidum veneno affords so simple and natural a solution of the passage that I think I shall hardly be required to discuss, much less to confute, the very strange *dictum* of Peerlkamp, " TUMIDUM ergo appellat, quia ipsa terra sub qua serpens latet est tumida, ex quo tumore simul serpentis magnitudo intelligitur," still less to show by argument that Horace when he used the word "intumescit" in his sixteenth Epode neither had our author in his mind, nor meant to indicate either the magnitude or the tumescence of his vipers, but solely to express the intumescence of the ground with the brood it was about to produce, an intumescence similar to the intumescence of the womb in pregnancy.

LINGUIS MICAT ORE TRISULCIS.—I have not examined any MSS. respecting this passage. Even should the authority of them all be against it, I do not know whether we should not accept the conjecture of Voss, viz., ORA.

479-495.

IPSE—COMPLENT

All commentators and translators divide this narrative into two distinct parts, making a new paragraph begin at AT DOMUS INTERIOR, and considering the words

LIMINA PERRUMPIT, POSTESQUE A CARDINE VELLIT
AERATOS

as descriptive, not of the actual and successful bursting in of the doors, but merely of an attempt to burst them in, which attempt does not succeed until, verse 492,

LABAT ARIETE CREBRO
IANUA, ET EMOTI PROCUMBUNT CARDINE POSTES.

Heyne's words are: "A CARDINE VELLIT: movet, labefactat, e cardine ut amoveat annititur. Nunc enim adhuc de conatu agitur."

Now, this is not according to the usual method of Virgil, who never begins with a hint or shadow of what is about to happen, and then brings gradually forward the event, but on the contrary always places the event full before the eyes first,

then ἐπεξεργάζεται, and explains by what means it has been
brought about, and then, as it were in a peroration, recapitulates
with a re-statement of the event, fuller and grander than at
first. And such is the method he has adopted on the present
occasion. Having given the brilliant picture of Pyrrhus and
his comrades, which is contained in the verses VESTIBULUM . . .
LACTANT, he informs us that Pyrrhus himself (IPSE) at the head
of his comrades seizes an axe, bursts through (PER-RUMPIT) the
doors, and forces the valves from the pivots. The event, *i. e.*,
the complete and successful forcing of the door, is thus in as
few words as possible laid before the eyes of the reader. But
this could not be done in a moment—required successive steps,
which the poet now sets about to describe particularly. First,
with the axe Pyrrhus cuts a panel out of the door:

        IAMQUE EXCISA TRABE FIRMA CAVAVIT
        ROBORA, ET INGENTEM LATO DEDIT ORE FENESTRAM.

This is the first step, and is attended by consequences which are
described before any mention is made of the second step; the
consequences are :

(1).   APPARET DOMUS INTUS, ET ATRIA LONGA PATESCUNT;
        APPARENT PRIAMI ET VETERUM PENETRALIA REGUM;
        ARMATOSQUE VIDENT STANTES IN LIMINE PRIMO.
(2).   AT DOMUS INTERIOR GEMITU MISEROQUE TUMULTU
        MISCETUR, PENITUSQUE CAVAE PLANGORIBUS AEDES
        FEMINEIS ULULANT ; FERIT AUREA SIDERA CLAMOR.
        TUM PAVIDAE TECTIS MATRES INGENTIBUS ERRANT,
        AMPLEXAEQUE TENENT POSTES, ATQUE OSCULA FIGUNT.

The first step and its consequences described, the next step
follows :

        INSTAT VI PATRIA PYRRHUS ; NEC CLAUSTRA—

viz., the CLAUSTRA in which he had already made the opening
or window with the axe—

        NEQUE IPSI
        CUSTODES SUFFERRE VALENT: LABAT ARIETE CREBRO
        IANUA, ET EMOTI PROCUMBUNT CARDINE POSTES

(*i. e.*, the battering ram is brought, and the doors levelled with
the ground); and thus the reader is put in full possession of all

the particulars necessary to be gone through (and which were actually gone through) in the performance of the act described at verse 480, as already performed. This done (and the peroration or winding up made, in the words EMOTI PROCUMBUNT CARDINE POSTES, which it will be observed are only a stronger enunciation of the previously enounced fact, verse 480), our author proceeds with the description of the consequences of this fact:

FIT VIA VI: RUMPUNT ADITUS, PRIMOSQUE TRUCIDANT
IMMISSI DANAI, ET LATE LOCA MILITE COMPLENT

[*the whole body of Danai burst in, butcher all they meet, and fill the house with soldiers*].

Nothing can be more complete and vivid than this picture, nothing more in conformity with Virgil's usual method of painting; on the contrary, nothing more confused and ill-imagined, nothing less like Virgil's usual style of painting, than the picture divided into two by the break placed by commentators and translators at PRIMO, and the commencement of a new paragraph at AT DOMUS INTERIOR.

The editors have introduced inextricable confusion into this wonderfully clear and distinct painting by dividing it, as just remarked, in the very middle, viz., at AT DOMUS INTERIOR, into two independent parts, led into this fatal error, it would seem, by the word AT, understood by them to indicate the commencement of a new action, while, in fact, it does no more than contrast DOMUS INTERIOR ... FIGUNT, with the immediately preceding APPARET ... LIMINE PRIMO, both descriptions being interposed as one intercalation between LATO DEDIT ORE FENESTRAM and INSTAT VI PATRIA. See Remm. on 5. 704, 659; 6. 743, 880.

PYRRHUS. Compare the exactly corresponding "At domus interior," 1. 641, where *at* again serves, not to indicate the commencement of a new action, but to contrast or connect the description "domus interior ... gentis" with "nec minus interea ... dei"—two counterpart or matching pictures, inserted side by side between Aeneas's introduction into the palace, verses 635 and 636, and the embassy of Achates, verse 647.

Until the sign of a new paragraph is removed from AT, the whole passage from IPSE INTER PRIMOS to COMPLENT will remain, what it has always been up to the present day, a mass of confusion.

IAMQUE, following the two verbs in the present, and belonging to the two verbs in the perfect tense, is equivalent to, *and see how much he has done already.*

ARMATOS (verse 485), " those already mentioned, verses 449, 450," Conington. No, no. Those were *outside* the door where the combat was then going on: these are a reserve *inside*.

POSTES ... CARDINE. The postes of the Romans were (as clearly appears from Lucr. 3. 370 :

> " praeterea si pro foribus sunt lumina nostra,
> iam magis exemptis oculis debere videtur
> cernere res animus, sublatis postibus ipsis."

Ovid, *Met.* 8. *638 :*

> " submissoque humiles intrarunt vertice postes."

Stat. *Silv.* 1. 4. 44 :

> " sic Ianus, clausoque libens se poste recepit"

[the door being closed, *i. e.*, having closed the door, retired]) the door itself, which, being always double, *i. e.*, having two valves meeting in the middle, was expressed by a noun plural. These valves were not fastened either to a door-case or to the wall of the house or building, but stood in the opening quite detached, and moved on pivots (cardines), one of which was inserted into the threshold, the other into the lintel. The word postes has passed into the Italian in the form of imposte : "imposta, legname che serve a chiudere l'uscio," Voc. Della Crusca.

LIMINA PERRUMPIT.—While the singular limen is the *sill* properly so called, the plural limina in the general use made of the word is the *entrance*, whether considered, as in 1. 452, the mere opening, or as that opening filled up with the stop or impediment, the fores. It is necessarily in this latter sense the word is used in our text, it not being possible perrumpere any but a closed or stopped up passage. The same word is used in the same sense, verse 508, " convulsa limina," not the threshold, not the open entrance, but the closed entrance, the **postes**, the **fores**. Compare Coripp. *de Laud. Iustin.* 1. 68:

> "et iam crebra manus veloci concita pulsu
> limina quassabat ductis munita catenis."

AERATOS.—Let the reader beware how he applies to aeratus either here or generally elsewhere the observation of Köne (*Sprache der Römischer Epiker*, p. 192): "aus erz sind die 'aeratae catenae' (Propert. 2. 16. 11), aus eisen die 'ferratos postes' (Hor. *Sat.* 1. 4. 61; Virg. *Aen.* 7. 622), aber weder aeneae noch ferreos passte in den vers." That the doors of Priam's palace are described by our author not as consisting of bronze (aereae) but as plated or otherwise strengthened with bronze (aeratae, in the proper sense of the word), is sufficiently plain from the terms **trabs** and ROBORA (terms peculiarly applicable to wood) applied to the same doors, in the very next clause, as well as from the facility with which Pyrrhus hews the said doors to pieces with an axe; also from the "auratas trabes" of the same palace only thirty lines previously, which can only be, *rafters of wood, gilt or ornamented with gold*. Compare 9. 463: "aeratasque acies in praelia cogit" [*not* troops consisting of aes, *but* troops accoutred in aes]; 10. 886:

> . . . "ter secum Troius heros
> immanem *aerato* circumfert tegmine silvam"

[*not* on his bronze shield, *but* on his shield plated or otherwise strengthened with bronze].

EXCISA TRABE.—" Arbore, ut 9. 87, propinqua scilicet regiae, eaque pro ariete utitur; cf. vs. 492," Wagner (*Praest.*). No, no; TRABE is not a neighbouring tree cut down by Pyrrhus in order to be used as a battering ram, but it is the wood (Germ. *holz*) of the door itself, which wood is hewed into a hole. Compare 6. 42:

> "excisum Euboicae latus ingens rupis in antrum,"

the side of the Euboean rock, not taken out in order to be used, but excavated, hollowed out; and so in our text, the wood of the door excavated, hollowed out into a hole by cutting, the ablative explaining the manner of the CAVAVIT, not the instrument with which the CAVAVIT was effected.

AT DOMUS INTERIOR.—AT contrasts the DOMUS INTERIOR (observe the comparative degree: *farther in*), and what is there happening, not with what is going on at or outside the door, *i. e.*, not with the bursting in of Pyrrhus and his comrades, but with the just-mentioned DOMUS INTUS (observe the positive degree: *just inside*), ATRIA LONGA, PENETRALIA REGUM, and ARMATOS STANTES IN LIMINE PRIMO. If a contrast between what was going on outside and the bursting open of the door had been intended, the word interea would have been added to AT DOMUS INTERIOR.

ATRIA LONGA . . . DOMUS INTERIOR . . . CAVAE AEDES.—The two main parts or divisions of which a Roman house consisted (for the plan is taken from a Roman, not a Grecian or Asiatic, house) are here indicated with great distinctness; the front part consisting mainly of the atrium, in the words ATRIA LONGA; the inner or back part, the cavaedium, in the words CAVAE AEDES. See Becker's *Gallus*, vol. 2. The double expression, INTERIOR DOMUS, CAVAE AEDES, reduced to plain prose, becomes the inner or back rooms, that is to say, those surrounding the cavaedium or inner court.

AEDES ULULANT.—Compare Soph. *Trachin.* 205:

CHOR. ανολολυξατω δομος εφεστιοις αλαλαγαις
ο μελλονυμφος.

Coripp. Johann. 6. 196:

. . . "*ululatibus* augent
ardua tecta sonos."

Isaiah, 14. 31: "Howl, O gate; cry, O city."

FERIT AUREA SIDERA CLAMOR.—SIDERA, not literally, *the stars*, but figuratively, *the sky*—the self-same phrase, "ferit aurea clamor sidera," being used, 11. 832, on occasion of the death of Camilla, which occurred in the day time. From sidera used in this sense comes sidereus, so often used to signify *of such beauty as belongs only to the sky, heaven, or celestial objects*.

AUREA, no more to be taken literally than FERIT or SIDERA,

is neither *of the colour of gold*, nor of course *of the material substance of gold*, but *beautifully bright and shining like gold; as handsome as gold*. The application of the term in this sense to the stars, sky, and even to the moon, is of the commonest. Compare Hor. *Epod. 17. 40*:

> . . . "tu proba
> perambulabis astra sidus *aureum*."

Aen. 3. 518:

> "armatumque *auro* circumspicit Oriona."

Ovid, *Met. 13. 587*:

> "omnibus inferior, quas sustinet *aureus* aether,
> . . . .
> diva tamen venio."

Georg. 1. 431: "vento semper rubet *aurea* Phoebe." Werner, *die Söhne des Thales*, th. 1, act 4, sc. 2:

> . . . "wenn morgen sich die sterne
> *vergolden*, Philipp, bin ich fern von dir."

H. Heine, *Neue Gedichte*:

> "sterne mit den *goldnen* füsschen
> wandeln droben bang und sacht,
> dass sie nicht die erde wecken,
> die da schlaft im schoos der nacht."

Rückert, *die Weisheit des Brahmanen, 17. 44*:

> "wozu sind all die stern' am himmel nur gemacht?
> mit *goldnem* flitter wol zu schmücken unsre nacht."

ARIETE (verse 492).—"Nolim accipere proprie, quippe quod inventum Troianis temporibus serius est," Heyne. To be sure, and the picture presented by the interpretation of Wagner, who will have the "aries" to be a neighbouring tree cut down for the purpose (TRABE EXCISA, verse 481) is mere caricature. ARIETE CREBRO, frequently repeated push, like that of a battering ram. Compare Sil. 11. 889:

> . . . "immissis pars caeca et concita frenis
> *arietat* in portas et duros obiice postes"

[batters at the gates]. The first qualification for a commentator of Virgil is not a knowledge of Buttman's *Lexilogus*, but a knowledge of the difference between prose and poetry, between literal and figurative, between body and soul. It is easier for flesh and blood to inherit the kingdom of God, than for a matter-of-fact expositor to enter into the meaning of Virgil.

FIT VIA VI.—Spoken not of Pyrrhus, but of the whole body of Danai, who now RUMPUNT ADITUS, &c.

496-517.

NON SIC—SEDEBANT

NON SIC... ARMENTA TRAHIT.—Compare *1 Chron. 14.11:* "Then David said, God hath broken in upon mine enemies by mine hand, like the breaking forth of waters." Schiller, *Braut von Messina:*

> "jene gewaltigen wetterbäche,
> aus des hagels unendlichen schlossen,
> aus den wolkenbrüchen zusammengeflossen,
> kommen finster gerauscht und geschossen
> reissen die brücken und reissen die damme
> donnernd mit fort im wogengeschwemme,
> nichts ist, das die gewaltigen hemme."

VIDI HECUBAM CENTUMQUE NURUS.—" Quinquaginta erant filiorum uxores s. nurus, ad quas accedunt totidem filiae," Wagner (*Praest.*). No pupil in the Kreutzschule could have calculated more exactly, or been more sure that if our author had had the good fortune to have one hundred and one tongues and one hundred and one voices, he would have been able to effect what he could not effect (*Georg. 2. 42*) with no more than one hundred tongues and one hundred voices. Servius, less arithmetical but more poetical than our modern commentators, amongst several guesses, hits by chance on the true meaning:

"finitus est numerus pro infinito." The hundred-handed Briareus, the hundred-gated city of Thebes, and the hundred-citied island of Crete are, as well as the still more famous hecatomb, examples of the same use of εκατον and centum. Almost any number from three upwards, especially ten, twenty, fifty, five hundred, a thousand, ten thousand, a million, may be, and is frequently, used in the same manner.

PROCUBUERE (verse 505).—Observe the effect of the emphatic position of this word at the beginning of the verse, and separated from the sequel by a complete and sudden pause. Compare "incidit," verse 467; and see Rem. on 2. 246.

CONVULSAQUE VIDIT LIMINA TECTORUM.—CONVULSA, *broken violently open, burst open, torn down, torn off the hinges.* Compare Plaut. *Amph. 4,* suppos. (Gronov.):

"quis tam vasto impetu has fores toto *convulsit* cardine?"

Plin. *Epist. 7. 19:* "ac mihi domus ipsa nutare, *convulsaque* sedibus suis ruitura supra videtur."

ARMA DIU, &c., . . . CINGITUR (verses 509-511). Compare Metast. *Regolo,* sc. ult. (Regolo, of himself):

. . . "Roma rammente
che il suo padre è mortal; che al fin vacilla
anch' ei sotto l'acciar."

AXE (verse 512). See Rem. on 6. 791.

LAURUS.—It is not accidentally or indifferently that our author places the laurel ("laurus nobilis") not only here in the court of Priam's palace, but (7. 59) in the court of Latinus's palace also, for we read (Plin. *H. N. 15. 30,* Sillig's ed.): "Laurus triumphis proprie. dicatur; vel gratissima domibus ianitrix Caesarum pontificumque; sola et domos exornat et *ante limina* excubat." Compare Dion Cass. 53. 16: και γαρ το τε [ελαβε Αυγουστος] τας δαφνας προ των βασιλειων αυτου προτιθεσθαι. Claud. *Rapt. Pros. 3. 74:*

" stabat praeterea luco dilectior omni
laurus, virgineos quondam quae fronde pudica
umbrabat thalamos."

PENATES.—"Aram Penatium," Heyne, following Servius.

No, but *the house, the dwelling;* because in a passage which may be assumed to be an adumbration of that before us, Martial (9. 61, ed. Schneid.) describes Caesar's platanus at Corduba as embracing not merely the "Penates," but "totos Penates," which can mean nothing else than the *whole house:*

"in Tartessiacis domus est notissima terris,
    qua dives placidum Corduba Baetin amat,
    vellera nativo pallent ubi flava metallo,
    et linit Hesperium bractea viva pecus;
acdibus in mediis *totos* amplexa *Penates*
    stat platanus densis Caesariana comis,
    hospitis invicti posuit quam dextera felix,
    coepit et ex illa crescere virga manu."

Compare Stat. *Silv.* 1. 1. 2, where the equestrian statue of Domition is described as " Latium complexa forum;" also, Stat. *Silv.* 1. 3. 59, and 2. 3. 1; and especially Claud. *Rapt. Pros.* 3. 74:

"stabat praeterea luco dilectior omni
laurus, virgineos quondam quae fronde pudica
umbrabat thalamos."

The passage being thus understood (1), a tenderness of sentiment is obtained not unlike that of Statius's *Silv.* 3. 5. 58:

. . . "non sic Philomela *Penates*
circuit *amplectens*,"

a tenderness wholly foreign to the picture of the laurel embracing the images with its shadow; (2), Virgil's account is made to tally better with the generally received tradition, that Priam was slain at the altar of Jupiter Herceus (Ovid, *Ibis,* 285:

. . . " ut illi,
cui nihil *Hercei* profuit *ara Iovis*");

and (3), the poet is no longer liable to the reproach that only three lines later he describes the daughters of Priam as embracing with their arms (AMPLEXAE) the self-same object which he here describes the laurel as embracing with its shadow (UMBRA COMPLEXA).

HIC HECUBA . . . SEDEBANT (vv. 515–517). Compare Marlowe, *Tamburlaine* (part 1, act 5, sc. 1, Tamburlaine to the virgins who come forward with laurel boughs and prayers for mercy):

> " what, are the turtles frayed out of their nests?
> alas! poor fools, must you be first shall feel
> the sworn destruction of Damascus?"

Aesch. *Suppl. ???* (Danaus desiring his daughters to take refuge at the altar):

> . . . εν αγνω δ' εσμος ως πελειαδων
> ιζεσθε, κιρκων των ομοπτερων φοβω,
> εχθρων ομαιμων και μιαινοντων γενος.

DIVUM AMPLEXAE SIMULACRA SEDEBANT. Compare Tacit. *Annal. 3. 61:* "Liberum patrem, bello victorem, supplicibus Amazonum, quae *aram insederant*, ignovisse"; Thuc. 3. 28: Dem. *de Corona, 31;* Soph. *Oed. Tyr. ?.*

519–523.

QUAE MENS TAM DIRA MISERRIME CONIUX
IMPULIT HIS CINGI TELIS AUT QUO RUIS INQUIT
NON TALI AUXILIO NEC DEFENSORIBUS ISTIS
TEMPUS EGET NON SI IPSE MEUS NUNC AFFORET HECTOR
HUC TANDEM CONCEDE HAEC ARA TUEBITUR OMNES

DEFENSORIBUS ISTIS.—" Durch den plur., obwohl von *einer* person zu verstehen, wird der begriff fein verallgemeinert, um einer härte, die man sagt, hiedurch das verletzende zu nehmen. ISTIS als pronom. der 2 person, *talibus qualis tu es*," Thiel. Gossrau, Forbiger (2nd ed., 1837), and (in a personal disputation I had with him on the subject in the year 1847: see Preface to " Twelve Years' Voyage") Wagner. Nothing can be farther from the meaning. The "defensores" of which Hecuba speaks, and which she says are not the defensores required by the necessity of the occasion, are not Priam—Priam being but one person could hardly be "defensores"—but the weapons wielded by Priam, the weapons which it alarms Hecuba to see Priam wield; and the picture with which we are presented in the person of Priam is not that of an old man too weak to defend with arms a cause which might have been successfully so defended by a younger and stronger man, but that of a weak old man who takes up arms in a cause in which arms, even although wielded by the youngest and strongest hands, are wholly incapable of affording help or defence—

> NON TALI AUXILIO NEC DEFENSORIBUS ISTIS
> TEMPUS EGET, NON SI IPSE MEUS NUNC AFFORET HECTOR—

and there is no resource left but the altar:

> HUC TANDEM CONCEDE; HAEC ARA TUEBITUR OMNES.

The identical sentiment is repeated in the very next book, verse 260:

> . . . " nec iam amplius armis,
> sed votis precibusque iubent exposcere pacem."

Compare Aesch. *Suppl. 203* (ed. Schütz) :

> αμεινον εστι παντος εινεκ', ω κοραι,
> παγον προσιζειν τωνδ' αγωνιων θεων.
> κρεισσον δε πυργου βωμος αρρηκτον σακος.

Heliodor. 8: Ευχαις, ουκ αιτιαις, εξιλεουται το κρειττον. Stat. *Theb. 4. 200* (ed. Müller) :

> " ' non haec apta mihi nitidis ornatibus,' inquit,
> ' tempora, nec miserae placeant insignia formae
> te sine; sat dubium coetu solante timorem
> fallere, et incultos aris adverrere crines.' "

Virgil, *Aen. 6. 37:*

> " non hoc ista sibi tempus spectacula poscit.
> nunc grege de intacto septem mactare iuvencos
> praestiterit, totidem lectas de more bidentes."

Ibid. 12. 156:

> " 'non lacrymis hoc tempus,' ait Saturnia Iuno;
> ' accelera, et fratrem, si quis modus, eripe morti.' "

Shakespeare, *Coriol. 1. 2:*

> . . . " for the dearth,
> the gods not the patricians make it; and
> your knees to them, not arms, must help."

Milton, *Comus, 611*:
"but here thy sword can do thee little stead;
for other arms and other weapons must
be those that quell the might of hellish charms."

And for the precisely opposite picture, compare Ovid, *Met. 6. 610* (of Procne):

. . . "fletumque sororis
corripiens, 'nou est lacrymis hic,' inquit, 'agendum,
sed ferro; sed si quid habes, quod vincere ferrum
possit.'"

Also, not very dissimilar, Claud. *in 3 Cons. Stilich. 268*:

. . . "non spicula poscit
iste labor: maneant clausis nunc sicca pharetris."

Also Lucan, 7. 87 (Pompey, of himself):

. . . "si milite Magno,
non duce, tempus eget, nil ultra fata morabor."

Herodian, 1. 8: ου πανηγυριζειν σοι καιρος, εφη, Κομμοδε νυν, ουδε θεαις και εορταις σχολαζειν· επικειται γαρ σου τοις αυχεσι το του Περεννιου ξιφος.

DEFENSORIBUS. The following are examples of the application of defensor to objects devoid of personality. In two of them, the objects to which the term is applied are actually, as in our text, arms. Caes. *Bell. Gall. 4. 17*: "Sublicae ad inferiorem partem fluminis obliquae adigebantur; quae, pro pariete subiectae, et cum omni opere coniunctae, vim fluminis exciperent: et alia [*qu*. aliae?] item supra pontem mediocri spatio: ut, si arborum trunci, sive naves, deiiciendi operis causa, essent a barbaris missae, *his defensoribus* earum rerum vis minueretur." Claudian, *in Rufin. 1. 79*:

. . . "haec [viz. Megaera] terruit Herculis ora,
et *defensores* terrarum polluit arcus."

Iscanus, *de bello Troiano, 6. 156*:

. . . "sed tot taedas, tot tela, secundus
sustinet Acacides, et *defensore* laborat
iam fessus clypeo."

Serenus Samonicus (ap. Burm. *Poet. Lat. Minor.*), 192:

"summa boni est alacres homini contingere visus,
quos quasi custodes *defensoresque* pericli
prospiciens summa natura locavit in arce."

By the same figure by which (1) Hecuba calls the arms wielded by Priam; (2), Caesar, the sublicae of a bridge; (3), Claudian, the bow of Hercules; (4), Iscanus, a shield; and (5), Serenus, the eyes, defensores, *defenders;* Ajax calls the sword which he has set upright in the ground, in order to throw himself upon it, σφαγευς, *executioner* (Soph. *Aj. 815*):

ο μεν σφαγευς εστηκεν, η τομωτατος
γενοιτ' αν,

and we call the piece of furniture which defends the floors of our rooms against the fires of our grates *fender*, i. e. *defender*, defensor.

ISTIS.—"Talibus qualis tu es," Thiel. The reference is as I have just shown not to Priam but to Priam's arms, and ISTIS is not contemptuous but simply demonstrative: *those arms*, exactly as Cic. *de Rep. 1. 37:* "'sed si vis, Laeli, dabo tibi testes nec nimis antiquos nec ullo modo barbaros.' L. '*Istos,*' inquit, '*volo*'" [*those are precisely what I want*].

QUAE MENS, &c. . . . AUT QUO RUIS? By a division of the compound question quo ruis his telis into its two components, quo ruis and quorsum haec tela, our author has secured on the one hand that free sailing room for his verse, that unconfined space for dactyl and spondee, for which we have already observed him to be always so solicitous; and on the other hand, sufficient place for ornament, without either loading, embarrassing, or complicating the structure. Had he been more studious of brevity and less of ease and grace and ornament, of the fine flow of his verse and the richness of the thought which it expressed, he had contented himself with the single compound question: quo ruis diris his cinctus telis? or quo ruis his cinctus telis? or even with the bare bald quo ruis his telis? and Virgil had been an heroic Persius. Less studious of brevity and more of ornamental richness and easy flowing verse, he had perhaps divided the compound question into three—*whither art thou rushing? why these arms? what dreadful thought has taken possession of thy mind?*—had ornamented not merely one of the three divisions, but the whole three, and Virgil had been an epic Ovid. Dividing, and not too much dividing, the question—into two, not three—our author has obtained sufficient, not too much, space both for ease of numbers and ornament of thought, and is neither Persius nor Ovid, but Virgil—

> . . . "anima, qualem neque candidiorem
> terra tulit ; neque cui me sit devinctior alter."

The very next following verse is constructed in a similar manner: NON TALI AUXILIO [*tempus eget*] being one, and NEC DEFENSORI-BUS ISTIS TEMPUS EGET the other, of two limbs into which, for the sake no less of ornament and variety than of ease of composition, the pregnant thought, *no use in arms now*, is divided.

AUXILIO. Compare Ovid, *Met.* 12. 88 (Cycnus to Achilles, explaining that he was invulnerable, not by means of his arms, but by means of his skin):

> . . . "non haec, quam cernis, equinis
> fulva iubis cassis, neque onus cava parma sinistrae
> *auxilio* mihi sunt ; decor est quaesitus ab istis.
> Mars quoque ob hoc capere arma solet. Removebitur omne
> tegminis officium : tamen indestrictus abibo,"

words which—if you alter "cernis" into cerno, and "mihi sunt" into tibi erunt, in order to suit the person of the speaker—become almost the very words of Virgil. Compare also Lucan, 4. 615:

> "ille [Antaeus], parum fidens pedibus contingere matrem,
> *auxilium* membris calidas infundit arenas"

[the help of the hot sand]. *Ibid.* 268:

> . . . "miles, non utile clausis
> *auxilium*, mactavit equos ;"

and Quint. Curt. 3. 11 (ed. Bipont.) : "*Arma* iacientes quae paullo ante ad tutelam corporum sumpserant ; adeo pavor etiam *auxilia* formidabat." *Aen.* 12. *378:* "auxilium ducto mucrone" [the help of his drawn sword]. Also *Aen.* 8. *376:*

> "non ullum *auxilium* miseris, non arma rogavi
> artis opisque tuae,"

where "auxilium" is the help afforded by the "arma" of the same line, exactly as in our text AUXILIO is the help afforded by the "defensores" (= arma) of the same line.

I crave the pardon of our parliamentary orators for an explanation which shows in what utter ignorance of its true meaning this passage is quoted vituperatively; also the pardon of my readers in general for having here repeated at full length the proofs of an interpretation which—first put forward by me five-and-twenty years ago in my translation of the first two books of the Aeneid, and twice since then, viz., in my "Twelve Years' Voyage" and in my "Adversaria Virgiliana"—has been received by Forbiger in his third edition, by Wagner in his edition of 1861, and generally by Virgilian editors both at home and abroad as the undoubted meaning. If in the beginning of this comment I have quoted the opinions of Virgilian editors antecedent to my publications on the subject, it is only in order that my reader may be enabled to fill up for himself the *lacuna* left by some editors, and notably by Wagner in his edition of 1861, respecting the source from which their new information has been derived—a precaution which, I am bound to say, it would have been wholly unnecessary for me to take either in this or any other instance if the publishers of editions of Virgil subsequent to my entrance into the lists had generally behaved towards me as honestly and honourably as Forbiger in Germany and Conington in England.

HAEC ARA, viz., Iovis Hercei; see Ovid, *Ibis*, 285:

"nec tibi subsidio sit praesens numen; ut illi,
cui nihil *Hercei* profuit *ara Iovis*."

Id. *Met. 13. 409:*

"exiguumque senis Priami *Ioris ara cruorem*
combiberat."

Ennius, *Andromache* (ed. Hessel.):

"haec omnia vidi inflammari,
Priamo vei vitam evitari,
Ioris arum sanguine turpari."

526-532.

ECCE AUTEM ELAPSUS PYRRHI DE CAEDE POLITES
UNUS NATORUM PRIAMI PER TELA PER HOSTES
PORTICIBUS LONGIS FUGIT ET VACUA ATRIA LUSTRAT
SAUCIUS ILLUM ARDENS INFESTO VULNERE PYRRHUS
INSEQUITUR IAM IAMQUE MANU TENET ET PREMIT HASTA
UT TANDEM ANTE OCULOS EVASIT ET ORA PARENTUM
CONCIDIT AC MULTO VITAM CUM SANGUINE FUDIT

VAR. LECT.

[*punct.*] TENET · ET PREMIT HASTA III P. Manut.; La Cerda; D. Heins.: N. Heins (1670); Heyne; Brunck; Wakefield; Wagner (ed. Heyn.)

[*punct.*] TENET ET PREMIT HASTA III Wagner (1861); Ladewig; Ribbeck.

ELAPSUS... FUGIT... LUSTRAT. The running is suitable for Polites, he being swift of foot, Hom. *Il. 2. 792:* πωδωκεηισι πεποιθως.

UT TANDEM (vs. 531) takes up the narrative dropped at SAUCIUS, and informs us that Polites—already presented to us as wounded, and fleeing from Pyrrhus (PYRRHI DE CAEDE ELAPSUS, SAUCIUS)—continues his flight until he reaches his parents' presence, and, there arrived, drops down dead. Nothing can be plainer than the connexion:

>ECCE AUTEM ELAPSUS PYRRHI DE CAEDE POLITES,
>UNUS NATORUM PRIAMI, PER TELA, PER HOSTES,
>PORTICIBUS LONGIS FUGIT, ET VACUA ATRIA LUSTRAT
>SAUCIUS.
>UT TANDEM ANTE OCULOS EVASIT ET ORA PARENTUM
>CONCIDIT, AC MULTO VITAM CUM SANGUINE FUDIT.

The picture, so far as Polites is concerned, is as simple and at the same time as clear and distinct, as any picture can possibly be. Words cannot describe more plainly. But there is another actor on the stage, whose action—although synchronous with that of Polites, yet being a distinct and different action—cannot be described synchronously, but must in description either precede, or follow, or be introduced in the middle. Being that of Polites' pursuer, it can neither precede nor follow; preceding, it would be unintelligible, impossible; following, it would be too late, the interest would be over. It is therefore placed in the middle, and the narrator suddenly leaves the one actor in the midst of his action, takes up and follows to the end the action of the second, and then returning to the action of the first proceeds with it also to the end, to that point where the two actions which had all along been synchronous terminate together. This is entirely according to our author's usual manner, for an example of which see the account of the storming of Priam's palace given in the same manner, the synchronous actions of besiegers and besieged being, by means of intermixture, *i. e.*, by means of rapid transition from one party to the other, carried on as much as possible together. There as here, readers, misled by the rapidity of transition, have fallen into the mistake of connecting together as parts or consequences of one action things which were parts or consequences of another. It is by such mistake arising from such cause that in our text UT TANDEM ... CONCIDIT has been connected with PREMIT HASTA, and Polites supposed to die not in consequence of his original wound, the wound of which when he first came into view he was already SAUCIUS, but in consequence of a new wound inflicted on him at the end of the chase, and imagined to be found described in PREMIT HASTA—" PREMIT HASTA, *durchbort ihn mit der lanze.* CONCIDIT, in folge der neuen, ihm jetzt beigebrachten, wunde," Ladewig.

ILLUM ARDENS INFESTO VULNERE PYRRHUS INSEQUITUR, IAM IAMQUE MANU TENET ET PREMIT HASTA. **Not**, as represented by Heyne's punctuation as well as by Wagner's in his edition of Heyne, ILLUM ARDENS INFESTO VULNERE PYRRHUS INSEQUITUR, IAM IAMQUE MANU TENET, ET PREMIT HASTA, *i.e.*, not three co-ordinate sentences, **but** ILLUM ARDENS INFESTO VULNERE PYRRHUS INSEQUITUR, IAM IAMQUE MANU TENET ET PREMIT HASTA, *i. e.*, two co-ordinate sentences, TENET and PREMIT being connected into one single sentence by ET, and both equally operated on by IAM IAMQUE; in other words, INSEQUITUR alone signifying what Pyrrhus does, while TENET and PREMIT signify what he is just on the point of doing, but does not do.

The sentence being thus analysed, we perceive, (**1**), the true force of UT TANDEM, viz., that those words refer not to any (impossible) continuation of the flight of Polites after he had been " pressus hasta," but to the continuation of the flight of Polites SAUCIUS with his first wound—a flight continued from the PORTICIBUS LONGIS and VACUA ATRIA to the very spot where his parents are sitting, viz., in the court-yard at the altar of Jupiter Herceus ; (**2**), why there is in the account of the death of Polites in verse 532 none, not even the slightest reference to the mode in which he had been, as alleged, "pressus hasta," "durchbort mit der lanze," but the description is limited to the mere statement that he fell, fell of a heap as we say, or altogether (CONCIDIT), and expired with a great loss of blood, the reason for such omission being that best of all reasons, that he had not been " pressus hasta " at all, but died of the effusion of blood which was the consequence of his previous wound, a wound not described because inflicted before he came on the stage; **and** (**3**), we perceive with what propriety Priam inveighs against Pyrrhus, not—as he should inveigh if Polites had been " pressus hasta " in his presence—for killing his son before his eyes, but, as well pointed out to me by my daughter, for making him see the death of his son—

QUI NATI CORAM ME CERNERE LETUM
FECISTI, ET PATRIOS FOEDASTI FUNERE VULTUS—

as if he had said : " who, not content with killing my son, with inflicting a mortal wound on my son, drovest him into my very presence to die " ; Priam, in conformity with the never enough to be admired sentiment of antiquity, meeting with fortitude and equanimity the calamity of his son's death as the *sors belli*, the will of heaven, the decree of fate, but rebelling and revolting against the barbarity which made him a witness of it.

IAM IAMQUE MANU TENET ET PREMIT HASTA.—Not *is every moment on the point of holding him in his hand and (actually) spears him*, but, IAM IAMQUE belonging no less to PREMIT than to HASTA, is *every moment on the point of holding him in his hand and spearing him.* Compare 12. 753, where "iam iamque tenet" is explained by "similisque tenenti increpuit malis morsuque elusus inani est;" and Ovid, *Met. 1. 533* (of Daphne pursued by Apollo):

> "ut canis in vacuo leporem cum Gallicus arvo
> vidit, et hic praedam pedibus petit, ille salutem.
> alter inhaesuro similis *iam iamque* tenere
> sperat, et extento *stringit* vestigia rostro:
> alter in ambiguo est, an sit deprensus, et ipsis
> morsibus eripitur, tangentiaque ora relinquit."

Iam iamque marks the succession of time, a thing which cannot be represented in a picture or statue. See Rem. on 2. 213. To represent the successive times of a narrative, as many pictures would be necessary as there are times in the narrative, as many statues as the number of times in the narrative multiplied, say by the mean number of the objects and actors at all the different times. Supposing the actors and objects to be represented as of no more than some small fractional part—say one-hundredth, or one five-hundredth, or one-thousandth part—of their apparent natural size, the entire surface of our planet cleared of everything now upon it would not afford sufficient space for the exhibition of those represented in the single pocket volume of the Aeneid or Iliad.

EVASIT, *came the whole way*, viz., the whole way just described (PER TELA, PER HOSTES, PORTICIBUS LONGIS FUGIT, ET VACUA ATRIA LUSTRAT), into the very presence of his parents. See Rem. on 2. 458.

CONCIDIT, *falls down all at once and* (as we say) *of a heap*. The word differs from procumbit, which is to lie stretched at full length. Compare Ovid, *Met. 8. 763:*

> . . . "ante aras ingens ubi victima taurus
> *concidit*, abrupta cruor e cervice profusus."

Ibid., 401:

> "*concidit* Ancaeus; glomerataque sanguine multo," &c.

VACUA.—Heyne is right; *deserted*, where there was no one

else but himself. Compare Tacit. *Ann. 11. 21:* "*Vacuis* per medium diei porticibus."

SAUCIUS, the emphatic word of the whole long sentence ECCE ... SAUCIUS (see Rem. on 2. 246), is not merely *wounded*, but *desperately wounded* and *hors de combat*. Compare Cic. *in Verr. act. 2*, lib. 1. 26: "Servi nonnulli vulnerantur; ipse Rubrius in turba *saucialur*." Vavassor, *de Vi et Usu*, etc.: "Saucius: *vulneratus;* prius apud Graecos τραυματιας, posterius τετρωμενος ... Proprie efferri *saucios* ex acie, *non vulneratos* historici dicere solent, qui melius quam ceteri Latine loquuntur." The same word is placed in the same effective position by Sil. 6. 66 (of Serranus):

> ... "miseramque parentem,
> et dulces tristi repetebat sorte penates,
> *saucius*, haud illi comitum super ullus," &c.

533-537.

HIC PRIAMUS QUAMQUAM IN MEDIA IAM MORTE TENETUR
NON TAMEN ABSTINUIT NEC VOCI IRAEQUE PEPERCIT
AT TIBI PRO SCELERE EXCLAMAT PRO TALIBUS AUSIS
DI SI QUA EST CAELO PIETAS QUAE TALIA CURET
PERSOLVANT GRATES DIGNAS

MEDIA IAM MORTE.—To be *in media morte* is to be in imminent danger of death; to have death as it were on every side round you, but not yet actually touching you. The expression is used indifferently of those who are so sick or so severely hurt or wounded as to be likely soon to die, *i. e.*, of those in whom a process which is to end in death has already begun, and of those with respect to whom the process which is to end in death has not actually begun, is only threatening and imminent. Accordingly the expression is applied, **firstly**, by Statius, (*a*), (*Theb.*

8. 728) to Tydeus, mortally wounded yet possessing strength enough to call for and gnaw the head of Melanippus:

"tunc tristes socii cupidum bellare (quis ardor!)
et poscentem hastas, *media*que *in morte* negantem
exspirare, trahunt, summique in margine campi
effultum, gemina latera inclinantia parma
ponunt, ac saevi rediturum ad praelia Martis
promittunt flentes;"

(*b*), (*Theb. 8. 187*) to Amphiaraus, still terrible although already half swallowed up by the yawning earth:

. . . "tunc etiam *media* de *morte* timendum
hostibus, infestaque abeuntem vidimus hasta;"

and (*c*), (*Silv. 2. 5. 17*) to a lion conquered and dying, but still able to fight:

. . . "mansere animi, virtusque cadenti
a *media* iam *morte* redit;"

and on the other hand it is applied, **secondly**, by Cicero *in Verrem*, lib. 5 (ed. Lamb. p. 190, 4) to malefactors tied to the stake, but still sound and unhurt, and afterwards liberated: "Ilos ad supplicium iam more maiorum traditos, et ad palum alligatos, ex *media morte* eripere ac liberare ausus es," where the meaning, if doubtful, would be placed beyond doubt by the exactly similar use of medius only a few lines later: "ut homines servos, ut ipse qui iudicarat, ut statim e *medio* supplicio dimiserit." Our author's use of the term corresponds not with Statius's but Cicero's; Priam is described as MEDIA IN MORTE, not because really and truly in the middle of death, or half dead, but because, although as yet unhurt, yet in such imminent and pressing danger as to be *as it were* in the middle of death. It is, no doubt, in the same sense the expression is used by Valerius Flaccus (3. 326), where Clyte, complaining that she had not had the satisfaction of being present when Jason killed Cyzicus, says:

"ast ego non *media* te saltem, Cyzice, vidi
tendentem mihi *morte* manus;"

meaning not the very moment in which he actually received the death wound, but that immediately preceding moment when the danger was so imminent and urgent as to cause him to stretch out his hands imploring help. The difficulty which the commentators laboured under was their old one, that of taking their author's words literally and prosaically instead of figuratively and poetically. They could not for the life of them see how Priam was in death at all, either in the beginning, middle, or end of it ("prima, media, postrema," Servius); all they saw was that he was in manifest and immediate danger of death, and hence Servius's " manifesta," and Heyne's and Wagner's (*Virg. Br. En.*) "praesenti mortis periculo"—Virgil's meaning all the while being, not that he was in manifest and immediate danger, but that, so manifest and immediate was his danger that he was (poetically, of course, not historically and in point of fact) in the very middle of death; that death, again, **not** being the death of his son, as Servius to relieve himself out of his embarrassment is fain to understand it (for his being in the middle of Polites' death, *i. e.*, surrounded by the bloody tragedy of his son's death, had rather been a reason for his not sparing, than for his sparing, his wrathful words: NEC VOCI IRAEQUE PEPERCIT), **but** his own death: as if Virgil had said that Priam, although so near to and sure of death as scarcely to belong any longer to the living (his deadly enemy approaching him with the bloody sword in his hand with which he has just slain his son), yet did not hesitate to do that which would soon put his belonging to the living out of question, viz., exasperate his enemy.

In the very sense in which Virgil here uses the expression media mors, Livy (8. 24) uses the expression "media fata:" "ut ferme fugiendo in media fata ruitur;" Statius, the expression medii Manes (*Theb. 2. 697*, ed. Müller—Tydeus addressing the sole survivor of the fifty of which the ambuscade had consisted):

"quisquis es Aonidum, quem crastina munere nostro
Manibus exemptum *mediis* Aurora videbit;"

Catullus, the expression medius turbo leti (*Epith. Pel. et Thet. 149*):

"certe ego te in *medio* versantem *turbine leti*
eripui;"

and Ammian (31. 13), the similar but much weaker expression, "Inter ipsa mortis confinia."

Extrema mors has the same relation to media mors as extrema to media, therefore expresses a greatly increased, much more imminent urgency either of death or of danger of death (as, 2. 446:

>   . . . "his se quando ultima cernunt,
>   *extrema* iam in *morte* parant defendere telis,"

with which compare Ammian. 16. 12: "Formidabilis manus, *extremae necessitatis* articulo circumventos, si iuvisset fors, ereptura")—nay, sometimes even death completed, as 11. 845 (Opis apostrophizing dead Camilla):

>   "non tamen indecorem tua te regina reliquit
>   *extrema* iam in *morte;* neque hoc sine nomine letum
>   per gentes erit, aut famam patieris inultae.
>   nam quicunque tuum violavit vulnere corpus
>   morte luet merita."

TENETUR, *is held* (*caught*), viz., as in a net, or other surrounding medium, out of which there is no possibility of flight or escape.

IN MEDIA . . . TENETUR. Compare Cic. *ad Att.* 11. 18: "*Tenemur undique*, neque iam quo minus serviamus recusamus," where the "undique" of Cicero corresponds to the MEDIA of our text; Aristoph. *Ranae, 469:* αλλα νυν εχει μεσος ("sed nunc medius teneris").

AT (vs. 535).—"Hoc loco est cum indignatione imprecantis; Terent. *Hecyr.* 1. 2. 59: 'At te dii deaeque perdant cum tuo istoc odio,'" Wagn. (1861). Neither in our text nor in the Terentian parallel is there more indignation or imprecation contained in the "at" than there is in the TIBI or the "te." The imprecation is in the whole sentence and context; the "at," as *at*, is indifferent, takes its colour from the context and is joined with simple praying, blessing, and cursing, all alike. Its use seems to be on all occasions to connect the subsequent with the preceding, whether that preceding has been actually expressed, as Tibull. 1. 73:

>   "*at* tu casta, precor, maneas; sanctique pudoris
>   assideat custos sedula semper anus;"

or is merely supposed to have passed through the mind of the speaker, as in our text, and Eurip. *Med.* 759 (ed. Fix) where the chorus, who like Priam in our text has not previously said a word, begins her prayer of good wishes or blessing with αλλα:

> αλλα σ' ο Μαιας πομπαιος αναξ
> πελασειε δομοις, ων τ' επινοιαν
> σπευδεις κατεχων πραξειας, επει
> γενναιος ανηρ,
> Αιγευ, παρ' εμοι δεδοκησαι.

SI QUA EST CAELO PIETAS.—Compare Shakesp. *Cymbeline*, 4. 6:

> . . . "but if there be
> yet left in heaven as small a drop of pity
> as a wren's eye, O gods, a part of it!"

Id. *Rom. and Jul.* 3. 5:

> "is there no pity sitting in the clouds
> that sees into the bottom of my grief!"

There needs no further proof than this single passage, how entirely different the pietas of the Romans was from our *piety*, how totally opposite "pius Aeneas" to "pious Aeneas." PIETAS here is precisely our *pity*, and the whole expression exists in Italian at the present day, as Goldoni, *Zelinda e Lindoro*, 3. 9: "Numi, assistetemi per pietà." See Remm. on 1. 14 and 607.

540-553.

AT—ENSEM

VAR. LECT.

ET ■ *Med.* (Fogg.) ■■■ Serv. (ed. Lion); Ven. 1470; Aldus (1514); P. Manut.

EX ■■■ Wakefield, *ex conj.*

EC ■■■ Ribbeck.

O *Vat., Rom., Ver., St. Gall.*

The connection of thought indicated by AT is: "Thou hast acted so, *but* Achilles acted differently; thou art worse than Achilles."

CORPUSQUE, &c., . . . REMISIT.—Compare Apollon. Rhod. 2. 966:

> ενθα ποτε προμολουσαν Αρητιαδα Μελανιππην
> ηρως Ηρακλεης ελοχησατο, και οι αποινα
> Ιππολυτη ζωστηρα πανσιολον εγγυαλιξεν
> αμφι κασιγνητης· ο δ᾽ απημονα πεμψεν οπισσω.

ERUBUIT, *blushed, was ashamed, was not* αναιδης. There is, perhaps, allusion to the βωμος αναιδειας on which the prosecutor stood in the Athenian court of justice, Zenob. *Proverb. 4. 36*: φησι Θεοφραστος εν τω περι Νομων Υβρεως και Αναιδειας παρα τοις Αθηναιοις ειναι βωμους. See Forchhammer, *Ind. Schol.* Kiel, 1843-4: "λιθος αναιδειας non est *impudentiae lapis*, sed *implacabilitatis* sive *negatae veniae*—qui vero accuset, is iam se nolle ostendit veniam dare, atque vel eam ob causam debet ex αναιδειας lapide perorare."*

IN MEA REGNA.—I think, not *into my kingdom*, in the literal sense, but in that secondary sense in which the same words might have been used by a private person. In the literal sense they had ill become the position in which Priam was at the time referred to. Compare *Ecl. 1. 67*:

> "en, unquam patrios longo post tempore fines,
> pauperis et tuguri congestum caespite culmen, ·
> post aliquot, *mea regna* videns, mirabor aristas?"

Georg. 3. 476:

> . . . "videat desertaque *regna*
> pastorum et longe saltus lateque vacantes."

And Lucan, 9. 458:

> "*regna* videt pauper Nasamon errantia vento."

I believe, indeed, the precise words mea regna are never used in any other than this secondary sense.

---

* The above from "Zenob." to the end is quoted from "Cambridge Journal of Philology," No. 2, p. 3 and p. 21, which whole passage is to be compared, as well as Pausan. 1. 28, 5, referred to, *ibid.*, p. 21.

CONIECIT, *threw with all his might* (see Rem. on "contorsit," 2. 52), but which nevertheless, his might being so little, did not tell, had no effect, did no damage, SINE ICTU.

RAUCO.—The ordinary adjunct. Compare Claud. *Bell. Gild.* 453:

> .... "an Mauri fremitum *raucos*que repulsus umbonum, et vestros passuri cominus enses?"

The addition of this word is for the purpose of showing the utmost effect of the stroke, viz., to make the shield ring.

PROTENUS AERE REPULSUM, ET SUMMO CLIPEI UMBONE PEPENDIT.—Not having been thrown with sufficient force to penetrate the brazen plate of the shield, the spear stuck in the outer coat (viz., in the leather), and not having sufficient support there to stand erect or perpendicular to the plane of the shield, drooped or hung down so as to form an acute angle with the plane of the shield below, and an obtuse angle above. That this is precisely the picture which our author wishes to present is declared by Silius's imitation (10. 115):

> "haesit multiplici non alte cuspis in auro,
> ac senium invalido dependens prodidit ictu."

SUMMO CLIPEI UMBONE.—Very precise: not merely in the shield, but in the boss or prominent central part of the shield (UMBONE); and not merely in the boss, but in the very top or most projecting part of the boss. There were two reasons, therefore, why the spear did not penetrate; first, because it was thrown without force (IMBELLE), and secondly, because it struck the very strongest part of the shield. Spears which penetrate the shield so as to wound are always described as striking the orae or thin part of the shield near the circumference. Compare 10. 474 (Turnus wounded through his shield by Pallas):

> "illa volans, humeri surgunt qua tegmina summa,
> incidit, atque viam clipei molita per *oras*,
> tandem etiam magno strinxit de corpore Turni,"

where we have the exactly opposite circumstances to those described in our text; the spear not only thrown with great force, but striking the shield towards the margin, and accordingly not only penetrating but wounding. Also 10. 588 :

> . . . " subit oras hasta per imas
> fulgentis clipei, tum laevum perforat inguen."

ILLI MEA TRISTIA FACTA DEGENEREMQUE NEOPTOLEMUM NARRARE MEMENTO.—ILLI, viz., PELIDAE. Compare Sil. 4. 286 (ed. Ruperti) :

> " cui consul : 'ferre haec umbris proavoque memento,
> quam procul occumbas Tarpeia sede, tibique
> haud licitum sacri Capitolia cernere montis.' "

The whole point is in ILLI—" tell that Pelides who behaved so well to you, how ill you have been treated by his son." Yet commentators have not been wanting to maintain that ILLI is not the pronoun but the adverb of place, and the meaning not that which I have just indicated, but " tell *there* (viz., there below in the shades where Pelides is) how badly you have been treated by the son of Pelides." See Donatus ad Terent. *Hec. 1. 2. 19 :*

> " nam *illic* haud licebat nisi praefinito loqui,"

where he says : " Legitur et *illi*, ut sit circumflexus accentus, et significet *illic*, ut ILLI MEA TRISTIA FACTA, et absolutum est." This is one of the not very rare cases in which the reader were better without any commentator—would be sure to go right if allowed to take his own way ; also one of the cases which show that the Donatus who commented on Terence, that Donatus whose comment on ILLI I have just quoted, was not Servius's Donatus, the comment of the latter on the passage being to the point-blank opposite effect : " 'Ibis,' inquit, 'ut patri meo ipse referas male gesta mea.' "

ENSEM (vs. 553) belongs to both verbs, CORUSCUM only to EXTULIT. EXTULIT (ENSEM) CORUSCUM, because the very act of raising and flourishing the sword made it flash ; ABDIDIT ENSEM (no longer CORUSCUM), because the very act of plunging it (or stowing it away : see Rem. on *Aen. 1. 56*) into the side caused it to cease to flash.

If it be not mere supererogation to refer to instances of a

similar beautiful accuracy of language in a writer whose language is always supereminently accurate, I would here refer the reader to the special apposition of "bellatrix" to "aurea cingula," and of "virgo" to "viris," *Aen. 1. 497;* to the junction of "Fortuna" with the two verbs "finxit" and "finget," and of "improba" with the latter only, *Aen. 2. 80;* and to the precise "intorserit hastam," "laeserit cuspide," *Aen. 2. 230, 231;* also to Remm. on vv. 270 and 689.

554-558.

HAEC FINIS PRIAMI FATORUM HIC EXITUS ILLUM
SORTE TULIT TROIAM INCENSAM ET PROLAPSA VIDENTEM
PERGAMA TOT QUONDAM POPULIS TERRISQUE SUPERBUM
REGNATOREM ASIAE IACET INGENS LITTORE TRUNCUS
AVULSUMQUE HUMERIS CAPUT ET SINE NOMINE CORPUS

VAR. LECT.

[*punct.*] PRIAMI FATORUM · HIC **I** *Med.* **III** P. Manut.; D. Heins.; N. Heins.; Philippe; Heyne; Brunck; Wakef.; Wagner (ed. Heyn., *Lect. Virg.* and *Praest.*); Dietsch; Kappes.

[*punct.*] PRIAMI · FATORUM HIC **III** Peerlkamp; Haeckermann; Ladewig; Haupt; Ribbeck.

So Ammianus Marcellinus (14. 11), finely, of Constantius Gallus Caesar: "Cervice abscissa, ereptaque vultus et capitis dignitate, cadaver est relictum informe, paullo ante urbibus et provinciis formidatum." Also Lucan (8. 710), much less finely, of Pompey the Great:

. . . "nullaque manente figura,
una nota est Magno capitis iactura revulsi."

HAEC FINIS . . . TULIT.—Not HAEC FINIS PRIAMI, but HAEC FINIS FATORUM PRIAMI, (*a*), because finis elsewhere in Virgil is always the end not of a person but of a thing. (***b***), because in the exactly corresponding passage of Tacitus (*Hist*. 1. *49*), "Hunc *exitum* habuit Ser. Galba, tribus et septuaginta annis, quinque principes prospera fortuna emensus, et alieno imperio felicior quam suo," it is not exitus fatorum but simply exitus. (***c***), because elsewhere in the same author it is invariably exitus of the person, not of the person's fates, as *Annal*. *1. 10:* "Sane Cassii et Brutorum *exitus* paternis inimicitiis datos." *Ibid.*, *4. 55:* "Atrociore semper fama erga dominantium *exitus*." (***d***), because HAEC FINIS PRIAMI had been if not absolutely disrespectful, at least much less respectful, towards Priam, than HAEC FINIS PRIAMI FATORUM. (***e***), because—the first clause ending with FATORUM and the second commencing with HIC—both clauses, the former especially, are more dignified, and the pause more acceptable both to mind and ear. (***f***), because the climax, the ascent from the fates of Priam in the first clause to Priam himself in the second, so impressive in the received structure, is wholly absent from the proposed. (***g***), because the repetition of the demonstrative in the like positions HAEC FINIS, HIC EXITUS, is more effective than in the unlike HAEC FINIS, FATORUM HIC EXITUS. (***h***), on account of the more perfect tallying of the clauses HAEC FINIS PRIAMI FATORUM, HIC EXITUS ILLUM SORTE TULIT (where SORTE balances FATORUM) in the same manner as HIC balances HAEC, and EXITUS, FINIS than of the two clauses HAEC FINIS PRIAMI, FATORUM HIC EXITUS ILLUM SORTE TULIT, where the whole weight both of FATORUM and SORTE is in the second clause, without any counterpoise at all in the first. (***i***), because FATORUM, tautological in the same clause with SORTE, expresses, in the same clause with FINIS, that the end spoken of is the end not of Priam, but of the fates of Priam, as if Virgil had said " here ends the history of Priam;" **and**, (***k***), because the citation by Gellius of HAEC FINIS PRIAMI FATORUM, without the context and without observation, is sufficient proof of the junction of FATORUM by Gellius and his contemporaries not with EXITUS but with FINIS. For all these reasons I adhere with Dietsch (*Theolog*. p. 23: "Minus recte FATORUM ad sequentia trahi mihi videtur, cum ita vis, quae in anastrophe est, deleatur, neque HAEC FINIS PRIAMI sine molestia sit, postremo vero per verba HAEC FINIS FATORUM legentes cum quadam gravitate ad vs. 506 revocentur") to the received structure and punctuation, and reject the innovation of Peerlkamp, Haeckermann, and Ribbeck, notwithstanding the argument which might, but has not yet been advanced in favour of it, viz., that it has a perfect parallel in τουτο Πομπηιου τελος, Plutarch's *epiphonema* of the closing scene of Pompey the Great, a closing scene so similar to that which our author has drawn for Priam as to call forth the observation of Servius on the latter: "Pompeii tangit historiam."

SORTE TULIT, *i. e.*, SORTE *fati* TULIT. Compare 12. 501: "nescia mens hominum *fati sortis*que futurae," *i.e.*, sortis quae e fato eveniet, sortis quam fatum dabit.

EXITUS SORTE [*fati*]. Compare Hom. *Il. 3. 309*: θανατοιο τελος πεπρωμενον.

INGENS LITTORE TRUNCUS AVULSUMQUE HUMERIS CAPUT ET SINE NOMINE CORPUS.—Only one of the nominatives, viz., TRUNCUS, belongs to IACET; the other two nominatives, CAPUT and CORPUS, have each their own verb, viz., *est*, understood. Compare *Aen. 1. 452*:

> "aerea cui gradibus surgebant limina, nexaeque
> aere trabes,"

where the structure is not "limina nexaeque trabes surgebant," but "limina surgebant, trabesque [*erant*] nexae." There should, therefore, be a semicolon at TRUNCUS.

SINE NOMINE.—*Not*, without name in the sense of appellation, *but* without name in the sense of honour or renown. That this and no other is the meaning is placed beyond doubt by the manifest imitation of Silius (*a*), 10. 209:

> "hic tibi finis erat, metas hic Aufidus aevi
> servabat *tacito*, non felix Curio, *leto*.
> namque, furens animi dum consternata moratur
> agmina, et oppositu membrorum sistere certat,
> in praeceps magna propulsus mole ruentum
> turbatis hauritur aquis, fundoque volutus
> Hadriaca iacuit *sine nomine mortis* arena."

where "sine nomine" is explained by Silius himself to be equivalent to "sine nomine mortis," and this again to be equivalent to "tacito leto." Compare also (***b***), Silius, 13. 4:

> ". . . "nulla laedens ubi gramina ripa
> Turia deducit tenuem *sine nomine* rivum,
> et tacite Tuscis *inglorius* affluit undis."

(***c***), Flor. 3. 16: "C. Gracchum hominem sine tribu, *sine nomine*." (***d***), *Aen.* 9. 343:

> ". . "ac multam in medio *sine nomine* plebem
> Fadumque, Herbesumque subit, Rhoetumque Abarimque
> ignaros,"

in which three latter places, persons or things said to be "sine nomine" are actually named. Also (***e***), 11. 846: "Sine nomine letum" [a death without renown, an inglorious death]. (***f***), Ovid, *Fast.* 4. 437:

> "illa legit calthas ; huic sunt violaria curae :
> illa papavereas subsecat usque comas.
> has, hyacinthe, tenes ; illas, amarante, moraris ;
> pars thyma, pars casiam, pars meliloton amant.
> plurima lecta rosa est ; et sunt *sine nomine* flores.
> ipsa crocos tenues, liliaque alba legit."

where "flores sine nomine" are not *flowers which have never received names*, but *inglorious flowers, flowers of little fame and note*, and therefore not to be enumerated along with the famous flowers already mentioned.

The body of Priam, therefore, lay on the shore SINE NOMINE, not, with Wagner, 1861, because it could not be distinguished whose body it was ("quia absciso capite iam cognosci non poterat cuius esset corpus"); but, with Nonius ("nomen, decus, dignitas ; *Aen. 2. 558:* SINE NOMINE CORPUS), because, although Priam's body, and known to be Priam's body, it had *no respect or honour*, was treated by the Greeks as if it had been the body of a man of no consequence, the carcase of a dog. See Remm. on 1. 613; 9. 343; 12. 514. The corresponding Greek expression is νώνυμος or ανώνυμος, as Hom. *Od. 13. 238* (of Ithaca):

ουδέ τι λιην ουτω νωνυμος εστιν. Eurip. *Hippol.* 1 :

πολλη μεν εν βροτοισι κουκ ανωνυμος
θεα κεκλημαι Κυπρις.

The corresponding English is *nameless*.

567-588.

IAM—FEREBAR

VAR. LECT.

IAM—FEREBAR II ½. III Aldus (1514); Junta (1537); P. Manut.; D. Heins.; N. Heins. (1670); Phil.; Wakef.; Pott.; Wagn. (ed. Heyn., ed. 1861), who without ever so much as having seen the MS. takes upon him, I know not on what hearsay, to inform his readers that these verses are contained in the Palatine; Lad.; Haupt.

IAM—FEREBAR OMITTED I Pal.; Med.; "In nullo ex iis veteribus codd. quos versavimus habentur," Pierius. II ½. III Venice, 1470.

IAM—FEREBAR OMITTED OR STIGMATIZED III Heyn.; Brunck; Peerl. (vv. 567-623); Gruppe; Ribb.

Concerning these verses, the following opinion has been expressed by Charles James Fox in a letter to Gilbert Wakefield, then a prisoner in Dorchester gaol (Russell's *Mem. of Fox*, vol. 4, p. 411): "If the lines omitted in the Medici MS. are spurious, they are, I think, the happiest imitation of Virgil's manner that I ever saw. I am indeed so unwilling to believe them any other than genuine, that rather than I would consent to such an opinion, I should be inclined to think that Virgil himself had written and afterwards erased them on account of their inconsistency with the account he gives of Helen in the Sixth Book." Mr. Fox should have said :—The verses are genuine, for none but a Virgil ever wrote them, and there never was but one Virgil. By that one only Virgil therefore they were written, and are absent from the more ancient MSS., because expunged along with the four introductory verses by Tucca and Varius, whose mutilation of the poem was antecedent not only to any MSS. of it now existing, but to any even so much as perusal of it after it had passed out of the capsule of the author (see Rem. on 2. 632). Wakefield, however, in his reply thus unqualifiedly accepts Fox's opinion : " Your supposition that the verses in *Aen. 2* were Virgil's own, and omitted by him, with the reason for that omission, pleases me entirely."

How has it happened that not Fox and Wakefield only, but all the propugners of these verses, have so entirely omitted to draw an argument in their favour from Hom. *Od. 20. 5 ?* There—

ενθ' Οδυσευς μνηστηρσι κακα φρονεων ενι θυμω
κειτ' εγρηγοροων· ται δ' εκ μεγαροιο γυναικες
ηϊσαν, αι μνηστηρσιν εμισγεσκοντο παρος περ,
αλληλησι γελω και ευφροσυνην παρεχουσαι.
του δ' ωρινετο θυμος ενι στηθεσσι φιλοισιν·
πολλα δε μερμηριζε κατα φρενα και κατα θυμον,
ηε μεταϊξας θανατον τευξειεν εκαστη,
η ετ' εω μνηστηρσιν υπερφιαλοισι μιγηναι
υστατα και πυματα. κραδιη δε οι ενδον υλακτει.
ως δε κυων αμαλησι περι σκυλακεσσι βεβωσα
ανδρ' αγνοιησασ' υλαει, μεμονεν τε μαχεσθαι,
ως ρα του ενδον υλακτει αγαιομενου κακα εργα.
στηθος δε πληξας κραδιην ηνιπαπε μυθω·
τετλαθι δη, κραδιη· και κυντερον αλλο ποτ' ετλης,
ηματι τω, οτε μοι μενος ασχετος ησθιε Κυκλωψ
ιφθιμους εταρους· συ δ' ετολμας, οφρα σε μητις
εξαγαγ' εξ αντροιο οϊομενον θανεεσθαι.
ως εφατ' εν στηθεσσι καθαπτομενος φιλον ητορ.
τω δε μαλ' εν πειση κραδιη μενε τετληυια
νωλεμεως.

562-576.

VITAM—POENAS

VAR. LECT. (vs. 561).

CIRCUM ME **III** D. Heins.
ME CIRCUM **III** P. Manut.; N. Heins. (1670); Heyne; Brunck; Wakef.;
Voss ; Heyne; Wagner (ed. Heyn., ed. 1861; see Wagner ad 11. 298);
Ladewig; Ribb.

VAR. LECT. (vs. 576).

SCELERATAS **III** P. Manut.; D. Heins.; N. Heins. (1670); Gesner; Heyne;
Brunck; Wakefield; Wagner; Ribb.
SCELERATAE **III** Heyne ("An SCELERATAE? ut malim"); Voss.

VITAM EXHALANTEM.—Compare *Bibl. Sacra, Lament. Ieremiae*,
2. 12: "Cum *exhalarent animas* suas in sinu matrum suarum."
The expression is exactly equivalent to vitam exspirantem,
and has descended into the Italian, as Ariost. *Orl. Fur.* 7. 76:

"e lo scudo mirabile tolse anco,
che non pur gli occhi abbarbagliar solea,
ma l' *anima* facea si venir manco,
che dal corpo *esalata* esser parea."

CUM LIMINA, &c., . . . ASPICIO: "LIMINA VESTAE, templum
Vestae in arce conditum," Forbiger, Ladewig. I think not;
first, because (see verse 632) Aeneas has not yet left the palace;
secondly, because the temple of Vesta on the arx being a
temple could not properly be denominated "secreta sedes;" and
thirdly, because there was in every royal palace, and especially
in Priam's, a sacred hearth, or hearth with sacred fire (εστια),
which, on account of its peculiar sanctity, afforded an inviolable
asylum to the fugitive. The LIMINA VESTAE of our text I understand to be that part of the palace in which the sacred hearth
was, that most interior, secret and sacred part of the palace, de-

nominated penetralia Vestae, or more briefly penetralia, or even Vesta, from the goddess whose peculiar seat it was, and in honour of whom the sacred fire, the εστια or Vesta, was kept there, perpetually burning. See 5. 744:

" Pergameumque Larem et canae *penetralia Vestae*
farre pio et plena supplex veneratur acerra."

9. 258 :

". . " per magnos, Nise, Penates
Assaracique Larem, et canae *penetralia Vestae*."

Hom. *Od.* 17. 155 :

ιστω νυν Ζευς πρωτα θεων, ξενιη τε τραπεζα,
ιστιη τ' Οδυσηος αμυμονος, ην αφικανω,

—the last example, an appeal to the sacredness of the same Vesta, which is made more than once elsewhere in the course of the poem. Callim. *Hymn. ad Delum,* 325 (apostrophizing Delos) :

ιστιη ω νησων, ευεστιε, χαιρε μεν αυτη,

where Spanheim : " Vestae autem simulacra . . . in iisdem Prytaneis, ac in privatis etiam aedibus, in earum penetrali seu media parte vulgo erant itidem sacrata. Hinc dicta quoque pridem *Vesta,* non solum in *penetralibus* habitare, ut apud Maronem, 5. 744, 'penetralia Vestae;' sed in Orphicis dudum ante, η μεσον οικον εχεις, . . . et apud Phornutum cap. de Cerere et Vesta, de hac, κατα μεσους ιδρυται τους οικους. . . . Unde quemadmodum aedes aut ara Apollinis Delphica, εστια μεσομφαλος, *ara* seu *sedes penetralis* apud veteres tragicos, Aeschylum, *Agam. 1065,* et alibi, haud semel appellata ; quod nempe urbs Delphi *orbis* haberetur iuxta poetam in Priapeiis *umbilicus :* ita haud minus *Delus* in medio Cycladum sita, immo *Cyclas* etiam, uti supra vidimus, et praeterea Latonae partu ac Apollinis natalibus et cultu veneranda, ιστιη νησων, et ευεστιος, *Vesta insularum* ac *fortunata,* hic dicitur."

This apartment, this " limina Vestae," being thus always in the innermost, least public, part of the building, . . . was of all places the most likely and most proper for Helen to take refuge in, not only on account of its secrecy and inviolability, but because it was so near at hand, in the very palace. Precisely because Helen's hiding place was so retired, is the explanation added how it happens that Aeneas discovered her :

<blockquote>
DANT CLARA INCENDIA LUCEM
ERRANTI, PASSIMQUE OCULOS PER CUNCTA FERENTI
</blockquote>

[surely *not* everywhere and through everything in the arx or in the city, *but* everywhere and through everything in the palace]. Precisely because the hiding place is so retired is Helen's hiding herself in it appropriately expressed by the words ABDIDERAT and LATENTEM, *put herself out of the way*, and *lurking*, expressions which had been less applicable if Helen's hiding place had been a public temple. And precisely because the secret hiding place was the εστια or sacred hearth, is the interference of Venus called for, less to hinder the unmanly act of killing a woman than to hinder the almost unheard-of impiety of killing an ικετης εφεστιος.

There is a peculiar propriety in Helen's taking refuge in the domestic Vesta, and thus rendering herself an ικετης εφεστιος. The domestic Vesta of the prince or other principal person afforded sure safeguard and protection to the stranger or to the culprit who, flying from the justice or revenge of his fellow-countrymen, was fortunate enough to reach such place of refuge, and Helen was both a stranger and a culprit :

<blockquote>
ILLA, SIBI INFESTOS EVERSA OB PERGAMA TEUCROS,
ET POENAS DANAUM, ET DESERTI CONIUGIS IRAS
PRAEMETUENS, TROIAE ET PATRIAE COMMUNIS ERINNYS,
ABDIDERAT SESE ATQUE ARIS INVISA SEDEBAT.
</blockquote>

In cases in which flight from home was impossible or not desirable, the guilty person used to take refuge in the same sanctuary, either for safety, or for the mere sake of hiding his shame from the eye of day, as Stat. *Theb. 1. 492* (of Oedipus) :

<blockquote>
" illum indulgentem tenebris, imaeque recessu
sedis, inaspectos caelo radiisque Penates
servantem, tamen assiduis circumvolat alis
saeva dies animi, scelerumque in pectore Dirae."
</blockquote>

In the houses of the poor there were no " limina Vestae " properly so called, no domestic sanctuary in which fire or at least a lamp was kept perpetually burning. The place of the sacred fire was in such houses filled by the kitchen hearth, which, following the primitive practice, was the εστια, the sacred refuge of the fugitive and stranger, as Sil. 6. 73:

> . . . . " quum membra cubili
> evolvens non tarda Marus . . . .
> . . . .
> procedit, renovata *focis* et *paupere Vesta*
> lumina praetendens."

The custom of the sacred or perpetual fire has, in common with so many other pagan observances, come down under a changed name to the present day, nay even to the present day varies in costliness in the direct ratio of the wealth of the individual votary; for while there is in every house in Rome a sacred light burning day and night before the likeness of the modern Vesta, it is only in palaces and churches this light radiates from a lamp or lamps of gold or silver, and serves to light a marble statue. In humbler dwellings it is a mere wick floating like a nurse's night-light on a little cup of oil, and serves to illuminate, not a marble statue, but a mere wood-cut on paper of the goddess, and is even sometimes obliged to perform the humbler, more useful, office of lighting a dark dirty stone stair or passage, or a dingy corner of an obscure shop, sometimes a wretched closet's still more wretched pallet.

SERVANTEM (vs. 568). See Rem. on 2. 450.

PRAEMETUENS.—"Fürchtete," Voss. "Temendo," Caro. "Dreads," Dryden—all omitting the PRAE, the force of which is, that her fear anticipated the anger, that she fled without waiting to see whether her fear were well founded or not. Compare Phaedr. 1. 16. 3:

> " ovem rogabat cervus modium tritici,
> lupo sponsore. at illa, *praemetuens* dolum," &c.

Metuere expresses the fear of an urgent or immediate, praemetuere of an uncertain or remote danger. The former word would express Helen's fear, if she was hiding from the Greeks, knowing them to be in actual pursuit of her; the latter expresses that sort of fear which leads Helen to hide herself without being sure that the Greeks will pursue her, or that they have even so much as a hostile feeling towards her. PRAEMETUENS INFESTOS TEUCROS, ET POENAS DANAUM ET DESERTI CONIUGIS IRAS, is therefore equivalent to *fearing that such might be the state of things;* while *metuens* INFESTOS TEUCROS, ET POENAS DANAUM, ET DESERTI CONIUGIS IRAS, would have been equivalent to saying that Helen knew that such was the state of things, knew that the Teucri *were* irritated against her, that her husband and the Danai were angry with her, and certainly would avenge themselves on her. The preposition PRAE is thus used with the greatest propriety, inasmuch as it expresses the precedence of the fear to the actual danger.

ABDIDERAT SESE ATQUE ARIS INVISA SEDEBAT.—The repetition, according to our author's usual manner (see Rem. on 1. 151), in a slightly changed form, of the preceding QUUM . . . ASPICIO, vss. 567-569.

INVISA (vs. 574), " unbemerkt," Ladewig. No ; but, as always elsewhere in Virgil, odiosa, *the hateful one,* and therefore praemetuens (vs. 573) not without reason. That this is the true import of the word seems to be placed beyond doubt by vs. 601 : " Tyndaridis facies *invisa* Lacaenae."

SCELERATAS* POENAS.—" Poenas de scelerata," La Cerda.

---

* It will be observed that the comment on this word rests on the acceptation of the term scelus in a wider and more general sense, to indicate, not absolute moral delinquency, but rather some circumstances of horror or the like accompanying the object to which it is applied. It is not, however, without some hesitation that I have adopted this view. If, as I formerly thought, the other interpretation be the correct one in this passage, then I would rather be inclined to read SCELERATAE with Voss, and not SCELERATAS—(1), because no parallel, so far as I know, has ever been adduced for the transference of the guilt of the offender to the punishment of the offence. Poenae may be crudeles, may be sanguineae, may be cruentae, but if I am not mistaken cannot be sceleratae unless there is scelus in taking them. If it be alleged that the guilt of the sinner is transferred to the place of his punishment in the expression " sceleratum limen," 6. 563, I reply that the transition from the wicked person to the wicked place is as easy and natural as the transition from the wicked person to the wicked punishment is forced and unnatural—a transition not to the near neighbouring thing, but to its point-blank opposite, the punishment being, in the direct ratio of the scelus, not sceleratae,

"Paullo insolentius pro *poenas a scelerata femina sumptas*, nam ut sint *poenae per scelus exactae*, alienum a loco est," Heyne. "Scelus futurum erat, interficere supplicem ad aras sedentem," Wagn. (*Praest.*), Ladewig. The poenae are not sceleratae because Helen is scelerata, such use of the word being contrary to its use in all the other places in which our author has used it, in every one of which the scelus expressed by sceleratus is the scelus of the subject of which sceleratus is predicated, as 6. 563 : " sceleratum limen ;" 12. 949 : " scelerato sanguine ;" 3. 60 : " scelerata terra ;" 7. 461 : " scelerata insania ;" 2. 231 : " sceleratam hastam ;" 9. 137 : " sceleratam gentem ;" *Georg. 2. 256 :* " sceleratum frigus." SCELERATAS POENAS is, therefore, poenae which are sceleratae in their own nature, and so far the explanation of Wagner and Ladewig is correct. But I differ *toto caelo* from those critics in the explanation of the scelus ascribed to the poenae. The poenae, as Heyne rightly observes, are not called sceleratae, as being *poenae exactae per scelus*. Aeneas, at the moment when the IRA enters his breast, thinks only of punishing Helen, and is so far from thinking that it is any crime to punish her, or that he is violating the sanctuary of Vesta in punishing her, that his reflection is: that although the act was no act of bravery in him, still it would be approved of, as no more than she deserved—

EXTINXISSE NEFAS TAMEN ET SUMPSISSE MERENTIS
LAUDABOR POENAS

[I shall be praised for having punished the wretch]. But if the poenae were sceleratae for the reason assigned by Wagner and Ladewig, sceleratae in the sense alluded to and disapproved

but iustae, aequae, and piae. **And**, (**2**), because nothing was easier than the mistake of SCELERATAS instead of SCELERATAE, the following word beginning with an s.

As analogues to SCELERATAE POENAS, we may compare 6. 542, "malorum poenas ;" 6. 422, " poenas amborum ;" also 11. 258, where there was like opportunity to use the contorted expression, but where nevertheless the simple, easy, straightforward opposite one, viz., " scelerum poenas," is preferred.

of by Heyne, viz., *per scelus exactae*, Aeneas, so far from being praised for having inflicted them, would have been condemned, would have incurred the displeasure both of men and gods. He would himself have been rendered sceleratus by the act. But it is not in this sense the poenae he was about to take were sceleratae: they were sceleratae in the sense which I have explained at full in my Remark on "scelus expendisse merentem," verse 229, in that sense in which every extreme and capital punishment is sceleratus, partakes in its own essential nature of wickedness. Improbus is used in a similar manner to express wickedness which is not moral, and the English word *wickedness* itself is not unfrequently used in the same manner, in such expressions, for instance, as : " he gave him a wicked blow," " he served him a wicked trick," " that is a wicked wind which is blowing to-day." In this sense the poenae Aeneas was about to inflict on Helen were sceleratae, poenae the infliction of which had not made him scelestus, would on the contrary have obtained the approbation of his countrymen, but which were in their abstract character, no matter where inflicted, or on whom, sceleratae, as being extreme, and from which all persons in their cool moments turn away with disgust and horror —precisely the sense in which sceleratus is applied by our author himself, *Georg. 2. 256*, to the coldness of the soil, "sceleratum frigus," exactly our *wicked, accursed, devilish, shocking, damned :* and so precisely we would say in English, of the vengeance wreaked on Helen, *damnable :* " He punished her damnably." And so Plin. *H. N. 25. 3 :* " Nec bestiarum solum ad nocendum *scelera* sunt, sed interim aquarum quoque et locorum." Plaut. *Pseud. 3. 2. 28 :*

" teritur sinapi *sceleratum :* illis qui terunt,
priusquam triverunt, oculi ut exstillent, facit."

Plaut. *Mostel. 3. 1. 1:*

" *scelestiorem* ego annum argento foenori
nunquam ullum vidi, quam hic mihi annus obtulit."

Plaut. *Amph. 192* (ed. Bothe) :

" ego tibi istam hodie *scelestam* comprimam linguam."

Cicer. ad. Att. 6. 1. (ed. Graev.) : "tu *scelestè* suspicaris ; ego αφελως scripsi." Sil. 3. 272 (ed. Rup.) :

  . . . " *sceleratαque* succis
  spicula dirigere, et ferrum infamare veneno."

See Rem. on 5. 793.

583 606.

NON—CALIGAT

NON ITA, ου δητ', Eurip. *Hec. 367* (ed. Porson).

NAMQUE ETSI, &c., . . . MEORUM.—In the exact coincidence of the sentiments here expressed by Aeneas with those expressed by Aruns when meditating the death of Camilla (*Aen. 11. 790, et seqq.*), Burmann and Heyne might have found a strong additional argument for the authenticity of this fine passage concerning Helen. The reader will, however, observe that the poet, although he has assigned similar sentiments to his hero and the coward Aruns while meditating similar acts, has been careful to draw a sufficiently broad distinction between the actual conduct of the one and that of the other. The hero is immediately diverted from and relinquishes his hasty purpose ; the coward persists in, and coolly executes, his deliberately formed plan.

EXSTINXISSE . . . MEORUM. The repetition in a slightly changed form of the preceding (vss. 575-6) EXARSERE . . . POENAS. See Rem. on 1. 151.

MERENTIS.—"Exquisite pro *a merente*," Heyne. "Strafe an der schuldigen," Ladewig. "Sumi MERENTES s. merito sumendas," Wagn. (*Praest.*) Wagner is certainly wrong that MERENTIS is the accusative ; Heyne and Ladewig so far right as that MERENTIS is the genitive, not however that it is equivalent to *a merente*, as if Virgil had said "POENAS SUMPSISSE *a merente*," "strafe an der schuldigen." MERENTIS is the simple genitive of possession depending on POENAS, POENAS MERENTIS, exactly as verse 576, SCELERATAE POENAS (according to Voss's reading); " malorum poenas ;" 9. 422, " poenas amborum." Compare verse 229 above : " scelus expendisse *merentem* Laocoonta ferunt ;" and, aptly quoted by Ladewig, Val. Flacc. 2. 101 :

" quocirca struit illa nefas, Lemnoque *merenti*
exitium furiale movet."

ANIMUMQUE EXPLESSE IUVABIT ULTRICIS FLAMMAE ET CINERES SATIASSE MEORUM.—This close juxtaposition of a moral flamma and a material CINERES has a bad effect, inasmuch as it suggests a relationship the farthest in the world from the author's thought, viz., that of cinders to flame. If the author perceived the unseasonable suggestion, he was called upon to take some pains to avoid it ; if he did not perceive it, it is another instance of an inadvertency respecting small matters, of which his great work affords but too many examples. See 2. 360 :

. . . " *nox* atra cava circumvolat umbra.
quis cladem illius *noctis*, quis funera fando
explicet ?"

where " illius " suggests an identity between " noctis " and the preceding " nox," than which nothing could be farther from the author's thought, " nox " being merely figurative, while " noctis " is real, material night. Also 1. 87 : " qua data porta *ruunt* . . . totumque . . . *ruunt*," where the same verb in the same person, number, and tense is applied in a transitive sense to the identical subject to which it has been applied, the line but one before, in an intransitive—whether observed by the author and left uncorrected as of small importance, or not observed at all, I shall not pretend to say.

CONFESSA DEAM.—Jocularly imitated by Petronius, p. 143 (ed. Hadrian.) : " Modo Bromium, interdum Lyaeum Euhyumque *confessus*."

QUANTA (vs. 592), *of as great size as*, i.e., *in her full magnitude*. See Rem. on 1. 756.

OBDUCTA TUENTI MORTALES HEBETAT VISUS, theme ; HUMIDA CIRCUM CALIGAT, variation. See Rem. on 1. 550.

608-618.

HIC—ARMA

VAR. LECT. (vs. 616).

LIMBO **II** ⁶⁄₈ (viz., Basle A and Munich 10719, in the latter of which it occurs as a second reading : it is the only example of a second reading which occurs in the whole of the second book). LIMBO is also quoted by Heyne as the second reading of *Moret. Sec.* **III** Servius ("alii LIMBO legunt"); "Twelve Years' Voyage," 1853; Ladewig, 2nd ed.; Haupt; Ribb.

NIMBO (or NYMBO) **I** *Pal., Med.* **II** ⁶⁵⁄₈₃. **III** Princ. Rom. 1473: Strasb. 1470 (Mentell.): Ven. 1470, 1471, 1472, 1475, 1486; Milan, 1475; Aldus (1514); Philippe; Heyn.; Brunck; Wakef.; Pott.: Wagn. (ed. Heyn., *V. L.* and *Praest.*), and all editors and commentators down to Ladewig, who adopted LIMBO from my "Twelve Years' Voyage."

UMBONE **II** ⅕.

O *Vat., Rom., Ver., St. Gall.*

With this fine picture of the gods giving their personal help towards the destruction of a city, compare the historical narrative, Tacit. *Ann. 13. 41:* "Adiicitur miraculum, velut numine oblatum; nam cuncta extra, tectis tenus, sole illustria fuere: quod moenibus cingebatur, ita repente atra nube coopertum, fulguribusque discretum est, ut, quasi infensantibus deis, exitio tradi crederetur."

Independently of the defence, of which Virgil's account of the taking of Troy is otherwise capable (see Rem. on vs. 5), the poet, calling in the hostile gods, and even Jupiter himself, to aid in the taking and destruction of the city, already (verse 351) deserted by its own gods, seems to be invulnerably armed against the assaults of those critics, who, with Napoleon at their head (see Remm. on vv. 15 and 299) insist that his whole narrative unstrategical, incredible, impossible.

PRIMA (vs. 613), the principal personage, the leader, the mover of the whole matter, princeps. As Juno, although thus expressly stated to be the leader, the mover of the whole matter (*i.e.*, of the destruction of the city), is yet not mentioned first in order, but placed in the middle between Neptune and Pallas, so Machaon (vs. 263), also stated to be the "primus," the mover of the whole matter, the principal actor, or taking the principal part among those enclosed in the wooden horse, is not mentioned first in order, but seventh, or nearly last. The same term prima, in the same sense and in a very similar connexion, is applied to the same Juno, *Aen. 1. 27*:

>   ". . . . " veterisque memor Saturnia belli,
> *prima* quod ad Troiam pro caris gesserat Argis."

FERRO ACCINCTA.—Not, literally, *girt with a sword, having a sword at her side* (" umgürtet mit stahl," Voss), which had been much too tame, too unbellicose a picture for the occasion, but — according to the secondary signification of the word accinctus —*equipped with a sword, armed with a sword*, or, as we say, *sword in hand*. Compare 9. 74:

> " atque omnis facibus pubes *accingitur* atris "

[not, surely, *with torches girded on*, but *armed with torches, torches in hand*]. See also 6. 570 (where see Rem.):

> " continuo sontes ultrix *accincta* flagello
> Tisiphone quatit insultans "

[not surely *with a whip in her girdle*, but *armed with a whip, whip in hand*]. Compare also the similar use of succinctus in conjunction with faces by Prudentius, *Psychom. 42*:

> " quam [Pudicitiam] patrias *succincta* faces Sodomita Libido
> aggreditur, piceamque ardenti sulphure pinum
> ingerit in faciem, pudibundaque lumina flammis
> appetit, et tetro tentat suffundere fumo "

[not, surely, *undergirt with torches*, but *equipped with torches, ready for action with torches*]. And see the *Comment. in libros Regum falso S. Eucherio ascript.* lib. 4 (De la Bigne, 5. 905): "Cuius temeritatem arrogantiae modesto sermone compescens rex Israel ait:

'Dicite ei, ne glorietur *accinctus*, aeque ut *discinctus*.' Aliud est autem *accinctus*, aliud *discinctus*, aliud *non accinctus*. *Accinctus* namque est qui cingulo circumdatus incedit: *discinctus* qui cingulum nuper deposuit, verbi gratia, vel balneum intraturus, vel lectum ascensurus, vel alteram tunicam forte induturus: *non accinctus*, qui, nuper tunica indutus, necdum se addita zonae circumpositione munivit. Sic ergo et in expeditione castrensi qui positus est recte *accinctus* nominatur, *i.e.*, armis indutus; qui pugna confecta victor domum rediit iure *discinctus* vocatur, quia nimirum depositis armis optatae pacis otium gerit; qui vero necdum pugnare, neque se ad certamen parare iam coeperat, merito *non accinctus* esse dicitur. Ait ergo rex Israel regi Syriae glorianti quasi iam cepisset Samariam, quam obsidere coeperat, 'Ne glorietur *accinctus* aeque ut *discinctus :*' ac 'si aperte dicat, 'Noli gloriari quasi iam victor bellici discriminis, qui adhuc in acie positus, quem victoria sequatur, ignoras.'"

These arguments are, as I think, sufficiently strong and decisive. The very picture, however, found by Voss in our text is actually presented by Silius, 9. 296:

"contra *cincta* latus ferro Saturnia Iuno,"

where, as *Aen. 11. 489:* "laterique accinxerat ensem," the addition of "latus" fixes the meaning to be, not *armed with*, but *girt with*. See Rem. on "succinctam pharetra," 1. 327.

ARCES PALLAS INSEDIT.—It is with peculiar propriety that Pallas is represented as taking possession of the arx, the arx having been her invention, and always (not alone at Troy, but elsewhere) her selected abode. Compare *Ecl. 2. 61:*

. . . . "Pallas, quas condidit *arces*,
ipsa colat."

Claud. *de Rapt. Pros. 2. 19:*

"et Pandionias quae cuspide protegit *arces*."

Catull. 64. 8:

"diva . . . retinens in summis urbibus *arces*."

RESPICE.—Not merely *look*, or *see*, but *look behind thee:*

Aspice (vs. 604), *look here before thee;* respice, *look there behind thee.* Compare Tibull. 2. 5. 21 :

> . . . "cum maestus ab alto
> Ilion ardentes *respiceret*que deos."

Observe also the effective position of the word immediately before the object to which it points, PALLAS ; and immediately after the words exciting expectation, IAM SUMMAS ARCES TRITONIA. See Rem. on verse 203.

LIMBO EFFULGENS ET GORGONE SAEVA.—I have myself personally examined only five MSS. with respect to this passage, viz., the oldest Gudian (No. 70), the two Leipzig, the Dresden, and No. 113 (Endlicher's Catal.) in the royal Library of Vienna, but in the whole five I have found NIMBO, which (see Foggini) is also the reading of the Medicean, and has been adopted without hesitation or exception, so far as I know, by all the editors and commentators. The explanation which the elder commentators have given us of this word is *halo* ("nube divina," Servius, La Cerda), against which the objection of Forbiger, "hic voc. nimbi significatus non nisi cadentis Latinitatis," seems to me to be conclusive. The more modern explanation of the word is that adopted by Heyne from Pomponius Sabinus : "nubes obscura qua illa cingitur ;" the effulgence of such obscure "nubes" being ascribed by Heyne to its reflexion of Pallas's aegis ("fulgentem aegidem tenet, a qua relucet nimbus"), and by Wagner to its reflexion of the flames of the burning city (" nimbus igitur ille, quem ut iratae deae atrum fuisse consentaneum est, fulgebat et rutilabat ab incendii flammis"), an interpretation which has been adopted and approved of by Forbiger.

I object, (**1**), that nimbus is never "nubes," but always that combination of darkness, heavy rain (or hail), wind, thunder and lightning, called in Germany *gewitter*, and in Italy *temporale*, but for which the English language possesses no more appropriate appellation than *thunder-storm.* See *Aen.* 5. 317 : "effusi nimbo similes" [*poured out*, surely not *like a cloud*, but *like a thunder-storm, a sudden shower of heavy rain*]. *Aen.* 2. 113 :

> . . . "toto sonuerunt aethere nimbi,"

[not, *clouds resounded over the whole sky*, but *thunder-storms resounded*]. Aen. 4. 161:

   . . . "insequitur commixta grandine nimbus"

[not, *a cloud mixed with hail*, or *a hail cloud, follows*, but *a hailstorm, a shower of hail, follows*]. Aen. 4. 120:

   "his ego nigrantem commixta grandine *nimbum*
   . . . .
   desuper infundam"

[not, *I will pour a cloud mixed with hail on them*, but *a hail-storm on them*]. (**2**), that there appears no reason, and no reason has been assigned, why Pallas should have a nimbus (whether understood to mean a cloud, or a storm) about her on this occasion. Such appendage had been equally useless, either for the purpose of inspiring terror, or for the purpose of concealment, she being (in common with the other gods introduced on the occasion, and who, it will be observed, had no nimbi) invisible to all human eyes except those of Aeneas alone, from which Venus had miraculously taken away OMNEM NUBEM QUAE MORTALES HEBETAT VISUS, and so rendered them able to see the invisible. **And**, (**3**), that Pallas could not correctly be represented as EFFULGENS NIMBO, whether the word be understood to mean (according to Heyne's erroneous definition of it) "nubes obscura," or (according to that which I have shown is its only true interpretation) *gewitter, temporale, thunder-shower, thunderstorm*, unless we admit the propriety of the expression (in the former case) *effulgent with darkness*, and (in the latter) *effulgent with the obscure cloak* in which gods were used sometimes for particular purposes to wrap themselves up, and hide themselves from observation, as Aen. 12. 416:

   . . . "Venus, *obscuro* faciem circumdata *nimbo*."

Ibid. 10. 634:

   . . . "agens hiemem, *nimbo* succincta per auras."

Despairing, therefore, of obtaining any good sense from the reading NIMBO, I look for a different reading, and being informed by Servius that "alii LIMBO legunt, ut (Aen. 4. 137): 'Sidoniam picto chlamydem circumdata *limbo*;'" and finding that information confirmed by Heyne (" LIMBO, *Moret. Sec.* pro var. lect."), I adopt LIMBO, and thus at once obtain, not merely an intelligible, but an admirable, sense—*Pallas* effulgent, neither with a dark cloud illuminated by her aegis or by flames of the burning city, nor with a dark thunderstorm, but with her limbus or *instita*, and her gorgon. Pallas is said to be effulgent with the "limbus," this part being the most splendid of the whole female dress; see the "limbus" of Dido, quoted by Servius above, and especially the "limbus" of the dress put by Thetis (Stat. *Achill.* 1. 325) on Achilles when she disguised him as a female for the court of Lycomedes :

> "aspicit ambiguum genitrix, cogitque volentem,
> innectitque sinus ; tunc colla rigentia mollit,
> summittitque graves humeros, et fortia laxat
> brachia, et impexos certo domat ordine crines,
> ac sua dilecta cervice monilia transfert,
> et picturato cohibet vestigia *limbo*,"

where it will be observed that the whole female dress of Achilles is placed before the eye of the reader by the "monilia" (representing the upper part) and the embroidered "limbus" (representing the lower), just as in our text the whole costume of Pallas is represented by the (effulgent) gorgon above and the effulgent "limbus" below.

If it was proper for Statius thus to put forward the "monilia" and "limbus" as representatives of the whole of Achilles' petticoats, it was still more proper for Virgil to use a similar representation in the case of Pallas, that goddess being remarkable for wearing (" pace deae dictum sit !") petticoats so long as to acquire the appellation of talares, *i.e.*, of coming down quite to her heels. See almost all her numerous statues.

Neither do I require to point out to the reader the necessity there was that Pallas, although invisible to all human eyes, should yet wear clothes, or the propriety with which those clothes, when she is rendered visible to Aeneas, are described to have been of a splendour suitable to the goddess (see below), and to the attitude in which she is represented, viz., that of standing mistress of the conquered citadel.

Similar to the effulgence of Pallas's "limbus" in our text is that of her palla in Claudian, *de Rapt. Pros.* 2. 25:

> ... "tantum stridentia colla
> Gorgonos obtentu *pallae fulgentis* inumbrat;"

and elsewhere I find a similar effulgence ascribed to other parts of the goddess's equipment. Thus (Claudian, *de Rapt. Pros.* 2. 226) her spear is so bright as to illuminate the chariot of Dis:

> ... "libratur in ictum
> fraxinus, et nigros *illuminat* obvia currus;"

her chariot (Auson. *Perioch.* 17. *Odyss.*) casts a red light over the sky:

> " iam caelum roseis *rutilat* Tritonia bigis;"

and (Claud. *Gigant.* 91) a similar light is cast by her gorgon:

> ... "Tritonia virgo
> prosilit, ostendens *rutila* cum gorgone pectus."

To LIMBO EFFULGENS ET GORGONE SAEVA thus understood as descriptive of the splendour of the goddess's dress, we have an exact parallel in *Aen.* 5. 132:

> ... "ipsique in puppibus auro
> ductores longe *effulgent* ostroque decori."

It would appear from the very ancient and remarkable statue of Minerva Polias, now in the Augusteum of Dresden, that the battle of the Giants described by Euripides (*Hecub. 466*), and by the author of *Ciris* (vs. 29), as embroidered on the peplum of Pallas, was not spread over the whole peplum, but confined to a clavus (limbus?), stripe, or border, represented on the statue as descending down the front of the person from the waist to the feet. For a view of this very striking statue, as well as for a separate view and description of the clavus, stripe, or border, descending down the front of its peplum, see Becker, *August. Dresd.* tabb. 9 and 10. Müller (*Minerva Polias*, p. 26) informs us, if I understand him right, that there is a similar band, or stripe, on the pepla of all the very ancient statues of the Minerva Polias: " Insignis maxime *clavus* quidam sive limes ceteris aliquanto latior de medio corpore decurrens, qui etiam apud populos Asiae maxime decorus habebatur."

SAEVA is predicated not (according to Servius's second interpretation) of Pallas, but (according to his first interpretation) of the gorgon : *first*, because the picture is thus more concentrated; *secondly*, because saeva (the Greek δεινη) is precisely the term applied to the gorgon both by Hesiod, *Scut. Hercul. 223*:

παν δε μεταφρενον ειχε καρη δεινοιο πελωρου
γοργους,

and Homer, *Il. 5. 741*:

εν δε τε γοργειη κεφαλη δεινοιο πελωρου
δεινη τε σμερδνη τε, Διος τερας αιγιοχοιο:

and, thirdly, because to apply to Pallas, in the positive degree only, the very term which had just (vers. 612) been applied to Juno in the superlative degree, had been an anti-climax of the worst kind.

Despairing to make any tolerable sense out of the received reading, I take the hint from Servius : "alii LIMBO legunt," and read LIMBO. Pallas is effulgent, neither with a " nubes divina" (Servius), for there is no instance of nimbus used in that sense either by Virgil or any of Virgil's cotemporaries, nor with a *dark* thundershower ("repentinae pluviae," Pomp. Sabin., Germ. *gewitter*, Ital. *temporale*), the only sense in which nimbus ever occurs in Virgil, but she is effulgent with her " limbus," *i. e.*, with the broad border of her peplum on which was depicted the battle of the Giants. See, in addition to the authors quoted three paragraphs back, in Buonarotti (*Osserv. sopra alcuni frammenti di vasi antichi*, p. 78), a figure of Pallas in which the limbus of the peplum occupies nearly the lower half of it. With such " limbus," either taken literally or as representing the whole female skirt or petticoat, Pallas is refulgent. Compare (*a*), Stat. *Achill. 1. 325*, where the whole female dress is thus represented by its most conspicuous and striking parts, the monilia above, and the embroidered limbus below. (*b*), Stat. *Theb. 6. 366*, where Apollo Musagetes is described as putting off (as soon as he had done playing on the lyre) the embroidered limbus, *i. e.*, the gown with embroidered border, which he had worn while playing. (*c*', especially Trebell.

Pollio, *Triginta Tyranni, 30*, where Zenobia appears before the assembly wearing a helmet and purple limbus : "Ad conciones galeata processit cum *limbo* purpureo, gemmis dependentibus per ultimam fimbriam" [a flounced purple skirt or petticoat]. (*d*), *Ibid. 14 :* "Eousque ut tunicae, et *limbi*, et paenulae matronales in familia eius hodieque sint, quae Alexandri effigiem de liciis variantibus monstrent," where also "limbi" can be nothing else than female skirts or petticoats. (*e*), Apollon. Rhod. 4. 940 :

αυτικ' ανασχομεναι λευκοις επι γουνασι πεζας.

And (*f*), Nonius: "*limbus*, muliebre vestimentum quod purpuram in imo habet."

The connection of "limbus" in either sense with EFFULGENS is not only appropriate, but according to Virgil's usual practice of representing his characters as effulgent with splendid dress, as 5. 132 ; 10. 539 ; 11. 489. Nor is the splendid "limbus" inappropriately joined as an object of terror with the gorgon, for see Prudent. *contra Symm. 2. 573:*

" nullane tristificis Tritonia noctua Charris
advolitans praesto esse deam praenuntia Crasso
prodidit ? aut Paphiam niveae vexere columbae,
cuius inauratum *tremeret* gens Persica *limbum ?* " *

where "limbum" is Venus's cestus—limbus being, as I may here incidentally observe, primarily *any broad stripe* (see Varro, fragm.: "mundus domus est . . . maxima rerum, quam quinque altitonae . . . fragmine zonae cingunt, . . . per quam *limbus* . . . pictus bis sex . . . signis stellimicantibus altus, . . . in obliquo aethere, lunae . . . bigas solisque receptat"), and only secondarily, and inasmuch as the border of a garment was usually ornamented and completed by a broad sewed-on stripe, *the border of a garment.*

LIMBO EFFULGENT.—Pallas is always effulgent. Her palla is fulgens, Claud. *Rapt. Pros. 2. 25;* her spear illuminates

---

* "Nimbum" has here in some editions taken the place of "limbum."

the whole chariot of Dis, *ibid. 2. 226;* her chariot casts a red light over the sky, Auson. *Perioch. 17. Odyss.;* her gorgon casts a red light, Claud. *Gigant. 91;* and she comes παμφαινουσα, Apollon. Rhod. 4. 1309, out of the head of Jupiter.

EFFULGENS.—So usually, properly, and even specially, is effulgence attributed to dress or equipment, that examples are not wanting of the single word effulgere used to signify *effulgent in dress.* Compare Claud. *6. Cons. Honor. 543:*

> " omne, Palatino quod pons a colle recedit
> Mulvius, et quantum licuit consurgere textis,
> una replet turbae facies: undare videres
> ima viris, altas *effulgere* matribus aedes."

By a similar substitution of *n* for *l*, most of the MSS. of Statius read "nymphas" instead of "lymphas," *Silv. 1. 3. 34* (of the villa of Vopiscus):

> " quid primum mediumve canam; quo fine quiescam?
> auratasne trabes, an Mauros undique postes,
> an picturata lucentia marmora vena
> mirer, an emissas per cuncta cubilia *lymphas?*"

621-631.

DIXERAT—RUINAM

SPISSIS NOCTIS SE CONDIDIT UMBRIS.—Peerlkamp objects: "CLARA INCENDIA obstant." Those who make such objections require more than is to be obtained from any poet. You must wink, or you cannot read, much less enjoy, poetry. The spectator in the theatre sits looking on, delighted at the performance, and shuts his eyes to the incongruities. If he does not, good-bye to the delight. The objection is of a piece with the rest of Peerlkamp's objections, which require nothing less than the recasting of every line of the *Aeneid*, with the view of rendering the style mathematically correct, and the necessary consequence of reducing it from poetry to prose, of substituting the common, vulgar, everyday light, for the gorgeous hues of the spectrum. See Rem. on "ignes iugales," 7. 320.

NUMINA MAGNA DEUM.—"Numen" is taken here not as at 1. 12, in its primary sense of will or pleasure, but in its secondary sense, viz., of the person of whom that will or pleasure is an attribute, exactly as in our expression: "the King's most excellent Majesty," meaning the most excellent and majestic king. NUMINA MAGNA DEUM therefore (literally and primarily *the gods' great wills*) is here equivalent to *the great willing and commanding gods*. See Rem. on "numine," 1. 12.

TUM VERO . . . TROIA.—Compare Pind. *Ol. 11. 34:*

και μεν ξεναπατας
Επεων βασιλευς οπιθεν
ου πολλον ιδε πατριδα πολυκτεανον υπο στερεω πυρι
πλαγαις τε σιδαρου βαθυν εις οχετον ατας
ιζοισαν εαν πολιν.

The manifest allusion to the original building of Troy, at the very moment of its overthrow, had been happier if it had not been forestalled by representation of Neptune himself engaged in overthrowing it, verse 610. The expression is repeated in a similar context and similarly constructed, almost identical, verse, 3. 2 :

. . . "ceciditque superbum
Ilium, et omnis humo fumat *Neptunia* Troia,"

where the allusion to the builder of Troy is happier, the picture of the same builder engaged in its overthrow being there less fresh in the recollection.

MINATUR.—Servius seems to be in the same doubt here as at 1. 166, and 2. 240, whether "minari" is to be taken in its primary or secondary sense: "MINATUR, aut eminet aut movetur," where by "movetur" can only be meant *threatens to fall* ("Cader' minaccia," Alfieri). That the former is meant, I have as little doubt here as on the two former occasions, and, as on those occasions, interpret the word: *towers, holds its head high;* an interpretation which has at least these two great advantages over its rival; first, that it is as entirely in conformity with the use of the term on both, especially on the first of those two former occasions, as the rival interpretation is in direct contradiction; and, secondly, that it is not to a tree immediately toppling over when the axe is laid to its root that *pius* Aeneas should compare the beleaguered city, but to a tree which continues to hold its head high and fearless (USQUE MINATUR) even while the axe is being laid to its root. See Rem. on 1. 166; 2. 240; 4. 88; 8. 668.

TREMEFACTA COMAM CONCUSSO VERTICE NUTAT, *nods with her leafy head*, viz., as a warrior with his crested and plumed helmet. Compare 9. 677:

> " ipsi intus dextra ac laeva pro turribus adstant
> armati ferro, et *cristis capita alta corusci*:
> quales aeriae liquentia flumina circum,
> sive Padi ripis, Athesim seu propter amoenum,
> consurgunt geminae quercus, intonsaque caelo
> attollunt capita, et *sublimi vertice nutant.*"

CONGEMUIT.—Not merely *groaned*, but *groaned loudly*; as it were *with all its force collected into one last effort*. See Rem. on vs. 52; 6. 634.

AVULSA.—" Evulsa," Ruaeus.

> . . . . " und schmetternd, den höhn entrottet, *hinabkracht*."
> Voss.
> . . . . " e dal suo giogo al fine
> o con parte del giogo *si divelgie*,
> o si scoscende."
> Caro.

No, but AVULSA, TRAXIT RUINAM IUGIS, *i.e.*, "ibi, in iugis:" *torn away with ropes from the stump where the axe had nearly (but not entirely) cut it through, fell there on the mountain.* AVULSA, sciz., funibus. Compare Ovid, *Met. 8. 774*:

> . . . " labefactaque tandem
> ictibus innumeris, adductaque *funibus* arbor
> corruit, et multam prostravit pondere silvam."

Thus the cadence—cracked, broken and limping, if the structure be

CONGEMUIT, TRAXITQUE, IUGIS AVULSA, RUINAM—

becomes fluent and sonorous:

CONGEMUIT, TRAXITQUE IUGIS, AVULSA, RUINAM ;

the ictus falling full upon VŬL.

632-633.

DESCENDO AC DUCENTE DEO FLAMMAM INTER ET HOSTES
EXPEDIOR

VAR. LECT.

DEA **I** *Ver.* DUCENTEDEA (DEO *a m. sec. superscr*). **II** cod. Canon.
(Butler). **III** " Legitur et DEO . . . Qui legunt DEO *fatum* volunt dictum . . . Qui vero legunt DEA *matri* adtribuunt Aeneae liberationem,"
Schol. Veron. (Keil's ed., p. 88, l. 29).

DEO **III** Servius ; " DUCENTE DEO, non DEA," Macrob. *Sat. 3. 8;* P. Manut. ;
D. Heins. ; N. Heins. ; Brunck ; Wakefield ; Heyne ; Voss; Wagn.
(*Praest.*) ; Ladewig.

O *Vat., Rom., St. Gall.*

DESCENDO.—Whence? If from the roof, he has been able from the roof not only to see Helen where she was hid in the interior of the temple of Vesta (LIMINA VESTAE SERVANTEM ; SECRETA IN SEDE LATENTEM ; ABDIDERAT SESE ; ARIS SEDEBAT), but to rush on her with his sword—" TALIA IACTABAM ET FURIATA MENTE FEREBAR . . . ALMA PARENS . . . DEXTRA PREHENSUM CONTINUIT." If from the arx why has there been no mention of his previous descent from the roof? In either case the difficulty is so great that I am fain to think that the original sequence has been

AD TERRAM MISERE AUT IGNIBUS AEGRA DEDERE
TUM VERO OMNE MIHI VISUM CONSIDERE IN IGNES,

a sequence affording this most natural connection of thought :—
" I look about ; I find myself alone. My companions have all

perished, and so at last I lose hope, give up everything for lost, and, descending from the roof from whence I have seen the city burning and the king killed, return home in order if possible to carry my father safe out of the city." Nothing can be better than this connexion of thought and this position of Aeneas's descent from the roof. On the other hand, nothing can be worse than the connexion of thought:—" I am left alone, Troy has been burnt, my companions have perished in the flames; I spy Helen in the temple of Vesta, and am prevented from killing her only by the intervention of my mother, who reproves me, and shows me the divinities personally occupied in overthrowing the city. Then and only then do I give up hope and descend;" as, in like manner, nothing can be worse than this position of DESCENDO, whether we consider the descent to be from the roof, in which case Aeneas has seen Helen from the roof, and had the interview with his mother on the roof, or whether we consider the descent to be from the arx, in which case we have no account either of Aeneas's descent from the roof, or of his feelings on finding himself alone on the roof after all his companions have perished—hear absolutely nothing of him, either of his thoughts or of his doings, from the time he finds himself alone on the roof till the time he is rushing on Helen hid in the temple of Vesta. Still further, in this connexion of thought and this position of DESCENDO, we have (**1**), Aeneas reminded by Venus (verse 596:

>   NON PRIUS ASPICIES UBI FESSUM AETATE PARENTEM
>   LIQUERIS ANCHISEN ? SUPERET CONIUXNE CREUSA
>   ASCANIUSQUE PUER ?)

of that which had occurred to himself before Venus made her appearance (verse 560 :

>   . . . SUBIIT CARI GENITORIS IMAGO
>   UT REGEM AEQUAEVUM CRUDELI VULNERE VIDI
>   VITAM EXHALANTEM ; SUBIIT DESERTA CREUSA,
>   ET DIREPTA DOMUS, ET PARVI CASUS IULI.

(**2**), we have the comparison AC VELUTI . . . RUINAM—unexceptionable if coming in immediate sequence after

>   AD TERRAM MISERE AUT IGNIBUS AEGRA DEDERE —

liable to have this strong exception taken to it, viz., that it forces on us an inevitable mental juxtaposition of the agents engaged in the destruction of Troy, the NUMINA MAGNA DEUM, and the agents engaged in felling the tree, the AGRICOLAE, nay of the instruments used, the "bipennes" of the one party and the "tridens" of the other, even of the grammatical pendants EMOTA and ACCISAM, ERUIT and ERUERE INSTANT. And (3), we have DEO the general term for divinity, and the very term which had rightly had a place in the sequence of thought in which no particular duty is introduced; we have, I say, this general term used in a sequence in which a particular duty has been introduced in so pointed a manner that the reader remains doubtful in which way to extricate himself from the ambiguity, whether by assuming that the particular divinity is referred to by the general term, or by finding Virgil guilty of ascribing to divinity in general what the whole context, with the exception of this single word, compels the reader to ascribe to the particular divinity so prominently placed before him at the very moment. For all these reasons I am strongly inclined to think that the original sequence of thought has been from

to
    AD TERRAM MISERE AUT IGNIBUS AEGRA DEDERE

    TUM VERO OMNE MIHI VISUM CONSIDERE IN IGNES,

that the in itself beautiful and truly Virgilian picture of Venus, Helen, and the deities inimical to Troy, has been an afterthought, not well dove-tailed in, and that this after-thought, if actually and in point of fact expunged by Tucca and Varius, was so expunged not at all on account of the unmanliness of Aeneas's intended onslaught on Helen, but altogether as an after-thought, which, however beautiful in itself, was so awkwardly filled in as rather to be an eyesore than an ornament.

644.

SIC O SIC POSITUM AFFATI DISCEDITE CORPUS

"Mortuum se effingit, componitque, ac si offerendus esset ad tumulum," La Cerda. "Dieses zurechtlegen der glieder und haende in gestreckte lage gehoert zu den heiligen letzten pflichten der verwandten . . . Dass Anchises es hier selbst thut, zeigt das freiwillige und feste seines entschlusses," Thiel. "Der zum sterben entschlossene Anchises hat sich selbst schon die lage eines verstorbenen gegeben," Ladewig. "*Sic positus* (ut 4. 681) quemadmodum mortui solent, rectus extentusque, Eurip. *Hipp*. 786 : ορθωσατ' εκτειναντες αθλιον νεκυν," Wagner (1861).

So Anchises stretches himself out stark and stiff and straight as if he were a laid-out corpse! A very pretty picture, indeed, especially as it is of a man who, while he thus stretches himself out stark and stiff and straight as if he were a laid-out corpse, tells us, at the same time, he will fight until he forces the enemy to kill him—IPSE MANU MORTEM INVENIAM. No, no; there is none of this child's play, this game of dead-and-alive, in the Aeneid. Anchises does not stretch himself out stark and stiff and straight as if he were a laid-out corpse ; but, throwing himself on the ground, or on a couch or sofa, or continuing to lie there, if he had been lying there previously, refuses to stir, and bids his friends take leave of him lying there, as they would take leave of him if he were lying dead: "Away," he says, "and save yourselves ; leave me here to die ; take leave of me as you would if I were laid here already dead, for you will never again see me alive." Compare Eurip. *Electr*. 1325 (Orestes telling Electra to take leave of him as if he were dead):

βαλε, προσπτυξον σωμα· θανοντος δ'
ως επι τυμβω καταθρηνησον,

and Val. Flacc. 1. 334 (Alcimede taking leave of Jason) : " et dulci iam nunc premo lumina dextra." Also Propert. 2. 34. 59

(ed. Hertzb.):

"me iuvet hesternis *positum* languere corollis,
quem tetigit iactu certus ad ossa deus;"

in not one of which cases does the individual act death, stretch himself out stiff and stark as if he were dead: all he does is to compare his lying, languishing, despairing, inert position, with the lying, inert position of a corpse. And, exactly so in our text: Anchises does not stretch himself out and act the laid-out corpse, but requests his friends to regard him as lying there already dead, and take leave of him accordingly: "Let this, oh! let this, be my death bed; take leave of me here for ever. The enemy will find me here and kill me in mercy and for the sake of my spoils. They shall not spare my life, for I will fight till I force them to kill me."

I by no means deny that positus has sometimes and even frequently the meaning assigned to it in this place by the commentators, is sometimes (*ex. gr.*, by Ovid, *Met.* 9. 502:

. . . "toroque
mortua componar, *positae*que det oscula frater;"

and even by our author himself, 11. 30:

"corpus ubi exanimi *positum* Pallantis Acoetes
servabat senior")

applied to the stretched, formally laid-out corpse, **but** that such meaning is inherent in the word, and therefore not to be ascribed to it except in those cases in which, as in the examples just adduced, the context shows that it is used in that special technical sense. But in our text the context shows the very contrary, shows that "positus" has not this special meaning of formally stretched, straightened, and laid-out, as dead bodies are stretched, straightened, and laid-out by the care of their surviving friends; but the much more ordinary, less special sense of *laid*, or *lying dead*, of which more ordinary, less special sense the following are examples: (*a*), Stat. *Theb.* 12. 288 (of Argia, searching for the dead body of Polynices on the field of battle):

. . . "visuque sagaci
rimatur *positos*, et corpora prona supinat
incumbens;"

(***b***), Stat. *Theb. 12. 359* (of Antigone) :

"quippe trucem campum, et *positus* quo pulvere frater
noverat,"

in neither of which passages will it be pretended that Polynices is described as formally laid out, straightened, and stretched, and not merely as laid or lying in his blood on the field of battle. Also, (***c***), Ovid, *Met. 13. 543* (Hecuba finding Polydorus's body washed on shore) :

"nunc *positi* spectat vultum, nunc vulnera nati,"

where it will as little be pretended by anyone that the stretched, straightened, laid-out position given to a corpse by the undertaker, and not the position in which the corpse happened to be laid, placed, or thrown by the sea, is meant. Compare also, (***d***), *Aen. 4. 681* : " sic te ut *posita* crudelis abessem," where the term is applied to Dido, not even yet dead but only dying ; and, (***e***), Stat. *Silv. 1. 4. 106* :

"dixerat : inveniunt *positos* iam segniter artus [Gallici]
pugnantemque animam : ritu se cingit uterque
Paeonio, monstrantque simul, parentque volentes ;
donec letiferas vario medicamine pestes,·
et suspecta mali ruperunt nubila somni,"

where it is applied to Gallicus, laid or lying on the sick bed. (***f***), Ovid, *Met. 3. 420* (of Narcissus) :

"spectat humi *positus* geminum, sua lumina, sidus."

And (***g***), Met. *Epist. 4. 97* :

"saepe sub ilicibus Venerem Cinyraque creatum
sustinuit *positos* quaelibet herba duos."

We might point out a thousand-and-one other instances in which it is applied to persons, in perfect health and vigour, laid or lying on the ground, in bed, on a sofa, no matter how. The words of the nuncius, then, in the *Hippolytus* directing the attendants to go and stretch and formally lay out the corpse of Phaedra :

ορθωσατ' εκτεινavτες αθλιον νεκυν,

by the citation of which Wagner has endeavoured to throw light on the picture, serve only to obscure and confuse it, the word positus not being used in the narrow and technical sense of laid out, straightened, and stretched, but in the wider, more general sense of laid or lying, and not at all containing the notion of death, not even with all the assistance afforded to it by the addition of corpus (for see "ponere corpus," even with the further addition of "humo," applied to persons in the perfect vigour of life and health, Ovid, *Amor. 3. 11* :

"ingenium dura *ponere corpus humo.*"

Id., *Art. Amat. 2. 523*:

"clausa tibi fuerit promissa ianua nocte,
perfer et immunda *ponere corpus humo*"),

but that notion being left to be gathered from the words of the context : AFFATI DISCEDITE ; MORTEM INVENIAM ; MISEREBITUR HOSTIS ; FACILIS IACTURA SEPULCRI, &c. ; and so far is the position taken by Anchises from being that in which the attendants are directed by the nuncius to place the dead body of Phaedra—

ορθωσατ' εκτειναντες αθλιον νεκυν—

and in which the chorus informs us the attendants proceed immediately to place it—

ηδη γαρ ως νεκρον νιν εκτεινουσι δη—

that it is the very opposite, viz., such uncared neglected position as had been assumed by Phaedra's body in the noose, or after it had been taken down from the noose and *before* the care directed by the nuncius had been bestowed on it.

To recapitulate : The words POSITUM CORPUS are equally applicable to any one of three states—laid (lying) alive ; laid (lying) dead ; and laid (lying) dead and formally straightened, stretched, and laid out. Which is the state meant in any particular case can only be shown by the context. In the case of Anchises the context plainly shows that the state meant is that of laid (lying) dead. Pity that the natural and pathetic should have been turned into the absurd and ridiculous ; that the universal destiny, the common lot of man, the position in which we are all sooner or later to be placed—viz., that of being left to die, left for dead—should be confounded with the particular attitude and set which it is the fashion to give to the body after it is dead!

CORPUS strengthens POSITUM. Anchises does not say, "take leave of me laid here, as you would take leave of me if I were laid here dead," but "take leave of the body (σωμα, Eurip. *Electr.*, just quoted), laid here as if it were dead."

SIC POSITUM, *so laid: so placed: in this position*, no matter what the position may be. Compare *Ecl. 2. 54*:

> "et vos, o lauri, carpam, et te, proxima myrte;
> sic positae quoniam suaves miscetis odores."

Aen. 4. 681: "sic te ut *posita* crudelis abessem." Hor. *Sat. 1. 2. 105*:

>   ". . . leporem venator ut alta
>   in nive sectetur, *positum* sic tangere nolit,
>   cantat."

(where Orelli: "In verbo autem *sic* inest notio: commode ac sine ullo labore leporem tolli posse"). Hor. *Carm. 2. 11. 13*:

> "cur non sub alta vel platano, vel hac
>   pinu *iacentes* sic temere . . .
>   potamus uncti?"

SIC, O SIC.—The O and the second SIC are added for the sake of pathos, and to show still more clearly that Anchises not merely bids his friends take leave of him where he was then laid, but bids them take leave of him as if he were laid there dead. We must punctuate SIC, O SIC, and not with the editors, Heyne, Brunck, Wakefield, Wagner (ed. Heyn. and 1861), Ladewig, SIC O, SIC. In order to express the pathos, the exclamation must go to the second SIC; otherwise there is an anticlimax.

645-649.

IPSE MANU MORTEM INVENIAM MISEREBITUR HOSTIS
EXUVIASQUE PETET FACILIS IACTURA SEPULCRI
IAMPRIDEM INVISUS DIVIS ET INUTILIS ANNOS
DEMOROR EX QUO ME DIVUM PATER ATQUE HOMINUM REX
FULMINIS AFFLAVIT VENTIS ET CONTIGIT IGNI

IPSE MANU.—"MANU hostis," Servius, Heyne. No; *I myself with my own hand*. Compare "ipsa manu" (*Georg.* 4. 329), *thou thyself with thine own hand;* "ipse manu" (*Aen.* 2. 320; 3. 372; 5. 241; 7. 143), *he himself with his own hand;* "ipsa manu" (7. 621), *she herself with her own hand;* "ille manu" (6. 395; 12. 899), *he with his hand;* "illa manu" (11. 816), *she with her hand*.

IPSE MANU MORTEM INVENIAM.—Not MORTEM MANU (which had been only *violent death*), but INVENIAM MANU, *will find by my hand*, i. e. *by fighting*. Compare verse 434: "meruisse manu;" 11. 116: "bellum finire manu;" Sil. 4. 47: "metui peperere manu." That it is death by fighting Anchises means, and not death by suicide ("Selbst werd' ich mich tödten," Voss. "*Manu mortem invenire* valet *manum sibi inferre*," Wagner, ed. Heyn.) appears sufficiently, first from the just-adduced examples of manu used in the sense of pugnando, and secondly from the immediately connected MISEREBITUR HOSTIS, EXUVIASQUE PETET—the enemy, in compassion to the wretched old man who endeavours to fight, will put an end to his trouble by killing him, and will be the more ready to do so in order to get possession of his spoils.

MISEREBITUR HOSTIS.—"Nullus dubito, quin post INVENIAM particula *aut* exciderit," Wagner. No, by no means; there is no division, no disjunction, no alternative. MISEREBITUR HOSTIS assigns the *how* he will find his death by fighting : the enemy will take pity on him and put him out of the way. Compare

11. 493 :

"ágite me, si qua est pietas, in me omnia tela
coniicite, o Rutuli, me primam absumite ferro;
aut tu, magne pater divum, miserere, tuoque
invisum hoc detrude caput sub Tartara telo ;"

also, 10. 676 :

. . . "vos o potius miserescite, venti ;
in rupes, in saxa—volens vos Turnus adoro —
ferte ratem, sacvisque vadis immittite syrtis,
quo neque me Rutuli, nec conscia fama sequatur."

It is not the old man whom the enemy will kill in compassion, but the old man *fighting* ; they will rightly judge that his only object is to be killed, not to survive his country and friends, and therefore they will kill him, to do which act of mercy they will have the additional motive, viz., of obtaining his spoils. The mistake committed by the commentators here is precisely the same as that which they have committed at verse 521. In neither case have they been able to see that the pitiable object was not the old man, but the old man reduced to the extremity of using arms.

MISEREBITUR HOSTIS. Compare Val. Flacc. 1. 323 (Alcimede lamenting the departure of Jason) :

. . . "si fata reducunt
te mihi, si trepidis placabile matribus aequor;
possum equidem lucemque pati, longumque timorem.
sin aliud Fortuna parat, miserere parentum,
mors bona, dum metus est, nec adhuc dolor."

FACILIS IACTURA SEPULCRI.—"Hoc a summa rerum omnium desperatione profectum ut ne sepulcri quidem iactura moveatur," Wagner (1861), Ladewig (1855). I think not ; inasmuch as, no matter how great the despair, the loss of the sepulchre was still to be lamented, that loss being the worst and last loss, and the care of the poor remains clinging even to the most unhappy, the most desperate. How then is the IACTURA SEPULCRI, this worst and last loss, so FACILIS to Anchises ? The explanation is to be found in what immediately follows. He had been smitten with lightning, and so marked out by Jove himself as a reprobate unworthy of sepulture 'IAMPRIDEM, &c.) Compare Festus,

Fragm. e cod. Farnes. (Mueller's Festus, p. 178): "In Numae Pompili regis legibus scriptum esse: 'Si hominem fulmen Iovis occisit, ne supra genua tollitor,' et alibi: 'homo si fulmine occisus est, ei iusta nulla fieri oportet;'" and again, p. 210: "Pestiferum fulgur dicitur, quo mors exiliumve significari solet." See also Artemidorus, *Oneirocr.* 2. 9 (ed. Reiff.): Ου γαρ οι κεραυνωθεντες μετατιθενται, αλλ' οπου αν υπο του πυρος καταληφθωσιν, εντανθα θαπτονται. Pers. 2. 27:

"triste iaces lucis evitandumque bidental."

The loss of a sepulchre now by the sacking of the city was a light loss, FACILIS IACTURA, to a man who, having been struck many years ago by Jove's lightning, had from that time lingered on, a useless castaway, hated by the gods, despised by men, and unworthy even of a sepulchre. If he lost the sepulchre now by the sacking of the city, it was no more than he might have expected ever since the day he was struck by Jove's lightning, on which day it had been better for him he had died (IAMPRIDEM DEMOROR ANNOS). So explained, the FACILIS IACTURA SEPULCRI, which has appeared to commentators so inconsistent with the religious character of Anchises, is not only not irreligious, but on the contrary in the highest degree religious, as a bowing to and submission of the entire will to the will of Jove. It is at the same time in the most perfect harmony with the changed feelings and conduct of the same eminently religious man, that as soon as convinced by two signs from heaven that he had been precipitate in forming his judgment of the disposition of Jove towards him, he should have allowed his son to rescue him.

FACILIS IACTURA SEPULCRI, exactly as Liv. 5. 39: "*Facilem iacturam* esse seniorum, relictae in urbi utique periturae turbae."

IAMPRIDEM.—This word and the sentence to which it belongs stand in the most intimate connexion with the immediately preceding. It is as if Anchises had said: "the loss of the sepulchre, great a loss as it is, is a light loss to one who has been so many years under the ban of the Omnipotent, and marked out by Him as undeserving of any respect and honour both during life and after death."

FULMINIS AFFLAVIT VENTIS ET CONTIGIT IGNI.—According

to the vague natural philosophy of the ancients, the noise of thunder was produced by the clashing of winds, on each other or on the clouds, as Claud. *in Rufin.* 2. 221:

> "quantum non Italo *percussa Ceraunia* fluctu;
> quantum non madidis *elisa tonitrua* Coris;"

and the thunderbolt itself (fulmen) consisted of ventus and of ignis, as Lucret. 6. 274:

> "hic, ubi *ventus*, eas idem qui cogit in unum
> forte locum quemvis, expressit multa vaporis
> semina, seque simul cum eo commiscuit *igni*;
> insinuatus ibei vortex vorsatur in alto,
> et calidcis acuit *fulmen* fornacibus intus."

And so not only the scholiast of the Veronese Palimpsest, commenting on our text (Keil's ed., p. 89, l. 9): "Ventumque igneum fulmen vocant," but our author himself, in his account of the manufacture of the thunderbolt by Vulcan, 8. 430: "rutili tres ignis et alitis Austri."

In the division of the simple thesis fulmine percussit into two distinct theses, each relating to a distinct constituent of the general subject ("fulmen"), our author has only exhibited his usual manner. See Rem. on l. 550. The "venti" being supposed to be the less, the "ignis" the more, solid part of the "fulmen," it is with the strictest propriety that AFFLAVIT is assigned to the former, and CONTIGIT to the latter. Compare Callim. *Hymn. in Dianam*, 116.:

> . . . απο δε φλογος ηψαο ποιης
> Μυσω εν Ουλυμπω· φαεος δ' ενηκας αϋτμην
> ασβεστου, τορα πατρος αποσταζουσι κεραυνοι.

Stat. *Theb.* 5. 586:

> . . . "moti tamen *aura* cucurrit
> *fulminis* et summas libavit vertice cristas."

And Sil. 1. 252 (ed. Rup.):

> "spectarunt Poeni tremuitque exercitus Astur,
> torquentem cum tela Iovem, permixtaque nimbis
> *fulmina*, et excussos *ventorum flatibus ignes*
> turbato transiret [Hannibal] equo."

AFFLAVIT, precisely our *blasted;* as Milton, *Par. Lost*, 4. 928: "the blasting, vollied thunder;" and the Italian *ventò*, as Dante: "col fulmine me ventò.". Compare also Liv. 28. 23: "ambusti afflatu vaporis;" Plin. *Paneg.* 90: "Utrumque nostrum ille optimi cuiusque spoliator et carnifex stragibus amicorum, et *in proximum iacto fulmine afflaverat;*" and, quoted by Wagner, Liv. 30. 6: "saucii afflatique incendio."

CONTIGIT.—According to the peculiar import of *con, struck violently, with force.*

653.

FATOQUE URGENTI INCUMBERE VELLET

I am not aware of a satisfactory explanation of this passage by any commentator. Servius's (ed. Lion) "Simile est ut *currentem incitare, praecipitantem impellere*" can hardly be called an explanation at all; at most and best tells what the Virgilian sentiment resembles; while Heyne's "*h. e.* exitium quod vel sic imminebat accelerare. *Urgent* quae instant; ut, quae casum minantur his si *incumbimus,* ea impellimus ut proruant" is a mere vague generalization from which the reader is left to collect if he can that Aeneas, in Heyne's opinion, implores his father not to push impending fate so hard as to bring it toppling over on himself and friends—a picture which, if it be verily the picture intended by Virgil, the reader will, I hope, have less difficulty in realising than I have.

But if Servius and his followers are so little precise as to afford no information at all, and put us off with sound in the place of sense, La Cerda is not only explicit but positive, and regards the INCUMBERE of Anchises on fate as beyond all doubt the incumbere of the suicide on the drawn sword ("Sumpta proculdubio locutio ab his qui incumbunt gladiis ut se interimant");

and La Cerda is followed, says Forbiger, for I have not the *Zeitschrift* before me, by Haeckermann: " INCUMBERE FATO, ex analogia locutionis *incumbere gladio, ferro.*" Plausible, however, as at first sight this explanation appears to be, and deservedly great as is my respect for both La Cerda and Haeckermann, I have found it impossible to reconcile myself to an allusion in INCUMBERE FATO to *incumbere ferro*, and preferred to remain in doubt until time, that great revealer of secrets, should perhaps throw in my way some truer parallel for INCUMBERE FATO than *incumbere ferro*. Nor had I long to wait, the desired parallel presenting itself almost immediately in "incumbere fortunae," Sil. 7. 241 (of Hannibal):

" *Fortunae* Libys *incumbit*, flatuque secundo
findit agens puppim"

[*leans on fortune, puts pressure on fortune so as to make it go on faster*]. This was the first true parallel which presented itself. The next was "instare fatis," Sil. 1. 268 (of the same Hannibal):

" ergo *instat fatis*, et rumpere foedera certus
qua datur interea Romam comprendere bello
gaudet, et extremis pulsat Capitolia terris"

[*presses on the fates*, viz., *so as to make them more faster*]. And the third was "addere cursum fatis," Sil. 12. 45:

" en qui nos segnes et nescire *addere cursum
fatis* iactastis"

[*to add speed to the fates, to make the fates go faster*]. Not only then were both La Cerda and Haeckermann wrong, entirely wrong, but Conington ("to lend his weight to the destiny that was bearing us down") was entirely wrong too, and old Servius was right, and understood his author well, however little pains he took to explain him intelligibly to the uninitiated.

URGENTI.—Is URGENTI transitive, either meaning, as it must mean with La Cerda and Haeckermann, *pressing on him* (Anchises), or meaning, as it means with Conington, *pressing on us* ("bearing us down")? or is URGENTI intransitive, as it is with Servius, and does it mean, as it means with Servius, merely *hastening?* I need hardly answer: intransitive, and means, with Servius, merely *hastening*. Compare Liv. 5. 22: "Quod decem aestates hiemesque continuas circumsessa [Veii] . . . postremo, iam *fato* tum denique *urgenti*, operibus tamen, non vi, expugnata est." Lucan, 10. 30 (of Alexander the Great):

> "perque Asiae populos *fatis urgentibus* actus
> humana cum strage ruit."

Virg. *Georg. 3. 199:*

> . . . "summaeque sonorem
> dant silvae, longique *urgent* ad littora fluctus."

URGENTI INCUMBERE.—Compare Plaut. *Aulul. 4. 1. 7:*

> "si herum videt superare amorem, hoc servi esse officium reor,
> retinere ad salutem; non cum quo *incumbat*, eo *impellere*,"

the "impellere" of which passage corresponds to the INCUMBERE of our text, and the "incumbat" of which passage corresponds to the URGENTI.

657–661.

MENE EFFERRE PEDEM GENITOR TE POSSE RELICTO
SPERASTI TANTUMQUE NEFAS PATRIO EXCIDIT ORE
SI NIHIL EX TANTA SUPERIS PLACET URBE RELINQUI
ET SEDET HOC ANIMO PERITURAEQUE ADDERE TROIAE
TEQUE TUOSQUE IUVAT PATET ISTI IANUA LETO

MENE EFFERRE . . . SPERASTI.—Not, *hast thou expected me to move my foot?* but *is it me (me, thy affectionate son) whom thou expectedst to move*, &c.? Compare 5. 848, and Rem.; and 1. 37, and Rem.

ET SEDET HOC ANIMO.—Compare 5. 418: "idque pio sedet Aeneae." The metaphor is taken from a balance, of which that scale in which the greater weight is placed is said *sedere*; see Tibull. 4. 1. 41:

" iusta pari premitur veluti cum pondere libra,
prona nec hac plus parte *sedet*, nec surgit ab illa."

PATET ISTI IANUA LETO.—" Ad talem mortem ab hoste accipiendam via patet; ea mors facile obtineri poterit. . . . Idem quod (645) IPSE MANU MORTEM INVENIAM," Heyne—confounding [with Thiel, who quotes Lucr. 1. 1104 :

" nam quacunque prius de parti corpora cesse
constitues, haec rebus erit pars *ianua lethi* ;"

Id. 3. 829 :

" haud igitur *lethi* praeclusa est *ianua* menti ;"

Id. 5. 374 :

" haud igitur *lethi* praeclusa est *ianua* caelo,"

as parallel and explanatory] the two very different, almost opposite, expressions, patet ianua lethi, ανεωγμεναι Αδου πυλαι, *the door of death is open* [Sil. 11. 186 (ed. Ruperti) :

. . . " nullo nos invida tanto
armavit natura bono, quam *ianua mortis*
quod *patet*, et vita non aequa exire potestas."

Val. Flacc. 3. 378 :

. . . " non si mortalia membra
sortitusque breves, et parvi tempora fati
perpetimur, socius superi quondam ignis Olympi,
fas ideo miscere neces, ferroque morantes
exigere hinc animas redituraque semina caelo.
quippe nec in ventos, nec in ultima solvimur ossa :
ira manet duratque dolor; cum deinde tremendi
ad solum venere Iovis, questuque nefandam
edocuere necem, *patet* ollis *ianua lethi*,
atque iterum remeare licet : comes una sororum
additur, et pariter terras atque aequora lustrant.
quisque suos sontes inimicaque pectora poenis
implicat, et varia meritos formidine pulsant."

Eurip. *Hipp.* 56 (of Hippolytus) :

. . . ου γαρ οιδ' ανεωγμενας πυλας
Αδου, φαος τε λοισθιον βλεπων τοδε·

Id. *Hecub.* 1 :

Ηκω, νεκρων κευθμωνα και σκοτου πυλας
λιπων, ιν' Αιδης χωρις ωκισται θεων,
Πολυδωρος, Εκαβης παις γεγως της Κισσεως,
Πριαμου τε πατρος],

and PATET IANUA LETO, *the door is open to death*, i. e., *open for death to enter in*. Compare Gul. Tyr. *Bell. Sacr. 15. 22 :* "Hoc vir audiens magnanimus, licet doloris angeretur immensitate, et *mortem* non dubitaret *adesse* pro foribus, imperiali tamen maiestate constanter observata, sprevit," &c.

Out of this confusion Mr. Conington in vain endeavours to extricate himself: " 'Leti ianua' and similar expressions occur repeatedly in Lucretius, *e. g.*, 5. 373, 'haud igitur leti praeclusa est ianua caelo.' Virgil has perhaps varied the image a little, though it is not clear whether he means the door that leads to death, or, as the dative would rather suggest, the door through which death may come. . . . The latter interpretation is favoured by two passages which Henry quotes—Plin. *Ep. 1. 18:* 'illa ianuam famae patefecit;' and Ter. *Heaut. 3. 1. 72 :* 'Quantam fenestram ad nequitiam patefeceris!'" Instead of saying "it is not clear whether," &c., Mr. Conington should have said it is perfectly clear and certain that the meaning is *the door for death to enter stands open ;* and instead of requoting my insufficient quotations of twenty years ago, might have quoted Ovid, *ex Pont. 2. 7. 37 :*

" sed quia res timida est omnis miser, et quia longo
tempore laetitiae *ianua* clausa meae est."

Id. *Fast. 5. 502 :* "hospitibus *ianua* nostra *patet.*" I need hardly point out to the reader how inharmonious—nay, how inconsistent both with the determination of Anchises to remain where he is, and with the announcement of Aeneas that Pyrrhus will be there immediately—are the words PATET ISTI IANUA LETO understood to mean, *the door to death is open to you, there is nothing to hinder you from going out to meet him ;* how perfectly consistent in the sense, *the door is open for death to enter*, the whole meaning being then: "You are determined to remain here and die : there is nothing to hinder you ; the door is open for death to enter in, and enter in he will immediately in the shape of Pyrrhus, who does not hesitate to butcher the son before the eyes of the father—the father at the altar."

670.

NUNQUAM OMNES HODIE MORIEMUR INULTI

– –

Commentators stumble over this passage more than they need.
"NUNQUAM pro *non*," says Aelius Donatus, quoting our text, ad
Terent. *Adelph.* 2. 1. 15. "NUNQUAM pro *non*," repeats Servius
(ed. Lion); and "NUNQUAM pro *non*," re-repeats Heyne—**all**
of them, in order to get rid of the apparent incongruity NUN-
QUAM—HODIE, content to reduce passion's strongest negative
NUNQUAM (*i. e.*, non-unquam, *never, not ever, not* for all time,
to the cool, common-place, simple negative non (*not* for the
present time, the time in which the negative is uttered). I
would not be fractious, but I must protest against this cutting
down of NUNQUAM, non unquam, into mere non, especially
of NUNQUAM in this emphatic position of first word in the sentence. I would not so deal even with Juvenal's "nunquamne
reponam"—how much less with the NUNQUAM of Aeneas, first
word of the short sentence with which the hero sums up as he
rushes forth to be revenged and die. Let us go back a little.
It was plain to Aeneas that the only safety either for himself or
his family was in flight. But his father was immovable in the
determination not to fly. He was himself equally determined
not to desert his father. The conclusion was obvious: death for
all—

HOC ERAT, ALMA PARENS, QUOD ME PER TELA, PER IGNES
ERIPIS, UT MEDIIS HOSTEM IN PENETRALIBUS, UTQUE
ASCANIUM, PATREMQUE MEUM, IUXTAQUE CREUSAM,
ALTERUM IN ALTERIUS MACTATOS SANGUINE CERNAM?

The thought is intolerable to Aeneas, and he calls for arms. He
will at least not sit there to see his whole family butchered and
be butchered himself along with them. He will have some
revenge. "*Never*," he cries, "shall we all die to-day unrevenged.
You are determined that we shall all die to-day. Be it so: but

it shall *never* be that we all die to-day unrevenged" [compare Sil. 4, p. 67:

"dii patrii . . . .
talin' me letho tanta inter praelia nuper
servastis ? fortunae animam hanc exscindere dextra
indignum est visum ? redde, o, me nate, periclis,
redde hosti, liceat bellanti arcessere mortem,
quam patriae fratrique probem"].

Aeneas's NUNQUAM is not in place of non, denies more strongly than it is possible for non to deny—denies not merely for the moment in which it is uttered, but for all future time. It is more impassioned than non in the very ratio in which it is less logical. Logic is the last thing emotion ever thinks of.

HODIE.—But commentators are always logical; and, disappointed—even Donatus himself—in cutting down NUNQUAM to mere non, change their hand, and letting NUNQUAM stand unshorn ("*Nunquam* plus asseverationis habet quam *non*, ut Virgilius: NUNQUAM OMNES HODIE MORIEMUR INULTI," Donatus ad Terent. *Andr. 4. 5. 7*), vent all their malice on HODIE: "*Hodie autem aut abundat, ut* NUNQUAM OMNES HODIE MORIEMUR INULTI [Donat. ad Terent. *Adelph. 4. 2. 31*, a hint which Voss taking, translates our text thus: 'nie doch sinken wir all' ungerächet dem tode!' and is praised by Thiel for so doing: 'Voss übersetzt mit recht HODIE *nicht*'], aut *nunquam hodie* pro *nullo tempore huius diei*, quia *nunquam* per se generale est"—the **former** of which interpretations, not fixing for any particular time, still less for to-day, either the slaughter of Aeneas and his family or the revenge which Aeneas promises both himself and family for that slaughter, deprives the scene of the interest and pathos attaching to inevitable immediately impending destruction avenged on the instant to the utmost ability of the sufferers; while the inordinate emphasis thrown on HODIE by the **latter**—"nullo tempore huius diei," *at no time of this day*—necessarily suggests at some time of some other day, a sentiment repudiated by the whole context.

But harsh and unmerited as has been the treatment which sometimes the NUNQUAM, at other times the HODIE, of our text has received from former commentators, harsher and still more unmerited that which both words at once have received at the hands of Mr. Conington, who, not content in his paraphrase of our text ("if my father dooms himself and the rest of the family to an unresisting death, I will not share it") with both cutting down NUNQUAM to mere non, and omitting HODIE altogether, refers us for further information to his note on *Ecl. 3. 49*, where we are told that "the phrase ['nunquam hodie'] is found in the comic writers . . . as an arch way of saying that a thing shall not be, and 'hodie' seems to be a sort of comic pleonasm." (!) Poor, almost forgotten Phaer knew better than either Donatus, or Voss, or Heyne, or Thiel, or Conington, and more than three hundred years ago (July, 1555) in Kilgerran forest, correctly and vigorously, without eke or omission, or exaggeration or perversion of any kind, translated: "never shall we die this day unvenged all." Compare Tacit. *Hist. 1. 29*: "ipsius imperii vicem doleo, si nobis aut perire *hodie* necesse est, aut, quod aeque apud bonos miserum est, occidere." Eurip. *Hipp. 41*:

> α δ' εις εμ' ημαρτηκε, τιμωρησομαι
> Ιππολυτον εν τηδ' ημερα.

Soph. *Oed. Col. 1611*:

> . . . ω τεκνα.
> ουκ εστ' εθ' υμιν τηδ' εν ημερα πατηρ.
> ολωλε γαρ δη παντα ταμα, κουκετι
> την δυσπονητον εξετ' αμφ' εμοι τροφην.

Soph. *Trach. 741*:

> τον ανδρα τον σον ισθι, τον δ' εμον λεγω
> πατερα, κατακτεινασα τηδ' εν ημερα.

And also—not correctly only, but conformably to the very commonest usage—Erasm. *Colloq. Opulent. Sordida*: "'Heus,' inquam, 'Orthogone, erit hodie pereundum fame?'"

672-684.

INSERTABAM—PASCI

VAR. LECT. (vs. 683).

MOLLI **I** *Ver.* **III** P. Manut.; La Cerda; D. Heins.; N. Heins. (1670): Philippe; Pott.; Wagn. (1845; *Lect. Virg.*); Wakef. (*Silv. Crit. 4*, p. 227).
MOLLIS **I** *Vat., Pal., Med.* **II.** cod. Canon. (Butler) (MOLLES); " In antiquis aliquot codd.," Pierius. **III** Heyne; Brunck; Wakef. (*in loco*); Wagn. (ed. Heyn. and *Praest.*); Thiel; Voss; Ladewig; Haupt; Ribb.; Con.
O *Rom., St. Gall.*

INSERTABAM.—Incorrect substitution of the frequentative for the ordinary form, merely because inserebam could not be fitted into an hexameter verse. See Köne, " Ueber die Sprache der Romisch. Epiker," p. 159. There is, however, this peculiar propriety in the word *insert*, used in whichever form, that the strap or handle of the shield through which the arm was passed was (as we are informed by Cael. Rhod. *ad locum*) technically denominated insertorium.

FUNDERE LUMEN APEX.—"Apex proprie dicitur in summo flaminis pileo virga lanata, hoc est, in cuius extremitate modica lana est; quod primum constat apud Albam Ascanium statuisse. Modo autem summitatem pilei intelligimus," Servius, followed by Burmann and Leopardi. An interpretation to which I object, (**1**), that if the fire had been in the cap, the first thing to do was to pull off the cap, and that nothing can be more ridiculous than the figure made by Iulus in the picture in the Vatican Fragment (reproduced in Pozzoli's [Romani e Peracchi's] *Dizionario della Favola*, tav. 72), where two attendants are represented pouring water on the cap on the top of Iulus's head; **and (2)**, that the "flammeus apex" which burned on the top of the head of Servius Tullius, and which was the prototype of the APEX of our text, was plainly not the apex or tuft of a cap, but an apex of flame, "flammeus apex;" Ovid, *Fast.* 6. 629:

> "signa dedit genitor tunc cum caput igne corusco
> contigit, inque comis *flammeus* arsit *apex;*"

Liv. 1. 39 : "Puero dormienti, cui Servio Tullio nomen fuit, *caput arsisse* ferunt, multorum in conspectu," in both which accounts, the prosaic no less than the poetic, the miraculous burning is not of a head-dress, but of the head itself or hair. Compare Hom. *Il. 18. 205* :

> αμφι δε οι κεφαλη νεφος εστεφε δια θεαων
> χρυσεον· εκ δ' αυτου δαιε φλογα παμφανοωσαν.

Val. Flacc. 3. 186:

> "accessere (nefas!) tenebris fallacibus acti
> Tyndaridae in sese: Castor prius ibat in ictus
> nescius; ast illos nova lux, *subitusque* diremit
> *frontis apex.*"

Claud. *4 Cons. Honor. 192* :

> . . . "ventura potestas
> claruit Ascanio, subita cum luce comarum
> innocuus flagraret *apex*, Phrygioque volutus
> vertice fatalis redimiret tempora candor."

Sil. 16. 118:

> "huic [Masinissae] fesso, quos dura fuga et nox suaserat atra,
> carpenti somnos subitus rutilante corusco
> vertice fulsit *apex*, crispamque involvere visa est
> mitis flamma comam, atque hirta se spargere fronte."

Also—an example of the application of the same term to the pointed summit of a real fire—Silius, 10. 556 :

> "tum, face coniecta, populatur fervidus ignis
> flagrantem molem, et, rupta caligine, in auras
> actus *apex* claro perfundit lumine campos."

The two substantives, APEX and FLAMMA, taken together present the precise picture which is afforded by "flammeus apex," Ovid, *Fast. 6. 630*, quoted above, exactly as in verse 722,

> "*veste* super fulvique insternor *pelle* leonis,"

the two substantives "veste" and "pelle" present the precise picture which had been afforded by veste pellicea. See Rem, on 721. The same words are united, with the same effect, 10. 270, where

"ardet apex capiti, cristisque a vertice flamma funditur"

is exactly equivalent to "flammeus apex ardet capiti, cristisque a vertice funditur." See Rem. on 10. 270.

TACTUQUE INNOXIA MOLLES.—TACTU INNOXIA, "unschädlich berührend," Voss. "Quae TACTU non nocet; nihil consumens," Forbiger. "TACTU innoxio," Conington. I think rather, *harmless to be touched: that would not harm you if you meddled with it;* just as *Georg. 3. 416*, "mala tactu vipera," where "mala tactu" seems to be the precise correlative of TACTU INNOXIA. If an active signification had been intended it is more probable the word employed would have been attactu, as 7. 350. It is at least remarkable that our author speaking of the viper being touched should use (*Georg. 3. 416*) as here the simple, and speaking of the viper touching should use (7. 350) the compound, word. Compare the Greek ευαφης, *good to be touched*, i. e., *smooth, or soft*.

This interpretation being adopted, the reading of the next word is determined to be not MOLLI, but, in conformity with the weight of MS. authority, either MOLLIS, as descriptive of FLAMMA, or MOLLES, as descriptive of COMAS. But MOLLIS is not wanting for FLAMMA, that subject being already sufficiently provided for in TACTU INNOXIA; and COMAS, otherwise without an epithet, requires some description. We come thus to choose MOLLES, and find our choice confirmed, first by the very similar "est molles flamma medullas" of the fourth book; secondly, by the proof left behind by Sidonius Apollinaris that the reading in his time was MOLLES (*Carm. 2. 114*):

"sic loquitur natura deos: cunctantis Iuli
lambebant *teneros* incendia blanda *capillos*;"

and thirdly, by the consideration that mollis is (see Forbiger *ad locum*) a very usual epithet for the hair.[*]

---

[*] [Among Dr. Henry's MSS. the following remark occurs, dated March, 1864.

689–691.

IUPITER OMNIPOTENS PRECIBUS SI FLECTERIS ULLIS
ASPICE NOS HOC TANTUM ET SI PIETATE MEREMUR
DA DEINDE AUXILIUM PATER ATQUE HAEC OMINA FIRMA

VAR. LECT.

[*punct.*] ASPICE NOS HOC TANTUM ┆ I *Vat.,** *Med.* (HOS), *Ver.* III D. Heins.; Wagner (ed. Heyn., ed. 1861); Lad.; Haupt; Ribb.
[*punct.*] ASPICE NOS ┆ HOC TANTUM ┆ III Venice, 1471; N. Heins.; Philippe; Heyne; Brunck; Wakef.; Pott.
[*punct.*] ASPICE NOS ┆ HOC TANTUM III Ven. 1475; P. Manut.
O *Rom., St. Gall.*

VAR. LECT.

AUXILIUM I *Vat., Pal., Med., Ver.* III Cynth. Cenet.; Rom. 1473; Jul. Scalig. *Poet. 3. 26*; P. Manut.; La Cerda; D. Heins.; N. Heins. (1671); Philippe; Heyne; Brunck; Wakef.; Pott.; Wagn. (ed. Heyn., *Lect. Virg.*, ed. 1861); Coningt.
AUGURIUM III Probus (ad *Eclog. 6. 31*); Peerlk; Keil (*Philol. Götting.* vol. 2, p. 166); Lad.; Haupt; Ribb.; Weidner.
O *Rom., St. Gall.*

---

and as I am not certain that the view given in the text embodies his final opinion, I here insert the other as a note.—ED.] MOLLI, not MOLLES—first, because the harmlessness of the flame requires to be expressed more fully than by the single word INNOXIA. Secondly, TACTU INNOXIA is a strange expression not at all analogous as alleged to "mala tactu," *Georg. 3. 416*, where "tactu" is passive, whereas TACTU in the construction TACTU INNOXIA is active. Thirdly, because we have the expression tactus mollis both in Ovid, *ex Ponto, 2. 7. 13:*

> "membra reformidant *mollem* quoque saucia *tactum,*"

and in Sil. 6. 91:

> . . . "nunc purgat vulnera lympha,
> nunc mulcet sucis; ligat inde, ac vellera *molli*
> circumdat *tactu,* et torpentes mitigat artus."

The reading, therefore, is MOLLI, and the structure LAMBERE TACTU MOLLI.

* Bottari, therefore, is incorrect in placing a point after NOS. There is no appearance at all in the MS. of a point in that situation.

Observe the words IUPITER OMNIPOTENS (expressive of the *power* to relieve, even in so desperate an extremity) joined to all the verbs in the sentence; the word PATER (moving to exert that power) joined only to the immediate prayer of the petition, DA DEINDE AUXILIUM, ATQUE HAEC OMINA FIRMA. See Rem. on verse 552.

ASPICE NOS; HOC TANTUM.—This punctuation, which is that of Nicholas Heinsius, renders ASPICE NOS, already emphatic by its position at the beginning of the line, still more emphatic by the sudden pause which separates it from the subsequent words; see Rem. on verse 246. Wagner removes the pause, and connects HOC TANTUM closely with ASPICE NOS : which arrangement —while it has the effect, first, of diminishing the emphasis of the emphatic words ASPICE NOS; and, secondly, of substituting for a simple, pathetic, passionate exclamation, one bound up with a cool, phlegmatic, lawyerlike condition or limitation—is directly opposed to Virgil's usual manner, which, as we have so often seen, is first to present us fully and boldly with the main thought, the grand conception, and then to modify, limit, soften down, adapt, or explain, afterwards. And so, precisely, on the present occasion, we have first the short, strong, emphatic ASPICE NOS, and then, after a pause, HOC TANTUM : *do but so much and I am sure of all the rest.*

ASPICE NOS, *look on us* (i. e., *in our trouble*) ; *see the trouble we are in*. *Look on us, see the trouble we are in, and I ask no more.* Compare Aesch. *Suppl.* 206 : Ζευς δε γεννητωρ ιδοι [not the vocative, nor addressed to God, but expressing a wish only : *may God look on us!*]. Eurip. *Hec. 808* (ed. Fix) (Hecuba speaking) :

ιδου με κάναθρησον οι' εχω κακα.

Prudent. *Cathem. Hymn. 3. 6:*

"huc nitido, precor, intuitu
flecte salutiferam faciem."

ASPICE.—The opinion was, that your cause was safe, your wishes acceded to, your prayer granted, if the god or other person to whom your prayer was addressed looked on you, especially if he looked on you with a mild and placid aspect. Compare

Aesch. *Suppl. 210* (chorus of Danaides) :

ιδοιτο [Ζευs] πρευμενουs απ' ομματοs.
κεινου θελοντοs εν τελευτησει ταδε.

Sil. 7. 239 :

" magnum illud, solisque datum, quos mitis euntes
Iupiter *aspexit*, magnum est, ex hoste reverti "

(with which contrast *Aen. 10. 473:*

" sic ait, atque *oculos* Rutulorum *reiicit* arvis").

Also Hesiod, *Theog. 81 :*

οντινα τιμησουσι Διοs κουραι μεγαλοιο,
γεινομενον τ' εσιδωσι διοτρεφεων βασιληων,
τω μεν επι γλωσση γλυκερην χειουσιν εερσην.

Pind. *Isthm. 2. 18* (ed. Dissen) :

εν Κρισα δ' ευρυσθενηs ειδ' Απολλων νιν
πορε τ' αγλαιαν
και τοθι

(where Dissen: "Benevole aspexit").

In Italy at the present day every supplication for alms by the commonest beggar is prefaced by the identical prayer " guardi," so little have manners changed in two thousand years, and so narrow the line of demarcation between worshipper and beggar; so insensibly does prayer merge in beggary.

Hoc TANTUM.—Compare Claud. *Bell. Gild. 314:*

" sed *tantum* permitte cadat: nil poscimus ultra."

Epitom. Iliados, 716 (of Dolon) :

" ille timore pavens, 'vitam concedite,' dixit.
' *hoc unum* satis est.' "

And—exactly parallel—Claud. *Rapt. Pros. 3. 298:*

. . . " liceat cognoscere sortem.
hoc tantum. liceat certos habuisse dolores."

Also Sil. 4. 407 :

" post me stato, viri, et pulsa formidine *tantum*
aspicite."

And Sil. 2. 230 : " spectacula *tantum* ferte, viri."

PIETATE, not *our piety*, viz., towards heaven, but *our tenderness*, viz., towards each other. See Rem. on *Aen. 1. 14.* Therefore the expression, ASPICE; *look on us, see what a picture of family affection we present;* and so, precisely, Ovid, *Trist. 3. 4. 35* (addressing his friend, from exile):

> " quae pro te ut voveam miti *pietate* mereris,
> haesuraque mihi tempus in omne fide "

[by your *brotherly kindness* and fidelity towards me].

AUGURIUM.—Notwithstanding the preponderance both of manuscript and editorial authority in favour of AUXILIUM, I am inclined to think that AUGURIUM is the true reading: (**1**), on account of the very parallel passage of Sil. 15. 143, where on the occasion of a first prodigy's being established by a second, sent as in our text by Jupiter himself, the word augurium is not only used but even repeated:

> . . . " bis terque coruscum
> addidit *augurio* fulmen pater, et vaga late
> per subitum moto strepuere tonitrua mundo.
> tum vero capere arma iubent, genibusque salutant
> summissi *augurium*, atque iret qua ducere divos
> perspicuum, et patrio monstraret semita signo."

And (**2**), because the identical expression, " da, pater, augurium," is used by our author himself, 3. 89:

> " da, pater, *augurium* atque animis illabere nostris."

Compare also 7. 259:

> . . . " dii nostra incepta secundent,
> *augurium*que suum;"

and Iscan. 2. 131:

> . . . " da, maxime, felix
> *auspicium*, laetum tribuas nubentibus omen."

693-698.

ET DE CAELO LAPSA PER UMBRAS
STELLA FACEM DUCENS MULTA CUM LUCE CUCURRIT
ILLAM SUMMA SUPER LABENTEM CULMINA TECTI
CERNIMUS IDAEA CLARAM SE CONDERE SILVA
SIGNANTEMQUE VIAS TUM LONGO LIMITE SULCUS
DAT LUCEM ET LATE CIRCUM LOCA SULFURE FUMANT

ET DE, &c., . . . CUCURRIT.—Compare S. Matth. *Evang.* 2. 9 : Και ιδου, ο αστηρ, ον ειδον εν τη ανατολη, προηγεν αυτους, εως ελθων εστη επανω ου ην το παιδιον. In "Saunders's News-Letter," of July 25, 1844, there is, in an extract from a letter, the following account of a meteor, seen almost on the same spot, and presenting precisely the same appearances as that seen by Aeneas :—" Constantinople, July 3.—On Sunday last, five minutes before sunset, we had a splendid sight here. The atmosphere was hazy, but without cloud. Thermometer about 90°. An immense meteor, like a gigantic Congreve rocket, darted, with a rushing noise, from east to west. Its lightning course was marked by a streak of fire, and, after a passage of some forty or fifty degrees, it burst like a bombshell, but without detonation, lighting up the hemisphere with the brilliancy of the noon-day sun. On its disappearance, a white vapour remained in its track, and was visible for nearly half an hour. Everybody thought it was just before his eyes, but it was seen by persons twelve and fifteen miles to the northward, in the same apparent position, and positively the self-same phenomenon. Many of the vulgar look upon it as a very bad omen, whilst others attribute it to the warm weather, which continues. The thermometer stands, at this moment, at 91° in the shade, and in the coolest spot could be selected."

SUMMA SUPER LABENTEM CULMINA TECTI.—Compare Apollon. Rhod. 1. 774 (ed. Beck), of Jason :

βη δ' ιμεναι προτι αστυ, φαεινω αστερι ισος,
ον ρα τε νηγατεησιν εεργομεναι καλυβησι
νυμφαι θηησαντο δομων υπεραντελλοντα,
και σφισι κυανεοιο δι' ηερος ομματα θελγει
καλον ερευθομενος, γανυται δε τε ηιθεοιο
παρθενος ιμειρουσα μετ' αλλοδαποισιν εοντος
ανδρασιν, ω κεν μιν μνηστην κομεωσι τοκηες.
τω ικελος προ πολησς ανα στιβον ηιεν ηρως.

CERNIMUS, &c.—Wagner (*Praest.*) and Forbiger, understanding the structure to be CLARAM SIGNANTEMQUE VIAS SE CONDERE, have removed the pause placed by the two Stephenses, the two Heinsii, and Heyne, after SILVA. The pause should undoubtedly be replaced, SIGNANTEM being connected by QUE, not with its unlike CLARAM, but with its like LABENTEM, and it being Virgil's usual method thus to connect a concluding or winding up clause, not with the immediately preceding clause, but with one more remote. See Remm. on 2. 148; 3. 571; 4..483; 5. 522.

SIGNANTEMQUE VIAS, *i.e.*, marking the way; which way, being towards Ida, signified to Aeneas that he was to take refuge in Ida. Compare (***a***) the way to the newly born Christ pointed out to the Magi by the star, Prudent. *Cathem. 12. 53:*

" exin sequuntur, perciti
fixis in altum vultibus,
qua stella sulcum traxerat
claramque *signabat viam*."

(***b***), the pigeons pointing out to Aeneas his way to the golden bough, 6. 198:

" observans, quae *signa ferant*, quo tendere pergant."

(***c***), the way marked for Acestes to heaven by the flaming arrow, 5. 525:

" namque volans liquidis in nubibus arsit arundo,
signavitque viam flammis."

(***d***), the way towards Africa pointed out to Scipio by the fiery snake in the sky, Sil. 15. 139:

> "ecce, per obliquum caeli squalentibus auro
> effulgens maculis, ferri inter nubila visus
> anguis, et ardenti radiare per aera sulco,
> quaque ad caeliferi tendit plaga littus Atlantis,
> perlabi resonante polo . . . .
> . . . .
> tum vero capere arma iubent, genibusque salutant
> summissi augurium, atque iret, qua ducere divos
> perspicuum, et patrio *monstraret semita signo*."

(*e*), the way marked by the admiral's ship for the rest of the fleet to follow, Senec. *Agam*. 427 :

> " signum recursus regia ut fulsit rate,
> et clara lentum remigem monuit tuba,
> aurata primas prora *designat vias*,
> aperitque cursus, mille quos puppes secent."

(*f*), the light placed on the turret by Hero to be "signa viae" to Leander crossing the Hellespont, Ovid, *Heroid*. 19. 35 :

> " protinus in summa vigilantia lumina turre
> ponimus, assuetae *signa* notamque *viae*."

(*g*), the way from this same Ida to the Grecian encampment pointed out to Hector and the Trojan army by a miraculous cloud of dust, Hom. *Il*. 12. 252 :

> . . . επι δε Ζευs τερπικεραυνοs
> ωρσεν απ' Ιδαιων ορεων ανεμοιο θυελλαν,
> η ρ' ιθυs νηων κονιην φερεν· αυταρ Αχαιων
> θελγε νοον, Τρωσιν δε και Εκτορι κυδοs οπαζεν.
> του περ δη τεραεσσι πεποιθοτεs, ηδε βιηφιν
> ρηγνυσθαι μεγα τειχοs Αχαιων πειρητιζον

(and so the Schol. of the Veronese Palimpsest (Keil's ed., p. 90, l. 21) : "Ait Troianos stellam ducem discessionis habuisse"). **And**, (*h*), Plut. in Caesar. : Τη δε προ της μαχης [of Pharsalia] νυκτι τας φυλακας εφοδευοντος αυτου, περι το μεσονυκτιον ωφθη λαμπας ουρανιου πυρος, ην υπερενεχθεισαν το Καισαρος στρατοπεδον, λαμπραν και φλογωδη γενομενην, εδοξεν εις το Πομπηιου καταπεσειν (thus indicating to him that he was to go towards Pompey, that he was to persist in his intention of fighting Pompey).

SIGNANTEM VIAS, not *drawing or marking a path or line in the sky*, but *marking, or signifying, or pointing out the route*, viz., for Aeneas, the method by which this is effected being explained in the immediately following words to be by drawing a long luminous furrow in the sky : TUM LONGO LIMITE SULCUS DAT LUCEM.

LIMITE, *track* or *path*. Contiguous properties being anciently, as still very generally on the continent of Europe, separated from each other, not by a fence, but merely by a narrow intermediate space, along which (in order not to trespass on the ground on either side) it was usual for those who had business in the neighbourhood to walk, the term limes, primarily signifying a boundary or limit, came by a natural and unavoidable transition to signify *a path, way*, or *track*. Compare Stat. *Theb.* 12. 240: " quoties amissus eunti limes?" [*how often the way or path lost?*]

702-714.

DI—CERERIS

DI PATRII.—Commentators being generally silent with respect to these words, the Virgilian student is left to himself to find out their meaning the best way he can. It occurs to him that it may be either *gods of my country*, or *gods of my fathers*. The difference, perhaps, is not great, but still he is curious to know which precisely was in Virgil's mind. If he has recourse to the translators he finds they are pretty well agreed that Virgil meant *gods of my country*—Surrey translating :

" o native gods ! your family defend ;"

Phaer:

" o contrey gods ! our house behold :"

Caro :

. . . "o de la patria
sacri numi Penati, a voi mi rendo ;"

Dryden:

> "keep, o my country gods! our dwelling place;"

and J. H. Voss, alone of translators of repute, rendering:

> . . . "ich folg' euch, götter der väter,
> wo ihr auch führt; erhaltet das haus."

Turning to Gesner's excellent lexicon he finds two separate and distinct adjectives patrius, one placed under the head pater and the other under the head patria, and our text cited as an example of the latter. He is quite persuaded, and for him it is to his country's gods Anchises commends his house and grandson. But let him beware. The minority or weaker side is shown by all experience to be oftener in the right than the majority or stronger side, and the present case constitutes no exception to the general rule. The DI PATRII of our text are the identical πατρωοι θεοι which Aeneas carries out of Troy on his shoulders along with his μητρωοι θεοι, or gods of his mothers, and therefore are and can only be gods of his fathers. Compare Xenoph. de Venat. 1. 15: Αινειας δε σωσας μεν τους πατρωους και μητρωους θεους, σωσας δε και αυτον τον πατερα, δοξαν ευσεβειας εξηνεγκατο, ωστε και οι πολεμιοι μονω εκεινω, ων εκρατησαν εν Τροια, εδοσαν μη συληθηναι.

But the student has not been left equally free with respect to the relation these words bear to the context. A period at ADSUM in the editions shuts off DI PATRII from DUCITIS, and throws those words wholly to SERVATE. In vain the bewildered student asks himself: Is not the DUCITIS no less than the SERVATE addressed to the DI PATRII? Is it not the DI PATRII who have just sent the guiding leading star, SIGNANTEM VIAS? Is it possible that DUCITIS can be addressed to Aeneas, Creusa, and Ascanius, and only SERVATE to the DI PATRII? that Anchises addresses in the first place his friends, and only in the second place his gods; begins with his friends and ends with his friends, and bundles his gods into a parenthesis in the middle? Again the commentators are silent, and of five translators three follow the editors, Surrey translating:

Phaer:
> " · now, now,' quod he, ' no longer I abide :
> follow I shall where ye me guide at hand.
> o native gods ! your family defend ; ' "

> " now, now, no more I let, lead where ye list, I will not swarve.
> o contrey gods, our house behold, my nevew safe preserve ; "

Dryden :
> " ' now, now,' said he, ' my son, no more delay ;
> I yield, I follow, where heaven shows the way ;
> keep (o my country gods !) our dwelling place ;' "

Caro :
> . . . " o de la patria
> sacri numi Penati, a voi mi rendo.
> voi questa casa, voi questo nipote
> mi conservate ;"

and J. H. Voss :
> . . . "ich folg' euch, götter der väter,
> wo ihr auch führt. erhaltet das haus, erhaltet den enkel."

Yes ; it is not only possible but certain, concludes the student, surrendering his common sense to the weight of authority, and continuing to do so until such time as editors shall perceive that there is no reason why the very first words Anchises utters after he has seen the guiding star should be cut off from the "affari deos" which the sight of that star prompted—that the structure is not : IAM IAM NULLA MORA EST ; SEQUOR ET QUA DUCITIS ADSUM. DI PATRII, SERVATE DOMUM, SERVATE NEPOTEM, but DI PATRII, IAM IAM NULLA MORA EST ; SEQUOR ET QUA DUCITIS ADSUM. SERVATE DOMUM, SERVATE NEPOTEM—and shall substitute a comma for the period they have placed at ADSUM.

VESTROQUE IN NUMINE TROIA EST.—" 'In tua,' inquit, 'pater carissime, in tua sumus custodia,'" Petron., p. 354 (ed. Hadr., Amst. 1669).

LONGE SERVET VESTIGIA CONIUX (VS. 711).—There seems to be no ground whatever for the charge which has so frequently been brought against Aeneas, that he deserted, or at least neglected, his wife. Comp. Ovid, *Heroid*. *7. 83* :

> " si quaeras, ubi sit formosi mater Iuli :
> occidit, a duro sola relicta viro."

It was necessary to divide the party, in order the better to escape observation by the Greeks; and not only the greater imbecility of, but stronger natural tie to, the father and the child, rendered it imperative to bestow the first and chief care on them. If Aeneas's direction that Creusa should keep, not merely behind, but far behind (LONGE SERVET VESTIGIA CONIUX), excite animadversion, I beg to suggest that it was indispensable that the separation should be to some considerable distance, not merely in order to ensure its being effectual for the purpose above mentioned, but in order to afford Creusa herself the chance of escape, in case of the miscarriage of those who led the way. With this account of Aeneas's loss of Creusa compare Göthe's not less charming description of Epimetheus's loss of Pandora, in his unfinished dramatic piece entitled *Pandora*.

TEMPLUM VETUSTUM DESERTAE CERERIS.—" Cuius templum erat desertum vetustate vel belli decennalis tempore," Heyne. No; Wagner's explanation is the correct one: " DESERTAE, quod templum habuit in loco infrequenti." The truth of this interpretation (rested by Wagner solely on the context, and the similar use made of the term desertus by other authors) seems to be established by the testimony of Vitruvius, that religion required that the temples of Ceres should be built outside the walls and in lonely situations ("Item Cereri, extra urbem loco, quo non semper homines, nisi per sacrificium, necesse habeant adire"); in order, no doubt (see the Emperor Julian's Letter to Libanius, *Epist. Mut. Graecan.* p. 148), to pay Ceres the especial compliment, that her worship should be apart from all secular concerns, not performed *en passant*.

The temple of Ceres outside Troy was therefore a fit place for the unobserved rendezvous of Aeneas and his party; as in real history the temple of Ceres outside Rome was a fit place for Piso (the intended successor to the empire) to wait unobserved until the conspirators should have despatched Nero: "Interim Piso apud aedem Cereris opperiretur, unde cum praefectus Fenius et ceteri accitum ferrent in castra," Tacit. *Annal.* 15. 53.

721-725.

HAEC FATUS LATOS HUMEROS SUBIECTAQUE COLLA
VESTE SUPER FULVIQUE INSTERNOR PELLE LEONIS
SUCCEDOQUE ONERI DEXTRAE SE PARVUS IULUS
IMPLICUIT SEQUITURQUE PATREM NON PASSIBUS AEQUIS
PONE SUBIT CONIUX FERIMUR PER OPACA LOCORUM

LATOS HUMEROS, &c.. . . . LEONIS.—"Instravit Aeneas humeris vestem, vestique pellem," Heyne.

"Breit' ich darauf ein gewand und die haut des gelblichen löwen."

VOSS.

Certainly, and for many reasons, not the meaning: (**1**), because Aeneas, about to undertake a perilous flight with his father and SACRA on his shoulders, should not load himself with two outside coverings when one was sufficient. (**2**), because Agamemnon, issuing out at night, puts on over his tunic only the lion's skin, Hom. *Il. 10. 23:*

αμφι δ' επειτα δαφοινον εεσσατο δερμα λεοντος,

and Dolon (*Il. 10. 334*) only the wolf's skin:

εσσατο δ' εκτοσθεν ρινον πολιοιο λυκοιο.

(**3**), because the lion's skin was the sole (outside) covering of Hercules, the rough block out of which courtly Aeneas is hewn. **And**, (**4**), because the construction by hendiadys, so usual with our author elsewhere [compare 9. 306:

" dat Niso Mnestheus *pellem* horrentesque leonis
exuvias,"

not two objects, viz., a skin and a lion's spoils, but the single object, a lion's skin, twice described] affords the unexceptionable meaning: rug, or cover of lion's skin.

VESTE FULVIQUE PELLE LEONIS, a rug of lion's skin. I say rug, not garment, because Aeneas represents himself as "superinstratus" with it, and SUPERINSTERNOR points directly to a rug such as is laid or spread upon a bed, or floor, or hearth, or table, or horse, not to a garment for the person. Compare Sil. 7 (p. 105) of Hannibal:

>   . . . "iam membra cubili
> erigit, et *fulvi* circumdat *pelle leonis*,
> qua *super instratos* proiectus gramine campi
> presserat ante *toros*,"

where we have not only the precise "fulvi pelle leonis" and "superinsternor" of our text, but the double use of the vestis, first as a rug to lie on, and then as a wrapper. See Rem. on 2. 682.

Vestis, generally, is any *outside* cover, whether of bed, table, or person. See Lucret. 2. 34:

> "nec calidae citius decedunt corpore febres,
> textilibus si in picturis ostroque rubenti
> iacteris, quam si plebeia in *veste* cubandum est."

Aen. 1. 643:

> "arte laboratae *vestes* ostroque superbo."

Celsus, *de Medicina*, 1. 3: "per autumnum vero, propter caeli varietatem, periculum maximum est. Itaque neque sine *veste* neque sine calceamentis prodire oportet." The corresponding Greek term ειμα is also applied to the coverings of the floor or ground, carpets, as Aesch. *Agam.* 921:

> μηδ' ειμασι στρωσασ' επιφθονον πορον
> τιθει.

INSTERNOR.—This word, properly applied to the εφιππια or covering of the horse (the modern saddle-cloth and ancient saddle; compare 7. 277:

> "*instratos* ostro alipedes pictisque tapetis")

shows unmistakeably Aeneas's tacit comparison of himself with a horse equipped for and receiving his rider on his back. The allusion is continued in SUCCEDO ONERI, the term succedere being commonly applied to horses or other animals yoked or put to a carriage or other burthen, as 3. 541:

> "sed tamen idem olim *curru succedere* sueti
> quadrupedes, et frena iugo concordia ferre."

Sequiturque patrem non passibus aequis.—The picture presented is that of the child in his father's hand, and striving to keep up with him; but, having shorter legs and taking shorter steps, not quite abreast with him, and trotting while the father walks. A similar picture, except that both parties are running, is presented by the words, "manu parvum nepotem trahit," 2. 320. Compare also Stat. *Theb. 5. 441*:

"audet iter magnique sequens vestigia mutat
Herculis, et tarda quamvis se mole ferentem
vix cursu tener *aequat* Hylas."

Hom. *Od. 15. 450*:

παιδα γαρ ανδρος εηος ενι μεγαροις ατιταλλω,
κερδαλεον δη τοιον, αμα τροχοωντα θυραζε·
τον κεν αγοιμ' επι νηος· ο δ' υμιν μυριον ωνον
αλφοι, οπη περασητε κατ' αλλοθροους ανθρωπους.

Sil. 4. 30:

. . . "dextra laevaque trahuntur
parvi, *non aequo comitantes ordine*, nati."

Val. Flacc. 1. 704:

. . "acrisona volucer cum Daedalus ora
prosiluit, iuxtaque *comes brevioribus alis*."

Senec. *ad Marciam, 11*: "Huc [ad mortem] omnis ista quae in foro litigat, in theatris desidet, in templis precatur turba, *dispari gradu* vadit" [*i.e.*, some quicker, some slower, some walking, some running].

Sequitur patrem [Iulus]; pone subit coniux.—Iulus has his hand in Aeneas's, and sequitur haud passibus aequis, goes along with Aeneas, keeps company with Aeneas: Creusa alone follows behind both. This meaning, viz., to go along with, to accompany as an inferior, to follow the lead of, without, however, being actually behind, is a very common one of sequi. See Senec. *Hippol. 844* (Theseus speaking):

. . . "heu, labor quantus fuit
Phlegethonte ab imo petere longinquum aethera,
pariterque mortem fugere, et Alcidem *sequi*!"

Ovid, *Amor. 2. 14. 1:*

> "quid iuvat immunes belli cessare puellas
> nec fera peltatas agmina velle *sequi*"

[*not* follow behind, *but* go along with as inferior]. *Ibid. 3. 8. 25:*

> "discite, qui sapitis, non quae nos scimus inertes,
> sed trepidas acies et fera castra *sequi*."

Ovid, *Fast. 1. 419:*

> "fastus inest pulchris, *sequiturque* superbia formam."

And our author himself, *Aen. 4. 384:* "*sequar* atris ignibus absens," where see Rem. The Greeks made a precisely similar use of ἐπεσθαι, as Hom. *Il. 16. 154* (of Achilles' horse Pedasus):

> ος και θνητος εων, επεθ' ιπποις αθανατοισι.

NON PASSIBUS AEQUIS, *not keeping pace with him.* Compare Val. Flacc. 3. 485:

> . . . "petit excelsas Tirynthius ornos;
> haeret Hylas lateri, *passu*sque moratur *iniquos.*"

Stat. *Theb. 11. 321* (of Jocasta):

> "non comites, non ferre ipsae *vestigia* natae
> *aequa* valent. tantum miserae dolor ultimus addit
> robur, et exsangues crudescunt luctibus anni."

FERIMUR PER OPACA LOCORUM.—OPACA, not *dark*, but only *shady*; not so dark but that one could see the way. Compare Plin. *Epist. 7. 21:* "Cubicula obductis velis *opaca*, nec tamen obscura, facio." Also Plin. *Epist. 8. 8:* "Modicus collis assurgit, antiqua cupressu nemorosus et *opacus.*"

729-759.

SUSPENSUM—AURAS

VAR. LECT. (vs. 738).

FATO NE **I** *Pal.* **II** ⅔. **III** Ven., 1471 and 1475; Mod.; R. Steph.; P. Manut.

FATONE **II** ₂⁷₂. **III** D. Heins.; N. Heins.; Philippe; Heyne; Pott.; Haupt; Wagn. (*Lect. Virg.* and *Praest.*).

FATO EST **III** Peerlk.; Dietsch; Lad.

FATO MI **III** Ribbeck.

VAR. LECT. (vs. 755).

ANIMO SIMUL **I** *Med.*

ANIMOS, SIMUL **III** P. Manut.; La Cerda; D. Heins.; N. Heins. (1670); Phil.; Heyn.; Brunck; Wakef.; Wagn. (ed. Heyn.)

ANIMO, SIMUL **I** *Pal.* (ANIMO* · SIMUL). **III** Voss; Lad.; Haupt; Wagn. (*Lect. Virg.* and ed. 1861); Ribb.

SUSPENSUM, "sollicitum," Servius, Heyne. No; SUSPENSUM is not "sollicitum," equivalent to *anxious, uneasy;* but *suspended, hung between hope and fear*, and so *irresolute, undecided, not knowing whether to go on or stop.* See Remm. on 2. 114, and 3. 372.

HEU! MISERO, &c., . . . INCERTUM (vss. 738-740).—" Excusationes istae ad triplex caput reducuntur; aut ad deos et fata, quae eripuerunt; aut ad Aeneam, qui non potuit animadvertere; aut ad Creusam, quae disparuit subsistens, errans, sedens prae lassitudine," La Cerda. "CONIUX [*mihi*] MISERO EREPTA CREUSA FATONE SUBSTITIT, *an* ERRAVIT DE VIA, *an* LASSA RESEDIT," Heyne; approved of both by Wunderlich and Forbiger. "Musste sie nach dem willen des schicksals stehen bleiben, um von den feinden getödtet zu werden," Ladewig. I agree, however, entirely with Servius: "FATO EREPTA CREUSA, SUBSTITITNE ERRAVITNE VIA." Aeneas is certain of

---

* Ribbeck has omitted the point.

one thing and of one thing only, viz., that Creusa was MISERO FATO EREPTA. How it happened that she was MISERO FATO EREPTA was entirely unknown to him—remained wrapt in obscurity; it might have been that she had stopped short, being afraid to go on, or that she had missed her way, or that she had grown weary, and sat down to rest. He could not tell in which of these three possible ways it had happened; but certain it was that she had been MISERO FATO EREPTA.

FATONE EREPTA CREUSA SUBSTITIT = SUBSTITITNE CREUSA EREPTA FATO, exactly as 10. 668 : " tanton' me crimine dignum duxisti " = " duxistine me dignum tanto crimine," not only FATONE and "tanton'," but SUBSTITIT and " duxisti " occupying the same positions both in their respective verses and respective sentences. See Rem. on " Pyrrhin' connubia servas?" 3. 319.

MISERO FATO EREPTA.—"*Mihi* MISERO EREPTA FATO," Heyne, Wunderlich, De Bulgaris, Wagner, Forbiger, and Conington. I have two reasons, however, for thinking that MISERO certainly belongs to FATO, and not to "mihi" understood : **First**, the personal pronoun is usually expressed when miser is applied to the speaker in the third case, as *Ecl. 2. 58 :* "heu! heu! quid volui *misero mihi?*" *Aen. 2. 70 :* " aut quid iam *misero mihi* denique restat?" *Aen. 10. 849 :* "heu! nunc *misero mihi* demum exitium infelix." Seeing that our author has thought it necessary to supply the personal pronoun to "misero" in these instances, in which there was no ambiguity to be apprehended from its omission, and yet has not supplied it in our text where there was the ambiguity arising from the near vicinity of FATO, I conclude that there is no pronoun at all to be supplied, and that the adjective really belongs (as at first sight it appears to do) to the substantive expressed ; compare, only three lines preceding,

HIC MIHI NESCIO QUOD TREPIDO MALE NUMEN AMICUM
CONFUSAM ERIPUIT MENTEM.

And secondly, FATO EREPTA, *without* the addition of MISERO, means *died a natural death* (see Livy, 3. 50 : "quod ad se attineat, uxorem sibi *fato ereptam ;*" also *Aen. 4. 696* and Rem.) : *with* the addition of MISERO, FATO EREPTA means *died a violent*

death, the only kind of death which can be meant by Aeneas. Compare *Aen. 4. 20:* "*miseri* post fata Sychaei." *Aen. 1. 225:* "*crudelia* secum fata Lyci." *Aen. 4. 696:*

> .... " peribat
> sed *misera* ante diem subitoque accensa furore."

DEFUIT (vs. 744), well opposed to VENIMUS; the two words of so opposite significations corresponding exactly to each other, not merely prosodiacally, but in emphasis arising from position, each being last word of its own clause, first word of its own verse, and separated by a pause from the sequel. See Rem. on "ora," 2. 247, and compare "substitit," 2. 243.

ET RURSUS CAPUT OBIECTARE PERICLIS.—Compare *Bibl. Sacr.* [Vulg.] *4. Regum, 25. 27:* "*Sublevavit* Evilmerodach rex Babylonis, anno quo regnare coeperat, *caput* Ioachin regis Iuda de carcere."

SIMUL IPSA SILENTIA TERRENT.—So Tacitus (*Hist. 3. 84*), not less finely of Vitellius: "In palatium regreditur, vastum desertumque . . . *terret solitudo et tacentes loci*." Compare also Schiller, *Braut von Messina:*

> " es schreckt mich selbst das wesenlose schweigen."

SI FORTE PEDEM, SI FORTE TULISSET.—Compare Ovid, *Heroid. 1.3. 164:*

> "*sive*, quod heu timeo! *sive* superstes eris."

EXSUPERANT FLAMMAE, FURIT AESTUS AD AURAS.—See Schiller, *Wilhelm Tell*, act 5, sc. 1:

> " die flamme prasselnd schon zum himmel schlug."

AURAS, the sky; exactly as *Ecl. 1. 57:*

> " hinc alta sub rupe canet frondator ad *auras;*"

and Claud. *Rapt. Pros.* p. 199: "quid incestis aperis Titanibus *auras?*" in both which passages "auras" is the sky; in the former, as in our text, literally and simply the sky, in the latter the sky figuratively, *i. e.*, the upper world, on which the sky looks down and shines, as contrasted with the lower world to which the Titans are condemned and on which the sky never looks down or shines. Compare also Ovid, 10. 178:

> " quem prius aerias libratum Phoebus in auras
> misit, et oppositas disiecit pondere nubes ;"

and Val. Flacc. 6. 56:

> . . . . " tandem dulces iam cassus in auras
> respicit, ac nulla caelum reparabile gaza,"

in the former of which passages " auras," simply and literally the sky, is repeated with a slight variation in " nubes," and in the latter of which passages " auras," simply and literally the sky, is repeated with a similar slight variation in " caelum."

769-779.

IMPLEVI—OLYMPI

IMPLEVI . . . VOCAVI.—Compare Orpheus calling on Eurydice in the fourth Georgic, and Pope's fine imitation (*Ode on St. Cecilia's Day*):

> " Eurydice the woods,
> Eurydice the floods,
> Eurydice the rocks and hollow mountains rung."

INFELIX SIMULACRUM (IPSIUS CREUSAE) theme; IPSIUS UMBRA CREUSAE, first variation; NOTA MAIOR IMAGO, second variation.

SIMULACRUM, *likeness*, *image*, *fac-simile*, nothing more. Compare Cicero, *de Invent. Rhet. 2. 1* (of Zeuxis) : " Helenae se pingere *simulacrum* velle dixit."

ET NOTA MAIOR IMAGO.—It is the beholder's fear makes the ghost appear larger than life. The real living Esmeralda, taken for her own ghost by Claude Frollo, appeared to be above her usual size, Victor Hugo, *Not. Dame, 9. 1*: " Elle lui parut plus grande que lorsqu' elle vivait." To a not very dissimilar fear is, no doubt, to be traced the notion of the superior size of the gods, if not, with Lucretius, the very notion of gods.

SIC AFFARI, theme; CURAS HIS DEMERE DICTIS, variation.

"FAS, *fatum;* 'non fatum, nec interpres fati, Iupiter,'" Wagner (*Praest.*), following Heinsius. And so Forbiger, who adds: "Ceterum ad FAS non supplendum verbum *est*, sed iungendum FAS SINIT." So also Voss, Thiel, and Conington. Neither the meaning of fas, nor the structure. (**1**), **not** the meaning of fas, for how would that meaning answer for Sinon, where he says, verse 157:

"*fas* mihi Graiorum sacrata resolvere iura,
fas odisse viros, atque omnia ferre sub auras,
si qua tegunt"?

How would it answer for Aeolus where he says to Juno, 1. 81: "mihi iussa capessere *fas* est?" How would it answer, verse 402, for "heu nihil invitis *fas* quenquam fidere divis?" or for 3. 55, where Polymnestor

"*fas* omne abrumpit, Polydorum obtruncat, &c.,"

or how would it answer in any one of the numerous places in which our author has used the word? No, no; FAS is here as everywhere *divine sanction, permission, license*, and differs from licet only in being more solemn and referring always to the permission granted by laws above human. While fatum is positive and obligatory, fas is permissive and optional; while fatum is what *must* happen, fas is what may. So far, therefore, from fas being equivalent to fatum, it is as directly opposed to it as permission is to obligation, as *may* to *must*. To do anything except according to fas involved responsibility and punishment, to do anything except according to fate was impossible. The relation of fas was to the innocence or guilt of the act in the eye of heaven, the relation of fatum was to the physical occurrence. The same act could therefore be, and in the case of every great crime actually was, at one and the same time contrary to fas and according to fatum; *ex. gr.*, Polymnestor murdering Polydorus "abrumpit omne fas," while he is all the time only fulfilling fatum. (**2**), **nor** is the structure FAS SINIT, because the SINIT, the permission, the lawfulness, is contained in the very notion FAS. In other words, it is impossible for FAS to permit, FAS itself being permission. The structure is FAS est, exactly as the structure is "fas est" both at verse 157 and verse 158, quoted above; as it is "fas est," *Georg. 4. 358*: "'fas illi limina divum tangere,' ait;" and as it is "fas est," 4. 350: "et nos *fas* extera quaerere regna." Nor is FAS est only the true structure, it is also the most emphatic; the pause after FAS throwing a very strong emphasis on that word (see Rem. on 2. 247), while, on the contrary, the structure FAS SINIT furnishes us with a sing-song line in which there is no prominent or emphatic word. Nor is the structure only the most emphatic; it affords also the most elegant line and most according to our author's usual manner (see Rem. on 3. 2; FAS and AUT ILLE SINIT SUPERI REGNATOR OLYMPI not being two permissive authorities, fate and fate's interpreter, Jupiter, but one permissive authority only, viz., Jupiter, the permission being expressed in FAS, and more fully explained and set out in ILLE SINIT SUPERI REGNATOR OLYMPI: in other words, FAS being the theme, of which ILLE SINIT SUPERI REGNATOR OLYMPI is the variation. (See Rem. on 1. 550). If I may use a very familiar illustration, Creusa says to Aeneas, "you are not allowed. Jupiter will not permit it," as a little sister says to her little brother, or a little schoolgirl to a little schoolboy, "you are not allowed to do that; papa (or the master) will be angry at you." See Rem. on "fata obstant," 6. 438, and on "immortale fas," 9. 95.

781-784.

ET TERRAM HESPERIAM VENIES UBI LYDIUS ARVA
INTER OPIMA VIRUM LENI FLUIT AGMINE TYBRIS
ILLIC RES LAETAE REGNUMQUE ET REGIA CONIUX
PARTA TIBI LACRYMAS DILECTAE PELLE CREUSAE

Ubi lydius, &c.—Comp. Schiller, *Wilhelm Tell*, act 2, sc. 2 : " wo jetzt die Muotta zwischen wiesen rinnt."

Arva opima.—" Terra fertilis," Donatus. " Fruitful fields," Surrey. No; opimus is not *fruitful*, but *in prime condition* ; in that condition, sciz., of which fruitfulness is the consequence. Land is opima (*in prime condition*, or *of the best quality*) before it bears, and even before the seed is put into it; it is not *fruitful* until it bears. Accordingly, both adjectives are applied by Cicero (*de imp. Pomp. 6*) to one and the same land : " regio opima *et fertilis* ;" and the opima arva of Virgil are exactly the πιειρα αρουρα of Homer, *Il. 18. 541* ; *Od. 2. 328*, and the πιειρα of Pind. *Nem. 1. 14* :

. . . αριστευοισαν ευκαρπου χθονος
Σικελιαν πιειραν.

Opimus has precisely the same meaning when applied to animals : viz., *in prime condition* : not, as incorrectly stated by Gesner, and even by Forcellini, *fat* (pinguis); fatness being only one of the qualities necessary to entitle an animal to be styled opimus. This primitive sense of opimus (to which its meanings in the expressions spolia opima, opima facundia, &c., are but secondary), is expressed in French by the phrase " en bon point."

Dryden has had his reward with the English reader for giving himself no trouble about such niceties, but substituting at once, for the Virgilian thought, whatever idea, suited *ad captum vulgi*, came first into his mind :

"where gentle Tiber from his bed beholds
the flowery meadows and the feeding folds."

Virgil is innocent of all but the first three words.
ARVA INTER OPIMA VIRUM.—With Heyne I refer VIRUM to
ARVA, and not with Burmann and Forcellini to OPIMA: (**1**),
because Virgil, on the other occasions on which he has used the
word opimus, has used it absolutely. (**2**), because opimus
in the forty examples of its use quoted by the industry of
Forcellini stands absolute in thirty-eight, and only in two is
connected with a case, which case is not the genitive, but the
ablative. (**3**), because, even though it had been the practice of
Virgil, or of other good authors, to join opimus to the genitive, the phrase OPIMA VIRUM were neither elegant nor poetic,
and had besides not failed to recal to a Roman reader or hearer
the " segetes virorum" of Cadmus, than which no allusion could
have been more *mal-a-propos*—Manil. 3. 8:

" Colchida nec referam vendentem regna parentis,
et lacerum fratrem stupro, *segetes*que *virorum*,
taurorumque truces flammas, vigilemque draconem."

(**4**), because OPIMA, taken absolutely, is in perfect unison with
the plain intention of the apparition, viz., to recommend Hesperia to Aeneas; taken in connexion with VIRUM, contradicts
that intention, a country being the less eligible to new settlers,
in the direct ratio in which it is already OPIMA VIRUM. (**5**), because we have (*Aen. 10. 141*):

. . . "ubi pinguia culta
exercentque viri. Pactolosque irrigat auro,"

where not only the structure, rhythm, and thought correspond
with those of our text, but even the separate word—"ubi" being
the same in both, and "pinguia" answering to OPIMA, "culta"
to ARVA, "viri" to VIRUM, "Pactolos" to TYBRIS, and "irrigat" to FLUIT. **And**, (**6**), because in the account of the fulfilment of the prophecy, 8. 63 (where we cannot but suppose our
text was present in a lively manner to our author's mind), it is
"pinguia culta."

ARVA VIRUM, as "saecula virum," *Georg. 2. 295.*

LENI FLUIT AGMINE.—It is difficult to determine in which of three possible senses "agmen" is here to be understood; whether in the sense of a body consisting of several parts and in motion, or in the sense of a body consisting of several parts, considered abstractedly from its motion, or in the sense of the motion of a body considered abstractedly, no matter whether consisting of several parts or not.

If in the first of these senses, we have the picture presented to us of the innumerable waters which make up the Tiber stream marching quietly and in good order through the country, the very picture, only less detailed, which we have at 9. 25, of the Ganges and Nile:

"Iamque omnis campis exercitus ibat apertis
. . . .
ceu septem surgens sedatis amnibus altus
per tacitum Ganges, aut pingui flumine Nilus
cum refluit campis et iam se condidit alveo."

If in the second sense we have the same picture, the motion of the compound body, the "agmen" being expressed not as in the former case twice, viz., both by AGMINE and by FLUIT, but by FLUIT alone. If in the third, we have no longer the picture of the waters composing the river, but only of the river alone flowing with gentle march, as Steph. Byz. (of the river Parthenius) : δια το ηρεμαιον και παρθενωδες του ρευματος·

ως ακαλα προρεων ως αβρη παρθενος εισι.

It is in the last of these senses, as the simplest, I think our author has used the expression AGMINE in our text; and Servius is right in his gloss: "LENI AGMINE, leni impetu." Compare 2. 212: "Illi *agmine* certo Laocoonta petunt," where "agmine certo" is *sure and steady march*, and where Servius is again right in his gloss, "itinere, impetu." See Rem. on 2. 212. That AGMINE in our text, no less than at verse 212 of this book, refers to motion only, and not at all to composite nature or aggregation, is shown further by the application by Silius, 14. 442, of agmen to the motion of a simple uncompounded body:

. . . . "tremulo venit *agmine cornus*,
et Neptunicolae transverberat ora Telonis."

DILECTAE, not merely *loved*, but *loved by choice* or *preference*. An exact knowledge of the meaning of this word enables us to observe the consolation which Creusa ministers to herself in the delicate opposition of DILECTAE CREUSAE to REGIA CONIUX PARTA.

785-802.

NON EGO—DIEM

VAR. LECT. (VS. 794.

SOMNO **I** *Med.* (Fogg.) **III** Serv.; Ven. 1470; Aldus (1514); P. Manut.
FUMO **III** Macrob. *Sat. 4. 5:* Manil. 1. 822; Wakefield. Compare *Aen.* 5. 740; *Georg.* ;. 199.
O *Vat., Rom., Ver., St. Gall.*

NON EGO ... NURUS. Compare Shakespeare, *Anton. and Cleop.*, act 5, sc. 2 (Cleopatra speaking):

     . . . "know, sir, that I
  will not wait pinioned at your master's court,
  nor once be chastised with the sober eye
  of dull Octavia. Shall they hoist me up,
  and show me to the shouting varlotry
  of censuring Rome?"

NON EGO ASPICIAM, AUT IBO; just as 3.42: "*non* Troia tulit, *aut* cruor hic manat." In both of these places our modern idiom would use (as Shakespeare, in the passage just quoted) the negative not the affirmative conjunction.

HAEC UBI DICTA, &c., ... IMAGO (vss. 790-793):

  " this having said, she left me all in tears,
  and minding much to speak; but she was gone,
  and subtly fled into the weightless air.
  Thrice raught I with mine arms to accoll her neck:

www.ingramcontent.com/pod-product-compliance
Lightning Source LLC
Chambersburg PA
CBHW030306240426
43673CB00040B/1081